# Oracle 11i
# E-Business Suite
## from the
# Front Lines

# Oracle 11i
# E-Business Suite
## from the
# Front Lines

## April J. Wells

# AUERBACH PUBLICATIONS

A CRC Press Company
Boca Raton   London   New York   Washington, D.C.

## Library of Congress Cataloging-in-Publication Data

Wells, April J.
   Oracle 11i E-Business Suite from the front lines / April J. Wells.
      p. cm.
   Includes index.
   ISBN 0-8493-1861-0
      1. Oracle (Computer file) 2. Oracle E-business suite. 3. Electronic commerce—Computer
   programs. I. Title

HF5548.323.O73.W45 2003
005.75′65—dc22                                                                                      2003062864

**Visit the Auerbach Publications Web site at www.auerbach-publications.com**

© 2004 by CRC Press LLC
Auerbach is an imprint of CRC Press LLC

No claim to original U.S. Government works
International Standard Book Number 0-8493-1861-0
Library of Congress Card Number 2003062864

# ACKNOWLEDGMENTS

There have been many people who have helped and encouraged me in bringing this book to life. This is the book that I would have given anything to have been able to find when I was looking down the long road to go live.

To Tricia Maupin, I would like to say thank you for letting me learn the hard way and for standing behind me and standing up for me when it mattered most. And to Arnie Goetz, thank you for saving me from my own good intentions.

I would like to thank Rich O'Hanley from CRC Press for giving me the chance to bring this dream to life. You have given me my big break, a chance that I never thought I would get. You have been there through all the questions. I hope this is just the beginning of our relationship together.

Rachel Carmichael, thank you for being brutally honest, but I did it anyway!

Mom, you told me I could do anything if I put my mind to it. I did it.

Most of all, I would like to thank my husband, Larry, and my children, Adam and Amandya. They have put up with me getting up early in the mornings and writing when no one else in the house was awake and going to sleep earlier than I needed to so I could get up and do it again. You have put up with me putting in long hours on my days off and weekends writing and working on this book when I know you wanted me to do other things with you. Larry, you have always encouraged me. Even when I was not sure that I could do it, you never doubted me. You pushed me when I did not think I could go on with it. To Adam and Amandya, I would like to say, this book is proof that if you have a dream and you always hold onto that dream, no matter how long, it really can come true. Never give up on your dreams and never let anyone make you believe that you cannot accomplish them.

# TABLE OF CONTENTS

# INTRODUCTION

When you are dealing with a product the size, complexity, and flexibility of the Oracle® E-Business Suite, Version 11i, the ideas of where to start, what to do (and what not to do), and where to turn for answers can be a daunting prospect. Through the process of bringing this book to life, I have come to realize that much of what you deal with in the new versions of what used to be loosely thought of as Oracle Financials (Financials) is somewhat like dealing with a desert or the surroundings; Oracle E-Business Suite 11i can look like a bleak, frightening, and desolate place. But to those with a trained eye and an open mind, it can be seen for the thing of efficiency and beauty that it is. All of the shapes, textures, pieces, and parts work together to create an environment that is perfectly suited to what it was created for. And if you are patient enough, you will be able to see the bright shining beauty of the desert in springtime, in flower, in all its glory (sometimes you really have to look for it, but it will be there). Those are the times when you question less the sanity of the decision to exist in this environment and enjoy your surroundings.

That is not to say that things do not happen to radically change the landscape. The winds of change blow endlessly in both environments. Both are acted upon by their surroundings, and both are robust enough to be able to survive even the cruelest circumstances and come back to thrive. Sometimes storms will alter the landscape in such a way that you are left trying to rediscover your navigation path. Other times the path is clear and easily navigable.

This book is designed to help you to find your path through the sometimes bleak, sometimes beautiful, always inconsistent desert landscape that can be Oracle E-Business Suite 11i (11i). It will help you through your day-to-day adventures in administration and includes tips, techniques, and practical advice from someone who has had her share of cactus spines and exposure along the trail. Included is information on AD (Active

Directory) Utilities, patching, cloning, and several of the newer features that 11i brings to market. It will assist you in finding your own path through the sometimes painful world that you now are walking through and hopefully will help you find the elegance in your surroundings.

## AUDIENCE AND SCOPE

This book is intended for anyone facing the task of administering Oracle E-Business Suite 11i. It is written primarily for those with limited experience with Oracle Applications but with some background in Oracle Database Administration. It is, however, a good reference for anyone wanting to learn more about the technical ins and outs of Oracle Applications (Applications), how it runs and how to live the life of an Apps DBA (database administrator). From the newest person whose management just asked her if she thought she could take over as the administrator for the new Oracle Apps installation to the veteran of several years, we all have things we can learn, things that we can have refreshed in our minds. Sometimes we just need a handy central reference to look to when a situation arises. Much of the information will be of particular interest to those administrators who have some background in older versions of Financials in helping to bring their existing knowledge base the added depth of how things have changed in 11i.

## HOW TO USE THIS BOOK

This book touches all aspects of what an Apps administrator does day to day. We will look at what is involved in installing a new 11i environment, what goes into upgrading from a 10.7 or an 11.0.3 release, and what happens during a migration from one maintenance release of 11i to another. Once you have it installed, what is entailed in patching, cloning, and exactly what are all of those AD Utilities that everyone is always talking about? What are all of the services that will be running on my middle tier and what do I do with these finicky Concurrent Managers? This book will provide you with real world hints and tips to help you with your day-to-day tuning, troubleshooting, and maintenance and will help you efficiently provide reliable service to your end users.

Managers, co-workers, and those who have to deal on a day-to-day basis with the Apps DBA will find this book helpful as a tool to understand what the Apps administrator is talking about and what that job looks like from the inside.

## Chapter 1: Introducing Apps

This introductory chapter explains what exactly this new suite of products (that have been packaged together and launched to be accessible through any browser anywhere) has to offer and what it means to the company and to the Apps DBA. It discusses the technical architecture and gives the reader a background in the fundamental language of the Oracle E-Business Suite as well as the language of the corporate environment in which it is used. It also touches on the responsibilities of the Apps DBA and how this role differs from that of a typical Oracle DBA.

## Chapter 2: What Is New in 11i, 8i, and 9i

This chapter discusses what new features not only the Oracle E-Business Suite brought with it, but the features of 8i and 9i that it takes advantage of, as well as those features that an Apps DBA can take advantage of in daily dealings with the system. Many of the new features are those which a DBA might deal with in day-to-day life, stressing the fact that an Apps DBA still maintains all of the awareness of the database and its operations as any other DBA does with the added attention to the details of Applications' middle tier of products.

## Chapter 3: The Surrounding Environment

Oracle E-Business Suite does not live in a vacuum and this chapter stresses those portions of the environment that touch the Oracle E-Business Suite and allow it to function to its fullest. Many of these are things that you may have had to deal with or have read about previously, but they are now impacting your life in an entirely new way. Some of these are things that you will probably never have dealt with before, but they will make your dealings with Oracle E-Business Suite in some ways easier and more intuitive, and in some ways more challenging and confusing. Some of the surrounding environmental pieces are geared particularly to those operating in a Windows® environment; some are universal to all operating systems.

## Chapter 4: Apache

Apache is the core of the Oracle 9iAS services. With its rather in-depth and flexible configuration files, directives, and containers, casual familiarity with the inner workings is something that the Apps administrator needs. This chapter will give you an overview of the inner workings of the Apache server that is at the heart of the Oracle Applications HTTP server.

## Chapter 5: Java and JServ

Extending the capabilities of Apache by means of the mod_jserv module, JavaServer pages, and other Java components, Oracle E-Business Suite makes extensive use of the newer Web programming standards. Without some understanding of what these are and what they could mean to you, your job as administrator could become significantly more difficult, especially when it comes to debugging problems. You will want to look to this chapter for information that will give you a better basic understanding of the way that Oracle uses Java and how it can impact your life.

## Chapter 6: Other Services

In addition to JServ and Apache, there are more services in 11i that you will work with frequently. Once running, many will cause you few concerns. Others may be more problematic. Several have been around for a long time. Several are new components of the core product, but were available as add-ons in previous releases. In this chapter, you will find information dealing with these components.

## Chapter 7: Printing

Printing is often one of the most misunderstood parts of how Oracle E-Business Suite works. Everyone takes for granted that when you tell a document to print, it is almost magically going to show up at the printer. In many programs that you use every day, this is almost true. With 11i you have to have a basic understanding of the inner workings of the way that the application and the printer interface via the operating system. While not an all-inclusive explanation of all of these inner workings, Chapter 7 will allow you to have a basic understanding, enough of an understanding that you can set up and troubleshoot printing as it occurs on the application.

## Chapter 8: AD and Other Utilities

Chapter 8 addresses the mystical sounding AD Utilities and some of the other handy utilities that you will find yourself dealing with often as you maintain your system. These utilities are often seen sprinkled throughout resumes and job listings for Apps professionals, and they look impressive and complicated. This chapter will acquaint you with the utilities that you will find becoming your friends as you navigate your way through the life of your system. After reading this chapter, you too will be able to liberally use words like ADADMIN and ADPATCH with ease and understand what you are talking about, what they do, and what to look for when a good utility goes bad.

## Chapter 9: Installing, Upgrading, and Migrating

How do you actually get the thing onto your system? Chapter 9 will give you hints on what to plan for in an upgrade or a migration. It will give you hints and tips on what to do to stay sane in an insane world and how to remember what you did later. There are different things to take into consideration with the different approaches to getting your system to the latest release of the Application. The path that you follow will have its own set of opportunities and problems and with the help of this chapter you will be ready to deal with them.

## Chapter 10: Patching

Patching is the mainstay of many Apps DBAs' existence. Chapter 10 addresses the pieces of a patch, what each does, what can break, and how to make the best use of your patching hours. There are suggestions on what to look for in the logs and how to manage what can quickly appear to become an unmanageable process. In this chapter you will find out how to merge many patches into a single patch to minimize impact to your system and find out when you cannot merge a patch no matter how enticing it looks. You will also look at patches that do not use ADPATCH to do their installation and find out the new manner of installing database patches.

## Chapter 11: Cloning

Plants do it, sheep have done it, and it is one of the more common things to occur on an Oracle E-Business Suite system — cloning. In Chapter 11 we look at logical times to clone, the main Oracle manners of cloning, and alternative ways to proceed through making an exact (or near) duplicate of one system into another environment. We also look at some of the ways that a clone can break and what to do if one does. There are some almost supported methods to fixing a clone gone bad and the more supported (but often less practical) way to accomplish the same ends.

## Chapter 12: Concurrent Managers and Concurrent Processing

One of the most powerful features of the Applications product suite is the ability to do Concurrent Processing. Concurrent Managers, Concurrent Programs, and the ability to do Concurrent Processing is one of the ways to turn your Online Transaction Processing system into a batch processing environment without having to make any changes to the parameters and without having to restart the instances or port the data to another environment. Concurrent Managers are often quirky, sometimes difficult to tune, and often tricky to report on. Chapter 12 gives you some ideas on how to tune your Concurrent Processes and make an already powerful feature work even better for you.

## Chapter 13: AutoConfig and Oracle Application Manager

Two of the latecomers to the 11i suite of products are the ability to run AutoConfig (automatic configuration) to maintain your system's configuration settings and use the Oracle Application Manager to monitor and manage different parts of your system. Throughout this chapter we look at the new features that help make your life easier and how you can make use of the tools that you are already paying for. Chapter 13 also provides you with some information on the alternatives that are available through third-party providers.

## Chapter 14: Odds and Ends

Chapter 14 brings you things that do not elegantly fit anywhere else, but do not really require a chapter of their own. In this chapter we look at dealing with Oracle Support and effective tuning methods you can use to determine bottlenecks in your system and printing, to name a few. In this chapter, you also get ideas of other places to look for information, where (other than directly from Oracle) to ask the pressing questions and get an answer from someone who has really been there, and what groups are available to assist you in your journey down the road to successful Apps administration.

Let the adventure begin.

# 1

# INTRODUCING APPS

## WHAT ARE ERP AND CRM?

To begin to understand more about the animal that you are going to be dealing with, and potentially be responsible for, it would help to have a basic understanding of ERP (Enterprise Resource Planning) and CRM (Customer Relationship Management) — the two main components in Oracle's E-Business Suite.

ERP is a process that helps you put any and all resources involved with an organization to the best possible use. ERP has had other names in its past iterations: Materials Resource Planning and Manufacturing Resource Planning. Manufacturing Resource Planning shows that, at its roots, it was used as a tool most often in a manufacturing environment. Typically, it was used in reference to a process with several discrete operations or discrete objects, many of which can be broken down further into atomic level objects or processes. An example would be a simple wooden bar stool. A bar stool with three legs, three dowels connecting those legs at a predefined space interval, and a round wooden seat. A process might be to drill the hole for leg one into the bottom of the seat piece. There would be three similar processes like that one, one for each leg into the seat. Each leg might have a process assigned to it of drilling two holes, each hole has a depth and a diameter and an angle in reference to the leg and an angle in reference to the other legs. The finished product (bar stool) as a whole has a demand for each component (e.g., legs, screws, seat) and you have a predefined amount that is allocated to waste. Tracking all of this information, as well as tracking those times when the projected numbers fall outside of the expected ranges are all things that historically were tracked by a MRP system either in a spreadsheet, in a notebook, or in early databases (usually with homegrown applications built as a front end).

ERP methodology has grown significantly from its manufacturing roots, although many times MRP is still the basis from which the implementation of an ERP system grows. Today the concept of ERP often refers to a broad set of activities that a company or an enterprise performs, both internally and externally. The computerized system that is often referred to when discussing the management of planning of an enterprise's resources (all resources, including money, physical, and people) is an integrated solution. Such a software system is typically made up of multiple modules that interact together, share information amongst themselves and each other, and provide management with a broad, all-encompassing picture of the entire enterprise. These systems can now be used to meet needs in any industry.

Within the software is stored the information that management needs to operate its business day to day. ERP software systems break down the departmental barriers that sometimes still exist in organizations and allow the information that may have been in silos before to be shared across the enterprise. Further, it takes a process-oriented view of the organization and uses that view to allow the organization to meet its goals by tightly integrating all aspects of the organization. With ERP software, a company can better integrate its entire supply chain, automate many of its processes, and reduce its lead times and exceptions to the process along the way.

CRM is the process of finding, getting, and retaining customers. It encompasses the methodologies, strategies, and other capabilities that help a company or enterprise organize and manage its customer relationships, as well as the software tools to help achieve those ends. Today, many companies focus on the wants and needs of the customer, so the ability to track information about the customer, learn from that information, and use that information to better serve the customer is crucial. CRM helps a company learn what works and what does not. It helps the company identify the profile of the most profitable customers, gain a deeper understanding of the most and least profitable customers, and will allow the company to target the most profitable customer profile when it is searching for new business. For companies that are forming alliances with business partners, CRM is centralizing information on the customer base in a way that can be shared between partners to help to create products to better serve the end user. Before, customer-centric information was likely already stored within the company. It was unlikely, however, that this information was stored in a central location or that it was easily accessible by multiple departments therefore reporting on customer information in an enterprisewide manner was nearly impossible. If it is difficult to report on, it is likely nearly impossible to perform analysis on.

CRM will help your customer base, and your reputation within that base, by allowing faster response to customer's inquiries because the information is centrally stored and accessible by the people who are interfacing with the customer.

## WHAT IS ORACLE E-BUSINESS SUITE?

Oracle E-Business Suite (i.e., Oracle Applications, Oracle Apps, Oracle Financials, Oracle Manufacturing, Oracle CRM) is the suite of products that used to be called Oracle Financials. Oracle Financials was first released in the late 1980s and has evolved into a full-fledged solution for enterprise processes for companies of nearly any size. The Oracle E-Business Suite contains over 55 integrated modules for financial management, supply chain management, manufacturing management, project management, human resources management, and sales force automation all pulled together to provide business automation. Oracle E-Business Suite combines ERP and CRM into one fully integrated package that can meet all of a company's needs. Oracle E-Business Suite can provide a company with business performance metrics, current financial ratios, profit and loss report summaries, and other information that can be tracked across departments, across product lines, even across geographies. It allows information to be shared across the enterprise. It further allows a company to centralize a single definition of what a customer is, what a supplier is, what an employee is, a business partner is, or product is, and maintaining this definition and its connected information across the enterprise. Oracle E-Business Suite allows upper management to access its business intelligence information and take immediate action when situations warrant it. The Customer Resource Management module allows a company to manage customer information, from leads to sales to revenue through multiple channels of input (e.g., Web, phone, mail order, or e-mail).

Oracle E-Business Suite also incorporates a powerful, flexible combination of state-of-the-art technology integrated to aid in rapid implementation. Various implementations in varying configurations can be found in shops with fewer than 200 employees to many of the Fortune 500 companies. Oracle Applications 11i also brings the evolution of the core technology, which saw its start with terminal emulation, to true Internet computing architecture. Where, in past releases, users needed some special piece of software installed on their workstations to run Financials (these could have included a terminal emulation package or Forms and Reports executables or the like), now the only piece of software that is really necessary to use Apps 11i is a Java-compliant browser. The only Oracle E-Business Suite specific software today that ends up on the end user's computer is a Java applet (JInitiator™ client platform) that is downloaded and cached the first time the PC connects to applications. This new, evolved architecture has opened the door for new modules and new functionality.

## Difference between an Apps DBA and a Regular DBA

The question is often raised: What is the difference between a regular Oracle DBA and an Apps DBA? While the answer may sound trite, the difference is what you make it. There are many different thoughts on this from many different people. Some people suggest that there is no difference and to an extent that is probably true. In reality, Apps DBAs are regular DBAs who have to remember and be concerned with a variety of additional influences. Further, Apps DBAs will likely work closer with other people, or teams of people, with whom they may never have been involved, before.

You, the Applications DBA, will be responsible for managing, sizing, maintaining, and tuning the database (just like any DBA). Your Apps database is an OLTP (online transaction processing) system. Along with the other responsibilities, go all of the wait and lock concerns that you would have in any transactional system. Oracle E-Business Suite also has some fairly hefty batch jobs (e.g., some creating reports, others bringing data in from outside sources, and still others doing massive calculations on the existing data). The scheduling and specifics of these jobs are not going to be under your control. You will have little to say about when they are kicked off or run. These jobs will be run at the discretion of the finance or accounting departments; therefore, it is important to maintain a harmonious working relationship with them and an open line of communication. Oracle E-Business Suite is also, potentially, a Business Intelligence System (BIS) and can have many of the same kinds of reports run against it that could be run on a data warehouse. After all, you are dealing with your company's financial data over time. This will be the kind of information that the executives want to run historic reports, trends, and what if scenarios on. Tuning will become a problem at some point for you. These factors combine to bring many sizing and performance concerns that go along with a reporting and a batch environment, an in-depth analysis system and a transactional system. What follows is a list of 11 things that you may want to consider as part of what it means to administer Oracle Applications and just a few of the jobs that you will have as you proceed through the often thorny environment that you now find yourself.

1. Get familiar with Concurrent Managers; there are no friendly manuals that you can read to help you with these or any in-depth

documents to help. Chapter 9 — Installation and Migration will help you along the way and will point you at some other information that may be of assistance.

2. Remember that, while you run mostly a transactional system with the end users entering row at a time information through the interface, you are not dealing with a true OLTP system. When a batch gets kicked off through a concurrent request is not usually under your control. An end user from the finance department may decide when to submit a payment batch and not realize that there may be ramifications to that decision. The more modules that you implement and the more people who have reason to submit a resource intensive batch process, results in a greater impact that these processes will have on your system. Excellent communications and coordination between you and all of the stakeholders will make your life easier.

3. Never apply a patch to the production databases unless you have tested it multiple times and get user acceptance testing done and end user sign off that the patch in question both fixed the problem that it was meant to fix (for a patch that is applied to fix a problem) and that it did not have any unforeseen side effects or break anything in the system (for all patches that are applied). Remember, it is quite likely your fault if a patch breaks production.

4. Document all the patches: the day applied, the reason for applying, the errors that they were supposed to solve, and the errors created after applying. Keep the logs of all the patches and do not ever erase them; Oracle will ask for that patch log after maybe six months when one of your current patches bombs. More on patch documentation and patching can be found in Chapter 10.

5. Remember that Oracle Applications is heavily indexed; rebuilding the indexes periodically will improve performance significantly. There is a Concurrent Process that will help you with performing this action. Try to schedule it for a time when there is a minimum of users on the system.

6. Monitor the rollback segments. This is probably one of the most important and one of the trickiest parts. This is particularly true if you have not implemented Automatic Undo Management. (See Chapter 2 — 11i, 8i, and 9i New Features for more on this Oracle 9i feature.) If, for example, a Concurrent Program fails because it is not able to allocate rollback segments, the whole program is rolled back and this can clog the CPU (central processing unit) because of the extreme backup of other programs in the concurrent queue. Often, this will leave behind interim tables and indexes that have to be cleaned up carefully and manually. Extreme care

must be taken with the interim tables as other programs may reuse them for reporting, posting, purging, or other functions.

7. Never attempt to add additional indexes for performance without first asking Oracle Support. It is Oracle's application and Oracle Support should know better than anyone if the addition of your proposed index is liable to make the core application perform worse. If you do attempt some changes, make sure that you document exactly what you did. The next patch you apply would quite probably identify the changes that you made and replace them with the canned functionality, placing you back at square one.

8. Understand how patch application works. You will be spending a great deal of time involved with some portion of patching: from planning which patches to apply, to acquiring the patches, to applying the patches, to testing and documenting post patching, just in time for the next time you start planning which patches to apply next. Chapter 10 — Patching will help with this.

9. Know that there will be many invalid objects any time that there are any changes made to the database. Any time you do anything that might have an affect on the database, check the number of invalid objects, and periodically run utlrp to recompile them. Utlrp.squ, located in the Oracle Home Directory's rdbms/admin subdirectory, is responsible for compiling invalid objects. When run as the 'SYS' user, it attempts to recompile all invalid objects to all schema owners. Anytime that you encounter a new error, check for invalids and recompile the database first before initiating an iTAR (Internet created Technical Assistance Request).

10. Understand Alerts. Especially understand Periodic and Event Alerts and understand how they differ from database triggers.

11. Remember, being an Apps DBA is pretty simple. With the exception of setting up printers (which can be tricky due to initialization settings) everything is fairly straightforward and you will learn quickly. You will soon become at ease in your environment.

You will create test and development databases (maybe more) and you will keep them refreshed by copying (cloning) the production database. How many instances you choose to create and maintain is enterprise dependent. Much of the decision on exactly how many databases will depend on what the business dictates. Minimally, I suggest having at least three complete and separate environments and four complete sets is even better. First, have a development environment where your developers can develop custom reports and custom PL/SQL (Procedure Language extension to Structured Query Language) packages to support those reports. This environment can be refreshed on a move up cycle or whenever the developers feel that the data is no longer representative of what is in production. This is likely the first environment into which to apply patches. Next, have a test environment where you apply patches before final user acceptance testing and user signoff. Test should be as close as possible to production data before a patching cycle starts, so that the end users can test with data as fresh as possible. Finally, you will have your production environment. Production is self-explanatory. Optimally, you will have a fourth environment: I will call it patching (if you installed the vision environment, you can use this for the patching environment). Patching is where you can apply patches and fix them when they break without having any impact on any of the users of the system. This is a place you can consider your playground. You can test out changes to the system without worrying if your changes are breaking anything or if they are having ill effects on what anyone else is doing.

Cloning (see Chapter 11) is making an exact duplicate environment (both the applications layer and the database layer) against which patches are applied and tested, reports are written and tested, upgrades start and are tested, and in which problems are fixed and the fixes tested all before any of these goes to production.

Patches, both ORACLE Applications and RDBMS (relational database management system) patches, will need to be applied and tested. These should start in the development database (unless you have one just for patching) and migrated to test and later to production. You will need to have a handle on how to patch, patch management, and version control of all of your individual systems.

Further, in your capacity as applications administrator, you can likely find yourself involved in the following roles:

- Oracle Applications DBA
- Capacity planning and sizing the hardware
- Architecture and design of the Applications system
- Installation of Applications 11i with respect to planned architecture
- Instance management
- Cloning Applications 11i and scripts
- Splitting and merging the nodes, single node to multiple node and vice versa
- Workflow installation and configuration and setting up test workflow
- Oracle WebServer (OWS), Oracle Application Server (OAS) tuning
- Tuning Apache
- Application security, post-implementation
- Tuning Concurrent Managers
- Tuning application UNIX server and identifying issues
- Tuning scripts and other Application troubleshooting

Finally, installs and upgrades will be your responsibility, as well as making sure those upgrades and installs are supported. Oracle Support does not support many release configurations and if you choose to install one of these configurations (e.g., 11.5.8 with a Version 8.0.6 database), you will likely not be able to rely on Oracle Support if something goes wrong. Oracle Support's solution will be to upgrade to a supported configuration. Always make sure that any installation or upgrade is a supported combination. This means the operating system (OS) version with the middle tier, the OS version with the database, and the middle tier with the database. Along with dealing with upgrades, you will need to know how to handle any customizations that were done to your system, so they can be handled in the upgrade process. This includes program units, interim tables, custom reports, and custom forms.

You also need to determine the timing and type (e.g., hot, cold, Recovery Manager, or any combination) of backups and when you can practice your recoveries. Remember, if you do not know (have not practiced) that you can recover using your backup method of choice, you do not have a backup and recovery plan. A backup is worthless if you cannot recover from it.

Most likely, you will be responsible for starting and stopping the Concurrent Managers and managing their functionality and performance. It may be your responsibility to create request sets for users to use to submit reports and batch jobs.

The help desk will probably turn to you when it is alerted to a problem. You will be the second tier support.

You may be called on to administer other pieces that are used in conjunction with your Apps install. These may include Discoverer, Forms and Reports, and other software used inhouse that interfaces with Oracle E-Business Suite. When custom programs, forms, or reports are created or altered, adding these to the system and registering them with Applications will also become something that you do. Again, this is where you will have to have a handle on versioning and version control.

Interim tables, their functions, and what they can and should do are also things that you will have to have a hand in, at some point. Interim tables are the means by which you get external data into your financials database from outside sources. These are the only tables that anyone should ever need to touch from a design standpoint.

Applications' middle tier and the database are intricately connected; that is part of what makes it such a powerful and complex piece of software. What affects one piece often affects others and usually affects the whole. If there are server problems on the database tier, they can become painfully obvious to your users accessing the Apps front end. If a form is not performing correctly, you could see performance issues on your database. Many times, following a patch installation, completely untouched forms and reports will change how they are acting or cease functioning. Concurrent Managers, regardless of what tier they reside on, can create their own sets of interesting problems.

You will also need to have a working knowledge of Oracle's Apache Server and the iAS Suite and their foibles on your OS. JServ, Apache, and the internals to iAS that come with Oracle Apps are what allow your users to access your system cleanly.

There are Forms and Reports Servers running on the middle tier. Those may become something that you need to maintain during a patch cycle or upgrade, if at no other time.

Metalink (http://metalink.oracle.com) is an invaluable tool that you will turn to on a regular basis. You will become better and better at finding notes and solutions to the problems that will be  laid at your doorstep. This is where you will download patches, research problems, and find considerable documentation and white papers. It will also be a source of much frustration, because an iTAR may be assigned to a very good analyst (which will make solving problems simpler) or to someone who will run you around in circles and add greatly to your frustration (which will likely make you wonder how any problem ever gets solved). Bear with it; in the end they are one of your best resources. Chapter 11 — Cloning will give you more information on what is involved in dealing with Oracle Support.

To better serve your end users, you will have to gain some basic understanding of the underlying structure and architecture. If there are other systems feeding your installation, you may need to understand where the data comes from and what could, potentially, go wrong in the transfer. You do not have to know everything about accounting and FASB (Financial Accounting Standards Board), but it does help to know things like AR is accounts receivable (money that is coming into your company), AP is accounts payable (money going out), and GL is general ledger (the accounts that the money goes into and out of).

If you are dealing with any Windows version as your middle tier, you will need to have a basic understanding of registry entries and how that can affect you and the differences in how path and environment variables are set. If you have multiple instances running on a Windows machine, the complexity of your install will be increased, the software components that come into play are increased, but some of the solutions to really weird problems can be simpler.

Besides you, who is responsible for what? It will be helpful to your organization to have a help desk to which the functionals and other technical people can turn when there is a problem, a point of contact. If you have one of these, it can add layers through which problems need to be routed that may be time consuming, but it also might be a way to centrally track if you are having ongoing similar types of problems and the resolutions to them.

System administrators (sysadmins) will most likely install, upgrade, or replace the OS and any of the hardware on which the pieces of your installation reside. They will monitor disk usage and physically perform the backups. A combination of administrators may also maintain and manage the physical printers and print queues. Although, defining those printers to the applications may be your responsibility.

Above all, you will be dealing with some of the most complex and powerful software that you may ever have been connected with. The parts of this application cannot be treated entirely independent of each other.

In short, an Apps DBA will need to know a little bit about a lot of things. This book will help you along the way.

# 2

---

# 11i, 8i, AND 9i NEW FEATURES

With the advent of Oracle E-Business Suite 11i, Oracle made use of some of the newer features of its 8i database and built new functionality into its 11i product suite. You should have some understanding of many of the ones that you may not necessarily be using or dealing with directly on a daily basis, because their functioning will impact you at some point.

## ORACLE 8i NEW FEATURES

### Cost Based Optimizer

While cost based optimization was released in Oracle 7, Oracle 8i brought with it significant improvements including many bug fixes and extended features. Oracle strongly suggests that everyone over Release 8i use the Cost Based Optimizer (CBO). They support Rule Based Optimizer (RBO) only for compatibility with existing applications. With the CBO, query optimization is calculated differently and the queries run more efficiently than under the RBO in past releases. In a non-Apps installation of the 8i database, you have the option to choose which optimization to use. In Apps 11i's Version 8i database, the preconfigured database installs CBO as the enabled optimization method and you have to allow it to use cost based optimization. The code that is written into this release of Apps was written to take advantage of the new algorithm and it is necessary that you allow it this freedom.

But what is the difference between the RBO and the CBO? The CBO is an expert system that figures all possible execution plans for a query and decides what each one's relative cost is dependent on the gathered statistics. This algorithm determines all execution plans based on available access paths and any hints that may have been used in the query. The execution plan with the lowest relative cost (based on estimated cost

11

proportional to the resources potentially used by the query) is the one that is processed. The weighted costs include network, throughput CPU, and disk input and output (I/O). CBO execution plans may not be reliable over different releases and Oracle makes no guarantees or apologies for any potential differences. The execution plan is only as good as the statistics on which it is based; therefore, it is vital that statistics be gathered regularly on all schema objects. There is a Concurrent Program that does this for you. A Concurrent Program is a program that runs as a batch job in the background (either on command or on a set schedule) while not impacting the end users' ability to work on transaction processing by a Concurrent Manager (a service that resides either on your database tier or on a middle tier). It can be run either manually on demand, or as a scheduled job and should be run on at least a weekly basis. Even with new, valid statistics, the CBO often still makes bad decisions. On the whole, however, it is a vast improvement over having to have all of the rules coded into the program logic.

The CBO has several relevant `init<SID>.ora` parameters. The parameters and their required (relative to Apps) and current values can be gathered by running a script that can be found under the `<FND_TOP>/sql` directory called `AFCHKCBO.sql` (this script comes in patch 1245516 if it is not already in your directory tree). A sample of the output can be seen in Table 2.1.

Often, the results of this query will have current values set to something other than the required value. If they are significantly different, you can enhance performance by changing the values.

One parameter that needs to be set is `optimizer_max_permu-tations` (maximum join permutations of tables in queries with join conditions). It has a default value of 80,000 and a range from 4 to nearly 4.3 billion. Leaving the value at the default, in effect, tells the CBO to consider that there are virtually no limits on `join` conditions. Setting the value to the Apps required value of 79,000 allows the optimizer to consider more than just the starting table in the query. By regularly maintaining statistics, you can better manage lower parse times for queries in the database.

`Optimizer_features_enabled` and `compatible` are compatibility parameters and the required values are considered lower limits of what can be expected. If your database is a release higher than this and all of the required parameters are compatible with the release you are on, it is safe (and often better) to make them higher than required (e.g., if required is 8.1.6 and you are set at 8.1.7, you should be safe in your parameters).

For the CBO to do its job efficiently and effectively, statistics need to be gathered regularly. How frequently statistics are gathered is open to

**Table 2.1   AFCHKCBO.sql Sample Output**

| Parameter Name | Current Value | Required Value |
|---|---|---|
| _sort_elimination_cost_ratio | 5 | 5 |
| _optimizer_mode_force | TRUE | TRUE |
| _fast_full_scan_enabled | FALSE | FALSE |
| _ordered_nested_loop | TRUE | TRUE |
| _complex_view_merging | TRUE | TRUE |
| _push_join_predicate | TRUE | TRUE |
| _use_column_stats_for_function | TRUE | TRUE |
| _push_join_union_view | TRUE | TRUE |
| _like_with_bind_as_equality | TRUE | TRUE |
| _or_expand_nvl_predicate | TRUE | TRUE |
| _table_scan_cost_plus_one | TRUE | TRUE |
| _optimizer_undo_changes | FALSE | FALSE |
| db_file_multiblock_read_count | 8 | 8 |
| optimizer_max_permutations | 79000 | 79000 |
| optimizer_mode | CHOOSE | CHOOSE |
| optimizer_percent_parallel | 0 | 0 |
| optimizer_features_enable | 8.1.6 | 8.1.6 |
| query_rewrite_enabled | TRUE | TRUE |
| compatible | 8.1.6 | 8.1.6 |
| always_anti_join | NESTED_LOOPS | NESTED_LOOPS |
| always_semi_join | NESTED_LOOPS | NESTED_LOOPS |
| sort_area_size | 5120000 | 512000 (**) |
| hash_area_size | 10240000 | 1024000 (**) |

Legend:
(**): Required value

some debate, some suggest that monthly is sufficient, others weekly. I gather statistics immediately after our company closes their accounting books. Further, I have scheduled a concurrent job to run every week, early on Monday morning before anyone gets into the system, to gather schema statistics for all schemas (other than sys). Fortunately, there are Concurrent Programs that you can schedule that call the FND_STATS package to gather statistics for you. Analyze all index columns, gather table statistics, back up table statistics, restore table statistics, gather column statistics, gather all column statistics, and gather schema statistics can be set to run on a defined schedule so that you do not have to worry about them getting done (more on Concurrent Managers and their jobs in Chapter 12).

## Materialized Views

Materialized views (MVs) are a materialization of frequently run, usually expensive queries. They are similar to standard views in that they are based on a predefined query and are similar to regular tables in that they take up storage, are queriable directly, and can be indexed on their own. MVs are an improved version of what used to be called Snapshots. There are some restrictions on what can and cannot be materialized. Typically MVs are used to precompute joins and to precalculate expensive functions on single or multiple tables like summarizing or aggregating data to allow queries to run faster. Oracle 11i has the ability to take advantage of this new 8i functionality. A few of the schemas (e.g., APPS, BIX, IBE, and the MSC) are installed with predefined MVs. These predefined MVs are not on a set refresh schedule; you will have to set that on your own. Table 2.2 is an example of a Create Materialized View statement and can give you a better idea on what you are dealing with. In particular, the Create Materialized View scripts in Oracle E-Business Suite create a MV based on a table with the same name. This registers the existing table as a MV.

This solution provides performance benefits, but does not permit query rewrite in all cases or support the ability to fast refresh the MV. Fast refresh means that, on a specific schedule, ON COMMIT of a transaction against the base table or on demand when the MV administrator invokes the refresh function, all changed rows and information are migrated via an interim MV log table to the materialized view. Because these underlying existing tables can be quite large and expensive to rebuild, if a table exists that provides the functionality desired and the end goal is to improve performance, registering MVs on existing tables should be used whenever possible. The single caveat is that the base table should exactly reflect the defining definition of the MV query at the time you register the view.

**Table 2.2   Create Materialized View Example**

```
CREATE MATERIALIZED VIEW ibe_sct_search_mv
   ON PREBUILT TABLE WITHOUT REDUCED PRECISION
   REFRESH complete on demand
   ENABLE QUERY REWRITE
   AS
   SELECT   *
   FROM ibe_sct_search_mv;
```

Because it shares similar attributes to a regular table, you have the option of partitioning the MV. This can be an extremely attractive option when the underlying tables are extremely large, and the resulting MV becomes large enough that queries on the MV become longer and longer. Not only does the MV benefit from the same features as the base table (including improved scalability, simplified administration, efficient use of local indexes), but it has the added benefit of being able to fast refresh on the partition boundary when the base table is updated on those same boundary lines.

When you create a MV, you have the option of specifying that the view be refreshed on demand or on commit. ON COMMIT refresh allows the MV to be refreshed every time a transaction commits on the base table, ensuring that the view always contains the most recent view of the data. The DBMS_MVIEW package provides three different types of refresh operations for dealing with MVs built with the on demand manner of refresh:

- DBMS_MVIEW.REFRESH allows for the refresh of one or more MVs.
- DBMS_MVIEW.REFRESH_ALL_MVIEWS refreshes all of the MVs that are owned by the calling schema.
- DBMS_MVIEW.REFRESH_DEPENDENT allows for the refresh of all table-based MVs that depend on a specific detail table or a specific list of detail tables.

An ON DEMAND refresh can only ever be refreshed by calling one of this package's procedures.

Refreshing a MV involves considerable sorting and requires temporary space to rebuild itself and its indexes. Because of this, it may not be wise to schedule your refreshes to occur at the same time. As these are database stored procedures, they can easily be scheduled to run via a Concurrent Manager job on a predefined schedule and can have a different schedule for each refresh job that you choose to define. The choice of when to refresh has to be based in part on business decisions on the required freshness of the Mview data compared with that of the base table. Remember that a full refresh truncates the MV table before inserting a new set of the full data volume of not only what was there before, but also what is there that has been added as well.

### Complete Refresh

A complete refresh, likely the option that would be best employed in the Apps instance, is also loosely defined as build immediate unless, as in the case of most canned Apps MVs, it is registered as being built on a prebuilt table. A complete refresh involves the complete rereading of the detail tables and reprocessing of all of the data from those tables. You should fully consider the resource ramifications (i.e., time and physical resources) involved before requesting it.

### Fast Refresh

Fast refresh is a more efficient means of refresh because it does not need to recompute the entire query used to create it to begin with. Fast refresh relies on the changes to the underlying data triggering the refresh of the MVs. Often this is accomplished by means of a third structure, a MV log, which is a trade-off between added maintenance of objects and the speed of refresh.

### ON COMMIT Refresh

The advantage of having a MV refresh ON COMMIT of a transaction on the base table is that the changes are automatically and immediately reflected in the MV. Further, this means that you never have to remember to refresh the view and your users will never access stale data. Depending on how busy your system is, one disadvantage is that it can add significant time to commit data.

When a MV is refreshed ON DEMAND, one of three refresh methods can be specified as shown in Table 2.3.

### Query Rewrite

Along with the ability to store the results of predefined queries in a physical structure and automate the maintenance of these structures, MVs allow you to take advantage of another Oracle 8i and newer feature —

**Table 2.3  Refresh Options for MVs**

| Refresh Option | Description |
| --- | --- |
| Refresh Complete | Refreshes the data by recalculating the MV's defining query every time refresh is run. |
| Refresh Fast | Refreshes the MV by incrementally applying all changes from the base table to the MV. |
| Refresh Force | Attempts a fast refresh. If that is not possible or if it fails, a complete refresh is done. Frequently this is the refresh option of choice since it allows Oracle to decide. Oracle attempts the fastest first. |

query rewrite. This feature checks the statistics that have been gathered in the database (e.g., tables and MVs) and the CBO uses those statistics to determine what queries can be rewritten to use the MVs, thus saving time. If you have any queries that make use of aggregation or summaries, you can store them in a MV and the optimizer will use them transparently. No end user or programmer need ever know that they exist. It is a trade-off between speed and storage, with the end user being the ultimate winner.

One major benefit of creating and going through the maintenance process of defining MVs is the ability to allow queries to take advantage of this rewrite capability. Query rewrite transforms a SQL statement that is written against a particular table, a set of tables, or views to be transformed into a statement accessing one or more MVs based upon the detail tables of the initial query. Because the transformation is transparent to the end user query, the MV can be dropped, added, refreshed, or altered at any time without adversely affecting the query in any way other than performance and without invalidating indexes or application code.

When the determination on whether to rewrite or not is made, several checks are performed on the query to decide if it is a candidate for rewrite or not. If the query fails a single check, it is not a candidate. The check and subsequent redirection can at times be costly in terms of response time and CPU utilization.

The CBO uses two different metrics to determine the rewritablity of a SQL statement. First, it checks to see if the query exactly matches the MV definition query. If it does match, it uses query rewrite. This is the only test that it can fail and still be a candidate for rewrite. If it does not exactly match the query, the CBO will compare joins, selections, data columns, groupings, and aggregate functions between the query and the MV. If it can in any portion of the query run faster using the MV, it will allow for the rewrite.

Ordinarily, the CBO optimizes each given query with and without attempting to rewrite the selects and chooses the least costly alternative to allow it to perform. When the CBO chooses to rewrite the query, it can rewrite the entire query or one or more of the query blocks within the query. The evaluation is done one block at a time. If it has to choose between two MVs on which to rewrite, it will choose the one that will cause the query to read the smallest amount of data to return the required information.

Since the optimization is based on the total cost of the statement, it is critical that statistics be gathered regularly to allow the CBO to make an informed decision.

## Database Resource Manager

Before Oracle introduced the Database Resource Manager (DRM), typically resource management and allocation (e.g., disk, memory, CPU, etc.) was left to the OS on which the database was running. This led to issues as the OS did not possess the ability to partition the machine's resources among tasks on priority bases and the Oracle RDBMS interactions with the OS were not always very symbiotic.

There can be significant overhead if there are several RDBMS servers on the box. Running each on its own Logical Partition, if even possible, would reduce some of the overhead associated with several engines running on one box, but would likely result in CPU contention in the end.

Scheduling and descheduling of servers is inefficient if left to the OS, particularly if the RDBMS is holding any latches servers.

Further, the OS is not built to efficiently manage database-specific resources. That is not its function; while it can do so to a significant extent, the efficiency and knowledge should be built into the database to manage this.

Oracle's DRM allows the DBA to have more control over how resources are managed than has typically been possible before. This improved control of resources enables you to provide better application performance and availability to the end users. DRM enables this by allowing you to guarantee a group of users a minimum amount of processing resources regardless of what others on the system are doing, to distribute processing by allotting different users or applications different percentages of CPU time based on their needs, to limit the degree of parallelism that one group is permitted to use over the permissions given to another group, and to set up the instance to allocate resources differently depending on what time of day it is. For instance, batch jobs are a lower priority during the day, but become a higher priority at night when there are less active users on the system.

The DRM comprises the following components, presented here with their basic functionality:

- Resource Consumer Group
  - Groups users' sessions with similar resource requirements
  - Controls the whole group's consumption
  - Allocates CPU among consumer group sessions

- Resource Allocation Plans
  - Allocates resources among consumer groups or plans
  - Contains directives that specify each consumer group's resource allocation
  - Groups the groups or plans together

- ■ Resource Allocation Methods
  - ■ Maintains the policies for each resource's allocation
  - ■ Determines what method is used when allocating to a group or a plan

- ■ Resource Plan Directives
  - ■ Assigns groups or subplans to a resource plan
  - ■ Allocates resources to groups in a plan by specifying parameters for each method
  - ■ Allows exactly one plan directive for each entry in the plan

A resource plan can reference other plans (i.e., subplans) and can be referenced by others. Figure 2.1 shows one possible configuration of plans and subplans.

Resource_manager_plan, the init.ora parameter that enables the resource manager, indicates what master resource plan and its associated subplans is to be used for the given instance at database startup. The alter system command can change the resource plan that is needed to be used at any time after startup. This means that you can dynamically change plans to meet batch and transactional processing demand without resorting to restarting the database.

The DBMS packages, DBMS_RESOURCE_MANAGER and DBMS_RESOURCE_MANAGER_PRIVS, can be called to facilitate the care and management of Resource Objects.

## Partitioning

Partitioning of tables has been available in previous releases of the database, but until release 11i, Apps did not take advantage of it. Partitioning breaks data in large tables and indexes down into smaller, more manageable chunks, logically grouped so that SQL statements can access the data in a single partition rather than having to parse the entire table. For very large tables, this can be a significant savings in both query processing and batch processing time.

There are two basic ways to partition in Oracle 8i: range or hash or a combination of these two. Range partitioning puts all of the data that fits between two boundaries into the same partition. Frequently the data is grouped by date, location, or other logical boundary. An example of range partitioning is every purchase order for the year 2001 or every widget that is in the Pittsburgh warehouse. Hash partitioning uses a hash function to determine where to store the data. Subpartitioning, or partitioning already partitioned data further, will speed data access up further and help evenly distribute data within the partition (thus helping to avoid

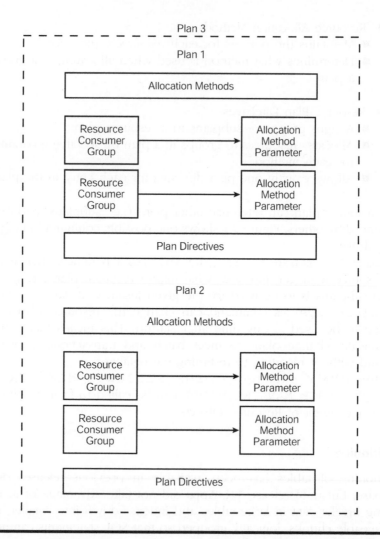

**Figure 2.1    Resource Manager Plan — Configuration of Plans and Subplans**

hot spots). Table 2.4, Table 2.5, and Table 2.6 show examples of using range partitioning. Table 2.4 is raw data, unpartitioned.

Table 2.5 is partitioned by date alone.

Table 2.6 shows the data partitioned by date and within date by location. The query to get all purchase orders in 2001 would run as effectively on either Table 2.4 or Table 2.5, however, the performance for all purchase orders for 2001 for the state of Pennsylvania would be much better on Table 2.6.

**Table 2.4   Partitioning Raw Data**

| PO_NUMBER | PO_DATE | PO_VENDOR | PO_LOCATION |
|---|---|---|---|
| 1234 | 10-Jun-02 | Smith's Office Supply | Pennsylvania |
| 2345 | 8-Jun-02 | Smith's Office Supply | Pennsylvania |
| 5678 | 7-Jul-02 | Smith's Office Supply | Ohio |
| 7891 | 4-Jul-01 | Smith's Office Supply | Ohio |
| 7410 | 8-Jun-02 | Smith's Office Supply | Colorado |
| 8520 | 28-Jun-02 | Smith's Office Supply | Mississippi |
| 9630 | 20-Jun-01 | Smith's Office Supply | Mississippi |
| 1478 | 14-Jan-02 | Smith's Office Supply | Colorado |
| 2589 | 23-Jan-03 | Smith's Office Supply | Tennessee |
| 3697 | 7-Sep-02 | Smith's Office Supply | Tennessee |

**Table 2.5   Partition by Date**

| PO_NUMBER | PO_DATE | PO_VENDOR | PO_LOCATION |
|---|---|---|---|
| 9630 | 20-Jun-01 | Smith's Office Supply | Mississippi |
| 7891 | 4-Jul-01 | Smith's Office Supply | Ohio |
| 1478 | 14-Jan-02 | Smith's Office Supply | Colorado |
| 2345 | 8-Jun-02 | Smith's Office Supply | Pennsylvania |
| 7410 | 8-Jun-02 | Smith's Office Supply | Colorado |
| 1234 | 10-Jun-02 | Smith's Office Supply | Pennsylvania |
| 8520 | 28-Jun-02 | Smith's Office Supply | Mississippi |
| 5678 | 7-Jul-02 | Smith's Office Supply | Ohio |
| 3697 | 7-Sep-02 | Smith's Office Supply | Tennessee |
| 2589 | 23-Jan-03 | Smith's Office Supply | Tennessee |

Partitioning can help you to balance I/O (depending on your disk configuration), separate different parts of the data or index for access and maintenance speed, and help provide the ability to restore parts of tables independently (leading to potentially shorter mean time to recover).

Several schemas in the predefined E-Business Suite database have tables that are partitioned and several more are large enough that they could be. You should keep this in mind when looking at ongoing, long-term maintenance, as you do not want one partition to hold the majority of your data, which defeats the purpose of partitioning.

**Table 2.6  Partition by Date, Subpartition by Location**

| PO_NUMBER | PO_DATE | PO_VENDOR | PO_LOCATION |
|---|---|---|---|
| 9630 | 20-Jun-01 | Smith's Office Supply | Mississippi |
| 7891 | 4-Jul-01 | Smith's Office Supply | Ohio |
| 1478 | 14-Jan-02 | Smith's Office Supply | Colorado |
| 7410 | 8-Jun-02 | Smith's Office Supply | Colorado |
| 2345 | 8-Jun-02 | Smith's Office Supply | Pennsylvania |
| 1234 | 10-Jun-02 | Smith's Office Supply | Pennsylvania |
| 8520 | 28-Jun-02 | Smith's Office Supply | Mississippi |
| 5678 | 7-Jul-02 | Smith's Office Supply | Ohio |
| 3697 | 7-Sep-02 | Smith's Office Supply | Tennessee |
| 2589 | 23-Jan-03 | Smith's Office Supply | Tennessee |

## Parallel Server

Oracle's Parallel Server harnesses the massive processing power of multiple interconnected (or clustered) computers. In a cluster, the united processing capability of each server combines to becomes a single computing environment. Each computer is considered a node and each node processes transactions against a single database. Parallel Server coordinates the access to the data from the nodes and provides for consistency and data integrity, providing a solution to speed access (several small processes running against the database is more efficient than one huge transaction), while helping to achieve high availability. With several nodes contributing to the whole, the failure tolerance is higher. If one node goes down, the slack gets picked up by the remaining nodes and redistributed. This lessened chance of hardware downtime implies higher availability of the database and of Applications to the end user.

A clustered environment is highly scalable. Throwing more users onto a system that has the processing power of several larger servers will show less of an impact than if those same users were added to a single server environment.

## Temporary Tables

Apps 11i now makes use of Oracle 8i's temporary tables feature. Temporary tables exist only for the duration of the session that owns them or for the duration of the transaction that creates them. They hold data privately, locked so only that session can update or modify it. These tables live only in memory and, because they are never written to disk, there is no redo associated with the Data Manipulation Language (DML) that is associated with the temporary table's data. Because there is no redo associated and because they are only accessible by the session that owns them, there are no DML locks required when doing data manipulation within them.

## Applications Manager for Oracle Enterprise Manager

The new Oracle Applications Manager (OAM) module for Oracle Enterprise Manager (OEM) allows administrators to better manage Oracle E-Business Suite systems from a central console. This console can be used for a wide variety of tasks including monitoring and tuning the running processes on the system. With the familiar look and feel of the other OEM products, it allows a DBA to make the leap between just DBA and Applications DBA.

## Invoker's Rights

In past releases, the addition of Multiple Reporting Currencies (MRC) and Multiple Sets of Books to the Oracle Applications architecture brought with it interesting challenges. In companies where these features were implemented, many of the packages that Apps makes use of had to be stored several times each in the database: once for each currency and once for each set of books. This led to longer upgrades and maintenance times as each of the copies had to be taken into account every time an upgrade was performed and every time a minipack or family pack patch was applied. Extra space was also required to store each additional copy of these in the database. This model, that of the user executing a stored procedure and having it execute under the authority of the owner of the package, was known as definer's rights (still the default execution method). The model assumed that an entire application would likely be built within one single Oracle account. Oracle Applications now has over 150 different schemas and owners, so this is not a realistic expectation.

Oracle 8i brings with it a functionality called invoker's rights. Invoker's rights allow each package to be stored once and accessed by different users, each user using their own synonym for the package or procedure and they are only permitted to perform those functions that their role or granted privileges allow them to perform and not the actions that the owner has the rights to perform. This is particularly powerful in the Oracle E-Business Suite, where the Apps schema may own packages that, if run as Apps, can see anything in the system. But if the purchasing department is allowed to see only the relevant personal information about a purchase order requester (e.g., name, department), but not update or delete any of it and that information is stored in the human resources (HR) tables, under definer's rights, purchasing would be able to change the values. Invoker's rights say that the package that queries the values from that table can be created with select, insert, update, and delete privileges, but only HR can insert, update, or delete and purchasing can select and only select, those columns from those tables that are relevant to a purchase order. The added safety of having a procedure or package defined with invoker's rights is that any unqualified call to the procedure will attempt to perform on the schema of the user calling the procedure. One package can now meet these needs, provide a more secure and efficient application, and have one central place for reusable code.

## Locally Managed Tablespaces

Until recent releases of the database, the space allocation for all objects was handled in the data dictionary. This could lead to performance problems as new extent allocation requires several single threaded recursive queries to be run on the System tables to find the free space, allocate it to the new extent, and then mark that space as used. The employee table needs another extent? Go check for free space in the free extents table. If there is free space, go ahead and allocate it to the employee table, but now you have to tell the used extents table that you now have one more used extent. These statements generated rollback, themselves causing further single threaded recursive statements to be generated: one row of redo for each insert, one row of redo for each delete, and a row of rollback for the row that is deleted. If you truncate a table (freeing all used extents) or drop a table (again, freeing all used extents), there would now be multiple rows inserted as available and deleted from being marked as used. These inserts and deletes would be occurring on the data dictionary and the corresponding redo would be happening at the same time. Locally managed tablespaces are tablespaces that use bitmaps to manage their own extents, rather than the data dictionary to do the management for them. These bitmaps keep track of what datafile blocks are used or free; each block of each datafile has its own bit in the bitmap that is switched on or off to show the allocation of each given block. Allocation of a block means flipping one bit from a 0 to a 1; deallocation means changing back from a 1 to a 0, with no rollback and no redo associated. Temporary Tablespaces and Rollback Tablespaces have significant amounts of allocation and deallocation and are therefore prime candidates for being locally managed. There is less chance for contention on these data dictionary tables if you do not have to go to them on a regular basis. Because they are self-managed and no Table updates are done, nearly no rollback information is generated. Further, the management of the extents tracks adjacent free space automatically. This means that there is no longer any need to manually coalesce free space (this is now automatic by design) and significantly reduces fragmentation (this is particularly true if you use uniform allocation).

In some Applications 11i installations, locally managed is the default way that tablespaces are built. In others, running dbms_space_admin.tablespace_migrate_to_local and passing it, the tablespace, as a parameter will allow you to migrate existing dictionary managed tablespace to locally managed ones.

### Diagnosing and Repairing Locally Managed Tablespace Problems

DBMS_SPACE_ADMIN is the package that provides database administrators with detection, diagnosis, and repair functionality for locally managed tablespaces. It cannot, under any circumstances, be used for dictionary managed tablespaces. This is also the procedure that you use when you are migrating from dictionary managed to locally managed and back again. The DBMS_SPACE_ADMIN package contains the following procedures:

- Segment_verify: This procedure verifies the consistency of the extent map for the segment. Does this tablespace currently require repair?
- Segment_corrupt: This procedure marks a segment as either corrupt or valid so that the appropriate recovery can be performed on it. This procedure can never be used on the system tablespace, as any corruptions found in that tablespace cannot be dropped.
- Segment_drop_corrupt: This procedure provides the ability to drop a segment currently marked as corrupt without reclaiming the space that was marked as corrupt. This can never be used on a locally managed system tablespace.
- Segment_dump: This procedure dumps the segment headers and extent map of any given segment.
- Tablespace_verify: This procedure verifies that the bitmaps and the extent maps for the segments in the tablespace are in sync.
- Tablespace_rebuild_bitmaps: If Tablespace_verify shows that the bitmaps are not in sync, use this procedure to rebuild the appropriate bitmaps. This procedure cannot be used on the system tablespace.
- Tablespace_fix_bitmaps: This procedure marks the appropriate data block address ranges to reflect their true status. They will be marked as free or used within the bitmap. This procedure cannot be used on a locally managed system tablespace.

- `Tablespace_migrate_from_local`: This procedure migrates the passed in locally managed tablespace to a dictionary managed tablespace. You cannot use this procedure to change a locally managed system tablespace to a dictionary managed system tablespace.
- `Tablespace_migrate_to_local`: This procedure migrates the passed dictionary managed tablespace to system managed tablespace. This procedure can be used on the system tablespace.
- `Tablespace_relocate_bitmaps`: This procedure relocates the bitmap portion of the specified tablespace (not the system tablespace) to the destination specified.
- `Tablespace_fix_segment_states`: If the migration of a tablespace gets aborted, from system failure, error condition, or because someone closed the session in which the migration was running, this procedure fixes the state of the segments in that tablespace.

None of these procedures should be used without a backup from which you can restore your system. Some of these procedures, if not used correctly, can result in lost and totally unrecoverable data. If you are not comfortable with what they are doing or exactly sure how to use them, do not hesitate to get the assistance of Oracle Support. It will be quicker to get help in not corrupting your data than it will in dealing with a severity 1 iTAR needed to fix the corruption.

How would you use these procedures? Let us look at some situations under which you might be able to use these. This is where you will find the drawbacks to having your tablespaces migrated to locally managed. No longer will all maintenance of the tablespace be taken care of by the system. No longer can you simply assume that there are no issues with your database just because there are no apparent problems. You will now have to run these package procedures to ensure the status of the tablespaces, identify any issues that may arise, and fix the issues after they are uncovered. It is a good administrative practice to attempt different scenarios with the `dbms_space_admin` and your own set of test locally managed tablespaces so there is not a panic situation if you have to run any of these procedures in a real problem situation.

1. You have decided to run the `tablespace_verify` procedure to find out if the bitmap and extent maps for the `IBED` tablespace have any issues. The results indicate that there are several blocks that show up as allocated in the bitmap, but that have no overlapping allocated segments in the extent map. What do you do?
   a. Call `dbms_space_admin.segment_dump` to dump the ranges that have been allocated to that segment.

b. For each of the dumped ranges, call dbms_space_ admin.tablespace_fix_bitmaps with the tablespace_extent_make_used option to mark the space as used.

c. Call dbms_space_admin.tablespace_rebuild_quotas to fix the quotas for that particular tablespace.

2. You are trying to unallocate a segment in the ARD tablespace and you are having problems dropping those segments. You discover that you cannot drop the segment because the segment blocks were marked as free and now the system has remarked them as corrupted. What can you do other than export the data from the tablespace, drop and recreate the tablespace, and reimport the information into the rebuilt tablespace?

a. Run dbms_space_admin.segment_verify with the optional parameter segment_verify_extents_global. If the results returned show no overlaps, proceed; otherwise, contact Oracle Support for assistance before proceeding.

b. Call dbms_space_admin.segment_dump to dump the ranges that are allocated to the segments.

c. For each of the ranges returned, call dbms_space_admin. tablespace_fix_bitmaps using the tablespace_ extent_make_free parameter to mark all appropriate spaces free.

d. Call dbms_space_admin.segment_drop_corrupt to drop the corrupt segment entries from the seg$ sys table.

e. Call dbms_space_admin.tablespace_rebuild_quotas to fix the quotas associated with the tablespace.

3. You have run dbms_space_admin.tablespace_verify and the results show that there is overlapping in the tablespace. Internal errors that you have become aware of indicate that there has to be some data sacrificed (e.g., there have been ORA-26082 errors when attempting to direct path load to one of the interim tables). You have to determine what objects overlap and which of these objects that you can afford to sacrifice.

a. Drop the table that you have chosen to sacrifice.

b. Optionally, run dbms_space_admin.segment_drop_corrupt.

c. Call dbms_space_admin.segment_verify on all of theobjects that t1 may have overlapped.

d. If necessary, run dbms_space_admin.tablespace_fix _bitmaps to mark the appropriate blocks as used.

e. Rerun dbms_space_admin.tablespace_verify to make sure that any overlap is gone.

4. You have determined that there is media corruption causing problems with bitmap blocks in your GLD tablespace.
   a. Call dbms_space_admin.tablespace_rebuild_bitmaps on either all bitmaps in the tablespace or only on the particular corrupt ones.
   b. Call dbms_space_admin.tablespace_rebuild_quotas.
   c. Call dbms_space_admin.tablespace_verify to make sure that the bitmaps in the tablespace are now in a consistent state.

5. Your implementation was done prior to Oracle packaging the Applications database with the parameters allowing all tablespaces to be built as locally managed. You have decided to migrate your entire database to locally managed tablespaces. How do you do this? The following code will assist you in migrating nonsystem tablespaces to locally managed tablespaces.

```
Set head off
Set echo off
Spool migrate.sql
Select 'execute
dbms_space_admin.tablespace_migrate_to_local('||
tablespace_name||');'   from v$tablespace where
tablespace_name = 'SYSTEM';
Spool off
Set head on
Set echo on
```

```
@migrate.sql
```

But what about migrating the sys and system tablespaces? In Oracle 9i it is not only supported but encouraged.

```
Execute
dbms_space_admin.tablespace_migrate_to_local
('SYSTEM');
```

Similar to the nonsystem tablespace, you use the dbms_space_admin procedure to do the migration. Before you start the migration procedure, there are several things that you need to take into account and make sure you have taken care of:

■ Have defined a default temporary tablespace that is not in the SYSTEM tablespace.
■ Have no dictionary managed rollback segment tablespace.

- Have at least one online rollback segment in a locally managed tablespace or migrated to Automatic Undo Management and that tablespace is online.
- Migrate any tablespaces to which you ever want the ability to perform write operations against in the future to locally managed. Once system tablespace has been migrated to locally managed, any tablespaces that were dictionary managed at the time of migration can no longer be opened for read/write access.
- Have all tablespaces other than SYSTEM and the undo or rollback containing tablespaces in read-only mode.
- Have a reliable cold backup of the database and have it available. This is always a safe precaution to take.
- Open the database in restricted mode for the duration of the procedure.

Once you have made sure that all of these conditions are met, you can safely proceed with the migration process. As soon as you have completed the migration of the system tablespace to locally managed, you should immediately test to make sure that your system can function with the new configuration. As soon as possible, take an additional cold backup of the database with the new configuration.

## 11i NEW FEATURES

### Internet Computing Architecture

Apps 11i is the first 100 percent fully Internet deployed version of the front end. Internet computing architecture distributes background processes across different nodes on the network. Oracle Apps 11i is typically deployed on three tiers (although the number of nodes varies). The database tier is where the database is housed. The desktop tier provides the graphical user interface (GUI). In the case of Apps 11i, this means the presentation layer via a plug-in to your standard browser.

On the middle, or application, tier is where the tools that manage the applications reside. This tier allows for a central installation location and eliminates the need to install client software on individual desktops. It also allows Apps to be scalable and limit bottlenecks in network traffic. This middle tier can reside on one or more nodes in the network.

### Forms Server

The Forms Server runs on the application tier and is the intermediary between the Forms Client (a Java applet run from the desktop) and the database. The two pieces exchange messages via a normal network connection. The presentation piece runs in any Java-enabled browser and manages the downloading, startup, and execution of the Forms client, which displays Apps screens, provides field validation, coordinates multi-window interaction, and data entry and validation features (e.g., lists of values and value lookups). The Forms Server also helps run the 9iAS server. This service helps to start the client's session over the intranet or Internet. It is possible to run multiple forms servers to do load balancing among network nodes.

## HTTP Server

### *Oracle Self-Service Web Applications*

Oracle Self-Service Web Applications (SSWA) product family allows users to perform fast, simple entering, updating, and transferring of information within an organization and within the application. Through this interface, and all of its components, customers can enter orders, enter billing disputes, or perform collection inquiries. It allows employees to change their own addresses, but not their salaries. It is designed for secure, self-service business transactions across an intranet, an extranet, or over the Internet. It has several components that can be implemented in many configurations to serve different definitions of end users (i.e., Oracle Web Employees, Oracle Web Customers, and Oracle Web Suppliers).

The architecture of OSSWA consists of the following components:

- Desktop Web browser (Java enabled).
- Oracle's rendition of the Apache HTTP server with Oracle specific extensions.
  - Mod_plsql is an Oracle specific module that routes all PL/SQL requests to the Oracle Universal Server through the Database Access Descriptors (DAD) file.
  - Mod_cgi provides for the execution of Common Gateway Interface (CGI) applications.
  - Mod_ssl deals with data security via cookies, encryption, and session expiration.
  - Mod_jserv routes servlets requests to JServ server engine, which then executes through Java Virtual Machine (JVM). This is one of the key, core components that you will deal with.
  - Mod_perl.

- HTML documents.
- JavaServer Pages (JSP)

- JavaBeans are reusable Java classes that have specific naming conventions for methods and variables. They perform well-defined tasks that are reused over and over (e.g., connecting, screen rendering).
- Java Servlets are small key components of server side Java development.

### Business Intelligence System

BIS is an integrated decision support system through which a manager can monitor recent business performance across multiple organizations, set tolerances, and perform some corrective actions if tolerances are exceeded. BIS works with the Discoverer™ Server and the Oracle Reports Server and runs via a Java applet that communicates with the HTTP Server, which in turn communicates with the Discoverer Server (to allow for ad-hoc analysis) or the Reports Server (for data analysis and queries using summary and aggregate data). To support the Discoverer/BIS interaction, it is necessary to create, in the database, a repository called the End User Layer (EUL) to house Discoverer workbooks and other metadata in the database.

### Personal Home Page

The Personal Home Page (PHP) is another addition to Apps in the 11i release. Your PHP provides a customizable interface between the user and the application. It allows one central page from which to link to all of your Applications responsibilities, access forms-based pieces of the application, SSWA, and BIS products. Through the PHP, you can navigate to anywhere in the system that you are permitted to work via a single log-on. It also allows you to have the freedom to change your password, access your work area, your reports, submit your concurrent requests, set preferences (Do you need Spanish to be your preferred language? PHP will tell all html and forms-based interfaces that is your preference) and contact Oracle from one central launch point.

Figure 2.2 shows an example of the PHP of one system administrator (sysadmin). What shows up on this page depends on what roles in the application the user is permitted to have.

### Product Global Scope

Oracle is committed to providing one product that meets global, regional, and local requirements for organizations of any size or definition. In previous releases, Oracle packaged one central product that conformed closely with U.S. standards (American English with accounting configured

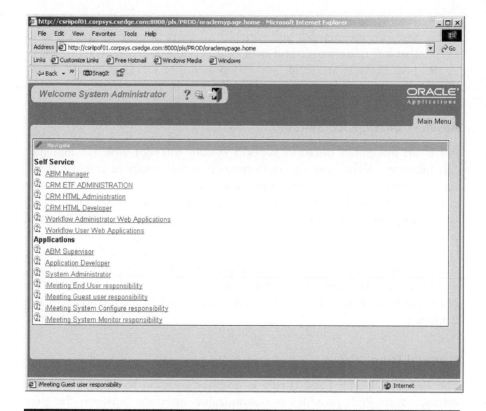

**Figure 2.2  Personal Home Page Example**

to closely adhere to generally accepted accounting principles, GAAP). Oracle packages extensions called localizations that could be added to the base product to provide additional languages of screens and reports, added software features, and added reports that met local statutory regulations. All of these features are now included in the single Oracle Applications product.

## Multiple Language Support

Oracle E-Business Suite's Forms and Reports are now packaged in more than 30 base languages so that people can see the screens in their language without need for an American English installation and then an added piece to allow someone installing in Paris, for example, to have to add customizations to view screens in their language. It also allows a company with employees who have different natural languages to be able to have the screens presented in their languages as well.

Release 10.7 required a customization to provide you with the ability to run Oracle Applications in more than one language. Release 11 had the ability to run in more than one, but still a limited number of languages. The number of languages is limited by the character set chosen. It still required that you input data in the base language, but the form presented to the user could be presented in a language of choice. Languages other than the base language again required costly customizations. Oracle 11i brings with it the ability to run the majority of the products in a multilingual environment. Support for the Unicode UTF8 character set allows the limit on the number of supported languages on a single Apps instance to be removed. UTF8 supports inclusion of all characters commonly used in all of the modern languages found worldwide.

The languages available at the database level are still reliant, to a large extent, on what character set is chosen at installation time. Rapid Install will lay down the database with a default character set of US7ASCII if you do not tell it that you want anything different. US7ASCII supports American English. If you need English and French or you need the ability to store numbers in Euros, you need to select WE8ISO8859P15 (a superset of US7ASCII). Inclusion of Japanese would require you to tell Rapid Install that you want to install in UTF8.

Careful consideration needs to be given to the decision of character set. If you choose US7ASCII and later realize that you needed the functionality of storing Euros or your company expands to the Czech Republic, it will mean an expensive and time-consuming character set conversion and an increase in the storage requirements for the data already stored in the database. For instance, US7ASCII takes up 7 bits; if German is required, the special characters native to German take up an additional bit; and if Japanese is a required language, each character requires 16 bits or 2 bytes for storage.

When the application tier is installed, Rapid Install also, by default, uses US7ASCII. Unless you tell it otherwise, you will be limited to this character set. To allow for ease of translation and lack of data loss, the character set on each tier should match, or be a superset of each other. The easiest way to ensure this is to install UTF8, as it is the only one that is a superset of all. While this may seem somewhat drastic, given your current circumstances, should it become necessary later to include data from another country, its inclusion in UTF8 will allow for a more elegant conversion. The only compatibility caveat to this is that the HTTP server and the browser of choice need to understand and support the same character set. If you are going to use UTF8, you must ensure that the desktop tier supports a font that is UTF8 compliant and make it available to all client machines. Further, the browser needs to be configured so that data inputted be able to be formatted in the required language and it needs to be able to handle any language specific display capabilities (right to left or special character shaping). The character set used is set by the HTTP server at connection time and users need to be aware that they cannot change character sets in their browser at any time during an Apps session.

One added benefit to the multiple language support of Apps 11i, is that it is possible to set up presentation and printing of external documents (e.g., purchase orders, invoices, bills of lading) to be in the preferred language. For example, you can print all French invoices at a given network printer in Paris, all Polish purchase orders to print in Poland, and all Spanish bills of lading to print at the user's printer in Madrid. *The System Administrator's Guide* will help you determine what is available for your release.

### *Multiple Organization Architecture*

Oracle E-Business Suite is designed with all of the flexibility and features needed to handle commercial and nonprofit organizations alike. It can work for any organizational structure, no matter how simple or complex. Because of the nearly infinite number of ways that a company can define itself, Apps contains, at its most basic, a general organizational model that can be customized to fit any definition. An important part of an Oracle E-Business Suite implementation is determining how closely your organization meets this generic definition and to what extent it needs expanding. This definition is usually done at the functional level and the only time that it needs to impact the technology side is in the implementation of features. Multi-Org (Multiple Organizations) is an 11i enhancement that allows for the support of multiple organizations within a single company and within a single database instance.

Multi-Org allows the business to dictate how any given transaction will flow through the different organizations within the business model. The defined organizations can be as narrow or as broad as the business dictates. Within a local company, an organization can be the finance, accounting, human resources, or purchasing departments. They can be defined as legal entities, balancing entities, operating units, inventory organization, HR organizations, different lines within a manufacturing company, client companies in an Application Service Provider environment, or units within divisions of a conglomerate. Any complex corporation today can be subdivided and therefore take advantage of the Multi-Org subsetting to define roles and responsibilities and to assist in the proper flow of information within the business. These more complex organizations can create multiple sets of books and each set of books can be complete with their own subledgers. This allows you to sell and ship what is sold to different legal entities or logical business entities across many sets of books. As stated above, this can also mean that within the same legal entity (itself within a single parent conglomerate), users can be separated within different operating units (e.g., HR, purchasing, accounting) and being assigned to these different units limits what data each user can or cannot see from other operating units. This feature adds an additional level of security as well.

Although the ability to define a Multiple-Organizations organizational structure has been included in releases as far back as Release 10.6 and has been standard since Release 10.7, 11i brought with it enhancements and flexibilities that make it simpler and more elegant to implement.

A global company will rely on Multi-Org as the basis of their Multiple Reporting Currencies.

### Multiple Reporting Currencies

MRC allows you to maintain your financial information in one base, functional currency and report on that information in others. This is done by defining your primary set of books and multiple other reporting sets of books. Examples of common uses for this are when you need to maintain records in the euro and report on transactions in local currency or when the parent company resides in the United States and maintains plants in the United States as well as in other countries and there is a need to report on information in different currencies for the different locations.

### Additional Global Features

Oracle Applications now supports many different ways to enter mail addresses based on the national address of that recipient. The same columns store the data, regardless of where the destination address is; however, the input screens can allow for the specifics of the destination country rather than requiring the address to be fitted into the U.S. Postal Service's standard format.

## ORACLE 9i NEW FEATURES

With all of the database enhancements that Oracle 8i brought to Oracle E-Business Suite over what was available in Oracle7, Oracle brought even more with the release of Oracle 9i. Oracle 9i database provides many new features to the RDBMS world that Oracle E-Business Suite administrator can take advantage of.

## Online Table Redefinition

By its inherent nature, Oracle Financials is designed to be a highly available system. If it is only part of your internal finance and accounting backbone, it is required by those directly connected with those functions to do their day-to-day jobs. It is the key to your company's financial future, as all of the financial information is maintained within its tables. If it is part of your E-business solution and any part of your company's store front on the Internet, its availability is even more critical, particularly if you are multinational.

In systems where high availability is a requirement, it is often necessary to redefine tables to improve performance, to provide added features, or to simply store related information that was not otherwise captured. While you should never attempt to make manual changes to any of the tables that belong to the core product, if you have any custom tables that your company relies on for reporting, for interfacing with outside data sources, or for any functionality that you have determined that Oracle E-Business Suite is lacking, you may find it necessary at some point to redefine one or more of your tables. In past releases, it was often necessary to make these tables unavailable to the end user for the duration of the redefinition. In Oracle 9i, this is no longer the case. Oracle now provides a means by which you can redefine tables online, making a significant improvement in availability in the system. With Online Table Redefinition, only a very small window exists where the table is not accessible to DML and this window is fixed in size regardless of the size or complexity of the table or the redefinition.

For example, you have a table that gets populated from an external source every hour and the process overwrites the previous hour's file. You need to make changes to the table so that one column (abc, for example) will be resized to be 100 varchar2 characters bigger, there will be 3 new columns (e.g., def, ghi, and jkl) and they will be defaulted to 10, 25, and 50, respectively, and the new definition will be range partitioned by the transaction location. Any one of these could be accomplished on its own, each might take a long time, and any of them may cause the table to be locked against update for the period of time that it takes to process the change. But if you process these changes via online redefinition, while it takes a little extra setup to prepare for the procedure, there need not be any interruption in service for the end user to notice.

### Steps for Online Table Redefinition

There are two methods for Online Table Redefinition. The preferred (and default) method for doing an Online Table Redefinition uses the primary key information to perform the redefinition. The only caveat to using this method is that the preredefined table and the postredefined table have to have the same primary key columns. The second uses the rowed method as the vehicle through which the redefinition is accomplished. Using this rowed method, you should not attempt to redefine an Index Organized Table. The end product, the redefined table, has one additional column that the initial table did not have. The hidden M_ROW$$ column is added to the table to facilitate this kind of redefinition and should be either marked as unused or (for a cleaner table) dropped after the redefinition is successfully completed.

The first step in online redefinition is to call the dbms_redefinition.can_redev_table () specifying the table name on which you want to perform the online redefinition as well as the method or redefinition you want to use if you are not using the default. If there is a reason why an online redefinition of the specified table cannot take place, an error will be raised by the procedure indicating why the table is not eligible for Online Table Redefinition.

Once you have determined that the table that you want to redefine is indeed a valid candidate for redefinition, you will have to create an empty interim table in the same schema as the table to be redefined with all of the desired attributes of the table that you want to have as an end product table, including leaving out and adding columns if necessary. This interim table should look exactly as the end table will look.

Table redefinition is an operation that can be performed in parallel. If you want to specify a degree of parallelism for the operation on both tables, you can alter the session in which you will perform the redefinition setting parallel= to the degree you want to attempt and Oracle will use parallel execution whenever it can in the redefinition process speeding the process up as much as it possibly can.

You can now start the table redefinition process by executing:

```
dbms_redefinition.start_redef_table(table_name,
interim_table_name, column mapping, redef method)
```

Table name and interim table name have to be present in the parameter list; the procedure cannot make this assumption. However, you can omit the column mappings for the columns that are mapped exactly the same in both tables (i.e., the names are unchanged in the interim table). If the method of redefinition is omitted, the default method is assumed, meaning that the procedure will attempt to use the primary key manner to redefinition.

Make sure that you have defined any triggers, indexes, grants, and constraints on the interim table that exist in the base table. Referential constraints that would in any way affect the base table, either as the parent or the child in any relationships, need to be created in a disabled state. Until the redefinition is complete, the triggers will be inactive and will not fire for the triggering event if it should occur. Once the redefinition is completed, the triggers, constraints, indexes, and grants associated with the interim table will replace those on the table being redefined, eliminating the need for you to manually go and redefine them after definition time. They will transfer in a fully enabled state at the end of the redefinition process.

You can now execute the dbms_redefintion.finish_ redev_table() procedure to allow for the successful completion of the redefinition of the original table. Again, during this procedure, there will be a small fixed window where the table will be locked against DML independent of the size and complexity of the table and ensuing processes. This procedure will complete the process, redefine the original table so that it has all of the attributes, triggers, constraints, indexes, and grants as the interim table had, and make sure that any referential constraints that were defined on the interim table will be created on the final table as enabled.

Now you can complete the optional step of dropping the hidden M_ROW$$ column that was included in the final table if you chose to use the rowed method of redefintion, using either of the following methods:

■ Alter table <your table> set unused M_ROW$$;
■ Alter table <your table> drop M_ROW$$;

As a result of this process you now have the following product in your system. The original table has been redefined and contains all desired attributes, constraints, and features. All indexes, constraints, grants, and triggers defined on the interim table are now defined on the base table as it was redefined. All referential constraints created as disabled on the interim table are now created on the end redefined table as enabled. All constraints, triggers, referential integrity (RI), and indexes on the original unredefined table have been transferred to the interim table and will be dropped when you choose to drop the interim table. And referential constraints that were built on the original version of the table are now on the interim table and are disabled. What is more important, though, all PL/SQL procedures, packages, and cursors defined on the original table are now invalidated. They will be revalidated, depending on how the table was changed, the next time that they are accessed. This validation can fail if the table definition has changed sufficiently to make the addition of programming logic a requirement in these program units.

If you are redefining a heavily accessed table, it is possible for there to have been a large amount of DML occurring on the base table during the redefinition process. This is one of the advantages of redefining online. If you know ahead of time that this is likely to occur, Oracle recommends that you periodically synchronize the interim table's data with the data from the original table. This is accomplished by periodically calling the `dbms_redefinition.sync_interim_table` () procedure, which allows the `dbms_redefinition.finish_redef_table` to finish faster, and reducing the overall time that it takes to complete the redefinition. The window of unavailability will still occur, as this is independent of the amount of data or the volume of transactions that have occurred during the process.

So what happens if there is an exception raised during the redefinition process or if you opt to abort the process? Call the `dbms_redefintion.abort_redef_table()` procedure to drop the temporary logs and tables that are associated with the redefinition process. You can then safely drop the interim table along with all of its associated objects and continue on as if nothing ever occurred.

Naturally, there are drawbacks:

■ Tables that have MVs and MV logs defined on them are not candidates for online redefinition.
■ Advanced Queuing tables cannot be redefined.
■ While an Index Organized Table can be redefined, its overflow table cannot.
■ Tables that have user-defined types cannot be redefined.
■ Tables containing `BFILE` columns are not candidates, nor are tables with long columns (although large objects (LOB), columns are acceptable).
■ The table cannot be part of a cluster.
■ The table cannot belong to `system` or `sys` and it cannot be a temporary table.
■ Horizontal subsetting of data cannot be handled in online redefinition.
■ Only simple expressions are permitted in mapping the columns from the base table to the interim table. These cannot include subqueries.
■ Now columns must not be declared as not null in the redefinition process. This has to be done after definition.
■ There can be no referential constraints between the base and interim tables.
■ Redefinition cannot be done `nologging`.

## Skip Scan Index

A composite index is an index that contains more than one column in the key. Typically a composite index can have significant improvements in selectivity and reductions in I/O. Two columns that have very poor selectivity can be combined to see significant improvements in selectivity. I/O can be reduced if the Oracle RDBMS can get the information that it requires by the use of an index, which can reduce the amount of time it would spend fetching blocks into memory to determine if the information it was looking for would be found in that block. Oracle has been able to use the index for an access path if the leading column of the index was used in the query. Typically columns in composite indexes are chosen because they:

- Occur frequently together in where clauses (on the all_objects table this is an index referencing owner and status: where owner='SYS' and status = 'INVALID').
- Are frequently found in and conditions (SYS and INVALID).
- Have higher selectivity when taken together than if they were taken alone (sys usually does not have a lot of invalid objects, but there are often many invalids and sys owns a lot of objects).
- Are almost always selected (the two or more columns) together.

For example, on the FND_CONCURRENT_PROCESSES table (the table in which Apps stores information about Concurrent Manager jobs), there is an index defined called fnd_concurrent_processes_n1. This index has three columns: queue_application_id, concurrent_queue_id, and process_status_code. The leading edge of the index would be the columns defined, left to right, in the list in the create index statement, and in the above list, as well. For Oracle to make use of this index, at least queue_application_id would have to be in the query. But running a query by process_status_code would (had there not already been an index built on that column alone) have caused, in all likelihood, a full table scan.

Index skip scans improve index usage considerably, because they allow the index to be used by nonleading columns as long as they participate in the index's makeup, because scanning the index blocks is still faster than scanning the table blocks to quickly locate pieces of information. The initial column in the index definition is, in effect, skipped by the query either because the information was not needed, or a qualifier could not be specified for the column. Skip scanning is particularly effective if there are a few distinct values in the leading column and more distinct values in the nonleading columns. In the case of the example index (owner = SYS and status = invalid) the reverse is true. To make full use of skip scanning, the index would be defined with status as the leading value (as in the case of all_objects, status can take on two values and in financials, owner can take on nearly 200). The query select count(*) from all_objects where owner = 'SYS' would skip the leading value of "status" in the index and perform a scan of the subindex, owner would provide the desired information in a more timely fashion.

## Transportable Tablespaces

Transportable Tablespaces are tablespaces within an Oracle database that can be defined to move data and structures from one database to another, simply by plugging the new tablespace into the alternative instance. This allows the data in the tables and the table structures to be moved without having to take the time for an extended outage. This may be a valid option when looking at cloning options and alternatives, when all you need to refresh is the data in the instances, and you have a limited number of modules configured. The tablespaces that are being transported can either be dictionary managed or locally managed, but dictionary managed tablespaces cannot be opened for write operations in a database with a locally managed system tablespace. Starting in Oracle 9i, the transported tablespaces can be of a different block size than the standard block size of the database into which they are being transported. Typically, Transportable Tablespaces are used for migrating information from an OLTP system into a data warehouse staging area, eliminating a significant part of the transformation process in the process. Further uses include:

■ Updating the data warehouses and data marts or reporting instances from staging areas
■ Loading data marts from the far larger central data warehouses
■ Archiving OLTP information and data warehouse information rather than dumping it to tape
■ Data publishing by pushing information to either (or both) internal or external customers
■ Enabling the ability to perform Tablespace Point-in-Time Recovery, where you recover a single tablespace to a specific point in time while allowing all of the rest of the database to be at a different point because the corruption was self-contained.

Moving a tablespace full of data can be much faster than performing an export/import on the tablespace level or an unload and load of the tablespace's data because there is no database level manipulation but rather is handled by directly copying the data files from one instance to another and then integrating the tablespace's structural information into the new database. Because you can choose to move any tablespaces, data or index, you can avoid having to rebuild indexes as you would likely have to do when either importing or loading the data directly into tables. Consistency is maintained while keeping time to an absolute minimum.

As with all of the new features, the advantages are tempered with certain limitations and Transportable Tablespaces are no exception:

- Both the source and target database must be on the same hardware platform and OS. You cannot use Transportable Tablespaces to move the database from RS-6000® AIX 5L to Intel® Based Windows 2000 or even between Intel® Based Linux and Intel® Based Windows 2000.
- Both the source and target database have to use the same character set and national character set. This is true even if one character set is a subset of the other.
- You cannot use Transportable Tablespaces to overlay a tablespace that already exists in the target database with the same name. This would imply that the only way that you could use these, at this point in time, would be to drop custom tables in their tablespaces from the target database and overlay where they used to be with the newly refreshed data from production or as a means for migrating similar structures from a well-tested test environment into production. Great care should be taken when you start attempting this and Oracle Support should be initially involved.
- Tablespaces containing certain kinds of structures are not candidates for transport. These structures include:
  - MVs used for replication
  - Function-based indexes
  - Scoped REFs
  - Advanced queues with multiple recipients that are at an 8.0 compatible level

If you are going to be transporting tablespaces with a different block size than the target database's standard block size, the compatible parameter has to be set to at least 9.0 on the target database. You do not have to be running the same Oracle version in both databases, so you could transport an Oracle 8i tablespace into a 9i database. Oracle guarantees that the Transportable Tablespace is compatible with the target database or an error condition will be signaled at the beginning of the transport plug-in operation. Transporting from an older database to a newer release of the database is always possible, as long as you meet the previously stated limitations. When creating and transporting Transportable Tablespace sets, Oracle determines the lowest compatibility level to which the target database needs to be set. When attempting to put the new tablespace into the target database, Oracle will throw an error if the compatibility level of the transportable set is higher than the compatibility level of the target. One solution might be to lower the compatibility level of the source database or to raise the compatibility level of the target database for the duration of the operation.

When you are ready to proceed with transporting a set of tablespaces, the following procedures should be followed.

Pick a set of self-contained tablespaces that you want to transport. There can be no logical or physical dependencies between the entire set of tablespaces and those structures outside of the set within the database. There can be no references from within the set pointing to structures outside the entire set that you are trying to transport. There can be no indexes inside the tablespace set on the tables that are not within the set that are not contained in tablespaces within the set (however indexes on tables in the tablespace set do not have to be included). You cannot have referential integrity that points to structures that are outside of the set (no child table or parent table can be outside of the transport set). However, you can choose not to include constraints and these tablespaces would be able to be included in a transport set. Tablespaces containing objects that have LOB columns or that point to LOBs outside of the tablespace set are not candidates for the transport operation. Have someone with the execute catalog role call the DBMS_TTS.TRANSPORT_SET_CHECK procedure to determine if the tablespace set is self-contained and able to be transported. You pass into the DBMS_TTS.TRANSPORT_SET_CHECK procedure the list of tablespaces in the tablespace set and indicate whether you want to have referential integrity and constraints included in the check.

After you have determined that you have a self-contained set of tablespaces, generate a transportable tablespace set that consists of the data files for the set of tablespaces being transported along with a file containing the structural information for the set of tablespaces to be transported. Make all of the tablespaces involved in the tablespace set read only:

```
Alter tablespace users_data read only;
Alter tablespace users_indexes read only;
```

You then have to invoke the export utility, specifying which tablespaces are in the transport set. While you are still using the export utility, you are exporting only the information that is contained in the data dictionary concerning the tablespaces in the tablespace set; therefore, this export, regardless of tablespace size, goes very rapidly.

```
Exp transport_tablespace=y tablespaces=(users_data,
users_indexes) triggers=y constraints=n grants=n
file=transport.dmp
```

You will be prompted for the user with whom to connect; connect with a user that has the sysdba privilege, typically if you have OS authentication it would look like the following:

```
Connect '/as sysdba'
```

You always have to specify tablespaces that are in your transport set. Triggers can be included. You must either specify `triggers = y` or `triggers = n`. If you choose `triggers = y`, then your triggers are exported without a validity check and this may cause compilation errors later during the subsequent import.

You need to specify whether or not referential integrity constraints and grants are to be exported. Specify the name of the export file that will contain the structural information.

If the tablespace sets that you are trying to transport are determined not to be self-contained at this point, the export fails and indicates that the failure is due to the transportable set not being self-contained. You must then resolve all violations and attempt this again.

Transport the tablespace set from the source database to the target database. This is accomplished by copying the data files along with the export information file to the target system, either using FTP, copy, `Tar` to tape and `untar` to the new location, or burning to CD and copying from the CD to the new location. Transport both the data files and the export files of those tablespaces to a central place that is accessible to the target database.

Plug the new tablespace into the target system. To do this, you invoke the import utility to plug the new information into the new database. If you are transporting a tablespace set that has a different block size than the standard block size of the target database receiving the tablespace set, you must have first set a `DB_nK_CACHE_SIZE` initialization parameter entry in the receiving database's parameter file matching the block size for the tablespace set. If it is not already included in the parameter file, the `DB_nK_CACHE_SIZE` parameter can be set using the `ALTER SYSTEM SET` statement. You plug the tablespace set into the target database and integrate the structural information using the import utility. Again, you are importing the data dictionary information only, so the import time will be minimal.

```
IMP TRANSPORT_TABLESPACE=y FILE=transport.dmp
    DATA FILES=('/db/users_dat.dbf','/db/
    users_idx.dbf') TABLESPACES=(users_dat,
    users_index) TTS_OWNERS=(users)FRO-
    MUSER=(users) TOUSER=(users)
```

At this point, if everything has successfully executed, all tablespaces have been copied and are now in read-only mode in the new database. You will need to check the import logs to determine that no errors have occurred.

Inputting the list of data files can be somewhat labor intensive, particularly if you have an extensive set of tablespaces in your transport set or if there are a large number of data files associated with the tablespaces.

If the list becomes prohibitively long (if it spans more than a line) you can put all of the parameters to import into a single file and use that file as a parfile (parameter file) and invoke import as follows:

```
IMP PARFILE='ajw_import'
```

The file `'ajw_import'` file would contain the following:

```
TRANSPORT_TABLESPACE=y FILE=transport.dmp
DATA FILES=('/db/users_dat.dbf','/db/
users_idx.dbf')
TABLESPACES=(users_dat, users_index)
TTS_OWNERS=(users)
FROMUSER=(users)  TOUSER=(users)
```

You can now put the Transported Tablespaces back into read/write mode.

```
Alter tablespace users_data read write;
Alter tablespace users_indexes read write;
```

## Online Table Reorganization

We have seen that we can redefine a table online, but one of the most resource intensive things that a DBA can do is to reorganize the tables. This is particularly true for a DBA who is responsible for an OLTP database that can far exceed 50 or 100 gigabytes in just the data. You can now perform reorganization of heap tables (that is those tables that are not index organized tables or external tables) online, while allowing users access to the data.

The online architecture provides you the ability to do any or all of the following:

- Any of the physical attributes of the table can be changed online.
- The table can be moved to a new tablespace.
- The table can be partitioned or partitions added.
- The table can be converted from one type of organization (such as a heap-organized) to another (such as index-organized).
- Column names, column types, and column sizes can be changed.
- Columns can be added, deleted, or merged online, although the primary key of the table cannot be modified online.
- Online creation and rebuilding of secondary indexes on index-organized tables is supported.
- Indexes can be created online and analyzed at the same time to save time and resources.

## List Partitioning

Recall that with Oracle 8i, you were able to partition tables and the indexes that went along with the tables. Oracle 9i brings an enhancement to the partitioning algorithm — list partitioning. List partitioning is used when you require explicit control over how the rows in a table are mapped to the partitions in the table. In this method of partitioning, you specify a list of discrete values for the partitioned columns in the description of each partition. This is vastly different from the way that range partitioning is handled in that you do not just specify an upper limit value and all values smaller than that value fall into the partition.

A good example of when list partitioning is appropriate is when you have a predescribed list of account numbers, department numbers, or other set of limited values that have particular meaning to your business and reside in some of the large tables in the database. As your financials instance grows, you may find more and more uses for list partitioning, or partitioning in general.

Range partitioning assumes that the data matches a natural range of values for the partition column. It is not possible to physically group together those out-of-range values. Hash partitioning allows absolutely no control over the distribution of data. In a hash partition, the data is distributed over various partitions using a system hash algorithm, making it impossible to logically group together the discrete data values for the partition columns into the particular partitions.

List partitioning allows you to group together unordered and not obviously related sets of data. All of the data for all of the departments that fall under a particular division could be partitioned together, allowing for quicker queries on that data by those falling into that set of departments. You can group the data together in a manner that matches the logic behind the business rules rather than using an arbitrary algorithm or having to manipulate the data to fit the algorithm.

One drawback is that, unlike hash or range partitioning, you cannot have multiple columns involved in the list of values in the partition list. If you choose to partition a column by list method, you are limited to a single column on the table on which to partition.

When you create the partitions in the list partition set you have to specify the method that you are using to partition, the column that will be involved, and the partition descriptions (each specifying a value list of literal discrete values) for the partitioning column that designate a row to be included in a particular partition. You cannot create an `all others into` parameter; you have to ennumerate all of the values that you anticipate being inserted into the table. An attempt to insert a value that does not fall into any existing partition will cause an error condition. Instead, you can define a default partition in which to place those rows that would otherwise not fall into a partition. This will allow you go back and determine commonalities in the data that is suddenly falling into the default partition and more effectively partition the data later. This means that, if you opt for using list partitions as a partitioning method, you will have to work even more closely with the end users of the system to head off problems when new values for the partitioned columns are added for expanded business reasons. If you look at the following definition of the GL_BALANCES (see Table 2.7), we might define a list partition on period name or, if you have multiple sets of books (multi-org), you might decide to list partition on set_of_books ID to segregate each set into its own partition.

Unlike range partitioning, in list partitioning there is no apparent sense of ordering between the different values that end up falling into any one partition.

Range or hash partitioning or composite partitioning are perfect methods for partitioning data for historical segregations or for striping. Primarily these are done for improved manageability and data placement and to add the ability to take advantage of parallelism when going after the data in the table. Often these ranges are done in data warehouses to segregate the data by date range, range of account numbers if they are sequential, or other information that can be easily chunked under a broad umbrella. Sales by month can be stored in a partition sales by years and within years, further partitioned by month. This allows administrators to be able to drop all of the data for a period of time based on business rules, suggesting that the company will retain only that sales information for the last ten years on the active database.

You can, however, take advantage of the advantages of both range partitioning and list partitioning by using a composite range/list method. This can allow for a two level hierarchy, the first level being a range of values and the second level being an enumerated list of values within that range. This form of composite partitioning would be well suited if you know that all departments in the range of 6000 to 6999 all report to a single upper management general manager, while the physical locations of the departments are disparate and seem to have no relation to each other. Department 6010 may be in Denver while 6020 is in Tampa and 6030 is in London. You would be able to take advantage of the speed in accessing all of the departments that the general manager manages. At the same time, you would be able to group together all of the information that belongs to a certain department by the commonality of that department. The definition of this kind of composite partitioning would follow the following method:

- Broad outer partitioning method: range.
- Partitioning column or columns to use for the range of values (you can use multiple columns in this outer range partition).

**Table 2.7   The GL_BALANCES Table**

| Name | Datatype | Size | Scale |
|------|----------|------|-------|
| SET_OF_BOOKS_ID | NUMBER | 15 | 0 |
| CODE_COMBINATION_ID | NUMBER | 15 | 0 |
| CURRENCY_CODE | VARCHAR2 | 15 | |
| PERIOD_NAME | VARCHAR2 | 15 | |
| ACTUAL_FLAG | VARCHAR2 | 1 | |
| LAST_UPDATE_DATE | DATE | 7 | |
| LAST_UPDATED_BY | NUMBER | 15 | 0 |
| BUDGET_VERSION_ID | NUMBER | 15 | 0 |
| ENCUMBRANCE_TYPE_ID | NUMBER | 15 | 0 |
| TRANSLATED_FLAG | VARCHAR2 | 1 | |
| REVALUATION_STATUS | VARCHAR2 | 1 | |
| PERIOD_TYPE | VARCHAR2 | 15 | |
| PERIOD_YEAR | NUMBER | 15 | 0 |
| PERIOD_NUM | NUMBER | 15 | 0 |
| PERIOD_NET_DR | NUMBER | | |
| PERIOD_NET_CR | NUMBER | | |
| PERIOD_TO_DATE_ADB | NUMBER | | |
| QUARTER_TO_DATE_DR | NUMBER | | |
| QUARTER_TO_DATE_CR | NUMBER | | |
| QUARTER_TO_DATE_ADB | NUMBER | | |
| YEAR_TO_DATE_ADB | NUMBER | | |
| PROJECT_TO_DATE_DR | NUMBER | | |
| PROJECT_TO_DATE_CR | NUMBER | | |
| PROJECT_TO_DATE_ADB | NUMBER | | |
| BEGIN_BALANCE_DR | NUMBER | | |
| BEGIN_BALANCE_CR | NUMBER | | |
| PERIOD_NET_DR_BEQ | NUMBER | | |
| PERIOD_NET_CR_BEQ | NUMBER | | |
| BEGIN_BALANCE_DR_BEQ | NUMBER | | |
| BEGIN_BALANCE_CR_BEQ | NUMBER | | |
| TEMPLATE_ID | NUMBER | 15 | 0 |
| ENCUMBRANCE_DOC_ID | NUMBER | 15 | 0 |
| ENCUMBRANCE_LINE_NUM | NUMBER | 15 | 0 |

■ Partition descriptions identifying partition bounds (including maximum value default partition).

■ Narrower subpartitioning method: list.

■ Subpartitioning column (list partition, one column).

■ Subpartition descriptions and for each description a value list of discrete literal values that will tell the table that a row qualifies to be included in the subpartition.

The outer partitions of range-list composite partitioned tables are logical structures only. The data is physically stored in the segments of the subpartitions of the table. The list subpartitions in the composite range list partition have similar characteristics to those of simple list partitions. You can specify a default list subpartition, just as you specify a default partition for list partitioning to assist you in your maintenance and in providing the best product possible for the end users.

## Dynamic SGA

Before Oracle 9i, there was a limited amount of tuning that you could do in the System Global Area (SGA). Now, you can exert more control over this part of the system. You can even do dynamic tuning while your instance is up and running. With the dynamic SGA structure, the size of the components of the SGA can be changed dynamically without having to shutdown the database. These structures over which you have extended control include the buffer cache, the large pool, and the process private memory that is allocated within the SGA.

Dynamic SGA limits how much virtual memory is available for use by Oracle and can be set at runtime. The instance can be started unconfigured, which allows the instance to grow and use more or less memory as the demand on the database changes. There is a maximum size that can be set to set upper bounds to which you will permit the SGA to grow. The parameter that allows for the bounding of the SGA is the sga_max_size parameter. This is the only parameter surrounding the use of the SGA that is fixed at database startup and can only be altered by restarting the database. As with a lot of the initialization parameters, Oracle looks at this value as a friendly suggestion, but if all of the components that are either specified or left at the default values sum up to a size larger than the value specified for the sga_max_size parameter, the parameter will be summarily ignored.

Optimally, the entire SGA for all instances on a box summed together should fit into physical memory. If it does not, virtual memory and paging space is used to store different parts of it, thereby decreasing the overall performance because of the increased disk I/O that is associated with operation.

The size of the SGA is determined by several initialization parameters. The following parameters most affect SGA size:

- DB_CACHE_SIZE: The size of the cache of the standard block size blocks.
- LOG_BUFFER: The log_buffer parameter designates the number of bytes that are allocated for the redo log buffer.
- SHARED_POOL_SIZE: The size in bytes of the area devoted to shared SQL and PL/SQL statements.
- LARGE_POOL_SIZE: This is the size of the large pool. The default is 0.

The total memory allocated to an instance's SGA is displayed on the screen when an instance's startup is processed, or when using OEM or SQL*Plus. You can deliberately display the size of the current instance's SGA using the SQL*Plus SHOW SGA statement.

With the new dynamic SGA, the unit of memory allocation is called a granule. Oracle allocates and tracks the memory used by each component in the SGA (i.e., the buffer cache, the shared pool, the Java pool, and the large pool) and all SGA free space in units of granules. In the SGA, memory is only allocated on the granule boundary, never in portions of granules.

Granule size in the SGA is determined by total overall SGA size. On most OSs and hardware platforms, the size of one granule is 4 MB if the total SGA size is less than 128 MB and 16 MB for any SGA larger than 128 MB. There are some platform dependent idiosyncrasies, most particularly on Windows NT/2000® platforms where the larger granule (for SGAs larger than 128 MB) is 8 MB instead of the typical 16 MB. The current granule size for a running database can be viewed using the V$SGA_DYNAMIC_COMPONENTS view. The same size is used for all dynamic components in the SGA. You can specify a size for these configurable components and when you do, it should be specified in a size that equates to a multiple of the current granule size. If you specify a size that is not a multiple of the current granule size, for example 13 MB on an SGA that is 100 MB, Oracle will round the size to the next largest granule boundary, allocating for the component 16 MB.

Oracle maintains information about these components and their allocated granules in what it calls a scoreboard. For every allocated and configured component for which at least one granule has been allocated, the scoreboard contains (1) the number of granules allocated to the component, (2) the description of any transactions that are currently pending against the component, (3) the target size in granules (you will have to do the math to determine how close it is to its boundary) and the progress made towards reaching its target size, and (4) the initial number of granules allocated to the component and the maximum number of granules that it can have. For operations on the database that can modify the number of granules, Oracle logs the operation, the target size, and start time to the affected SGA component in the scoreboard and updates the progress field until the running process completes. When the process completes, the scoreboard gets updated, sets the current size with the target size, clears the target size and progress fields, and allows the DBA to see how the number of granules allocated changed. Oracle then alters the initialization parameters to reflect how much of the SGA is currently in use.

The scoreboard is, in effect, a circular buffer that contains the last 100 operations made to the scoreboard. The fixed views show the state of the scoreboard at any given time and the current contents to the 100-operation limit of its size.

Information about current and on-going SGA resize-affecting operations can be found in the V$SGA_CURRENT_RESIZE_OPS view, information about those last 100 completed SGA resize operations can be found in the V$SGA_RESIZE_OPS view, and the amount of SGA memory that is currently left available for future dynamic SGA resize operations can be found in the V$SGA_DYNAMIC_FREE_MEMORY view.

You can allocate granules at startup. When the instance starts up, Oracle reads the values in the parameter file (the init.ora or the spfile) and determines what settings it expects to be able to allocate based on the OS's memory limits. Oracle then allocates virtual address space for the SGA. SGA_MAX_SIZE is read from the initialization file and the values for the malleable components are rounded to the next highest granule.

You can grow a component's SGA use by using the Alter System command. If you are using spfile, remember that you need to determine if you want this change to be just for the current instance of the database or if you want it to persist through the next shutdown and pass the scope parameters to the alter command based on that decision. Oracle will take your newly suggested size, round it to the nearest multiple of granules, and add or subtract granules to meet this target size. Oracle will, in this case, stop allocating granules when it comes to the SGA_MAX_SIZE boundary. It will only allocate those free granules that it knows it can safely allocate and will not be able to handle any request that would cross that boundary.

```
SQL*Plus: Release 9.2.0.2.0 - Production on Wed
Jul 16 08:09:35 2003
Copyright (c) 1982, 2002, Oracle Corporation.  All
rights reserved.
Connected to an idle instance.
SQL> ORACLE instance started.
```

```
Total System Global Area 110100536 bytes
Fixed Size                  741432 bytes
Variable Size             92274688 bytes
Database Buffers          16777216 bytes
Redo Buffers                307200 bytes
Database mounted.
Database opened.
SQL> Disconnected from Oracle 9i Enterprise Edition
Release 9.2.0.2.0 - 64bit Production
With the Partitioning, OLAP and Oracle Data Mining
options
JServer Release 9.2.0.2.0 - Production
```

## Multiple Block Sizes

New in Oracle 9i, you are no longer tied to the standard block size that is defined at database creation time. Now nonstandard block sizes can be used when creating tablespaces so you can intelligently decide what size to make tablespaces based on what you will be putting in those tablespaces. Have you ever wanted to be able to put indexes into a 16K block size, but your database was created with a standard block size of 4K for performance improvement? Now you can. You can define the standard block size of the database and nonstandard block sizes in discrete values of powers of 2 (2K, 4K, 8K, 16K, 32K). There are some platform specific limitations on the maximum block size, so these are general values and may not necessarily be available depending on what OS your database is residing on. This feature is particularly useful when you are transporting tablespaces between databases created with different standard block sizes, but also can have significant ramifications if you are looking at tuning.

When a tablespace is created using the create tablespace statement, you can use the "blocksize" keyword to specify the size in kilobytes of the blocks that you want to use for that tablespace. To define a table in this manner, first you will have had to define the buffer cache in the SGA that will be dedicated to processing information from components of that block size. The initialization parameters connected with enabling this feature affect the amount of memory that gets allocated in the SGA. With the exception of sga_max_size (the static initialization parameter), all of the parameters that deal with this ability are dynamic and alterable with the alter system command. The size of your SGA could grow or shrink considerably based on the values specified for these dynamic parameters.

The block size of the System tablespace is set when the database is created; it is the db_block_size and can only be changed by recreating the database. Most other tablespaces will use this size as well, unless you deliberately tell them otherwise at creation time. You can specify five total block sizes, including the standard block size for most databases on most platforms.

Before you can create an alternatively block-sized tablespace, you have to create the subcaches (although they are not a part of the size of the db_cache, they are called subcaches) for each of the block sizes that you believe you will need to use. If you find the need later to add another one, they can be added as well as altered while the database is running. DB_nK_CACHE_SIZE needs to be set, replacing the "n" with the number of kilobytes that is being defined as the block size. DB_16K_CACHE_SIZE would be the cache size parameter for the database cache dedicated to handling the objects created in the 16K block size tablespace.

Smaller block sizes are better for small rows with a lot of random accessed information because it tends to reduce block contention. Smaller block sizes also have fairly large space overhead (block header information) due to the metadata that has to be stored. It is not recommended for tables that have large rows where there might only be a few rows able to be stored for each block or for row chaining when not even a single row fits into a block.

Larger block sizes have lower metadata overhead, so there is more usable space to store data. You can utilize this more data per block feature because you can read more rows into the buffer cache with every block retrieved in a single I/O. They are good for tables with high sequential read access, full table scans, or very large rows (especially rows containing LOB (large objects)/BLOB (binary large objects)/CLOB (character large objects) data). However, they can waste space in the buffer cache if you are doing random access reads on tables with small rows that reside in tablespaces that have a large block size. A good example is when you pull in information from a tablespace that has an 8K block size and there is only a 50-byte row size. In this case, you will have potentially wasted 7950 bytes in the buffer cache when doing random access on the table. Further, they may not be good for certain index blocks used in a heavily accessed OLTP environment, because they may tend to increase block contention on the index leaf blocks. Depending on the number of users and the volume of data, you may want to consider them.

Temporary Tablespaces have to be created in the standard block size of the database.

When using partitioning, all partitions of a partitioned table, even those in separate tablespaces, must reside in tablespaces of the same block size. This means if you create the first partition as 8K, all partitions of that table must be 8K.

## Cursor Sharing

Although cursor sharing is not new to Oracle 9i, it has seen significant improvements in recent releases. Initially cursor sharing was set as:

```
Cursor_sharing = exact
```

This meant that any SQL statement that had identically matching text in the SQL area could use the same execution plan. But only statements that were textually identical could make use of this feature. This exactness extended to white space, bind variable values, and literal values; they had to be indexically identical.

The `force` setting was introduced in Oracle 8i, allowing (causing) vaguely similar statements to use the same execution plan. This can have the effect of severely degrading performance as it may deteriorate the execution plan of the SQL already in the SQL area and allowing suboptimal plans to be used instead or recalculating the plan. Force should be used only when the trade-offs between the new plans in total outweigh the drawbacks of the performance previously.

In Oracle 9i, the `similar` setting was brought into the equation allowing for a middle ground between hardly ever using them and nearly always using the ability. In short, `similar` will force similar statements (including the values in the bind variables) to share the SQL area without deteriorating execution plans.

You will want to set `Cursor_sharing = similar` if you have many similar SQL statements executed in an environment. Because much of what is done in Oracle E-Business Suite is repetitious, and the only difference between the statements is often the values in the `update` or `where` clause, making use of the `similar` setting will likely show performance improvements to much of the application. While the optimal solution would be to have everything written with sharable SQL code, `Cursor_sharing` will significantly reduce the amount of resources required of the system and will lower the number of hard parses required. Soft parses, the parses of the shared pool, may rise somewhat as Oracle will look there first to see if there is an existent cursor that can be used to apply to the current statement. `Similar` may slow down queries marginally if a significant amount of literals are used in the query. Overall, setting `Cursor_sharing` to `similar` should reduce memory usage, speed up parse times, and reduce overall latch contention.

A statement is considered similar if the statements are identical except for some literals, although a textual similarity does not guarantee sharing. Cursor sharing will have the effect of making the CBO determine if it is a close enough match to something that exists in the shared pool to make it able to use the same `explain` plan.

## External Tables

How do you get external information integrated into your database? Do you have a set of custom tables that you load, probably via SQL*Ldr and then, from there, drag into the database using the Oracle E-Business Suite utilities? Do you import information into custom tables for use in generating reports that combine this information with information resident in the Apps database? There might be an easier way.

Oracle 9i brought with it a new enhancement called external tables. External tables allow data in an OS's flat file to be accessed as if it were a standard Oracle unindexed table set to read-only access. You simply need to define the metadata about the external table to the Oracle Data Dictionary and tell Oracle how the columns in the file are mapped to perceived columns in the end table. Oracle makes no assumptions about the data in the external table; it simply allows for the access of the data in a more simplified and intuitive manner than might otherwise be available. The definition to Oracle includes the keywords "organization external" in the `create table` statement.

To use external tables, the user or owner of the tables has to have the following system level privileges, so care should be taken to ensure that limited users have this ability. It may be wise not to let some of them know exactly what access they have.

- Alter any table.
- Select any table.
- Read access on the OS directory containing the file.
- Write access on the OS directory containing the file.

Write access on the directory is required for bad files, log files, and discard files.

## Automatic Undo Management

In previous versions of the database, rollback information (the preimage of the data involved in active transactions) was stored in Rollback Segments. The preimages were used so that Oracle understood what the data looked like before any changes were made to it so that if there was a rollback situation, it could be handled elegantly. Oracle also uses this information to provide other sessions' transactions a read consistent view of the data.

Traditionally, management of these Rollback Segments was labor intensive and the sizing of the segments was tedious and prone to error. Frequently batch processes would experience ORA-01555 (Snapshot too old) errors because the read consistent view of the data would get aged out of the segments when another process was trying to access that view of the data.

## SPFILEs

A new parameter file has been brought into the picture in Oracle 9i. The Server Parameter File (spfile) is more like a binary repository for the initialization parameters for an Oracle database instance. It is a file located on the server (server part of the name) that holds not only what the parameter file (pfile) (the init.ora) used to contain, but other parameters as well that are persistent across shutdowns as well as instantaneously captures systemwide changes that are made during runtime. Any time that you issue an alter system command, the statements that you issue get written by default to the spfile as well (eliminating the need to manually edit the init.ora file with those values). The file initially gets built based on the init.ora file and appears, when viewed in a text editor, to be a typical text file; however, due to its binary nature, it should never be edited in this manner.

As of Oracle 9i, the default behavior of the database at startup time is to read the spfile, if one exists, to find its initialization parameters, resorting to a pfile only if no spfile exists or if the pfile= command is included in the startup command.

To migrate your instance to spfile while it is running, issue the command:

```
Create spfile=$ORACLE_HOME/dbs/initVISspfile.ora
from pfile=$ORACLE_HOME/dbs/initVIS.ora
```

Or

```
Create spfile from
pfile=$ORACLE_HOME/dbs/initVIS.ora
```

at the sql prompt while logged in as sysdba or sysoper. The database can either be started or not started at the time that the command is issued. From that point on, you can start your instance with the newly created spfile. You can choose to deliberately name your spfile, however, it is Oracle's suggestion that you allow the database server to default the name and location of the parameter file; this will allow the database to know the default location and will ease the administration of the database.

Comments from the pfile, if they were located on the same line as the parameter, are retained in the spfile while all other comments are ignored. Further, the parameters are alphabetized making the parameters and values easier to find from the OS level.

Values for the initialization parameters are altered in the database instance as well as in the spfile based on the values set during an alter system command to the database. If you want to override this default behavior, you can specify the scope that you want the values to take. If you want to make a change to the running instance and not allow the change to make to the spfile, you can use the `scope=memory` parameter to the `alter system` command. This will allow you to dynamically alter the values based on database conditions while maintaining the default behavior. The converse is true as well. If you want to make the changes to just the spfile, allowing the current settings to apply to the current running instance of the database, but to change that behavior when the database is next restarted, you can provide the `scope=spfile` parameter to the `alter system` command. `Scope=spfile` applies to parameters that are only alterable at startup of the database (like compatible). `Scope=both` is the default behavior and makes the changes to the running instance and to the spfile at the same time. Also, if you want the behavior to only be in effect for those sessions connecting after the parameter gets changed, but the old behavior to be in effect for those sessions that are already connected, you can use the deferred keyword following the scope parameter to make this change possible.

If you need to remove a parameter from the spfile, you will need to provide the `alter system` command, setting the given parameter to a zero length string, altering it back to its default value and removing it from the spfile (typically the spfile holds only those parameters that are no longer at their default values). If the parameter in question has a Boolean value or a numeric value, you need to reset those back to their default values, as they will not take a zero value string.

## Resumable Space Allocation

Have you had an operation in Oracle Financials ever error out and rollback because of space related issues (either running out of space in a data file, hitting maximum extents, or preset limits on the amount of data that a schema is able to store in any particular tablespace)? Have these errors caused problems for you or for your end users and you would love to be able to make it possible to recover from those errors without having to recapture the data that was in process at the time? Now you can. With Oracle 9i, Oracle provides a means for suspending a session's activities and resuming it later, after a space related error has been taken care of. This is particularly important in activities that are long running and data intensive. Enabled by the DBA, Resumable Space Allocation allows the statements for which it is enabled to halt at the onset of a space related problem and to be restarted at exactly the same point after the space issue has been resolved or when a predefined amount of time has passed for timeout.

## Online Index Rebuild

Have you gone through the exercise of having to rebuild indexes on some of the quickly changing tables in your Oracle E-Business Suite environment? If so, you will recognize how much easier and more time effective (especially for a 24/7 shop), the ability to rebuild indexes online while the database base tables are still available for insert, update, delete, and query by the end users would be. In Oracle 9i, you now have the ability to rebuild indexes online while allowing the information in the base table to be accessed by the end users. Rebuilding indexes in this manner will allow you to move them to a different tablespace (perhaps one with different space characteristics like a different block size) while the underlying data continues to use the old index definition for accessing the information.

## Character Set Scanner

The Character Set Scanner, new in Oracle 9i, can provide a quick assessment of the feasibility of and raise any potential issues that you might find in changing the character set of your Oracle database from its existing character set to a new database character set. The scanner checks all of the character-based data in the database and analyzes it for all of the effects and any problems that may be encountered in changing the character set encoding. At the end of the scan, the scanner generates a summary report of its findings and provides the scope of work that would be required to convert to the new character set. Based on the information in the report, you can better determine the level of effort that will be needed to do the conversion. You can make a more informed decision as to the advisability of making a voluntary change as opposed to one that is driven by the business expanding into new areas.

# 3

---

# THE SURROUNDING ENVIRONMENT

Oracle E-Business Suite is a large and unwieldy piece of software. The database, with very little data, requires 30 gigabytes of disk space and will grow from there depending on the size and complexity of your installation, your organization, and the modules that you install. The application tier can comprise 10 gigabytes or more of disk space, depending on how your installation is configured. An upgrade patch can easily be over 1 gigabyte to download and over 7 gigabytes unzipped. But Oracle E-Business Suite is only part of the story.

While the Apps installation itself comprises a significant amount of time, space, and other resources, there are several other pieces that are involved. Some pieces of software need to be installed regardless of where you are installing, others are OS dependent, and (in the case of the UNIXes) some are provider dependent.

One piece of software that you need to have installed on your system, regardless of what OS you are running, is Sun's JDK™ (Java Development Kit) Version 1.3.x. JDK, also known as Java 2 SDK (standard development kit) Standard edition, is required by Apps 11i to be installed on all tiers. It can be obtained from several download sites, depending on the OS or systems that you are running on:

- Windows http://java.sun.com/j2se/1.3/download .html
- Solaris (SPARC) http://java.sun.com/products/archive/
- HP-UX http://www.hp.com/products1/unix/java/java2/sdkrte1_3/ downloads/index.html
- Tru 64 http://h18012.www1.hp.com/java/download/index.html
- Linux http://java.sun.com/j2se/1.3/download.html
- AIX http://www.ibm.com/java/jdk/aix/index.html

Oracle recommends that you always download the latest maintenance release of the JDK version that you are installing. The third digit in the number string denotes maintenance releases and patch releases are signified by the fourth set of numbers. That means that 1.3.1_02 would be Version 1.3, Maintenance Pack 1, and Patch Release 02.

For AIX, you will have to go to the Developer kit downloads section: in the available downloads section, pick the AIX platform, register, and download the correct version.

You want to size your environments with at least the minimum hardware requirements that Oracle suggests. Keep in mind, though, that 11i installations take approximately 30 percent more space than 10 or 11 installations did. They take approximately 10 percent more bandwidth on the network (they are bringing virtually everything over the network to your browser). Never forget the axiom that more is better. It is true when it comes to the Oracle E-Business Suite installation. More RAM, more disk space, and more bandwidth over which to travel, all of these will improve your performance and the satisfaction of your end user with the end product.

There are also specific things that are particular to an implementation on any individual OS. Some are things just to keep in mind, things to do differently with one over another, things that may or may not add cost to your implementation.

## WINDOWS

Windows NT or Windows 2000 installations are entirely different kinds of animals. Where nearly everything in a UNIX installation is self-contained either in the installation or within the OS, there are several additional pieces that need to exist in an NT/2000 environment. There are different concepts that you have to deal with and different concerns that have to be taken into account. If you are installing on Windows 2000, you will need to be at Service Pack 1 or greater for Server, Advanced Server, and DataCenter editions. However, some of the components of Oracle E-Business Suite require you to be at other service packs, minimally. You will need to go to the highest minimum that you can get to in order to run. For example, if you are going to run Oracle Alerts, you are required to be at Service Pack 2 or higher and have Exchange Server with Service Pack 4 or greater, as well as either Windows Messaging (Messaging Application Programming Interface or MAPI) or Outlook® e-mail without the Security Update. You will have to deliberately install MAPI if you are running on Windows 2000. MAPI was installed with the NT OS, but is not a part of Windows 2000. Assistance with either of these two products can be gotten from Microsoft support (http://www.microsoft.com). Further, if you are going to run CRM

Call Center Applications, you will need to run an Entegrity Solutions Corporation product called Gradient PC-DCE v4.0 (http://www2.entegrity.com) to run the following products:

- Campaign Plus
- Predictive
- Call Center Connections
- IVR Integrator

## FAT

You will, possibly, have the decision to make over running on FAT (file allocation table) partitions or NTFS (NT file system) partitions. While you may see some small performance gains in running on NTFS, where you will see significant improvements is in security when using NTFS over FAT. FAT partitions' content can be accessed by anyone who can access the box. NTFS partitions' data can have their contents' access restricted to those defined as DBA accounts only.

## Considerations

When downloading updates or patches or installing utilities or required auxiliary programs, make sure that you create a place to download that does not contain spaces in the name. Do not download them to "Program Files," "Oracle Downloads," or "Download Files." Do not take the defaults on paths or filenames in some of the installations. You want to keep your path as short as you possibly can and spaces tend to make the installations have problems. Remember, Oracle E-Business Suite components were probably programmed first against a UNIX OS.

The minimum OS and service pack requirements in the Oracle documentation are for Oracle only. You may have to upgrade to a higher release or service pack to meet the JDK requirements for certified versions. For installing JDK, you will want to follow the installation instructions provided and reference Metalink documents on installing.

## Additional Tools Required

There are several extra pieces of software that you will need to acquire, install, and maintain in order do get your Apps to install on a Windows platform. It is critical to remember that you should not install any of these extra pieces of software under what is known as your APPL_TOP directory. This directory houses 90 percent of your installed products for Applications, but cannot contain your auxiliary software. Relinking becomes problematic if there is anything there other than what Apps expects to be there. There are other reasons for not putting anything that is not core to the installations into the Applications directory tree, not the least of which is that when you clone (see Chapter 11) many of these directories get emptied out and you will lose your products and have to reinstall and reconfigure. Enough can happen in a clone without deliberately adding to the problems.

### Microsoft Visual C++

Oracle on Windows requires a certain release of the Visual C++® compiler. You will have to get and install Microsoft Visual C++, Version 6.0 and Service Pack 3 or higher (available from Microsoft resellers) before you can install Apps. It is important that you not exceed the requirements in this case. Do not install Visual C++ 7.0 (also known as Visual Studio.NET). Not only is it not supported, it does not work and the errors that occur when you install do not lead to any logical conclusions. It may be difficult to get a copy of this software, depending on where you live and who your resellers are, but you need Version 6.0. The service pack can be anything 3 or higher; just do not exceed Version 6.0.

This is an installation that will try to create a path that contains spaces. Do not take the defaults. A good alternative is to install it into a directory with a simple name. C:\CPP or C:\VisC are examples without spaces that will clue you or someone else into what they are later.

It is important that you segregate your auxiliary programs from your core Apps installation. Do not put anything in the same directory structure installs with Oracle E-Business Suite. This will make upgrades, patching, and cloning much cleaner and easier.

You do not have to worry about being able to code in C or C++. This is the compiler that Apps wants to have available for its use on Windows platforms.

### MKS Toolkit

Oracle products are usually released on a UNIX platform first. Many of the scripts that run the internals of Oracle's E-Business Suite were written in Perl (Practical Extraction and Report Language) shell scripts and make use of other features that are native to the UNIX environment. These pieces work best the way they were originally written, but that meant that there needed to be a mechanism that would allow those pieces to run well under the Windows environment. Enter MKS Toolkit™ family products.

MKS Toolkit brings a UNIX environment to a Windows server. It allows you to utilize a selection of different command environments, adding the availability of Korn shell, C shell, or Tclsh to the standard Windows command prompt. You can access remote servers using Secure Shell utilities, Remote Shell utilities, telnet, or xterm (secsh, scp, sftp, rsh, rexec, rlogin are just a few of the utilities that are added to your Windows repertoire). Scheduling is more robust and flexible with MKS Toolkit as well. Further, you can take your choice of command line utilities for running things on a schedule (i.e., at, batch, crontab, taskrun). Symbolic Linking is supported under this add-on. It allows you to build notification automation into your processes and scripts, so that you can run something on a schedule and have the program notify you (by smtpmail or mapimail) if it encounters problems. Tape commands and compression utilities are enhanced by running MKS, as are a variety of utilities and access files of different types using tar, pax, cpio, zip, unzip, gzip, and gunzip, thereby extending what you can do with any other zip/extract utility that might be on your server. Also, for those with a preference for UNIX tools, you can use VI editor and ls commands. To see what processes are running on your server, you can use ps.

The minimum version that you need to acquire for your installation is MKS Toolkit, Version 6.1a, which is available from http: //www.mks.com. Any from the line of the Developer series (for Developers, Professional Developers, or Enterprise Developers) can be installed; choose the one that fits your situation.

### GNU Make

Finally, you will need to download and install GNU make, Version 3.77 or higher (but not 3.79.0), available from http://www.gnu.org. Install it by following the README that comes with the download to ensure that the tool is properly created. Also, if GNU make creates a file that is named make.exe, you must rename it to gnumake.exe for Apps to be able to use it. If this means naming it the same as another file on your system, make sure that you rename that file as a backup first.

### Windows Registry and Getting the Environment Set

If you are installing on a Windows machine and you are not comfortable navigating the registry settings, you will need to become comfortable if only to find out what settings are there. The registry is the primary place that Windows NT and Windows 2000 store the information for the system environment. Oracle E-Business Suite looks into the registry to determine values assigned to the variables for the Apps instance that you are working in; it stores the values in a file under the APPL_TOP called apps.cmd (Table 3.1 shows an excerpt from a Vis instance's apps.cmd file).

The AD Utilities use this information (along with the information in files and in the database) to make sure that they are running in the environment that you expect them to be running in. This becomes particularly important if you have more than one instance running on a machine. For example, if you have your Vis instance and your Development instance on the same middle tier, then you have different values required for the same variable name, dependent on which environment you are working in.

Apps.cmd is created (or recreated if you have to make changes to registry variables) when you run adregenv.exe (AD Utility to regenerate variables). Adregen is used to copy all of the pertinent registry variables under the <SID APPL_TOP> registry tree into the cmd file, which will then be located under the APPL_TOP.

Environment variables are the way to reassign values to the same variable. Oracle stores its variables in a file under the APPL_TOP (c:\visappl, for example) in a file called <instance>.cmd (vis.cmd for the Vis instance). A sample of an excerpt from one such Vis.cmd can be seen in Table 3.2.

The VIS.cmd calls the ADOVARS.cmd file. Table 3.3 shows a section out of the ADOVARS.cmd file.

Envshell.cmd is what you run when you want to run utilities at the command line and need to be sure that you have sourced the environment variables before hand. Table 3.4 shows an excerpt envshell.cmd script and Figure 3.1 the resulting command window.

Envshell.cmd calls the <SID>.cmd file. This makes the calling chain Envshell.cmd calls VIS.cmd which in turn calls ADOVARS.cmd. If you need to set environment variables within an existing command window, you can call appsora.cmd (see Table 3.5) and set the variables that you need to access the correct environment on the system.

## Installing Multiple Environments

Installing more than one instance of Oracle E-Business Suite on one physical machine (or on one physical set of machines) is often done to consolidate resources. Oracle supports the practice, but strongly suggests against it for the Production instance. Production should be installed and maintained on a box all its own, particularly for a Windows OS. Installing Test, Demo (VIS), and Development all on the same box, however, is managable.

Oracle suggests there are several ways to accomplish this. You can install up to three instances on one server with one run of the Rapid

**Table 3.1   Vis Instance's `apps.cmd` file**

```
apps.cmd
set APPL_CONFIG=VIS
set PLATFORM=WIN_NT
set APPL_TOP=c:\visappl
set FNDNAM=APPS
set GWYUID=APPLSYSPUB/PUB
set FND_TOP=c:\visappl\fnd\11.5.0
set SHT_TOP=c:\visappl\sht\11.5.0
.
.
.
set APPLBIN=bin
set APPLDOC=docs
set APPLFRM=forms
set APPLGRAF=graphs
set APPLIMG=images
set APPLINC=include
.
.
.
set APPLPLUS=plus80
set APPLIMP=imp80
set APPLLDR=sqlldr80
set APPLSHAR=AU FF DT CUA
set APPLFULL=FND AD ALR AX AK XLA GL RG AP FA AR AS
PA CN PER PAY SSP BEN HXT OTA INV PO CHV BOM ENG MRP
CRP WIP CZ PJM FLM MSC XTR RHX QA CS CE
set JAVA_TOP=c:\viscomn\java
set CLASSPATH=c:\viscomn\java\jdbc111.zip;d:\ora-
cle\devlcomn\java;d:\oracle\devl-
comn\java\apps.zip;d:\oracle\devl-
comn\util\jre\1.1.8\lib\rt.jar
set OAH_TOP=c:\viscomn
set OAD_TOP=c:\viscomn
set OAM_TOP=c:\viscomn\java\oracle\apps
set OA_HTML=c:\viscomn\html
.
.
.
set XIT_ALR=ALR115W.DLL
set XIT_AS=AS115W.DLL
set XIT_DT=DT115W.DLL
set XIT_ENG=ENG115W.DLL
set XIT_OFA=FA115W.DLL
.
.
.
```

**Table 3.2    Vis.cmd**

```
Vis.cmd
set APPL_CONFIG=VIS
set APPLFENV=VIS.env
set PLATFORM=WIN_NT
set APPL_TOP=d:\visappl
set FNDNAM=APPS
set GWYUID=APPLSYSPUB/PUB
set APPCPNAM=REQID
set APPLMAIL=NONE
set FND_TOP=d:\visappl\fnd\11.5.0
set AU_TOP=d:\visappl\au\11.5.0
set AD_TOP=d:\visappl\ad\11.5.0
set AK_TOP=d:\visappl\ak\11.5.0
set AHL_TOP=d:\visappl\ahl\11.5.0
set AHM_TOP=d:\visappl\ahm\11.5.0
.

.

.
set MSR_TOP=d:\visappl\msr\11.5.0
set OKR_TOP=d:\visappl\okr\11.5.0
set
PATH=d:\visappl\au\11.5.0\bin;d:\visappl\fnd\11.5.0\bi
n;d:\visappl\ad\11.5.0\bin;%path%
set APPLDCP=OFF
set APPLCSF=d:\viscomn/admin
set AFSYSCSI=N/A
set APPLLOG=log/VIS
set APPLOUT=out/VIS
set APPLTMP=d:\viscomn\temp
set APPLPTMP=c:\temp
set APPLBIN=bin
set APPLDOC=docs
set CCMNUMDBRETRIES=10
set CCMORAHOME=d:\visora\8.0.6
set LOCAL=VIS
.

.

.
set XIT_PAY=PAY115W.DLL
set XIT_PO=PO115W.DLL
set XIT_WIP=WIP115W.DLL
set NLS_LANG=American_America.WE8ISO8859P1
set NLS_DATE_FORMAT=DD-MON-RR
```

*-- continued*

**Table 3.2 (continued) Vis.cmd**

```
set NLS_NUMERIC_CHARACTERS=.,
set NLS_SORT=binary
set REPORTS60_TMP=d:\viscomn\temp
set
REPORTS60_PATH=d:\visappl\au\11.5.0\plsql;d:\visappl\f
nd\11.5.0\reports;d:\visappl\au\11.5.0\reports;d:\visa
ppl\au\11.5.0\graphs
set GRAPHICS60_PATH=d:\visappl\au\11.5.0\graphs
set ORAPLSQLLOADPATH=d:\visappl\au\11.5.0\graphs
set FORMS60_MAPPING=http://csriizof01.corp-
sys.csedge.com:8001/OA_TEMP
set CNTL_BREAK=ON
set FORMS60_MESSAGE_ENCRYPTION=TRUE
set FORMS60_OUTPUT=%APPLTMP%
set FORMS_OUTPUT=%APPLTMP%
set FORMS60_SESSION=TRUE
set ORACLE_TERM=vt220
set FORMS60_APPSLIBS=APPCORE FNDSQF APPDAYPK APPFLDR
GLCORE HR_GEN HR_SPEC ARXCOVER
set FORMS60_FORCE_MENU_MNEMONICS=0
set
FORMS60_PATH=d:\visappl\au\11.5.0\resource;d:\visappl\
au\11.5.0\plsql
set FORMS60_OAM_FRD=OFF
call d:\visappl\admin\adovars.cmd
set FORMS60_WEB_CONFIG_FILE=%OA_HTML%\bin\appsweb.cfg
set REPORTS60_USEREXIT=%AU_TOP%\bin\APPR60UE.dll
set REPORTS60_PRE="&5555"
set REPORTS60_POST="&5556"
IF NOT EXIST%AU_TOP%\bin\FNDCORE.dll (
   ECHO The%AU_TOP%\bin\FNDCORE.dll not found
   GOTO theend
)
COPY%AU_TOP%\bin\FNDCORE.dll%AD_TOP%\bin
:theend
```

Installer, selecting the box for up to three instances on the Select Applications Instances screen of the installer, and either accepting the defaults or customizing the names, locations, and types of databases that you would like to install. Following this path, you will want to carefully review the values for the separate sets of parameters before proceeding with the installation. If at all possible, I suggest following this route of installation. It seems to be the cleanest, with the installer

**Table 3.3  Envshell.cmd**

```
envshell.cmd
SET LOCAL=VIS
SET PATH=c:\mks\mksnt;C:\WINNT;C:\WINNT\system32
IF NOT EXIST d:\visora\8.0.6\VIS.cmd GOTO skiporacmd
CALL dd:\visora\8.0.6\VIS.cmd
IF NOT EXIST d:\visappl\VIS.cmd GOTO nobatfiles
CALL d:\visappl\VIS.cmd
IF NOT EXIST c:\cpp\VC98\bin\vcvars32.bat GOTO
nobatfiles
CALL c:\cpp\VC98\bin\vcvars32.bat
:skiporacmd
:nobatfiles
START cmd.exe
GOTO theend
:noconfigfiles
:theend
```

taking care of many of the details for you. If you did not do it this way, it is the way that Oracle Support will suggest you should have done it when you call in for support. Documentation, however, leaves the method up to you. A second alternative is to install a first instance on the server and go back later to install the subsequent ones. If you follow this path, you will need to make sure that the instance name, directory names (for APPL_TOP, COMMON_TOP, and ORACLE_HOME), all port numbers, and the configuration filename are all unique for this instance. Further, you will have to consolidate the Net8 Configuration files for your listener.ora and your tnsnames.ora manually, merge them into one file with all pieces of all instance accounted for, and place those files into the most recently installed instance's %ORACLE_HOME%/net80/admin directory. To stay on the safe side, I back up all of the individual files in all of the admin directories and copy the merged version into each. That way I know that they are consistent and that no matter what happens the instances are going to be using the same one. You may find that, if you upgrade, the order changes and the instance that was the most recently installed is no longer the master. Having all of the controlling files the same in all instances will help ensure that the users will not face unnecessary downtime.

**Table 3.4   Adovars.cmd**

```
ADOVARS.cmd
set JAVA_TOP=c:\viscomn\java
set OA_JRE_TOP=c:\viscomn\util\jre\1.1.8
set AF_JRE_TOP=c:\viscomn\util\jre\1.1.8
set ORACLE_HOME=c:\visora\8.0.6
set
CLASSPATH=%OA_JRE_TOP%\lib\rt.jar;%OA_JRE_TOP%\lib\i18
n.jar;%JAVA_TOP%\apps-
borg.zip;%JAVA_TOP%\apps.zip;c:\visora\8.0.6\form
s60\java;%JAVA_TOP%
set
AF_CLASSPATH=%OA_JRE_TOP%\lib\rt.jar;%OA_JRE_TOP%
\lib\i18n.jar;%JAVA_TOP%\apps-
borg.zip;%JAVA_TOP%\apps.zip;c:\visora\8.0.6\form
s60\java;%JAVA_TOP%
set
LD_LIBRARY_PATH=%OA_JRE_TOP%\lib;%ORACLE_HOME%\li
b;%LD_LIBRARY_PATH%
set OAH_TOP=c:\viscomn
set OAD_TOP=c:\viscomn
set OAM_TOP=%JAVA_TOP%\oracle\apps
set ADJREOPTS=-mx256m
set ADJVAPRG=c:\visora\8.0.6\jdk\bin\java.exe
set AFJVAPRG=c:\visora\8.0.6\jdk\bin\java.exe
set OA_HTML=%OAH_TOP%\html
set OA_SECURE=%OAH_TOP%\secure
set OA_MEDIA=%OAM_TOP%\media
set OA_DOC=%OAD_TOP%\doc
set OA_JAVA=%JAVA_TOP%
set oa_htmlbin=%OA_HTML%\bin
```

## Printing

Another idiosyncrasy of your installation being on Windows, Concurrent Managers have to be able to access networked printers. Because the Concurrent Manager starts by default using the internal system account and this account does not have access to network printers, you have to enable printing through the Concurrent Managers, thus allowing printing to run successfully for end user reports. To do this, you have to become comfortable with other Windows utilities.

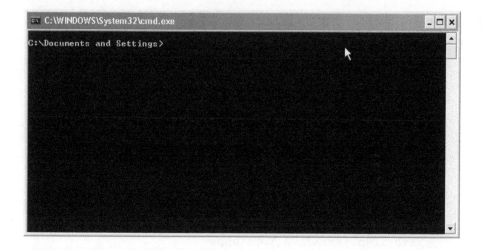

**Figure 3.1    Command Window from** envshell.cmd

1. Navigate to Control Panel and open the Services window. From the Services list, highlight the Concurrent Manager service for the current instance (OracleConcMGRVIS). Right click on the service and select the Log In tab. Select the This Account radio button and enter a user ID and password to start the Concurrent Manager and click OK. The user that you have chosen has to have administration rights to the computer.
2. Define a printer. Use the Add Printer option to define a printer or more than one printer for the account you assigned to the Concurrent Manager.
3. Restart the Concurrent Manager.

## Manual Services

There are several services that may be created by the Rapid Installer, depending on what version you use for your base installation, to provide functionality that is not currently in the Oracle E-Business Suite product. These services are set to be started manually by default. There is no need for you to start them and no need to change them to start automatically. Starting them does not appear to do anything or to cause conflicts anywhere. The services are Oracle<SID>_HOMEClientCache, Oracle <SID>_HOMECMAdmin, Oracle<SID>_HOMECMan, and Oracle_HOME1HttpServer.

**Table 3.5 Appsora.cmd**

```
Appsora.cmd
SET LOCAL=vis
SET
PATH=c:\mks\mksnt;C:\WINNT;C:\WINNT\system32
REM Run the vis.cmd file to set the environment
REM to point correctly to the vis APPL_CONFIG
IF NOT EXIST c:\visora\8.0.6\vis.cmd GOTO nocon-
figfiles
CALL c:\visora\8.0.6\vis.cmd
IF NOT EXIST c:\visappl\vis.cmd GOTO noconfig-
files
CALL c:\visappl\vis.cmd
IF NOT EXIST c:\cpp\VC98\bin\vcvars32.bat GOTO
nobatfiles
CALL c:\cpp\VC98\bin\vcvars32.bat
GOTO theend
:noconfigfiles
ECHO This script requires the following files:
ECHO
ECHO       c:\visora\8.0.6\vis.cmd
ECHO       c:\visappl\vis.cmd
ECHO
GOTO theend
:nobatfiles
ECHO This script requires the following files:
ECHO       c:\cpp\VC98\bin\vcvars32.bat
:theend
```

## Sun SPARC

The requirement for the Sun SPARC installation is similar to the others in that it requires JDK 1.3 (Java 2 SDK Standard Edition j2se). It also requires that the server be running Solaris™ 2.6 or 2.8 operating system.

## Considerations

### LD_LIBRARY_PATH

SPARC makes use of dynamic libraries when it goes through the relinking process, as well as when it is in the process of execution. The LD_LIBRARY_PATH environment variable is what enables the system to locate these libraries. The location of these libraries is customizable and the particular installation of SPARC may have them elsewhere, but the default settings for LD_LIBRARY_PATH are as follows:

```
EXPORT $LD_LIBRARY_PATH =
/usr/dt/lib:/usr/openwin/lib:${ORACLE_HOME}/lib:$
{ORACLE_HOME}/network/jre11/lib/spare/
native_threads
```

Where /usr/dt/lib and /usr/openwin/lib are directories containing the X Windows dynamic libraries that are needed by the Oracle products and may be in different directory structures and where {ORACLE_HOME} is the full path to where your RDBMS binaries are installed. {ORACLE_HOME} can be substituted with its variable name as well. You can reset the values in the LD_LIBRARY_PATH by changing its values in the $ORACLE_HOME/VIS.env file where VIS is the system ID (SID) of the given instance.

The value for LD_LIBRARY_PATH gets set in three places. First, in the $APPL_TOP/admin the ADOVARS.env file, it gets set with a command similar to:

```
LD_LIBRARY_PATH=$ORACLE_HOME/network/jre11/lib/sparc\
/native_threads:${LD_LIBRARY_PATH:=} and export
LD_LIBRARY_PATH
```

It also gets set with the command set/usr/dt/lib:/usr/X11R6/lib:/usr/openwin/lib followed by:

```
export LD_LIBRARY_PATH
```

Finally, it gets set in the /$TWO_TASK.env file located in $ORACLE_HOME, in both the 8.0.6 and *i*AS directories with:

```
LD_LIBRARY_PATH="$ORACLE_HOME/lib:$ORACLE_HOME/thr
lib: \
```

On the Database server, it also is set in the $ORACLE_SID.env file (VIS.env) located in the $ORACLE_HOME directory and the command there will be similar to:

```
LD_LIBRARY_PATH="$ORACLE_HOME/lib:/usr/dt/lib:/usr
/openwin/lib"export LD_LIBRARY_PATH
```

If you need to change the value of LD_LIBRARY_PATH, the changes need to be made in any or all of the following files: ADOVARS.ENV, VIS.ENV in both the ORACLE_HOME/8.0.6 and in the ORACLE_HOME/iAS directories, and any file in the directory tree that has the string LD_LIBRARY_PATH in it. Back up any files that you plan on changing before implementing the changes.

If you are AutoConfig enabled, you can change the values centrally using the Context Editor; updating the adovars LD_LIBRARY_PATH field, the iAS OH LD_LIBRARY_PATH library field, and the iAS ORACLE_HOME LD_LIBRARY_PATH, and running AutoConfig to perpetuate the changes. I suggest backing up the directory tree before you run either the Context Editor or AutoConfig.

### Printers

Printer registration is much simpler in the UNIX environment than it is under Windows. Before printers can be registered and used under Apps, they need to be defined to the OS. You need to find its system name to be able to use it. To find the names of the printers that are defined to Sun SPARC you can run the following command:

```
$ lpstat -p
```

### HP-UX

HP-UX installations that need to be done on an OS version for HP 9000 Series HP-UX machines are HP-UX 11.0 for either 32 bit or 64 bit with (minimally) the PHSS_23823, PHSS_24301, and PHSS_24303 patches applied on all involved nodes and the maxdisz kernel parameter set to at least 130 MB. The OS patches (much like Oracle patches) become superceded occasionally, so have the sysadmin make sure you have been set up with the right ones. You will need, at minimum, 650 MB of temporary space to run the installation. The default temporary directory is /tmp. If there is not sufficient space in /tmp, you can redirect the temporary directory to another path by setting both the $temp and the $tmp to a directory that does have sufficient space. For instance, if there is extra space in the home directory of the Oracle user that you have chosen to own the installed files (visora for example), you can do the following:

```
Export temp =/usr/home/visora
Export tmp = $temp
```

This will enable you to run the installation program, provided that there is at least 50 MB in the /tmp directory.

As with Sun SPARC, the LD_LIBRARY_PATH environment variable needs to be set to the location of the dynamic link libraries needed for execution and relinking processes. Setting this variable is taken care of in the ADOVARS.ENV script located under the $APPL_TOP/admin directory (for instance, /oracle/visappl/admin). Further additions to the ADOVARS.ENV file for HP-UX include the setting of the SHLIB_PATH = <VISORA>/8.0.6/lib.

### Java on HP-UX

On the HP 9000 Series HP-UX, JDK comes as part of SDK.

The `swinstall` utility allows any existing installation of JDK to be overwritten by a newer version. If there is already a JDK installation on your HP-UX HTTP server node that is an older release of the newer version (required by Apps) and you do not wish to overwrite your existing installation, work with your sysadmin to install the Apps JDK into a location other than the default before running Rapid Install.

If your installation requires maintaining different Rapid Install environments on the same server, Oracle suggests that you make independent installations of JDK for each environment on the server. This can be accomplished in several ways. You could copy the new installation into the `APACHE_TOP` directory after Rapid Install has finished. (It would be safe here; cloning does not interact with this directory structure.) Or you can alter where the symbolic link points and recreate it to point to the independent installation location.

### Printers

Also similar to SPARC, the HP-UX command to determine what printers are defined to the OS is:

```
$ lpstat -p
```

### Other Required Software

If you are going to work with Oracle Constraint Based Optimization, Work-in-Progress (WIP), or Manufacturing Scheduling (WPS), there are some added requirements if your Concurrent Processing server node is running HP-UX. To run any of these products on the HP 9000 Series HP-UX system, you will need to install a C++ compiler that is Version A.03.15 or higher. This is only a requirement on the node running the Concurrent Managers. This compiler version can be obtained from HP (http://h21007. www2.hp.com/dspp/tech/tech_TechSoftwareDetailPage_IDX/1,1703,1740, 00.html). When you install this compiler, the `PATH` variable of the `applmgr` user needs to include the path to the `aCC` executable:

```
libcplex.a library optimization
```

The "ILOG Cplex" library `libcplex.a` should be to increase performance of the C++ based products (i.e., MSO, WPS, and WIP). The `libcplex.a` library file is located in the `$SHT_TOP/lib/ilog` directory on all nondatabase servers and it is optimized for the PA-RISC 1.1 architecture. There is a backup of this file in the `$SHT_TOP/lib/ilog/ cplex_PA-RISC1.1`. If the Apps server is using PA-RISC 2.0 architecture, you can replace `libcplex.a` from the `$SHT_TOP/lib/ilog` directory with an optimized one. For the PA-RISC architecture, the optimized version would likely be `$SHT_TOP/lib/ilog/cplex_PA-RISC2.0/libcplex.a`.

**Table 3.6 Output Interpretation of /usr/bin/getconf _SC_CPU_VERSION**

| If the Output is | Associated PA-RISC Version | Optimization Action Required |
|---|---|---|
| 528 | PA-RISC 1.1 | None |
| 529 | PA-RISC 1.1 | None |
| 532 | PA-RISC 2.0 | Copy $SHT_TOP/lib/ilog/cplex_PARISC2.0/libcplex.a to $SHT_TOP/lib/ilog/libcplex.a and replace existing file. |

If you want to determine the PA-RISC architecture version on your Oracle E-Business Suite server system, the following command will assist you in determining it:

```
$/usr/bin/getconf _SC_CPU_VERSION
```

The numeric output of this command corresponds to a PA-RISC version, its corresponding PA-RISC version is in the second column, and any optimization actions required are in column three of Table 3.6.

### Tru64

The Compaq Tru64 UNIX required OSs are Tru64 UNIX V4.0.f, g; V5.0; V5.0a; or V5.1.

### LD_LIBRARY_PATH

Tru64 makes similar use of dynamic libraries when it goes through the relinking and execution processes. The LD_LIBRARY_PATH environment variable enables the system to locate these libraries and the location of these libraries is customizable. Your particular installation may have them elsewhere, but the default settings for LD_LIBRARY_PATH are as follows:

```
EXPORT $LD_LIBRARY_PATH =/usr/dt/lib:/usr/open-
win/lib:${ORACLE_HOME}/lib:${ORACLE_HOME}/net-
work/jre11/lib/spare/native_threads
```

Where /usr/dt/lib and /usr/openwin/lib are directories containing the X Windows dynamic libraries that are needed by the Oracle products and may be in different directory structures, where {ORACLE_HOME} is the full path to where your RDBMS binaries are installed, {ORACLE_HOME} can be substituted with its variable name as well. You can reset the values in the LD_LIBRARY_PATH by changing its values in the $ORACLE_HOME/VIS.env and in the $APPL_TOP/admin/ADOVARS.ENV files where VIS is the SID of the given instance.

### Mount Point Ownership for Multi-Node Multi-User Installation

Before you run Rapid Install, make sure that either you or the sysadmin creates your mount point directories in the OS that you will specify to the Rapid Install utility as the top-level mount points (i.e., VISAPPL, VISCOMN, VISORA). When creating these mount point directories, and before you run Rapid Install, make sure that the owning username and group ID is the same as the one you are going to specify within Rapid Install. For example, if your APPL_TOP (VISAPPL for the Vision Demo instance) mount point directory has ownership vismgr:system when you run ls -al, all the subsequent directories created by Rapid Install and files created under the VISAPPL directory will have ownership as vismgr:system even if you have specified vismgr as the owner and dba as the group within Rapid Install. You or the sysadmins should change the ownership to vismgr:dba before you start the Rapid Install.

### Printers

Registering printers in Applications is similar to the other UNIX-based installations; the Oracle Applications sysadmin needs to know each printer's name as it is known to the OS. To find these names in Tru64, enter the following command:

```
$ lpstat -p
```

### Resource Limits

For all nodes involved in your installation that are running Tru64, you will need to check the size of the resource limit for the data area and make sure that it is set to the size of the virtual memory. For example, for the Korn shell, entering the following command will allow you to see the resource limits for all resources:

```
ulimit -a
time(seconds)      unlimited
file(blocks)       unlimited
data(Kbytes)          131072
  .
  .
vmemory(kbytes)      1048576
```

You will want to set (or have your sysadmin set) the size of the data area to the size of the vmemory area by entering:

```
$ ulimit -d 1048576
```

If this is not resized so that data area = virtual memory area, relinking executables for different Oracle E-Business Suite products may fail.

### Temp Directories

The installation of Applications Release 11i for Tru64 UNIX requires at least 650 MB of temporary disk space. I have never seen an installation only take the minimum amount of temporary space, so allocating high would not hurt. The default location for this temporary space and associated files is the /tmp directory. If there is not enough disk space available in the /tmp directory, you can redirect the temporary files to a location where there is sufficient space. This is accomplished by setting the $TEMP and $TMPDIR environment variables to another directory where you know that there will be sufficient space. You will still need at least 50 MB in the /tmp directory that is not redirectable.

### Additional Software Required by Individual Components

If you are implementing *i*Payment by using CyberCash for CRM 11i, *you will need to refer to CyberCash to acquire the version of the* CyberCash Merchant Connection Kit (MCK) that is supported on Tru64. You can find information for CyberCash at the following Web site:

```
http://www.cybercash.com
```

If you are implementing Oracle Constraint Based Optimization, Work in Progress (WIP), and/or Manufacturing Scheduling (WPS), and you are running Tru64, Version 4.0f or 5.0, there are additional requirements for the Concurrent Manager server. To use these products on Tru64 UNIX, you will need to install the Compaq C++ Run-Time Library Redistribution Kit on the Concurrent Manager server. You can obtain this kit from http://www.tru64unix.compaq.com/cplus/index.html.You want to download the CXXREDIST*.tar file and follow the instructions on the Web site to install the product appropriately.

### Intel Linux

### Operating System Version

Because of the flexibility in the Linux OS and because there are so many flavors of Linux, keeping up with all of the versions you can have is nearly impossible. As of early 2003, Red Hat had desupported Version 6.2, but Oracle was still supporting its 11.5.3 customers running on this version. The default version of the kernel, with the exception of SuSE 7.0, is supported; SuSE 7.0 customers should upgrade their kernel to 2.2.19.

If you are running 11i up to Release 6 and you are running Oracle 9i, you must have your database and middle tier on separate machines.

### Operating System Patch Requirements

Open Motif, Version 2.1 is required for all versions of Intel Linux running Apps 11i. Obtaining this should not be a problem, as all currently supported Linux versions include this version with their installation CDs; however, not all distributions install this by default. You can also obtain the latest Open Motif 2.1 binary or source packages from the Metro Link Web site at `http://www.metrolink.com/products/motif/open_motif2-1-30.html` or directly from Open Group's official Open Motif Web site at `http://www.opengroup.org/openmotif/`. For two node or multi-node installations, it is only required that this be installed on the node or nodes that will be housing the Concurrent Managers, Forms Server, and HTTP Server.

### LD_LIBRARY_PATH Environment Variable

The Linux OS is no different than the versions of UNIX in its use of dynamic libraries in the process of relinking and execution. The LD_LIBRARY_PATH is the variable responsible for maintaining the list of libraries. Again in Linux, the variable is set in the following two files:

```
$APPL_TOP/admin/adovars.env file
$ORACLE_HOME/VIS.env
```

### Printers

To find out the names of the defined printers at the OS level so you can define those printers to the applications, issue the following command at the Linux command prompt:

```
$/usr/sbin/lpc status
```

### Linux Temporary Directories and Files

To install Release 11i of the Oracle E-Business Suite on a Linux platform, you will need at least 1.3 GB of temporary space. The default location in Linux, as in UNIX, is the /tmp directory. If there is insufficient space in that directory, you can redirect the temporary files to another location by the following commands:

```
Export TEMP=<your other directory>
Export TMPDIR=<your other directory>
```

You will still need to have at least 50 MB available under the /tmp directory for the installation to run.

### Additional Software Required for Individual Components

If you are going to implement *i*Payment using CyberCash for 11i's CRM, you will need to check the CyberCash Web site and determine if your platform is supported for the MCK. You can find this out from the following Web site: http://www.cybercash.com; however, as of early 2003, it was not supported for SuSE 7.0. For those SuSE clients affected, and wishing an alternative to the CyberCash product that can use the iPayment functionality and flexibility, you can refer to the Oracle iPayment Concepts and Procedures documentation that can be found on the Documentation CD for your installation.

### JDK Note

Occasionally, when installing Sun's SDK 1.3.1 on SuSE 7.0 using rpm command, the following error can occur:

```
$ rpm -ivh - force jdk1.3.1.i386.rpm
ERROR: failed dependencies
glibc>=2.1.2-11 is needed by jdk1.3.1-fcs
```

If you get this error, using the -nodeps option of the rpm command will allow it to install successfully:

```
$ rpm -ivh -nodeps jdk1.3.1.i386.rpm
```

### AIX

### Operating System Version and Patch Requirements

For AIX installations, there are two supported options for OS version. You can either be on AIX 4.3.3 or AIX 5x. There are several required OS patches that may or may not have been installed. There are different requirements for different components of the installation. You should double-check with Oracle Support on Metalink to make sure that your sysadmin has all of the patches installed that are required for your installation configuration.

## LD_LIBRARY_PATH

AIX is a UNIX-based OS and, therefore, requires the LD_LIBRARY_PATH environment variable to be set to the libraries needed for Apps to run and relink when based on this platform. The two Oracle E-Business Suite files that are responsible for maintaining this variable are:

```
$APPL_TOP/admin/adovars.env
$ORACLE_HOME/VIS.env
```

### Printers

To find out the names of the defined printers at the OS level so you can define those printers to the applications, issue the following command at the AIX command prompt:

```
$ lsallq
```

## ULIMIT

For all AIX nodes involved in your installation, check the sizes of the resource limits. The minimum resource limits on data, stack, and memory should be no less than 256,000 KB.

### Temporary Directories and Files

AIX installation of Oracle Applications, Release 11i requires a minimum of 650 MB of temporary disk space, 50 MB of which has to be in the default directory, /tmp. If there is not 650 MB free under the /tmp directory, you can redirect the installation's temporary files by setting both the $TEMP and the $TEMPDIR values to another directory on your system where there is sufficient space to complete the installation. This can be accomplished by the following commands:

```
Export TEMP=<your directory>
Export TMPDIR=<your directory>
```

### Additional Software Required for Individual Components

If you are implementing *i*Payment for CRM 11i using CyberCash, refer to the CyberCash Web site for a list of supported platforms and releases for the CyberCash MCK at http://www.cybercash.com. As of early 2003, AIX systems are not supported with CyberCash MCK; however, there are plans to support that in future releases. For alternatives to CyberCash that can use the *i*Payment functionality, please check the Field Installable Servlets section under *i*Payment Servlets portion of the *i*Payment Architectural Overview topic in the *Oracle iPayment Concepts and Procedures* documentation that can be found on the *Documentation Library CD* that came with your installation.

If you are going to use MSO, WPS, or WIP on AIX, you need either the IBM C++ Compiler 3.6.6 or higher or VisualAge C++ Professional, Version 5.0 with C++ Redistributable Tools installed on the node that will be running your Concurrent Managers. These utilities, VisualAge or IBM C++, include the tools necessary to run WIP, WPS, and MSO, such as linkxlC and munch. You can perform the following checks to make sure that the IBM compiler version is installed:

' 1. Verify that the compiler is installed finding the /usr/ibmcxx directory (or the imbcxx directory in another path). If this directory exists, check the README.C++ file that will be in that directory to make sure that Version 3.6.6 is what is installed.
2. If 3.6.6 is installed, verify that linkxlC is in /usr/ibmcxx/bin (or the <your path>/ibmcxx/bin directory).
3. Verify that munch is in /usr/ibmcxx/exe/aix43 (or the <your path>/ibmcxx/exe/aix43 directory), and that there is a symbolic link pointing to its location that exists in its parent directory (/usr/ibmcxx/exe).

If you are not running the IBM C++ compiler, you can perform the following steps to determine if you have VisualAge C++ V5.0 or newer installed:

1. Verify that the /vacpp subdirectory exists somewhere on your system. If it does, read the README file located in that directory to make sure that what you have installed is Version 5.0 or newer.
2. If you can find that directory, verify that linkxlC is located in /vacpp/bin.
3. Verify that much is located in /vacpp/exe/aix43 and that a symbolic link points to it and that the link exists in the parent directory (/vacpp/exe).
4. Make sure that linkxlC (whichever version of C++ you have installed) is included in your PATH setting. If you are installing this on a node that has multiple users, make sure that this setting exists for in the environment owned by your applmgr user.

If neither of these C++ compilers are installed or you have a version less than what is required, you can purchase and install the IMB C++ Compiler or you can download and install the VisualAge C++ Professional, Version 5.0 with Redistributable Tools from the IBM Web site:

```
http://www-3.ibm.com/software/awdtools/vacpp/
service/csd.html
```

If you choose the VisualAge option and you opt to download and install Redistributable Tools, you or your sysadmin will need to perform the following steps:

1. Locate the Redistributable Filesets section on the IBM Web site.
2. Download VisualAge C++ Professional V5.0 C++ Redistributable Tools.
3. Within the download, locate VisualAge C++ for AIX 5.0.2.1 runtime PTF.
4. Further, download the VisualAge C++ 5.0.2.1 or higher version compiler PTF.
5. Read the README provided by IBM on how to apply the downloaded package and PTF.
6. After you have applied the package and PTF, verify that you now have a /vacpp subdirectory, that it has been installed, and that the path to the /vacpp/bin directory is in your PATH.

# 4

## APACHE

Oracle E-Business Suite uses as its Internet engine a scaled down version of the Oracle 9iAS product. The full installation of 9iAS is a suite of products including a Web server, security features, and many add-on modules to assist you in your job of serving Web content to your customers. Oracle Financials version is scaled down, with fewer bells and whistles, but is still a complex set of products.

### ORACLE HTTP SERVER

At the core of Oracle's 9iAS product (either the scaled down or the full, robust version) is Oracle's version of its HTTP Server, a simple Web server based on the Apache Web Server. Apache documentation is widely available and there are several good books available if you want to know, in depth, what Apache is about, what it does, and what you can do with all of its features. Here we will touch on what core components you will need to be aware of and to some extent comfortable with, as they apply to the Oracle E-Business Suite.

Running the Apache version that ships with Oracle E-Business Suite does not require that you know all there is to know about Apache, only the pieces that you are likely to be concerned with on a somewhat routine basis. This chapter will, among other things, give you the information that you will need to maintain and configure this Apache-based set of services and help you troubleshoot some problems that you may find along the way.

Figure 4.1 shows, graphically, the basic directory structure that your Vision or other installation may have. You can extrapolate from here for your other environments.

There are several files directly related to Apache that you will need to work with. Some are configuration files, some security files, and

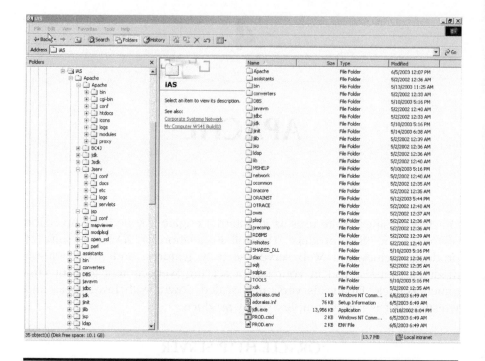

**Figure 4.1    Directory Structure**

some are your logs. All are in the directories under /visora/
iAS/Apache/Apache and usually located in the logically named
subdirectories. The primary configuration file, and the file from which
all of the other configuration files get called, is the httpd.conf file.
A basic understanding of this file and what directives and containers
are in it will help you to understand some of what is going on with
Apache and will help you if you should need to open an iTAR with
Oracle Support about anything with the Apache setup.

Running as an integral part of Apache is an include module called
mod_jserv.so or just JServ. JServ, an open source servlet engine, brings
with it the ability to communicate and accept servlet requests and to
perform extensive Java related tasks through the Applications interface.
The JVM™ (Java Virtual Machine)  interface that runs is called JServer.
While the Oracle HTTP Server that runs in the Oracle E-Business Suite is
not as broadly functional as the one that runs within 9iAS V9.0.2, it brings
with it full functionality and the ability to expand the capabilities of your
server and to grow as the product suite and certification grows. While
the engine behind Version 9.0.2 of the Application Server is Oracle 9iAS
Containers for J2EE (OC4J), JServ was the primary servlet environment in
earlier releases of Oracle 9i Application Server (1.0.2.2.2 is a case in point).

The flexibility that it brings to the configuration, though, does not come without complexity to configuration interaction.

The configuration files are made up of variables and directives. A directive is a command that conveys information to the Apache server on specific actions to take in certain situations.

## Httpd.conf

The `httpd.conf` file is one of the primary configuration files for your Apache service. It is a long file divided into three sections and each section has configurable parameters. Each section has a narrower focus than the section before, starting out with the overall operations and narrowing to the narrowest parameters. The values and variables found within this file and the files that it calls build upon each other. This file is commented somewhat extensively; however, if you do not know anything about what you are doing to begin with, you could soon find yourself lost in the somewhat terse, often limited information.

### Global Environment

Section 1 is the Global Environment section. This section's directives affect how Apache operates overall. Things in this section tell Apache, mostly, about itself: where to find its log and configuration files, how many requests it can handle concurrently, and other things about its global environment.

### ServerType

The `ServerType` variable can only ever have one of two values. If you are running on a Windows platform, you can only have one of the two. A Windows `ServerType` has to have a value of standalone; a UNIX platform can either be standalone or `inetd`.

### ServerType Standalone

### ServerRoot

The `ServerRoot` directive gives the uppermost directory under which Apache and its files can be found. It is important that the path not end with a trailing slash. Also important, do not alter the direction which the slashes appear in the path. If you are maintaining a Windows environment, the path may look odd, but it needs to stay that way.

```
ServerRoot "d:\visora\iAS/Apache/Apache"
```

### LockFile

The LockFile directive specifies the full path, including the filename, to the LockFile. The LockFile is a file that Apache uses if it has been compiled with either the USE_FCNTRL_SERIALIZED_ACCEPT or the USE_FLOCK_SERIALIZED_ACCEPT parameter. Very often, this directive will be commented out. This directive is best left at its original value in this file; alter it only if the value in the ServerRoot directive is to be NFS (network file system) mounted. The LockFile has to be stored on a local disk and never on a NFS disk. If you need to find somewhere local to locate this file, it is best not to locate this file in a directory to which everyone has write access (like /var/temp or /usr/tmp). Putting this file in a location to which the world can freely write could leave your company open to denial of service attack. Again, make a note to not change the direction of the slashes after the *i*AS directory.

```
LockFile
d:\visora\iAS/Apache/Apache/logs/httpd.lock
```

### PidFile

The PidFile directive specifies a log file in which the server records the process identification (pid) number under which it was started. You can "more" this file from a command prompt through either UNIX or the MKS toolkit, or you can make a copy of it and open the copy if you are on a Windows machine. You cannot open the file directly. Do not try to edit this file. Again, never change the direction of the slashes in the directory paths in any of these directives.

```
PidFile d:\visora\iAS/Apache/Apache/logs/httpd.pid
```

### ScoreBoardFile

The ScoreBoardFile directive specifies a log file containing information on internal server processes. It is a file that Apache uses to communicate between the parent server processes and any child processes. This file (and therefore this directive) is not required on every platform. The easiest way to find out if it is required on your platform is to start Apache and determine if the file is created. If it is created, it is needed. This file is created in the logs directory of the ServerRoot with all of the other log files. If you have multiple Apache server processes running on your server and your platform requires a scoreboard file, it is important that each server process have its own scoreboard file and that the same scoreboard file is not written to by more than one instance of Apache.

```
ScoreBoardFile
d:\visora\iAS/Apache/Apache/logs/httpd.scoreboard
```

## ResourceConfig

The `ResourceConfig` directive specifies a configuration file that likely will not contain any directives. There are several of these files that are holdovers from previous versions of Apache. You will, in all likelihood, have one of these files, but it will probably contain only the header comments. All of the directives and their associated information that would have been in this file have been migrated over time to the `httpd.conf` file. You will find this file in the `conf` directory under `ServerRoot`. `Srm.conf` is not big and while it is not really used, I would probably not clean it up, but leave it where it is.

    conf/srm.conf

## AccessConfig

The `AccessConfig` directive specifies another configuration file that likely will not contain any directives. You will probably have one of these files as well, but it will contain only the header comments. All of the directives and their associated information that would have been in this file have been migrated over time to the `httpd.conf` file. You will find this file in the `conf` directory under `ServerRoot`. `Access.conf` is another small file that can be left in place.

    conf/access.conf

## Timeout

The `Timeout` directive is the number of seconds that Apache will wait for a `get,` `put,` or `post` command or the amount of time between ACKs (acknowledgments of TCP-IP packet receipt) before a time-out occurs. Apache has plans to break this out into several configurable directives, similar to this one, but one each for `gets,` for `puts,` for `posts,` and for ACKs.

    Timeout 300

## KeepAlive

The `KeepAlive` directive allows Apache to determine if it should allow persistent connections or not. A persistent connection is usually only implemented for pipelining data from one server to the requesting client. Typically, the Web server will close the connection after returning the data that is requested, although this is never apparent to the end user. If it is set to on, `KeepAlive` allows more than one request per connection, off will cause Apache to allow only one request per connection. Allowing multiple requests to be sent over the same TCP-IP (Transmission Control Protocol/Internet Protocol) connection can cause up to 50 percent lower latency times for HTML documents, particularly if the documents are graphic heavy. Because we are dealing with Oracle Financials, which is not graphics intensive, but is Java based, deciding to set this directive in either fashion is a judgment call based on network traffic more than anything. KeepAlive and the following two directives MaxKeepAlive Requests and KeepAliveTimeout should be addressed as a group.

```
KeepAlive On
```

### MaxKeepAliveRequests

The MaxKeepAliveRequests directive value is the maximum number of requests that Apache will allow during persistent connections. If this is set to 0, it will allow an unlimited number of requests. This makes some kind of intuitive sense, as there is no apparent reason that anyone would want to run a Web server that allowed no one to connect. Setting a higher value for this directive allows for better performance. This directive limits the number of requests that Apache will allow per connection if the KeepAlive directive is set to on.

```
MaxKeepAliveRequests 500
```

### KeepAliveTimeout

The KeepAliveTimeout directive sets the number of seconds that Apache will wait from the end of the current request to the arrival of the next request coming from the same client through the same connection. Once any request has been received, this value comes into play. Setting this number too high may cause performance problems, particulary in a server that is heavily loaded as more of the server processes will be dedicated to waiting for subsequent requests from idle clients than to accepting new requests.

```
KeepAliveTimeout 15
```

### MinSpareServers and MaxSpareServers

The MinSpareServers  and MaxSpareServers directives work together regulating the server pool size. Apache dynamically adapts to load by attempting to maintain enough server processes to handle that load. Apache will periodically query for the number of servers waiting for a request. If it determines that there are fewer idle child server processes than the value for MinSpareServers, it will create enough more child processes to bring the number up to this minimum value. If it determines that there are more idle processes than the value of Max-SpareServers, it allows those above this value to die off. The default settings are usually sufficient for most configurations and tuning should only ever potentially need to be done only on extremely busy sites.

One note to remember, these are spare servers. This means that they are not currently handling requests. Neither the MinSpareServers nor the MaxSpareServers parameter in any way affect the total maximum number of requests that can be handled by the server. Further, this directive has no effect on a Windows-based machine, so tuning the numbers if your Apache is running on Windows will have no effect and the defaults should be left alone.

```
MinSpareServers  5
MaxSpareServers  10
```

### StartServers

The StartServers directive indicates the number of servers that Apache starts initially on startup. The number of servers started is dynamically controlled by Apache and is determined by load; therefore, the default should be reasonable. On a Windows server, this directive has no effect as there is always one child that handles all requests and each of those requests are handled by separate threads. ThreadsPerChild directive has a similar effect on Windows as this directive does on UNIX. Apache on Windows is somewhat less configurable than it is on other OSs.

```
StartServers  5
```

### MaxClients

The MaxClients directive limits the total number of servers running and the number of clients that can connect simultaneously. If this number of consecutive live connections is ever reached, subsequent connection attempts will be locked out. Typically connections to your server will no longer be active after the completion of a put or a get command. Setting this directive too low can have adverse effects on your implementation particularly if your implementation in any way sits on the Internet and is accessible by outside clients. Those connection attempts that try and are locked out will typically be queued up and handled by a child process after it is freed up. The maximum number that can be queued up is based on the ListenBacklog directive. The MaxClients directive acts as a brake to keep a runaway server from taking the system down. If you need to configure Apache to handle more than 256 clients, you will need to edit HARD_SERVER_LIMIT entry in the httpd.h header file and recompile Apache.

```
MaxClients  150
```

### MaxRequestsPerChild

The `MaxRequestsPerChild` directive is the number of requests that each child is allowed to process before that child dies. The child process will elegantly exit so that there are no problems connected to prolonged use. Problems associated with allowing a single child process to handle too many requests are often connected to memory leaks or other resources problems, particularly in the libraries. Although this directive is not usually needed, there are some places where it will help. Assigning a finite value to this directive will reduce the number of processes that remain after the load is reduced on a busy server. A value of 0 for this directive means that there are unlimited requests. Setting the value to around 1000 or 1500 should be sufficient for most configurations. It is important to note that this value does not include the `KeepAlive` requests. For example, if a child process receives an initial request, then 15 or 20 subsequent requests from the same client over the same connection, would count as one request toward that child reaching this value. On a Windows platform, it is strongly advised that this directive be set to 0 (unlimited) because if a non-0 value is ever reached, the child process (the only child process remember, all processes are then handled by thread) dies and needs to be respawned, requiring a reread the configuration files. While the time involved would be minimal with this action, it could result in unexpected behavior if there are modifications to any of the configuration files that were not intended to be implemented yet.

```
MaxRequestsPerChild 1000
```

### Listens

The `Listens` directive allows you to instruct Apache to listen to specific IP (Internet Protocol) address and port combinations in addition to the default. This is redefining the default action of listening to all IP interfaces on the port assigned in the `Port` directive. Listen can be used instead of `BindAddress` and `Port` combinations. If you assign `Listen` the value of a port only, it will listen to the newly assigned port (or ports) on all IP interfaces instead of just the port given in the `Port` directive. To avoid denial of service problems you can use IP addresses in the `Listen` directive. The first example shows a configuration listening to all IP interfaces on two separate ports:

```
Listen 80
Listen 8000
```

If you want to limit the server to accepting connections to two IP interfaces, one with port 80, the other on port 8000, your `Listen` directive would look like the following:

```
Listen 12.34.56.78:80
Listen 12.34.56.72:8000
```

## BindAddress

The BindAddress directive gives you the ability to support virtual hosts. It is used to tell the server which IP address to listen on. It can contain a "*" (listen to all IP addresses), an IP address, or a fully qualified Internet domain name.

```
BindAddress *
```

## Dynamic Shared Object Support

Apache is a modular program that allows you, the administrator, to choose the functionality to be included in the server by selecting a set of modules that bring the functionality with them that is required by the implementation. These modules can be compiled into the Apache binary, requiring a recompile if additional modules need to be added, or they can be compiled as Dynamic Shared Objects (DSO) that exist independent of the binary file, after the server has been built, by using the Apache Extension Tool (axps).

There are modules that are minimally required to be compiled into the binaries and others that can be allowed to stand alone. It is required that a module, mod_so.c and the main body module, core.c be compiled statically into Apache's core. Mod_so.c and core.c are the only two modules that have to be compiled into the core file and cannot be put into the DSO directive. Once the initial compilation including the mod_so.c module is complete, other modules can be placed into a DSO. Enabling this functionality is accomplished via Apache's configuration command –enable-<module>=shared option. Once the module is compiled in this manner, it will be a file with the naming convention mod_<module>.so that can be loaded dynamically into Apache runtime via the LoadModule directive in the httpd.conf file (this is a directive that comes with the mod_so.c module) at startup or restart.

DSO has several advantages. Flexibility is the chief advantage. By using these objects, you can run different server instances (e.g., standard Apache, secure SSL version, minimal server, PHP2, mod_per version, etc.) with a single installation. Pulling in third party modules to add features and flexibility easily extends what Apache can do. Some of these modules can include mod_plsql (required for running many of the Applications programs), mod_perl, and mod_fastcgi.

Not all platforms support dynamic loading of code into the address space. Because Apache pulls these modules in at runtime, it has to resolve symbolic links if they exist.

### ExtendedStatus

The ExtendedStatus directive controls Apache's choice to provide full status information or to simply generate basic status information when the server-status handler gets called. Default is off. Off has the effect of leaving the ExtendedStatus directive commented out. The detailed information returned and the values of ExtendedStatus required for it to be returned are found in Table 4.1.

        ExtendedStatus On

### Main Server Environment

Section 2 of the httpd.conf file specifies the configuration of the main server. The main server is the one that picks up all requests that are not picked up by a virtual host definition. The directives and values in this section also give defaults to any containers that could be used by a virtual host later on. This will provide a default expected action, but will allow for the flexibility of adding custom configurations for each additional

**Table 4.1   Extended Status Directive Statuses**

| Status Information | ExtendedStatus Setting Required |
|---|---|
| Number of children serving requests | Off or on |
| Number of idle children | Off or on |
| Server time started (or restarted) and the total time it has been running | Off or on |
| Status of each child | On |
| Number of requests that child has performed and the total number of bytes served by the child | On |
| Number of accesses and bytes served | On |
| Average number of requests per second | On |
| Number of bytes served per second | On |
| Average number of bytes per request | On |
| Current per child CPU percentage | On |
| Total CPU percentage used by Apache | On |
| Current hosts and requests being processed by each | On |

virtual host. Any directives in this section could be found inside of a virtual host (<Virtual Host>) definition in Section 3. Redefining the directives in the Virtual Host section overrides the settings and values in the Main Server Environment directives.

## Port

The Port directive specifies which port the server listens on. This directive gets configured during your installation and, unless you are running more than one instance of Apache on your server, it will likely never need to be altered. If you intend to run on ports with numbers lower than 1023, you will need to run Apache Web Server initially as root (on UNIX) or as administrator (Windows). If you are running with a ServerType directive of inetd on UNIX, this directive will have no effect.

```
Port 11111
```

## User/Group

The User/Group directive set specifies the name or number of the user and group that will be used to run Apache. On Sun, you should specify User "nouser" and Group "nogroup." On HP-UX, you may or may not be able to use shared memory as "nobody." There is a suggested workaround if this is the case. You will need to create User "www" and use that user as the one who will run Apache. If you want Apache to run as a different user or group than these values, you will need to start Apache as root or administrator (for Windows) initially, allowing it to be switched later. Be extremely cautious. Some UNIX version kernels refuse to set the group (setgid) or IPC_SET (semctl) to an unsigned Group value over 60,000. If you find this to be the case in your system, do not use the Group "nobody." If you are running with a ServerType directive of inetd on UNIX, this directive will have no effect.

```
User nobody
Group nobody
```

## ServerAdmin

The ServerAdmin directive can be used to set the default e-mail address that is included in some of the error messages and pages that the server generates. It is through this mechanism that users outside your immediate company accessing your server will know who to contact and know how to contact you if they encounter problems. Leaving it at the default will provide you with fewer sleepless moments, but presents a highly unprofessional front.

```
ServerAdmin you@yourcompany.com
```

### ServerName

The `ServerName` directive is what you would use if you were planning on setting up a server with the canonical name of something other than what you wanted to use for Web services. It is a common practice to name the server one thing, but to alias it in a Domain Name System (DNS) server with another name. This allows you to list your Web service under one name while maintaining any actual named server machines under that alias in DNS and changing out the server as needed. This not only provides you with an ability to switch out servers easier, but also allows for some obfuscation of names, adding a potential layer of security. It also allows you to maintain a duplicate backup server and allows the sysadmins to perform upgrades on servers transparently; it also allows you to restore your server to another machine at another site in the event of a disaster and not be concerned with the true server's name and then you can switch it back again at the home site. The `ServerName` directive in the `httpd.conf` file sets the host name of the server, further allowing redirection URLs. If there is no value set in this directive, the server tries to extrapolate the server's name from its own IP address. While this may work in theory, it is likely not going to work in all cases and the name that it may return may not be the preferred host name of the server. If you are using name-based virtual hosts, specifying the `ServerName` inside of the `<VirtualHost>` directive body specifies what host name will be needed in the requests `Host:Port` header to match the particular virtual host.

Remember, you cannot just invent host names and put them in this directive and hope they work. You have to have defined in DNS a valid name for your host even if there is no alias for it. If you do not understand how DNS works and you do not know what valid names your server can take on, work with your network administrators to either create one that you both agree on or determine one that has already been assigned. If there is not currently a valid value in DNS for your server, other than its canonical name, you can place its IP address here for the value of the directive. Anyone, including all end users of your system, will then need to access Apps using this address.

```
ServerName myserver.mydomain.mycompany.com
```

### DocumentRoot

When Apache decides what file to serve for a given request, its default behavior is to append the URL path for the request to the trailing end of the value specified in this directive. The `DocumentRoot` directive, therefore, sets the uppermost directory in the tree out of which Apache will serve its Web pages. If this directive is coupled with the ServerName directive, it will alias the path to the pages with the name specified in the ServerName; otherwise, it will append the path from the requested URL to the document root. This is only the default directory out of which Apache will serve pages. You can use symbolic links and further aliases to point to other locations from which you want to serve them. It is important that you not end the value for this directive with a trailing "/." A different DocumentRoot can be specified for different virtual hosts.

```
DocumentRoot "d:\viscomn\portal"
```

To allow for different levels of security at the Apache level, each directory that Apache can access can be configured differently with respect to what services and features are enabled or disabled based on directory (and applying to its subdirectories). Initially, you configure the default value to be very restrictive with respect to what is and is not allowed.

It is important here to remember that you are, at this point, setting many values to disabled. You will need to enable them deliberately further on. If things do not work as anticipated, you may need to check that the functionality has been enabled.

The first directive set says that from the root directory no one is allowed to follow symbolic links:

```
<Directory/>
     Options  FollowSymLinks
     AllowOverride  None
</Directory>
```

Now, you set your document root up to allow the ability to list an index of all files in your directory tree. This directive will give anyone who wants it the ability to list all of the files in your directory tree. This may have its advantages, in that it allows easy drill down access to find files via a browser, but remember that this also gives people the ability to find any files via a browser and gain a broader understanding of your environment via the understanding of the way in which these accessible files are laid out. They may not have the ability to find the location of those files in any other way and someone malicious could find a way to exploit this ability.

Directory gives the upper bounds of the directory tree to which you are granting this ability.

The Options portion of the command is the explicit option or options that you are enabling. In this case, the ability to follow symbolic links.

AllowOverride controls which options the .htaccess file has the ability to override (these files are security files that can allow you to limit the access that any particular user or group of users might have).

Order controls the order in which to determine who is allowed to retrieve information from the server. By default, Apache allows access to everyone. Depending on your circumstances, this may or may not be the action that you would like it to take. You can use the `Order` parameter to limit access to certain information to a single machine, to a domain or subdomain, or any combination of those situations. Adding a line below `Allow` specifying `Deny` from 123.46 (if you had 123.45 and 123.46 as the two subnets that had machines that could access your Apps) would limit what the users of any machine with an IP of 123.46.\*.\* could see.

`Allow` specifies who explicitly can retrieve the information:

```
<Directory "d:\viscomn\portal">
   Options Indexes FollowSymLinks MultiViews
   AllowOverride None
   Order allow, deny
   Allow from all
</Directory>
```

### UserDir

The `UserDir` directive sets a specific directory to append onto a user's home directory if a `~<user>` type request is received. If the following were to be the entry for this directive, only `user1`, `user2`, and `user3` would have a `UserDir` privilege due to the initial `UserDir` being designated as disabled. In many cases, Apache will allow you to determine that you will be granting access in the Least Privileges model. Least Privilege allows that users should only be granted the amount of privilege that will permit them to perform the given job but no more.

```
UserDir disabled
UserDir enabled user1 user2 user3
```

If you wanted to allow all users to have this access ability except `user4`, `user5`, and `user6`, you would put in the following directives:

```
UserDir enabled
UserDir disabled user4 user5 user6
```

This directive is, in all probability, commented out in your Apps Apache `httpd.conf` file and it would probably be best to leave it that way. Opening access up further than is necessary in the configuration of Apps Apache would be best left to contacting Oracle Support if it is necessary. Necessity would probably be tied to certain customization situations.

```
#UserDir public_html
```

The following code shows how to configure `UserDir` directive directories for a site where the specified directories are open for read-only access. This is a commented out example from a working `httpd.conf` file. It allows `gets` and `posts` (for posting from a form), but denies everyone from putting, deleting, patching, copying, moving, locking, or unlocking any files in that directory through that interface. It is only through the Web interface that this is true. If the files are accessible to too broad an audience at the server level, people will be able to perform these actions directly on the server.

```
#<Directory/home/*/public_html>
#       AllowOverride FileInfo AuthConfig Limit
#    Options MultiViews Indexes SymLinksIfOwnerMatch
IncludesNoExec
#       <Limit GET POST OPTIONS PROPFIND>
#            Order allow,deny
#            Allow from all
#       </Limit>
#       <Limit PUT DELETE PATCH PROPPATCH MKCOL COPY
MOVE LOCK UNLOCK>
#            Order deny,allow
#            Deny from all
#       </Limit>
#</Directory>
```

### *DirectoryIndex*

The DirectoryIndex directive specifies a list of resources that Apache will look for in a client request for an index of a directory. Achieving this result is accomplished by placing a trailing "/" at the end of the URL string. Figure 4.2 shows the result of having the DirectoryIndex directive set to a file without a relative path and having the Options Index set in the DirectoryRoot such that a user could view an index of all of the files in the specified directory.

```
DirectoryIndex index.html
```

If your httpd.conf file set the DirectoryIndex value as above, then entering http://myserver/docs would return a value of http://myserver/docs/index.html if that file exists. If index.htm exists in that directory, but not index.html, or if no version exists in that directory, the result of a similar search can be seen in Figure 4.2, which lists all files in the respective directory.

If, however, users always specify a relative path, or a full valid path to a default file, even if the Options Index is set in the DirectoryRoot directive, they will have returned to them a valid Web page. This directive can take on several values if they are specified in a space-delimited list. If you make sure that in at least one of these places there is a valid default html file (index.htm or index.html), you will ensure that no one will be able to get directory listings of your whole directory structure by simply navigating through browser pages.

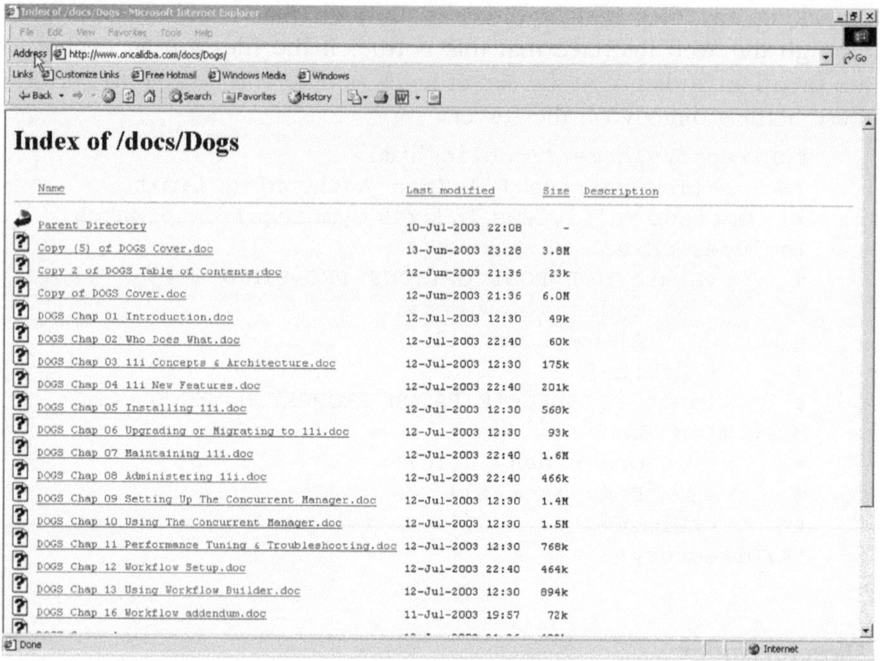

**Figure 4.2  Results of a DirectoryIndex Directive**

```
DirectoryIndex  index.html
index.txt/OA_HTML/US/index.html/OA_HTML/US/index.htm
```

## AccessFileName

The `AccessFileName` directive specifies the name of the file for which Apache will look in each directory for any directory specific access control information. This feature can allow you to limit the access of any user or group of users to the contents of that directory. It is not necessary that the file be named `.htaccess`, this is what it is named by convention. Following conventions has its advantages and its disadvantages. Following conventions allows anyone walking into your environment to be able to quickly and easily gain understanding of some of the security measures that you have in place by determining the locations of these files and accessing the information that they contain. By the same logic, this means the same thing to anyone who would gain inappropriate access to the server and alter the contents of these files or determine what access people have to the different directory structures. If you want to name it `.config` or `.secure` or `.buffy` or `.hank`, you can name it whatever you want. As long as you maintain the same naming standard throughout, and put that name in the `AccessFileName` directive, you should not have any problems.

The .htaccess files provide a simple way to make configuration changes on a directory-by-directory basis. A file by this name and containing one or more configuration directives (and there are many directives that can be placed in it) is placed in a particular document directory. The directives apply to that directory and all of its subdirectories. The directives available to be placed in this file are many of the same directives that can be found in the major configuration files for Apache and JServ environments.

    `AccessFileName.htaccess`

The `.htaccess` file is a simple text file just like `httpd.conf` file that is more of a script that Apache loads and runs than a simple file. The naming convention reflects the UNIX origination of Apache. Beginning with a dot (inferring that in UNIX environment it is typically somewhat hidden), `.htaccess` is the full filename. There is nothing before the dot and it does not get connected in any way to any other file. Similar to the `.profile` file, it just is.

Although placing a `.htaccess` file in a directory affects that directory and all subdirectories below it, you can change the control information in the lower directories by placing still more `.htaccess` files in those directories as well. Apache will locate the nearest `.htaccess` file and use that file's directives as the basis for its access control.

Before you go off and plant `.htaccess` everywhere, read through the following description and make sure you do not do anything redundant. It is possible to cause an infinite loop of redirects or errors if you place something too unusual in the `.htaccess`. There are three primary reasons that you should seriously consider not using an override file, despite how inviting it looks to directory-based access control.

One reason to avoid the use of an override file is the performance hit that can occur when one is used. When `AllowOverride` is set to allow the use of `.htaccess` files (whatever you choose to name them), Apache will look in every directory it accesses for a `.htaccess` file. Thus, permitting this file to be used once causes a performance hit (no matter how minimal in most cases, the overall degradation can be high on a busy site), whether or not you actually even use them. Also contributing to performance degradation is the fact that access files get loaded every time a document is requested. If there is not an access file in the directory that you are accessing a document from, Apache looks in all higher level directories in search of an access file that might have an affect on the contents of the current access directory. If there is such a file in the directory that you are accessing, it will check the upper level directories anyway to see if there might be a directive in one of their access files (there or not) that might impact the current directory. This means that if a user requests a file out of the `/www/htdocs/example` directory and this feature is enabled, Apache must look for all of the following files:

```
/.htaccess
/www/.htaccess
/www/htdocs/.htaccess
/www/htdocs/example/.htaccess
```

Another consideration concerns security. By using this directive, you are permitting users to modify server configuration, which may result in situations and changes over which you have very little or no control. Carefully consider whether or not you really want to be giving users this privilege. While this may be granting more security that you intend, it may also be limiting a user's ability to accomplish a job, leading to the unnecessary logging of self-imposed support requests. While there are situations where I fully believe that iTARs and Metalink are very valuable tools, if there is any way to limit the need to deal with a support analyst, I am all for it.

Any directive and any measure that you can implement via a `.htaccess` file can be implemented via the `httpd.conf` configuration file. Since you have access to and control of that file, you should take advantage of the elegance and simplicity (and limit the holes and hits) that using one central file can provide.

Some sites do not allow use of `.htaccess` files, since (depending on what the files are doing) they can dramatically slow down a server that is overloaded with domains if they are all using `.htaccess` files. I cannot stress this enough: **You need to make sure you are allowed to use** `.htaccess` **before you actually use it.** Some things that the `.htaccess` file can do can compromise a server's configuration that has been specifically set up by the administrator, so do not get yourself into trouble.

> **Caution:** Your `.htaccess` file will not work if there is a blank line above the first line that you type in. Be careful when editing it; if one of the lines in the file is so long that the editor you are using has to wrap it down to the next line it may cause inconsistent results.

The lines immediately following the `AccessFileName` directive (separated only by comments) prevent the contents of the `.htaccess` files from being viewed by clients via the Web. Because your `.htaccess` file contains control and authorization information for the directories on your server, you do not want most people to have access to this file for security reasons.

This directive says, "if I am using a .htaccess file, regardless of where that file is located, if the file starts with ".ht" do not let anyone view the contents." It is good to construct this directive in this manner, as many sites create password files that are often named something like .htpasswd and this directive will protect people from not only viewing the .htaccess file, but will also prevent them from unauthorized viewing of these other files as well.

```
<Files ~ "^\.ht">
     Order allow,deny
     Deny from all
</Files>
```

## CacheNegotiatedDocs

The CacheNegotiatedDocs directive suggests to the proxy servers that they not cache documents by overriding the default Apache action of sending a Pragma: no-cache command along with each document that it sends on the basis of content. The default action is to have this command commented out in the httpd.conf file (telling the proxy servers that they should follow the typical performance). As you are dealing with continually changing information in your environment, leaving this at its default behavior is advised.

```
#CacheNegotiatedDocs
```

## UseCanonicalName

There are many situations in which Apache has to construct self-referential URLs (a URL that refers back to the same server that the call is coming from). If the UseCanonicalName directive is set to on, Apache uses the ServerName and Port directives to construct the canonical name for the server which it then uses in all self-referential URLs.

There are three values that UseCanonicalName can take: off, on, and DNS. The DNS value is intended to be used with mass IP-based virtual hosting to support clients that are still using setups that do not provide a host value. Remember that you may be dealing with backward compatibility issues. With this UseCanonicalName set to DNS, Apache has to do a reverse DNS lookup to resolve what server the IP address references and this can cause some degree of performance degradation.

If UseCanonicalName is set to off, Apache will form the self-referential URLs using the host name and port only if the client supplies them; otherwise, it will use the canonical name.

The default for this directive is to be set to on.

If you are using a server with a short name (often the name of the Web server machine is www or www1) and the user enters http://www/mydirectory Apache (with UseCanonicalName set to on), the request will be redirected to http://www.company.com/mydir. With UseCanonicalName set to off, it would redirect the request to literally the directory and file that the user typed.

```
UseCanonicalName On
```

### TypesConfig

The TypesConfig directive specifies where Apache can go to find the typing configuration file. Typically this file is named mime.types and usually requires no editing. The filename that is given as the value for TypesConfig is always relative to the value that you provided for ServerRoot, so you do not have to provide the full path to the file providing it is within the same directory tree that ServerRoot is the root for.

Entries in mime.types contain references to the type and a space-delimited list of filename extensions and it appears mime.types allows the browser to understand what plug-in or application you want to associate with what extension that your users may access.

```
type/subtype file_extenetion1 file_extenetion2
file_extenetion3…
```

While you can add types to this file if needed for local use, it is highly recommended that you use the AddType directive in the httpd.conf file to accomplish this.

```
d:\visora\iAS/Apache/Apache/conf/mime.types
```

Example of entries that you might find in the mime.types file:

```
application/vnd.koan
application/vnd.lotus-1-2-3
application/vnd.lotus-approach
application/vnd.lotus-freelance
application/vnd.lotus-notes
application/vnd.lotus-organizer
application/vnd.lotus-screencam
application/vnd.lotus-wordpro
application/vnd.mediastation.cdkey
application/vnd.meridian-slingshot
application/vnd.mif        mif
```

### *DefaultType*

If Apache cannot determine what type a file is from its extension (or if it is extensionless or its extension is not located in either an AddType directive or in the mime.types file), it will use the value assigned to this directive to determine what kind of file to assume (right or wrong) that it is. If most of the content of your server is flat text files or HTML documents, you can safely set this to text/plain. If, however, much of your content is binary format (e.g., applications, images) you might want to set it to application/octet-stream. This will keep the browser from trying to display an unknown image format or application with an undefined extension as text. This occasionally happened in the early- to mid-1990s when new types were coming out frequently and older browsers did not know what to do with them. Historically this was located in the srm.conf file, but has now been migrated to httpd.conf.

```
DefaultType text/plain
```

### *MIMEMagicFile*

The mod_mime_magic module allows Apache to use various hints that can be found in the first few bytes of a file to attempt to determine its type if it cannot make that determination in any other way. The MIMEMagicFile directive enables this module's use. The default file containing the hints for mod_mime_magic is located in the ServerRoot/conf directory and is named magic. This module is not part of the default server and it needs to be added in the DSO section with a LoadModule directive or recompiled into the server. The MIMEMagicFile directive is enclosed within an <IfModule> container so that the directive is ignored if the module to which it refers is not loaded.

```
<IfModule mod_mime_magic.c>
    MIMEMagicFile d:\visora\iAS/Apache/Apache/conf/magic
</IfModule>
```

Example entries that might be seen in the magic file:

```
0      lelong      0x0064732E
>12    lelong      1              audio/x-dec-basic
>12    lelong      2              audio/x-dec-basic
>12    lelong      3              audio/x-dec-basic
>12    lelong      4              audio/x-dec-basic
>12    lelong      5              audio/x-dec-basic
>12    lelong      6              audio/x-dec-basic
>12    lelong      7              audio/x-dec-basic
```

It is highly unlikely that you would ever edit this file and it would be wise to only do so with the full support and knowledge of Oracle Support.

### HostnameLookups

The `HostnameLookups` directive enables DNS lookups so that the host name can be logged and used (often this is required in CGI in its `remote_host` variable). `HostnameLookups` can take on three values: on, off, and double. Double allows Apache to do a double reverse DNS; after the first (reverse) lookup is done to retrieve the host name from DNS, another forward lookup is done to verify that result. At least one of the IP addresses in the forward lookup must match the original address. Regardless of the value of `HostnameLookup`, when `mod_access` module is being used, a double reverse lookup is done for added security (although the result in this case may not always be available to CGI for use in its variables). The default (and default value used by Apps) currently is off, saving on often unnecessary network traffic and considerable latency time observed by users by virtue of Apache doing the reverse lookup.

```
HostnameLookups Off
```

### ErrorLog

The `ErrorLog` directive specifies the location of the error log file containing Apache's errors. If the path does not begin with either a drive specification (for Windows users) or a "/" for UNIX/Linux users, the path is assumed to be relative to the `ServerRoot` directive value. This is the default assumption in many cases within this file and the files that it calls. If the file path begins with a "|", it is assumed that it is the command that Apache is supposed to use to spawn the error log. With Apache, regardless of what platform you are on, do not change the directions of any of the slashes in the path.

```
ErrorLog d:\visora\iAS/Apache/Apache/logs/error_log
```

### LogLevel

The `LogLevel` directive adjusts the amount of detail and the level of information that gets recorded in the `ErrorLog` log file. Table 4.2 shows the levels available and what level of detail goes along with each. They are listed in the table in order of decreasing significance of information. Whatever level is specified, all messages from that level and every level of increased significance is recorded in the file. This means that critical log level information will include alert level messages and emergency messages as well. It also means that `info` will include `notice`, `warn`,

**Table 4.2   LogLevel Levels Available**

| LogLevel | Meaning |
|---|---|
| emerg | Emergencies—system is unusable. |
| alert | Action must be taken immediately. |
| crit | Critical conditions exist and should be addressed. |
| error | Error conditions (some of these errors are expected). |
| warn | Warning conditions. |
| notice | Normal but significant condition exists. |
| info | Informational entries will be written. |
| debug | Debugging level messages. |

error, critical, alert, and emergency. This may be more information than you are intending so be careful with its use. It is highly suggested that a level of at least critical be maintained.

Apps defaults the value to warn, which causes a verbose and lengthy log file that often contains irrelevant information. A level of error should be sufficient to alert you to things that may not be running correctly but will limit what is likely not of interest to you. Oracle Support will often have you reset this value to allow for the gathering of more information if you find that you are experiencing difficulties in your environment. Make sure that you change it back later or you will find that you have extremely large log files.

```
LogLevel warn
```

Custom logs are written in a customizable format, may be directly written to a file, or indirectly by means of an external program. The LogFormat directive specifies the format in which those custom files are written. Table 4.3 provides the English interpretation of what the variable values that can be used in the string specify.

```
LogFormat "%h%l%u%t \"%r\"%>s%b \"%{Referer}i\"
\"%{User-Agent}i\"" combined
LogFormat "%h%l%u%t \"%r\"%>s%b" common
LogFormat "%{Referer}i ->%U" referrer
LogFormat "%{User-agent} i" agent
```

## CustomLog

The CustomLog directive specifies the location and format that the access, agent, and referrer log files should have. The formats—common, agent, and referrers—refer back to the format above with the trailing tag bearing

**Table 4.3    English Interpretations LogFormat Variable**

| Format Variable | English Interpretation |
|---|---|
| `%P` | The process ID of the child process. |
| `%p` | Canonical port of serving server. |
| `%{< FOOBAR >}o` | Contents of Foobar with header line(s). |
| `%{< FOOBAR >}n` | Contents of note Foobar other module. |
| `%m` | Request method. |
| `%l` | Remote log name. |
| `%{<FOOBAR>}I` | Contents of variable Foobar with header line(s). |
| `%H` | Request protocol. |
| `%h` | Remote host. |
| `%f` | Filename. |
| `%{< FOOBAR >}e:` | Contents of environment variable FOOBAR. |
| `%c` | Connection status at response time. "X" = Connection aborted before completion. "+" = Connection kept alive after response. "-" = Connection closed after response. |
| `%b` | Bytes sent not including headers in CLF or Common Log File format. |
| `%B` | Bytes sent not including headers. |
| `%A` | Local IP address. |
| `%q` | Query string. |
| `%r` | First line of request. |
| `%s` | Status or original request. |
| `%t` | Common log format time. |
| `%{Format}t` | Time formatted. |
| `%T` | Request served time in seconds. |
| `%u` | Remote user (may not be valid). |
| `%U` | URL path requested without query string. |
| `%V` | Server name per UseCanonicalName directive. |
| `%v` | Canonical ServerName requesting server. |
| `%a` | Remote IP address. |

that name. Uncomment those logs that you want to maintain on your system. If you want to have all of this information (agent, access, and referrer) stored in a single file, you can comment out even the common one in this list and uncomment the combined.

```
CustomLog
/export/home/hays/my_apache/apache_1.3.11/logs/acc
ess_log common
#CustomLog
/export/home/hays/my_apache/apache_1.3.11/logs/ref
erer_log referer
#CustomLog
/export/home/hays/my_apache/apache_1.3.11/logs/age
nt_log agent
#CustomLog
/export/home/hays/my_apache/apache_1.3.11/logs/acc
ess_log combined
```

### ServerSignature

The ServerSignature directive provides the ability for Apache to place a trailing footer line under any server-generated documents. This line (available with ServerSignature value of on or e-mail) is particularly useful when placed in error message pages. It will place a line informing the user of the server version number, serving host, and, if the directive is given the value of e-mail, a mailto: link that will direct e-mail to the address specified in the ServerAdmin directive. In Oracle E-Business Suite (where many users are internal), this is often a handy way to allow users to quickly send you where they are and what their error conditions were. If you have implemented any of the "i" modules (e.g., iReceivables, iStore, iProcurement) this may become an e-mail headache unless you redirect the e-mail address to a central problem resolution address that is used only for this purpose. Remember, this value can be overridden in the Virtual Host section by a virtual host container directive, so you can specify that internal customers can send e-mail but limit what external customers are permitted to do. The default for this directive is off.

```
ServerSignature On
```

### Alias

The Alias directive comes as part of the mod_alias module and provides the means to allow manipulation and control of URLs when requests are processed by Apache server. Again, this module either needs to be compiled into the Apache core or be included in the DSO include directive. Alias is used to create a map between URL strings and file system paths, particularly those paths outside of the DocumentRoot tree structure. A trailing "/" (as in /icons/ in the example below) forces Apache to require that exact string including the trailing slash to be a part of the referencing URL string; a reference to /icons/ would redirect, a reference to /icons would not. That means that a reference to http://myserver.mycompany.com/icons/mail.ico would result in the server retrieving the mail.ico icon file from the http://myserver.mycompany.com/export/home/hays/my_apache/apache_1.3.11/ icons directory. The directory container following the Alias directive allows security to be placed on the redirect directory if needed.

```
Alias/icons/"d:\visex-
tras\extras/Apache/Apache/icons/"
<Directory "d:\visex-
tras\extras/Apache/Apache/icons/"
     Options Indexes MultiViews
     AllowOverride None
     Order allow,deny
     Allow from all
</Directory>
```

### ScriptAlias

The ScriptAlias directive provides the same functionality and behaviors as the Alias directive, but for primarily CGI scripts. It refers to the target directory typically containing CGI scripts that will be processed by the mod_cgi module's CGI script handler.

```
ScriptAlias/cgi-bin/"d:\visex-
tras\extras/Apache/Apache/cgi-bin/"
<Directory "d:\visextras\extras/Apache/Apache/cgi-
bin">
     AllowOverride None
     Options None
     Order allow,deny
     Allow from all
</Directory>
```

### Redirect

The Redirect directive maps an old URL into a new one. This allows you to redirect requests to new locations of old files without having to recode all links in all referring documents. The new URL is returned to the calling client and the client then attempts to retrieve the document again with the new address. The format for this directive is Redirect OldURL NewURL. This should not be used instead of fixing all known references, but should be a stopgap measure to make sure that anything that you have not found gets redirected properly to new locations.

```
Redirect http://myserver.my.company.com/thisold-
page.html http://myserver.my.company.com/new-
path/to/thisoldpage.html
```

### IndexOptions

The IndexOptions directive specifies the behavior of directory indexing. Valid formatting can either be IndexOptions option option option or IndexOptions +option +option -option depending on which Apache version you are dealing with. The "+|–" syntax became available with Apache 1.3.3 and is likely available in your implementation; however, the regular syntax will work as well. Options for this directive are in Table 4.4.

### IndexOptions FancyIndexing

This can be further narrowed to directory specific IndexOptions as follows:

```
<Directory/OA_HTML/docs>
      IndexOptions FancyIndexing
</Directory>
<Directory/OA_HTML/docs/spec>
      IndexOptions ScanHTMLTitles
</Directory>
```

The "+" and "–" prefixes attached to a keyword are applied to the current IndexOptions settings whether they are inherited from a higher level directory or are directly applied just on this directory. If an unprefixed option is processed, it has the effect of clearing out all of the inherited options and all incremental settings that have been acquired so far. This includes all options in the same IndexOptions directive. It does allow the further acquiring of options from that point forward, however. For example, if you have the following set of IndexOptions directives, you will process ScanHTMLTitles, add the IconsAreLinks option, then clear both of those options out because FancyIndexing is neither yes nor no, only exists and is therefore on. At this point you have the equivalent of IndexOptions FancyIndexing. Processing the next directive with the option +SupressSize has the net effect of having a single directive of IndexOptions FancyIndexing +SupressSize.

```
IndexOptions +ScanHTMLTitles –IconsAreLinks Fancy-
Indexing
IndexOptions +SupressSize
```

**Table 4.4    IndexOptions Options**

| Option | Option Description |
|---|---|
| DescriptionWidth=[n \| *] | Width of description column in number of characters. |
| FancyIndexing | Enables fancy indexing of directories (setting this option will enable the ability to add many of the other options). |
| FoldersFirst | Subdirectories appear first in listing followed by files. Only available if FancyIndexing. |
| IconHeight[=pixels] | Causes the server to include height and width attributes in the IMG or Image tag for the icon so browsers can precalculate the page layout instead of waiting for all images to load. |
| IconsAreLinks | Makes icons part of anchor for the filename. Available only with FancyIndexing. |
| IconWidth[=pixels] | Works together with IconHeight. |
| IgnoreCase | Filenames sorted in case insensitive manner. Available only with FancyIndexing. |
| NameWidth=[n \| *] | Specify width of the filename column in bytes. "*" Indicates that the column is automatically sized to longest filename allowing you to not have to do any recalculation when you add files to a directory. |
| ScanHTMLTitles | Allows extraction of the title from HTML documents for FancyIndexing (can be CPU and I/O intensive). |
| SuppressColumnSorting | Column headings made into links for sorting. Available only with FancyIndexing. |
| SuppressDescription | Suppresses the file description. Available only with FancyIndexing. |
| SuppressHTMLPreamble | Causes the display to start with the header file contents, provided that the header file contains appropriate HTML instructions. |
| SuppressLastModified | Suppresses the display of the last modification date. Available only with FancyIndexing. |
| SuppressSize | Suppresses the file size. Available only with FancyIndexing. |
| TrackModified | This returns the Last Modified and E Tag values for the listed directory in the HTTP header. This option is best used for UNIX servers due to the way that Windows does formatting. |

## AddIcon

The AddIcon directive instructs the server what icon you want to have shown for each different type of file, filename, or extension. These directives also only apply for those directories for which FancyIndexing is defined as an option.

```
AddIconByEncoding (CMP,/icons/compressed.gif) x-
compress x-gzip
AddIconByType (TXT,/icons/text.gif) text/*
AddIconByType (IMG,/icons/image2.gif) image/*
AddIconByType (SND,/icons/sound2.gif) audio/*
AddIconByType (VID,/icons/movie.gif) video/*
AddIcon /icons/binary.gif.bin.exe
AddIcon /icons/binhex.gif.hqx
AddIcon /icons/tar.gif.tar
AddIcon /icons/world2.gif.wrl.wrl.gz.vrml.vrm.iv
AddIcon /icons/compressed.gif.Z.z.tgz.gz.zip
```

## DefaultIcon

The DefaultIcon directive sets a generic default icon to display for files when Apache cannot determine what other icon should be used. This directive is only applicable for use with IndexOptions Fancy-Indexing.

```
DefaultIcon /icons/unknown.gif
```

## AddDescription

The AddDescription directive allows Apache to place a particular defined short description in the display for any file or directory in server generated index lists. This allows users to have an understanding of what kind of file they are dealing with, if that is important to you. It can become a maintenance problem if you have an extensive list of file extensions that you want to maintain in this section. This directive is only applicable for use with IndexOptions FancyIndexing.

```
AddDescription "GZIP compressed document."gz
AddDescription "tape archive."tar
AddDescription "GZIP compressed tar archive."tgz
```

## ReadmeName

The ReadmeName directive instructs Apache what README file, by default, to look for in the given directory. This assumes that you want to provide the ability for a user to access the README files in your directories and gain the information that might be in there. Not a bad idea for well-informed internal users, but it might be ill advised for a user coming in from the outside of your company who might have the intention to use this information for illicit means. It will start by looking for `file-name.htm` or `filename.html` then if it does not find either one, it will look for `filename.txt`.

```
ReadmeName  README
```

### HeaderName

The `HeaderName` directive instructs Apache what filename to insert at the top of an index listing. Apache will by default start by looking for `filename.htm` or `filename.html`. Then, if it does not find either one, it will look for `filename.txt`.

```
HeaderName  HEADER
```

### IndexIgnore

The `IndexIgnore` directive adds additional files to the list it maintains of files that it should hide when listing the contents of a directory. The argument to this directive is a space-separated list of file extensions, partial filenames, and wildcarded filenames or extensions (shell script style wildcarding), expressions, or full filenames that you want Apache to ignore. Any value added to this directive adds to the list of files that Apache ignores, rather than replacing that list. By default the full list contains ".". This means that the `.htaccess` or the `.htpass` files would be excluded from any index listing. The inclusion of the READMEs in this list counteracts anything that might have been accomplished in the `ReadMeName` directive.

```
IndexIgnore  README readme*.conf.properties
```

### AddEncoding

The `AddEncoding` directive allows Apache to allow certain browsers (those with the capabilities to do so) to uncompress information. It maps the given filename extensions to specific encoding types. Anything added by means of this directive will add to the existing list instead of replacing it unless that extension already exists in the Apache maintained list. If Apache already has an extension of the given type in its internal list, setting this directive will override those values; so care must be taken to ensure that you are not overriding anything that you do not intend to. The following examples would direct Apache that anything with a `gz` or `tgz` extension would be read as encoded using `x-gzip` encoding and anything with a Z extension would be interpreted as being encoded with x-compress. The extension is case insensitive and can be entered with or without the leading dot.

```
AddEncoding x-compress Z
AddEncoding x-gzip gz tgz
```

## AddLanguage

The AddLanguage directive allows you to instruct Apache what language to infer a given document is written in. This adds the flexibility of allowing developers to be writing documents in the language they are going to be accessed in. You can then use content negotiation to give the browser a file that it can interpret. With the global nature of many businesses and the support that Oracle now builds into its product for more and more languages, this setting allows you to build customized interfaces into extensions to your system into the language format of the users who will be accessing that information.

The suffix does not have to be the same as the language keyword. For example, Polish would be pl if following net-standard coding, but you can use AddLanguage pl.po to limit the ambiguity that may result for developers between Polish spoken-written language and Perl scripts. The following lists typical defaults for these languages: Danish (da), Dutch (nl), English (en), Estonian (ee), French (fr), German (de), Greek-Modern (el), Italian (it), Portuguese (pt), Luxembourgeois (ltz), Spanish (es), Swedish (sv), Catalan (ca), Czech (cz). And this list adds to that default list:

```
AddLanguage da.dk
AddLanguage nl.nl
AddLanguage en.en
AddLanguage et.ee
AddLanguage fr.fr
AddLanguage de.de
AddLanguage el.el
AddLanguage it.it
AddLanguage pt.pt
AddLanguage ltz.lu
AddLanguage ca.ca
AddLanguage es.es
AddLanguage sv.se
AddLanguage cz.cz
```

### LanguagePriority

The LanguagePriority directive instructs Apache in the precedence of languages to present in case the requesting client (the end user's browser) does not have a preference set. This directive assists content negotiation in case it is determined that more than one language could be used. The list is in order of decreasing preference. In this case, the precedent order is English, Spanish, and French.

```
LanguagePriority en es fr
```

### AddType

The AddType directive allows you to extend the functionality of mime.types without having to resort to editing the mime.types file. Adding types to this list is the preferred method of adding functionality. AddTypes maps the given file extension to a specific content type. These types are typically added for functionality that is not currently part of the Apache distribution. As the Internet grows, this is an easy place to add the functionality of the newer technology without necessarily having to upgrade every time a new function is released.

```
#AddType application/x-httpd-php3  .php3
#AddType application/x-httpd-php3-source  .phps
#AddType application/x-httpd-php  .php
#AddType application/x-httpd-php-source  .phps
AddType application/x-tar  .tgz
```

### AddHandler

The AddHandler  directive allows you to map a certain file extension to a certain existing handler or to a downloadable plug-in. There are mappings already in place in Apache for most existing file types. If you map an extension that already exists in the Apache chore list to another handler, it will override the default value already in the default. Care must be taken to ensure that you do not create unanticipated side effects.

```
#AddHandler cgi-script .cgi
#AddType text/html .shtml
#AddHandler server-parsed .shtml
```

### Action

The Action directive provides you the means to define media types that will be executed by whatever interpreter is defined for that extension whenever a file with that call's extension gets accessed. This allows some file extensions to be handled by one certain CGI script while a different script handles another. While the previous few directives are very useful if a little risky to alter, this one will allow you to provide a far higher level of flexibility with the inclusion of newer versions of interpreters while allowing previous versions to continue to function successfully until a migration to the newer technology can take place.

```
Action image/gif/cgi-bin/images.cgi
AddHandler my-file-type.xyz
Action my-file-type/cgi-bin/program.cgi
```

### MetaDir

The `MetaDir` directive specifies the directory where Apache can find metadata information files. These files contain additional HTTP headers that can be included when sending a document and are usually located within a hidden subdirectory of the upper level directory housing the files for which access is being attempted. If the value that is assigned to `MetaDir` is just a dot ("."), Apache will attempt to look within the same directory as the file being accessed. Again, the dot notation means that the directory is hidden unless accessed via the proper method (`ls -al`).

```
MetaDir.metainfo
```

### MetaSuffix

The `MetaSuffix` directive works with the `MetaDir` directive to fully provide Apache with the extension of the file within the `MetaDir` directive that contains the meta information. The default file extension for this directive is the `.meta` extension, but by setting this directive you can reassign this suffix to whatever you choose to use.

```
#MetaSuffix.meta
```

### BrowserMatch

The `BrowserMatch` directive modifies the normal behavior that a browser will have in response to certain HTTP requests. Because you cannot always determine what brand or version of a browser that a client might be using, these directives can customize the response that Apache will use when it serves content to the different browsers that call. For example, `KeepAlive` is not always stable for a Mozilla/2-based browser (Netscape 2 and other browsers that use the same type base code). Internet Explorer Version 4.0b2 is known to have a somewhat incompatible implementation of HTTP 1.1 such that it also does not fully support `KeepAlive`. One of the things that any Web developer has to keep in mind when developing content is to build for the least common denominator. Build your content to be accessible by anyone from anywhere. While this is something that is usually easily remembered in most cases, this feature can also assist your implementation to become more accessible to users of the system who have disabilities that would possibly mean that they could not use the site otherwise (vision impaired, for example).

```
BrowserMatch "Mozilla/2" nokeepalive
BrowserMatch "MSIE 4\.0b2;" nokeepalive downgrade-
1.0 force-response-1.0
BrowserMatch "RealPlayer 4\.0" force-response-1.0
BrowserMatch "Java/1\.0" force-response-1.0
BrowserMatch "JDK/1\.0" force-response-1.0
```

### Allow Server Reports

The `ServerStatus` directive in a location container will allow server status reports to be presented to the browser for viewing if they have the URL configuration of `http://myserver/server-status`. You will need to alter this container directive, changing the `your_domain.com` to your particular domain and uncomment it to make this directive work.

```
#<Location/server-info>
#       SetHandler server-info
#       Order deny,allow
#       Deny from all
#       Allow from.your_domain.com
#</Location>
```

### ProxyRequests

A proxy server is a server or service that sits between a client machine and a real or regular server (e.g., your Oracle E-Business Suite server). The proxy server's job is to intercept requests made to the regular server and try to fill the request. If the proxy server cannot fill the request on its own, the request gets forwarded on to the Applications Server. The `mod_proxy` module provides a proxy cache for Apache.

The `ProxyRequests` directive allows (`on`) or prevents (`off`) Apache from functioning as a proxy server. Setting this directive to off does not prevent you from being able to use other proxy servers. If you want to enable `ProxyRequests`, uncomment the following container enclosed directives; before you do, make sure you have secured your server. An open proxy server can be very dangerous.

```
<Directory proxy:*>
   Order Deny,Allow
   Deny from all
   Allow from mycompany.com
</Directory>
```

Once it has been secured, uncomment the following:

```
#<IfModule mod_proxy.c>
#ProxyRequests On
#
#<Directory proxy:*>
#       Order deny,allow
#       Deny from all
#       Allow from.your_domain.com
#</Directory>
```

Notice the beginning line in the previous example is the command IfModule <module name>. This is the beginning of an IfModule container. This container continues and includes everything that appears in the file through the /IfModule command. In this case, all following commands apply in some way to the proxy settings on the server.

### ProxyVia

The ProxyVia directive controls the flow of requests along a chain of proxy servers. Primarily, it is used to help deal with the handling of Via: HTTP headers. Table 4.5 shows the possible settings that Proxy-Via can take on and the meaning to the server and the end user for those settings.

```
#ProxyVia On
```

### CacheRoot

The CacheRoot directive specifies the name of the directory that will contain cache files for the server; it must be a directory to which the HTTP Server can write. While setting CacheRoot enables proxy caching,

**Table 4.5   Possible ProxyVia Settings**

| Setting | Meaning |
| --- | --- |
| Off | No special processing is performed. Requests or replies containing a Via: header are passed through unchanged. This is the default setting. |
| On | Each request and reply processed will have a Via: header line appended for this host. |
| Full | Each Via: header line appended by this server will have the Apache server version shown as a Via: comment field. |
| Block | Every proxy request will have all of its existing Via: header lines removed and no new lines will be generated. |

without it you can still continue to have proxy functionality (if Proxy-Requests is set to on) but no caching functionality would be available.

```
#CacheRoot "d:\visora/Apache/Apache/proxy"
```

### CacheSize

The CacheSize directive specifies the desired space usage of the cache specified in the CacheRoot directive in kilobytes. While it may grow somewhat beyond this size, Apache's garbage collection will delete files until it is back at or below this number. If you are going to use cache, set this value to at least 20 to 40 percent below the actual amount of space allocated to the CacheRoot directory.

```
#CacheSize 5
```

### CacheGcInterval

The CacheGcInterval directive specifies the number of hours after which the Apache service should check the cache and delete files above the space usage specified in the CacheSize directive. Many of these directives come in sets and build upon each other to provide full functionality and full control. This directive accepts a float value, so 1.5 is a valid value and garbage collection will occur (if this is the value that you choose to set for the directive) every 90 minutes. If this is left unset while the previous two are set, no garbage collection will occur and the cache in the CacheDir will grow until it runs out of space, making CacheSize irrelevant.

```
#CacheGcInterval 4
```

### CacheMaxExpire

The CacheMaxExpire directive specifies the maximum number of hours a cached document will be allowed to be maintained on the proxy cache server before a new request is directed directly to the primary server. Any document in the cache could be, at most, this number of hours out of date.

```
#CacheMaxExpire 24
```

### CacheLastModifiedFactor

The CacheLastModifiedFactor directive helps Apache determine the expiration date for a document for which the originating HTTP Server did not supply an expiration date. The formula for this calculation is:

```
Expiration-period = time-in-hours-since-last-
modification * CacheLastModifiedFactor
```

If a document has a last modified date of a week ago (168 hours) and a CacheLastModiedFactor of 0.1, that would mean that the Expiration Period for that particular page would end after 16.8 hours.

```
EP = 168 *.1 = 16.8
```

If the result of this calculation is larger than CacheMaxExpire, CacheMaxExpire prevails. Again, this directive really applies only if you are using caching on the server.

```
#CacheLastModifiedFactor 0.1
```

### CacheDefaultExpire

The CacheDefaultExpire directive specifies a default expiration time in hours of a document that gets fetched into the cache via a protocol that does not support expiration times. The CacheMaxExpire does not override this setting.

```
#CacheDefaultExpire 1
```

### NoCache

The NoCache directive specifies a list of words, host names, and or domain names (space separated) from which this proxy server does not cache documents. If Apache can determine the domain name–IP connection for a domain contained in this list, addressing it by its IP would have the same effect on the caching (or not caching) of documents as having it referenced by name. Setting NoCache to "*" has the effect of disabling caching completely.

```
#NoCache a_domain.com another_domain.edu
joes.garage_sale.com
```

This is the end of the IfModule container and the end of the directives that are only in effect if the server is going to have the proxy server settings turned on. This is how you can apply some kind of if, then, or else logic to the directives, adding flexibility to the server and to your environment.

```
#</IfModule>
```

### Virtual Hosts

Section 3 of the httpd.conf file is the Virtual Hosts section. You configure containers and directives in this section that will allow you to maintain multiple domains and host names on one machine, differentiated by apparent host name. If there are several companies sharing a Web server, each will likely want to have their own domain without requiring visitors to know extraneous path information. Apache supports both IP-based and name-based virtual hosts. Virtual host containers are set up for different hosts.

*Virtual host* refers to the practice of maintaining more than one server service on one physical machine, each service differentiated by its apparent host name. One common example is in cases where different companies are sharing a physical Web server, yet it is highly desirable that each company has its own domain. The physical box may be named Bullwinkle; Company 1 may have licensed its domain www.mycompany.com and Company 2 may have licensed www.yourcompany.com. These individual domains can coexist on the same server through the implementation of each by way of Virtual Host directives.

*IP-based* implies that the server that you are dealing with **must have a different, distinct IP address for each IP-based virtual host that you intend to configure**. This is usually achieved by configuring the physical machine to have several physical network connections or to use one of the virtual interfaces that are supported by most OSs. IP-based virtual hosts make use of the IP address of the incoming connection to determine which virtual host it needs to serve. Therefore it is necessary to have a separate IP address for each separate host or for each domain.

*Name-based virtual hosting* relies on the client making the request to deliver the host name as part of the HTTP header that it sends. This allows many different hosts and many different domains to use the same IP address. Name-based virtual hosting is typically simpler to implement. You simply need to work with your networking people to configure the DNS server to map each host name to the correct IP address. Then you configure the Apache HTTP Server to recognize these different host names and test the resolution of the names to the correct places. Name-based virtual hosting would make the network folks at your company somewhat happier as it eases demand for one of the scarcest commodities in many corporations, IP addresses. Therefore, if you are going to be using virtual hosting in any way, you should attempt to use name-based virtual hosting unless there is a specific and compelling reason to choose IP-based virtual hosting.

The <VirtualHost> and </VirtualHost> container tags are used to enclose each group of directives that applies to each particular virtual host. Any directive that is allowed to be in a virtual host may be included between these two tags. Addr can be the IP address of the virtual host or a fully qualified domain name for the IP address of the virtual host.

Each virtual host must correspond to a different IP address, a different port number, or a different host name for the server. In the case of a different IP address, the server must be configured to accept packets for multiple addresses. This is particularly important if the machine you are dealing with does not have multiple physical network interfaces; it needs to be accomplished using `ifconfig alias` command (if your OS supports it).

```
#NameVirtualHost 12.34.56.78:80
#NameVirtualHost 12.34.56.78
```

Nearly any Apache directive can go into a virtual host container. If you put a directive into one of these containers, the value that you specify here overrides any value that you may have specified anywhere else and overrides the default values. Careful planning is necessary if you are considering using this section.

```
#<VirtualHost ip.address.of.host.some_domain.com>
#      ServerAdmin webmaster@host.some_domain.com
#      DocumentRoot /www/docs/host.some_domain.com
#      ServerName host.some_domain.com
#      ErrorLog logs/host.some_domain.com-error_log
#   CustomLog logs/host.some_domain.com-access_log
common
#</VirtualHost>
#<VirtualHost _default_:*>
#</VirtualHost>
```

# 5

---

# JSERV

Java is the platform independent, interactive programming language of the Web. Oracle 11i harnesses the power and flexibility of the Java language and Java extensions to allow the entire application to be served up as a thin client through a browser. It also harnesses the Java database capabilities along with the Java enabled front end to bring added features and added power to Oracle Applications.

## JSERV

JServ allows you to include Java servlets in the Oracle E-Business Suite application. It is a servlet engine that allows Apache to serve the nondatabase driven JSP to a requesting browser. Recall that the database driven JSP are delegated to the mod_ose module that is an Oracle provided module. JServ is an Apache standard module. Its functionality is available through the mod_jserv module plug-in. Requests for Java pages are routed through the mod_jserv module to Apache and from Apache through the module back to the requesting user.

While Apache is no longer offering new releases of the JServ product and is currently in maintenance mode (meaning that well tested patches could be released but not major updates), JServ remains a stable and useful tool. Providing complete environment independence, JServ is a server application that is responsible for serving requests made, translating the servlet requests, and forwarding them to the correct servlet engine.

## VOCABULARY

Before we venture too far in to the world of Java servlets, we probably need a small taste of the vocabulary that surrounds these highly flexible inclusions.

## Servlet

A servlet is a Java-based server-side small application (or a single Java class) that runs inside of a Web server. It accepts client provided input, responds to the request based on that input, and dynamically generates the output based on those inputs. Servlets are roughly equivalent to a file in the Web server environment.

## Servlet Engine

The servlet engine is the part of the application that executes the servlet, forwards the client's request for data to the requested servlet, and then routes the response back to the client application. Apache JServ is the servlet engine that is relevant in this case. The Apache JServ engine is completely written in Java and is a stand-alone server (not necessarily requiring a Web server to allow it to function, although the routing of requests is much simpler through this mechanism).

## Servlet Repository

A servlet repository is a collection of servlets, either in a directory or in an archive. Often the archive is a zip file, more often it is a jar file (jar being a Java archive format similar to zip but available only to Java). The Web equivalent is roughly a directory.

## Servlet Zone

A servlet zone is the location where the servlets live during their life cycle. It defines the security environment to where the servlet is restricted and allows for the logical separation between different groups of servlets. Also a collection of repositories that share a common context. It is the JServ version of the Web server's virtual host concept.

## Servlet Life Cycle

Every servlet must go through a certain execution path. This path starts at the point where the servlet is called and ends when the information is returned to the calling client. It is composed of an initialization phase, execution phase, and destruction phase.

### Initialization Phase

In the initialization phase, the servlet engine loads the servlet's `.class` file into the JVM's memory space, converts the loaded file into a valid object, and initializes it. This step allocates the resources that will be required by the servlet for execution. The Java programming method associated with this part of the life cycle is the `init()` method.

### Execution Phase

Once the servlet is instantiated into JVM memory, it is combined with all of the passed parameters from the calling client to form a request object. The request object is processed and the information to be returned to the calling client is assembled into a response object within this phase. This phase's method would be the `service (ServletRequest, Servlet-Response)` method.

### Destruction Phase

Once the servlet has run and provided suitable output to the client, it cleans up after itself. In the destruction phase, resources that were allocated are returned to the system and the engine shuts down gracefully. The method associated with this portion of the life cycle would be the `destroy ()` method.

Configuration and inclusion of JServ in your environment is accomplished by configuring the `Jserv.conf` file and the `Jserv.properties` file along with their includes in the Apache include file tree. Figure 5.1 shows an example of the files called by `httpd.conf` in an Oracle E-Business Suite configuration.

## CONFIGURATION

Configuration of the highly flexible JServ environment is accomplished through the combination of the `httpd.conf` file that we looked at in Chapter 4 — Apache, the `Jserv.properties` and `Jserv.conf` file, and the `zone.properties` files and the smaller files that they call.

We can look at the `jserv.properties` file and the `jserv.conf` file to see the directives within them that you will find useful to understand.

### Jserv.properties

The `jserv.properties` file should be either appended to the end of the `httpd.conf` file or, preferably, called from that file and maintained on its own for modularity and ease of configuration and debugging.

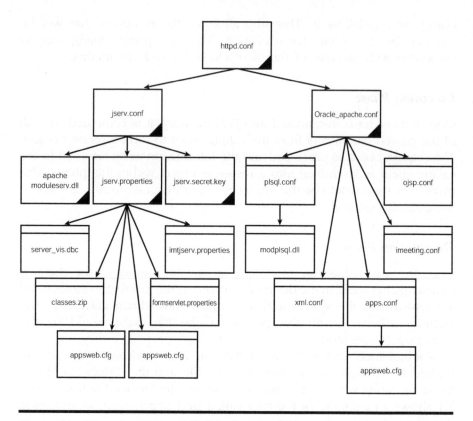

**Figure 5.1   Example of Files Called by httpd.conf**

## LoadModule

For Apache on Windows to know that it needs to load the JServ module into the system, you need to call it in with a `LoadModule` command:

```
LoadModule jserv_module
"%s_topDir%\JServ\ApacheModuleJServ.dll"
```

For UNIX, use a similar `LoadModule` command:

```
#LoadModule jserv_module libexec/mod_jserv.so
```

Again, using containers to modularize the code, even within the `Jserv.properties` file, the following container (`IfModule`) will contain all of the logic that is in play until the ending of the container code:

```
<IfModule mod_jserv.c>
```

## AppsJServManual

AppsJServManual instructs Apache whether or not to start the Apache JServ. Counterintuitively, default is off, meaning that JServ is autostarted. On means that it has to be started manually.

```
ApJServManual off
```

## ApJServProperties

ApJServProperties provides you with the properties filename for the Apache JServ when it is running in automatic mode. If JServ is running in manual mode, the directive is ignored. It can be entered in absolute terms for added readability or in relative terms using the environment variables.

```
ApJServProperties
"D:\visora\iAS\Apache\Jserv\conf\jserv.properties"
```

## ApJServLogFile

ApJServLogFile is the log file that is relative to the Apache root directory. You can use environment variables to reference the location of this file, but absolute paths are recommended for readability and main-tainability. Not to be confused with the log file that is referenced elsewhere in the jserv.properties file, this log file is specific to the C portion of the Apache JServ module. If you are running this tier on a UNIX environment, the owner of the JVM process must have write permissions on the directory that this directive points to. If this directive is disabled, the defaulting error log will be appended into the Apache error log.

```
ApJServLogFile
"D:\visora\iAS\Apache\JServ\logs\mod_jserv.log"
```

## ApJServLogLevel

ApJServLogLevel sets the logging level for this module. If unset, it defaults to info and can take on the values (in decreasing amounts of detail placed into the log) debug, info, notice, warn, error, critical, alert, emerg. As with other log levels, remember that all of the values from the lower levels are included in the upper levels of logging. It is recommended that this be set to at least error. Leaving it at info might cause you to accumulate very large logs and have to wade through irrelevant information in search of problems.

```
ApJServLogLevel notice
```

### ApJServDefaultProtocol

ApJServDefaultProtocol signifies the protocol that is used by this host to connect to the Apache JServ module. Extensive information is available in the Oracle documentation on what values this directive can take on and what meanings are attached to each of those protocols. The default is ajpv12. Unless you have a pressing need to use a different protocol, it would be better to leave this as it is until you have a better handle on what your system is doing and how it is going to be used.

```
ApJServDefaultProtocol ajpv12
```

### ApJServDefaultHost

ApJServDefaultHost is the default host on which the Apache JServ is running. This defaults to localhost and should probably be left at that unless you become comfortable with changing it. It can also be safely set to the name to which your machine is referred in the URL that starts your E-Business system session.

```
ApJServDefaultHost localhost
```

### ApJServDefaultPort

ApJServDefaultPort is the port on which Apache JServ is listening. This port is protocol dependent, which is another reason to leave the protocol alone until you have a comfort level with the alterations that you can make to these files and directives. Mismatches between this port and its associated protocol can cause a system to be unaccessable. The default port for the ajpv12 protocol is 8007.

```
ApJServDefaultPort 8007
```

### ApJServVMTimeout

ApJServVMTimeout is the amount of time that you should give the JVM to startup as well as the amount of time to wait to ping the JVM to make sure that it is running and alive. The default is 10 seconds, which may be sufficient in many cases. If you are running a slower server or a heavy workload, you may want to increase the value. This can be done safely within reason. Making incremental increases to determine when performance is acceptable is recommended when making alterations.

```
ApJServVMTimeout 10
```

### ApJServProtocolParameter

ApJServProtocolParameter is currently a useless directive; it is provided to pass parameter values to specified protocols. Currently, its value defaults to none. When there are protocols built that can handle this functionality, the syntax will be in the form that follows:

```
# Syntax: ApJServProtocolParameter [protocol name]
[parameter] [value]
```

This directive is only included to provide positioning for future protocols. At this time, do not attempt to edit the values if any are set.

### ApJServSecretKey

The `ApJServSecretKey` directive provides the location of the Apache JServ secret key file relative to the Apache root directory. It is critical that you know what you are going to accomplish by changing this value. The default location of this file is within the `conf` directory within the `jserv` tree. It is very important to remember that if the authentication gets set to disabled, everyone on the machine (not just this module) will be able to connect to your servlet engine and execute a servlet. By bypassing the Web server's restrictions you may be accomplishing something that you fully intended to achieve, but you may be disabling many security features unintentionally. It is important that you examine Oracle's documentation closely before you make any alterations to this directive. For readability, you should make the path to the file absolute rather than using the environment variables.

```
ApJServSecretKey
D:\visora\iAS\Apache\jserv\conf\jserv.secret.key
```

### ApJServMount

`ApJServMount` defines the mount point for servlet zones in your implementation. The syntax is:

```
ApJServMount [name] [jserv-url]
```

The default is none. Name refers to the name of the Apache path to mount the `jserv-url` on and `jserv-url` is something similar to `protocol://host:port/zone` (`http://myserver.my.company.com:8010/zone`). If no protocol, host, or port is defined in this directive, the values from `ApJServDefaultProtocol`, `ApJServDefaultHost`, or `ApJServDefaultPort` are used to derive these values. If there is no zone specified, the zone name will be the very first subdirectory of the particular called servlet.

```
ApJServMount/servlets/root
ApJServMount/servlet/root
```

### ApJServMountCopy

The `ApJServMountCopy` directive's value determines whether the virtual host inherits the base host mount points or not. The default is on. This directive is only meaningful if virtual hosting is being used; if not, the directive is ignored.

```
ApJServMountCopy on
```

### ApJServAction

`ApJServAction` allows for the execution of a servlet and the passing of filenames with the proper extensions in the `PATH_TRANSLATED` property of the referenced servlet's request. The default for this directive is none and the directive is used extensively if you are dealing with external tools in your configuration. If you do not know if you should alter these values, do not. You will soon be able to determine if the tools that you are dealing with require alteration.

```
#ApJServAction.jsp/servlets/org.gjt.jsp.JSPServlet
#ApJServAction.gsp/servlets/com.bitme-
chanic.gsp.GspServlet
#ApJServAction.jhtml/servlets/org.apache.
servlet.ssi.SSI
#ApJServAction.xml/serv-
lets/org.apache.cocoon.Cocoon
```

The following code enables the Apache JServ status handler of the URLs that you call (for example, `http://myserver.my.com-pany.com:8010/jserv/`). Remember that status handlers provide information to be displayed to the Web page when the URL is accessed with the trailing slash. It is important that you take measures to secure this ability, particularly in a production environment. Either comment out the container completely (invoking the default behavior of deny all) or make sure that you change the deny directive to deny or restrict access to this page. Only set the allow, from a particular set of trusted (and innumerate) IP addresses, if you have need to monitor this for any reason to provide information to support. A better solution would be to allow only from the server console and secure access to that console. Not securing this directive could allow any user to access restricted information about your servlets, their initialization parameters, JDBC passwords, or other highly sensitive information. Only sysadmins and Apps administrators have the need to know any of this information.

```
<Location/jserv/>
   SetHandler jserv-status
   order deny,allow
   deny from all
   allow from 123.45.6.789
</Location>
```

You are now at the end of both the `Jserv.properties` file and the module container code.

```
</IfModule>
```

## Apache JServ Configuration

Called from Apache's configuration file, the next JServ file that is of great importance to Applications is the `JSERV.CONF` file. This file has two significant differences compared to other configuration files. Commas are used in `JSERV.CONF` as token separators and directives can take on multiple values that are presented as a comma-separated list of values.

This file is separated into sections, similar to the way that `httpd.conf` was. The first provides information on the execution of JServ.

## Execution Parameters

### Wrapper.bin

The `wrapper.bin` directive points the environment to the Java executable in the configuration. This is the path to the JVM interpreter. The full path, as opposed to relative path, should be used if the interpreter location is not in your path. For maintainability and ease of understanding, it would be a good idea to provide the full path, as well:

```
wrapper.bin=d:\visora\iAS\Apache\jdk\bin\java.exe
```

There are optional parameters that can get passed to the Java interpreter. The default is none and should be sufficient for most configurations. Seek assistance from Oracle Support when making decisions about starting to add parameters to the file.

Apache JServ entry point class is included within this section and is a parameter that should not be changed. Identified as a `wrapper.class` directive with a default of `org.apache.jserv.JServ`, it often takes on that value and does not appear as a definitive parameter in the file.

### Wrapper.path

The `wrapper.path` directive sets the path environment value that gets passed into the JVM. Values, if they are innumerated, are separated with a ":" on UNIX platforms and ";" on Windows. The default values for this are typically sufficient for most environments and carry general default values of:

UNIX
```
/bin:/usr/bin:/usr/local/bin
```

Windows
```
"c:\<windows-directory>;c:\<windows-system-
directory>"
```

Under the Windows OS, the directories will have automatically been configured during setup of the system to match the relevant directories on your particular system.

### Wrapper.classpath

The `wrapper.classpath` directive determines the environment variables that get passed to the JVM. The default is none as Sun's Java suite already includes a default classpath, but in this case there are often values that are included in even the most generic implementation. If you are operating on UNIX, values that are concatenated without being tagged with additional `wrapper.classpath` directives will be separated using a ":" and on Windows with ";". The JVM has to be able to find SDK, as well as the JServ classes, any utility classes that you have opted to use in your servlets, and any that your developers have chosen to add to the servlets that they have coded to customize your environment. If there are any classes that you want to be able to automatically reload after any modifications, the classes cannot be included within the classpath that gets passed into the JVM or in the classpath that you use to start the Apache server. Any modifications made to those classpaths that are included in that manner will require the restarting of the Apache Server to take effect.

```
wrapper.classpath=d:\
visora\iAS\Apache\jdk\lib\tools.jar
wrapper.classpath=d:\
visora\iAS\Apache\JServ\ApacheJServ.jar
wrapper.classpath=d:\
visora\iAS\Apache\Jsdk\lib\jsdk.jar
```

### Wrapper.env

The `wrapper.env` directive allows for further passing of environment variables into the JVM. Typically, these variables will be passed in by appending their particular values by adding to the end of the already defined PATH variable. The default is none on UNIX systems and the default on Windows is SystemDrive and SystemRoot (again configured with the appropriate values for those parameters on the initial installation and configuration of the software). While the defaults may be sufficient, it is not uncommon for there to be added values, often because the PATH on Windows is getting long and adding these values here will allow the base PATH to maintain minimally long.

```
wrapper.env=PATH=d:\visora\iAS\bin
```

### Wrapper.env.copy

In the case of the wrapper.env.copy directive, these are values that get copied from the caller (the calling program) into the JVM. The default is false and usually the default is all that is used.

### Wrapper.env.copyall

Similar to wrapper.env.copy, the wrapper.env.copyall signifies that all values sent from the caller should be copied into the JVM. The default is false and it is often left at the default value until there is a pressing need to alter this action. In both wrapper.env.copy and the wrapper.env.copyall directives, false means that the environment variables of the calling environment are not copied in. If you are finding that you are having strange exceptions in your environment like UnsatisfiedLinkError errors, setting these two directives to true, at least temporarily, may help you find the problem and configure the other directives to include the missing variables.

### Wrapper.protocol

The wrapper.protocol directive provides the protocol that is used for signal handling to the JVM. This should match the ApJServDefault-Protocol directive from the jserv.properties file. As with the ApJServDefaultProtocol, the default of ajpv12 should be used (unless you are sure of what you are doing) and should be sufficient in most implementations.

### General Parameters

The parameters and directives in this section are general in nature and are typically overridden by other directives, but they provide the default values for many parameters.

### BindAddress

BindAddress is the directive that provides Apache JServ with the information about what IP addresses or host name that it should listen to (or bind to). A machine that has multiple IP addresses would use this directive to set the value that would be the single IP address to be used by this instance of Apache. If you set its value to localhost, the IP will be resolved to the IP address that has been configured for your localhost on the machine. This will allow multiple instances of Apache JServ to listen on the same port number but can direct that port to different IP addresses. You should only change the BindAddress information if you are sure of what you are doing. It could allow JServ to be wide open on the Internet, opening an unintended security breech in the system. Understand that in this case, JServ should be allowed to answer only to Apache mod_jserv, so leaving it set to localhost (typically the same IP address on every machine and only reachable from internal to that machine) is a good choice.

```
bindaddress=localhost
```

### Port

Port, in this case, is set to the port on which Apache JServ listens. It defaults to 8007 and typically Port can be left at its default, particularly if you have only one instance of JServ running on a server and it is set to localhost.

```
port=8007
```

### Zones

Zones is the servlet zones parameter which lists the zones that Apache JServ manages. Typically in an Oracle E-Business Suite implementation, there is one zone per instance. However, if there is more than one, they will be provided in a comma-separated list. The default is none.

```
zones=root
```

Coupled closely with the Zones are the configuration files, one for each zone. The configuration files default to none, as the zones default to none. Typically, the file that is the configuration file for the zones in an Oracle E-Business Suite implementation is the zone.properties file. For maintenance and ease of understanding, you should make sure that you use absolute pathing in the value for this parameter.

```
root.properties=d:\visora\iAS\Apache\JServ\
servlets\zone.properties
```

## Pool

The `Pool` directive enables or disables the use of a thread pool. Extreme care must be exercised if you are going to attempt to use this feature, as it has not been extensively tested in an Oracle E-Business Suite setting and it may generate deadlocks. Even if you can get it to work reliably in a test environment, you should be very careful using it in a production environment. While it defaults to false, it would be safer to make sure that it is deliberately set to false.

```
pool=false
```

## Pool.capacity

If `Pool` is set to true, `pool.capacity` is set to the number of idle threads that the pool may contain. It is set to an integer value, as partial threads do not make a lot of sense. If used, it defaults to 10. If `Pool` is set to false, regardless of the value that this is set to, it is ignored. If you choose to use `Pool`, this number should be set fairly low based on server load. An extremely busy, loaded server could have it set somewhat higher to handle bursts of activity. But again great care should be taken before implementing these directives.

```
pool.capacity=10
```

## Pool.controller

Only if you have chosen to set `pool = true`, does `pool.controller` come into play. `Pool.controller` indicates which controller should be used to control the level of recycled threads in the pool. Even if you have set `Pool` to true, it is safe to leave this at its default value, `.apache.java.recycle.DefaultController,` unless a specific recycle behavior is required. If `Pool` is set to false, `pool.controller` is ignored regardless of its value.

```
pool.controller=org.apache.java.recycle.
DefaultController
```

## Security.selfservlet

`Security.selfservlet` is the first security parameter that you are likely to encounter in your file. This directive enables or disables the execution of `org.apache.jserv.JServ` as a servlet. While it defaults to false because access to the information that it could provide should be restricted, it is often set to true in an Oracle E-Business Suite implementation. Take care when testing it if you choose to alter the behavior that is set up by the installation. Because execution of Apache JServ itself as a servlet is filtered by the Web server by default, for this service to work, you will have to make sure that it is enabled not only here, but within the Apache configuration files as well. This service is useful for installation and configuration information as it provides extensive feedback about the precise configuration of Apache JServ, which is why it should be disabled when installation and configuration processes are complete.

```
security.selfservlet=true
```

### Security.maxConnections

The `security.maxConnections` directive gets set to the maximum number of socket connections that Apache JServ is to be permitted to handle simultaneously. When making alterations to this directive, you need to be sure that the OS has enough file descriptors to allow for the number to which this gets set. It defaults to 50 and this should be enough to handle most configurations.

```
security.maxConnections=50
```

### Security.backlog

The `security.backlog` directive is another security setting that allows for extreme fine tuning of the JServ service. Until you have a comfortable familiarity with JServ and with the server load and inner workings of your server, it is wise to leave this directive commented out.

```
# security.backlog=5
```

### Security.allowedAddresses

The `security.allowedAddresses` directive provides a list of IP addresses that are allowed to connect to the Apache JServ. This directive assists in security filtering of possibly unsecured connections and still avoids the overhead of connection authentication. Be careful if you choose to alter the settings of this directive if it is set. Use only `security.allowedAddresses=DISABLED` if you are sure of what you are doing as this setting could open up your JServ to connections from the entire Internet. There is always the need in E-Business Suite setups to allow your Apache Server the ability to make this connection. Default is 127.0.0.1 which is, in effect, setting it to localhost and only allowing the computer on which it is resident to run the JServ service. If more than one IP address is to be granted this access, they should be provided in a comma-separated list.

```
#security.allowedAddresses=127.0.0.1
```

## Security.authentication

The security.authentication directive either enables or disables connection authentication. Unauthenticated connections tend to be a little faster since the authentication handshake has to be performed any time that an authenticated connection connects. Authentication is disabled by default because Apache and Oracle tend to believe that connection restriction from all IP addresses except the localhost reduces the time that it takes you to initially get JServ to run. If you anticipate other addresses connecting and you are not sure that you trust all of them, you should enable this parameter to prevent untrusted execution of your local servlets. If authentication is disabled and the IP address sending the request is trusted, then everyone on that machine can execute any of your servlets.

```
security.authentication=false
```

## Security.secretKey

The security.secretKey directive provides the authentication secret key that is passed as a file that must be kept secure and must be exactly the same as those used by clients to authenticate themselves. Typically there is a secret key and a public key involved. This directive defaults to none and, if provided, should use absolute pathing to make maintenance and readability easier.

```
security.secretKey=d:\visora\iAS\Apache\JServ\
servlets\jserv.secret.key
```

## Security.challengeSize

The security.challengeSize directive provides the length in bytes of a randomly generated challenge string that is used to authenticate connections. A value of 5 (also the default) is the lowest possible value to ensure a safe level of security while reducing connection creation overhead. The higher the number, the more secure the connection and the higher the overhead experience on every connection attempt.

```
security.challengeSize=5
```

## Log

The Log directive is the first logging parameter, takes a value of true or false (true enables server logging by Apache JServ), and allows for the enabling and disabling of Apache JServ logging. Logging tends to be a resource expensive and intensive operation when looked at in comparison to performance. If fast execution is a high concern, you should severely limit the amount of logging that is allowed to take place and you may choose to turn it off entirely. If all log channels are enabled, this log may become extremely large, as each servlet request can generate many kilobytes of log. Some channels are provided for debugging purposes only and should always be disabled in production environments.

```
log=true
```

### Log.file

`Log.file` provides the fully qualified path and filename to which to set the trace log file. To limit confusion and aid in maintainability, use absolute pathing when specifying the location of this file. This is not the log file that is specified in the `jserv.conf` file, but is the log file that is dedicated to the Java portion of Apache JServ.

On UNIX, the owner of the JVM process needs to have write permission to the location of this file. That means if Apache is running as nobody, then the file and its directory need to have their permissions set such that the nobody user is able to write to it consistently.

```
log.file=d:\visora\iAS\Apache\JServ\logs\jserv.log
```

### Log.timestamp

`Log.timestamp` enables the time stamp to be presented in the log file before the log message is provided. This makes it easier to locate the time stamp of the message and to locate the end of one day and the beginning of the next. If you know that something happened on a specific day, you can quickly locate that day and examine the log file for messages in connection with the situation.

```
log.timestamp=true
```

### Log.dateFormat

`Log.dateFormat` tells the Apache JServ logging mechanism the format in which to present the log.

```
log.dateFormat=[dd/MM/yyyy HH:mm:ss:SSS zz]
```

### Log.queue.maxage and log.queue.maxsize

Since all messages are logged to the log file by means of a thread running with only mimimal priority at the OS level, it is critical that this thread periodically get its chance to run and log messages to the log file. If it never gets to process its messages, the queue will overflow and will typically result in an `OutOfMemoryError` situation. To help eliminate the possibility of this occurring, two directives are presented: `log.queue.maxage` and `log.queue.maxsize`.`Log.queue.maxage` defines the maximum time that a logged message is permitted to remain in the queue before it gets written out to the log file. `Log.queue.maxsize` defines the maximum number of messages that are permitted to be in the queue at any one time.

When one of these limits is exceeded, the log file message stating that fact is generated, and the log queue is flushed to the log in a separate thread. Seeing such a message in the log file means that your system is either not performing as anticipated or you have a runaway loop somewhere and it is generating a lot of messages. The defaults are not optimal and you will likely need to do considerable tweaking.

```
# WARNING: Default values are lousy, you probably
want to tweak them and
# report the results back to the development team.
  log.queue.maxage  = 5000
  log.queue.maxsize = 1000
```

## Log.channel

`Log.channel` enables or disables logging the channel name. It defaults to false, disabling the channel name.

```
log.channel=false
```

## Log.channel.info

`Log.channel.info` provides a large volume of informational messages. It is unlikely that you would want to allow this to be enabled for an extended period of time in a production environment. It has limited usefulness in any environment unless you are using it to assist you with working through a problem. Default is to not log, meaning false.

```
log.channel.info=true
```

## Log.channel.servletException

`Log.channel.servletException` signifies that all exceptions caught during servlet service will logged to the log. You would likely want to maintain this one as true in all environments so you can capture error conditions and determine the cause of an apparent ongoing problem.

```
log.channel.servletException=true
```

### Log.channel.jservException

`Log.channel.jservException` is another useful exception logging channel. This one logs all exceptions that are raised internally to JServ. If this is set to true, it will assist with alerting you to trouble areas on your system.

```
log.channel.jservException=true
```

### Log.channel.warning

`Log.channel.warning` allows logging of all of the important messages that may indicate a problem, but that allow JServ to continue running. Closer examination of these messages helps you determine if you have problem areas in your system. You should allow this one to continue to run in all environments.

```
log.channel.warning=true
```

### Log.channel.servletLog

With `log.channel.servletLog` enabled, all messages that get generated by servlets will be logged in the log file. To help you determine if you have trouble areas in your environment, you should leave this one set to true in all environments.

```
log.channel.servletLog=true
```

### Log.channel.critical

`Log.channel.critical` allows for the capture of all critical event errors that are raised by an issue that causes JServ to stop. This one should be enabled in all environments.

```
log.channel.critical=true
```

### Log.channel.debug

The `log.channel.debug` channel is provided only for internal debugging purposes. It is unlikely that you would want this to be enabled in your production environment (or in any environment) during periods of normal operation. In the event that you have problems that require volumes of information to debug (usually this will be at the request of Oracle Support), you can always reenable it.

```
log.channel.debug=false
```

## *Wrapper.classpath Directives*

The following are `wrapper.classpath` directives that allow the inclusion of many different components into your Applications environment. Typically these are installed either at installation time or at patching time and should be left intact. The only time that this may not be true is if there is an order problem with them and you have to reorder the order that the entries are found in the file.

Oracle XSQL Servlet
```
wrapper.classpath=d:\visora\iAS/lib/oraclexsql.jar
```

Oracle JDBC (8.1.7)
```
wrapper.classpath=d:\visora\iAS/jdbc/lib/classes12.zip
```

Oracle XML Parser V2 (with XSLT Engine)
```
wrapper.classpath=d:\visora\iAS/lib/xmlparserv2.jar
```

Oracle XML SQL Components for Java
```
wrapper.classpath=d:\visora\iAS/rdbms/jlib/xsu12.jar
```

XSQLConfig.xml File location
```
wrapper.classpath=d:\visora\iAS/xdk/lib
```

Oracle Servlet
```
wrapper.classpath=d:\visora\iAS\jsp\lib\servlet22.jar
```

Oracle Java Server Pages
```
wrapper.classpath=d:\visora\iAS\jsp\lib\ojsp.jar
```

Oracle Util
```
wrapper.classpath=d:\visora\iAS\jsp\lib\ojsputil.jar
```

Oracle Java SQL
```
wrapper.classpath=d:\visora\iAS\sqlj\lib\translator.zip
```

Oracle JDBC
```
wrapper.classpath=d:\visora\iAS\jdbc\lib\classes12.zip
```

Oracle Messaging
```
wrapper.classpath=d:\visora\iAS\rdbms\jlib\aqapi11.jar
wrapper.classpath=d:\visora\iAS\rdbms\jlib\
jmscommon.jar
```

OJSP environment settings

```
wrapper.env=ORACLE_HOME=d:\visora\iAS
```

This directive should be modified to reflect the location of the SID for your Web server in your environment.

```
wrapper.env=LD_LIBRARY_PATH=d:\visora\iAS\lib
wrapper.classpath=d:\visora\iAS\Apache\BC4J\
lib\oraclexmlsql.jar
wrapper.classpath=d:\visora\iAS\Apache\BC4J\
lib\jboorasql.zip
wrapper.classpath=d:\visora\iAS\Apache\BC4J\
lib\jndi.jar
wrapper.classpath=d:\visora\iAS\Apache\BC4J\
lib\jbomt.zip
wrapper.classpath=d:\visora\iAS\Apache\BC4J\
lib\javax_ejb.zip
wrapper.classpath=d:\visora\iAS\Apache\BC4J\
lib\jdev-rt.zip
wrapper.classpath=d:\visora\iAS\Apache\BC4J\
lib\jbohtml.zip
wrapper.classpath=d:\visora\iAS\Apache\Apache\
htdocs\OnlineOrders_html
wrapper.classpath=d:\visora\iAS\Apache\Apache\
htdocs\OnlineOrders_html\OnlineOrders.jar
wrapper.classpath=d:\visora\iAS\Apache\BC4J\
lib\connectionmanager.zip
wrapper.classpath=d:\visora\iAS\Apache\BC4J\lib\jb
odatum12.zip
```

This is now the end of the `jserv.properties` file.

### Zones.Properties

Remember the `Zones` directive and the configuration file for the zones? The next `include`, called in at that point in the `jserv.properties` file, is the `zones.properties` file. This section lays out the entries in the `zones.properties` file.

### *Repositories*

The `Repositories` directive provides a list of servlet repositories that are controlled by the servlet zone. Recall that it is possible for there to be more than one zone in a configuration and that each zone is configured and controlled by its one properties file. Classes that you want the ability to load and reload upon modification should be placed in this repository.

```
repositories=d:\visora\iAS/Apache/JServ/
servlets,d:\oracle\devlcomn\java/apps.zip
```

### Autoreload.classes

The `autoreload.classes` directive enables or disables the auto reloading of servlet classes. It defaults to true.

```
autoreload.classes=false
```

### Autoreload.file

`Autoreload.file` allows or disallows for the auto reloading of properties and other loaded resources into the zone. It defaults to true. Most of these directives should only be altered from the Oracle configured values once you have become comfortable with what they do and how they perform.

```
autoreload.file=false
```

### Init.timeout

The `init.timeout` directive sets the number of milliseconds that the server should allow to pass before it gives up on initializing the servlet. A value of zero indicates that it should never give up and that there is no limit to the number of milliseconds that should be allowed to pass. Default is 10,000 milliseconds or 10 seconds.

```
init.timeout=10000
```

### Destroy.timeout

`Destroy.timeout` sets the number of milliseconds that the server should wait before giving up on destroying a servlet after it has performed its function or stopped functioning. Again, a value of zero indicates that it should never stop waiting and the default value of 10,000 means it should wait for 10 seconds.

```
destroy.timeout=10000
```

### Session.useCookies

The `session.useCookies` directive instructs the server whether or not to allow the use of cookies to maintain session state. If set to false, the `response.encodeUrl()` method will always be the method used to maintain the state. If this directive is allowed to be set to true, the servlet engine will attempt to set a cookie when `request.getSession(true)` is called. Setting this to true is one of the reasons that you should always allow cookies to be enabled through your browser for the zones that are likely to be serving up your Oracle E-Business Suite.

```
session.useCookies=true
```

### Session.topleveldomain

Session.topleveldomain is the domain in which the particular server responsible for this zone resides. It is likely the same domain in which all of your servers reside. If you are unsure if this location is correct double-check with your internal networking people.

```
session.topleveldomain=.domain.company.com
```

### Session.timeout

Session.timeout sets the number of milliseconds that the server should wait before invalidating unused sessions. This directive allows for the graceful cleanup of sessions that have errored out and not been cleaned up as a part of an elegant shutdown. It defaults to 1,800,000 milliseconds or 30 minutes.

```
session.timeout=600000
```

### Session.checkFrequency

Session.checkFrequency sets the frequency at which the server checks for timed out sessions. It defaults to 3000 milliseconds or 30 seconds.

```
session.checkFrequency=30000
```

### Single Thread Model Servlets

Single Thread Model (STM) servlets allow programmers to not worry about multi-threading when they are writing their code. This is common when servlet programmers begin to program in multi-threaded manner, but do not take multi-threading into account. They rely on the STM mode, because they do not know how or do not want to learn how to write multi-thread safe code. This usually means that your system will get hit with performance issues, information sharing issues, or issues arising because your servlets are being used in a multi-user environment. While Oracle E-Business Suite (out of the box) takes multi-threaded environments into account, this is another place you have to be very careful when you start customizing your environment that you do not shoot yourself in the foot.

### SingleThreadModelServlet.initialCapacity

`SingleThreadModelServlet.initialCapacity` sets the initial capacity of the STM servlets in your zone. It defaults to 5.

```
singleThreadModelServlet.initialCapacity=5
```

### SingleThreadModelServlet.incrementCapacity

`SingleThreadModelServlet.incrementCapacity` allows you to set the number of servlet instances that should be added to the pool, if the pool should be found empty. Again, it defaults to 5.

```
singleThreadModelServlet.incrementCapacity=5
```

### SingleThreadModelServlet.maximumCapacity

`SingleThreadModelServlet.maximumCapacity` sets the maximum capacity of the STM pool. This is a safety check feature that prevents runaway environments. Care should be taken on tuning this, particularly when customizations are involved.

```
singleThreadModelServlet.maximumCapacity=10
```

## Servlet Properties

The following are servlet parameters. When keyword "classname" is specified, it means that a Java dot-formatter full classname should be used there without the `.class` extension. If you want to pass private initialization data to the servlet, Apache allows for the use of a separate file named `<servlet classname>.initArgs` in the same directory as the servlet.

### Servlets.startup

`Servlets.startup` denotes a list of servlets that should be launched on startup. These can either be classnames or aliases and the default is none. The servlets can either be presented in a comma-separated list or with the `servlets.startup` directive on each line.

```
servlets.startup=oracle.apps.icx.common.
InitSystemProperties
servlets.startup=oracle.apps.ecx.oxta.
TransportAgentMain
```

The following list defines aliases from which servlets are able to be invoked. Each alias allows for a new instance of the servlet. If a servlet is invoked by a classname and then invoked by an alias, it will result in two instances of the servlet being created. Make sure that this is the way you want this to work.

```
servlet.CatalogTemplates.code=oracle.apps.icx.
catalog.ui.DownloadServlet
servlet.ibyscheduler.code=oracle.apps.iby.
scheduler.PSReqHandler
servlet.ibyecapp.code=oracle.apps.iby.
ecservlet.ECServlet
servlet.oramipp_lop.code=
oracle.apps.iby.bep.loop.LoopBackServlet
```

### Servlets.default.initArgs

`Servlets.default.initArgs` lists out the parameters that are passed to each of the servlets called on your system. You should put configuration information in here that is common to all servlets on your system. The value of this property is a comma-delimited list of `name=value` pairs accessed by the servlet via the `getInitParameter()` method. Default is none. In Apps, `FND_TOP` parameters should be allowed to be placed into this directive.

```
servlets.default.
initArgs=FND_TOP=d:\visappl\fnd\11.5.0
```

### Servlet.oracle Properties

The following directive properties define the initialization parameters that are available for each servlet that gets invoked on the system by using its classname. Again, it defaults to none.

```
servlet.oracle.jsp.JspServlet.initArgs=
translate_params=true,developer_mode=false,page_re
pository_root= d:\viscomn/html/_pages
servlet.oracle.jsp.JspServlet.ini-
tArgs=alias_translation=true
servlet.oracle.apps.icx.common.InitSystemProperties.
initArgs=initFile=
d:\visora\iAS/Apache/Jserv/etc/ssp_init.txt
```

### Initialization Properties

The following directive properties define the initialization parameters that are available for each servlet that is invoked by its alias. This separation of these two sets of initialization parameters allows you to pass different parameters based on how the servlets are called.

Oracle Applications Manager
```
servlet.weboam.code=oracle.apps.oam.
servlet.ui.OAMServlet
```

Manadatory Cabo settings; do not modify these.
```
servlet.weboam.initArgs=oracle.cabo.servlet.
pageBroker=oracle.apps.oam.servlet.ui.
oamUIXPageBroker
servlet.weboam.initArgs=oracle.cabo.servlet.
loginPage=oam/oamLogin
servlet.weboam.initArgs=oracle.cabo.servlet.
loggedInKey=oracle.apps.oam.oamUserData
```

End of mandatory settings.
```
servlet.weboam.initArgs=oracle.cabo.servlet.
xml.UIXPATH=d:\viscomn/html
servlet.weboam.initArgs=oracle.apps.oam.logger.
path=d:\ viscom/html/oam
servlet.weboam.initArgs=oracle.apps.oam.logger.
filename=weboam.log
servlet.weboam.initArgs=oracle.apps.oam.trace=off
servlet.weboam.initArgs=oracle.apps.oam.logger.
history=on
servlet.weboam.initArgs=oracle.apps.oam.
dbInitParams.path=d:\ viscom/html/oam/config
servlet.weboam.initArgs=oracle.apps.oam.
dbInitParams.filename=dbInitParams.xml
servlet.weboam.initArgs=oracle.apps.oam.
standalone=on
servlet.weboam.initArgs=oracle.
apps.oam.sqlplus_home=d:\visora\iAS
servlet.framework.code=oracle.apps.fnd.
framework.provider.OAFrameworkHttpProvider
servlet.framework.initArgs=dbcFileName=d:\
visappl\fnd\11.5.0/secure/server_sid.dbc
servlet.framework.initArgs=sessiontimeout=1800000
servlet.framework.initArgs=appPath=/OA_HTML
servlet.framework.initArgs=appRealPath=d:\
viscomn/html
```

MapViewer OMSLauncher
```
servlet.oms.code=oracle.spatial.mapserver.
omslauncher
servlet.oms.initArgs=remote_name=mapviewer,
oms_config_file=d:\visora\iAS/Apache/mapviewer/
conf/mapViewerConfig.xml,registry_port=9800
```

WEBADI Servlet

```
servlet.BneSnoopServlet.code=oracle.
apps.bne.framework.BneSnoopServlet
servlet.BneProxy.code=oracle.
apps.bne.share.BneProxy
servlet.BneComponentService.code=oracle.
apps.bne.integrator.component.BneComponentService
servlet.BneDocumentService.code= oracle.
apps.bne.integrator.document.BneDocumentService
servlet.BneApplicationService.code=oracle.
apps.bne.webui.BneApplicationService
servlet.BneCaboTestServlet.code=oracle.
apps.bne.framework.BneCaboTestServlet
servlet.BneUploaderService.code=oracle.
apps.bne.integrator.upload.BneUploaderService
```

Sourcing Servlet

```
servlet.fndgfm.code=oracle.apps.pon.attachments.
Fndgfm
servlet.MonitorServlet.code=oracle.apps.pon.auctions.
monitor.MonitorServlet
```

JServ can provide you with extensive flexibility and is a very powerful and maintainable service.

# 6

## OTHER SERVICES

There are several other services that come along with Oracle E-Business Suite that have not been touched on yet. All of these work together to provide the overall integrated picture of the suite. Each component by itself is a powerful tool that could, in other circumstances, be used on its own to provide nearly total solutions to many company problems, but together they answer nearly any question that thousands of companies worldwide have every day.

### FORMS

The Apps Forms Server is the service that provides the infrastructure that enables forms to run and to be served up to the end user via the Web interface. It is the event driven interface from the front-end form to the database that produces the interface result that the end users see when they are presented with somewhere that data input is required. It assists in field level validations, the presentation of Lists of Values, and the multiple documents interface that allows you the ease of navigating between several open windows without actually having to close any of them (the simple click adjusts the focus from one to the other while allowing all other open windows to remain running in the background). The Forms Server typically installs on one of the middle tier servers and has as its primary job, the presentation of forms via the Apps Interface.

Built with Oracle Forms, Release 6*i*, the forms in Applications 11i are simple to understand and follow a well established set of Oracle E-Business Suite programming standards.

The Forms Server, as the underlying engine that sends Applications Forms to the Web, is one of the main underlying pieces of the application; it is the primary location where the business logic, business rules, and data management logic reside. Forms has been a core component of

Oracle Financials from the very beginning and the Forms Server now provides the ability to no longer require client server architecture, but to have the same forms served up through the thin client browser-based architecture.

In the old client server model, the runtime component is responsible for painting the GUI form to the screen, for containing all application code (e.g., the FMX file, the PLL libraries) as well as the entire runtime component for accessing the database. In the Forms Server model, the form still contains all application code, but now the application code continues to sit on the middle tier server rather than having to be installed on each individual client machine. The Forms Server and the browser work together to provide the GUI interface to the client. While this is a somewhat cosmetic change in how things basically work, it also means that there is a lesser load on the client, but a higher impact on the network as now the image of the screen has to be transmitted on the browser.

Because there is the potential for several users to access the same form at exactly the same time, the Forms Server has to provide the ability to cache the common information in a common memory area and allow for the only difference to be the data that is accessed through the interface.

### Administering the Forms Server

You are provided with a simple set of scripts that should be used to start up and shut down the Oracle Forms Server. Located in the `%COMMON_TOP%` directory under `admin\scripts` (`admin\scripts\ <SID>` once you move to AutoConfig), these commands can be called in batch or individually at the command line to startup and shut down the services.

> `forms60_server start <optional>parameters`

To ensure direction of any errors to a specific log file:

> `forms60_server start log=\usr\logs\forms_server.log`

To shut down the server:

> `forms60_server stop`

To test your Forms Server from the Web:

> `http://yourhost.your.`
> `company.com:8010t/dev60html/runform.htm`

The Forms Server comprises a set of executables that are responsible for different aspects of the different forms that are encountered in your application interface. These executables are located within the `$ORACLE_HOME\bin` directory of your middle tier machine where the Forms Server is running. Table 6.1 gives a brief explanation of the components and the executables responsible.

**Table 6.1  Oracle Forms Executables**

| Component | Executable Name |
| --- | --- |
| Oracle Forms CGI | f60cgi |
| Oracle Forms Listener | f60webm |
| Oracle Forms Server | f60srvm |
| Oracle Forms Web Cartridge | f60webc.so |

## REPORTS SERVER

Working closely on the middle tier with the Forms Server is the Reports Server. They work in similar manners to each other, simply providing different outputs to the end user. Reports used to be called from the client with the data request simply being the transferred information, where now both the report interface as well as the end data has to be returned to the browser. Typical applications run as a combination of forms and reports (forms being the interactive and input agent into the database where inserts, updates, and deletes occur and reports being where static content data is returned for viewing). The reports engine is one of the components at the heart of Concurrent Processing along with PL/SQL stored procedures that drive many of the reports that users run.

Much like the Forms Server, you can start and stop the services with simple scripts and test the Oracle Reports Server from the Web.

To start up the server:

```
reports60_server start
```

To shut down the Reports Server:

```
reports60_server stop
```

To test the Reports Server's functionality from the Web:

```
http://server.your.company.com:8010/dev60html/
runrep.htm
```

Much like the Forms Server, the Reports Server's executables reside in the %ORACLE_HOME\bin directory and Table 6.2 provides a brief description of the components and the executables that are responsible for it.

## ORACLE SELF-SERVICE WEB APPLICATIONS

The OSSWA (ICX is the abbreviation for the product set) architecture is made up of a Web browser, the Apache powered HTTP Server, HTML documents and Java components (i.e., JSP, JavaBeans, servlets), and an extensive set of PL/SQL functions and procedures that access information

**Table 6.2 Reports Executables**

| Component | Executable Name |
|---|---|
| Reports CGI Executable | rwcgi60 |
| Multi-Tier Server | rwmts60 |
| Queue Viewer | rwrqv60 |
| Reports Client | rwcli60 |
| Reports WebCartridge | rwows60.so |

in the Web Applications Dictionary and display the elements in dynamic pages.

## Vocabulary

What, more new words? Not to a great extent, no. In this case, it is the way that these words, most of which we have already become acquainted with, are used in connection with this part of the application.

## HTTP Server

The HTTP Server provides the communication services from the database and the other services on the middle tier to the Web browser.

## CGI

Common Gateway Interface or CGI is an industry standard means by which many applications are run via the Web. In real world examples, many sites have guest books that they want people to sign when they visit. These guest books are very often programmed using the CGI interface. Mod_cgi is the Apache module that allows for the execution of CGI components in the Applications interface.

## Flow

A flow is a series of data displaying Web pages that are bound together by a complex set of definitions. In many cases, these flows can be grouped together and thought of as an inquiry.

## HTTP

Hypertext Transfer Protocol is the transfer protocol used to request documents from the Web server.

## HTML

Hypertext Markup Language is the encoding format for presenting Web pages to the browser in a way that allows them to display nicely. These pages may contain text, graphics, and references to (links to) other programs, files, and hypertext documents. HTML is a subset of SGML or the Standard Generalized Markup Language.

## JavaBeans

JavaBeans are special Java classes that have specific rules and naming conventions for its methods and variables. These reusable components perform well-defined tasks that are repeated over and over within an application.

## JavaScript

JavaScript is a scripting language that adds powerful extensions to standard HTML without having to rely on CGI interface. These are responsible for the scrolling messages that you see at the bottom of some Web pages. There is no need to interpret this coding in any way; a standard browser interprets it. While not very robust, it is useful in cases where light programming will suffice.

## JavaServer Pages (JSP)

JavaServer Pages allow the embedding of servlet code within a standard HTLM document. A JSP is similar to server side includes.

## Java Servlets

Java servlets are small, pluggable programs that are extensions to a server that will enhance that server's functionality and are the key components in server side Java development. Mod_jserv Apache module is the servlet engine that allows for the inclusion of these servlets in the application.

## Web Applications Dictionary

The Web Applications Dictionary is, conceptually, an active data dictionary that utilizes a Forms-based interface. This data dictionary (not to be confused with the Oracle Data Dictionary) stores the specific information about the OSSWA data. This includes the information about the prompts, languages, navigation, and security that is inherent in the OSSWA.

Using this dictionary and its interface, you can define the rules that define the manner in which a flow acts for a particular user. You can specify the way that you want the HTML document to behave, object content that associates the business views and PL/SQL, the hyper text business flows between objects, and page content including fields and selection criteria.

The Web Applications Dictionary can also be viewed as a real-time execution engine that retrieves relevant information from the database. This engine allows OSSWA to retrieve database data that supports the creation and presentation of dynamic HTML documents and is considered to be one of the AD modules.

## Web Browser

One of the most important and most visible components to the world is the Web browser. The browser you choose must support frames, tables and JavaScript. (Internet Explorer supports the most features dependably.)

## Web Inquiries

A Web inquiry (or a flow from above) is a series of hyper-linked Web pages, many of which are predefined in the application based on business inquiry process. Defined within the Web Application Dictionary, one of the most common uses for these flows is to drill out from one piece of information further detailed data that went into making up that information (e.g., the purchase order that resulted in an invoice).

## Web Transactions

A Web transaction is the interface through which a user enters data that gets stored within the client machine using the JavaScript technology. When the user chooses to commit the data, it gets passed to the PL/SQL agent that executes a PL/SQL procedure or set of procedures to store that data in temporary tables that are owned by the product schema on the database. These temporary tables or open interface tables (the only tables that OSSWA has the ability to interface with) rely on the open interface programs to do all validations and referential integrity checking.

## Oracle Workflow

Workflows can be considered to be business flows that allow the end users to be automatically sent the information that they need in their position to adequately be prepared to make decisions. Depending on your version, Workflows can be defined through the Workflow Builder, a GUI interface that allows users to define their own business processes and activities that will be provided based on their security within the application. These definitions can also be created within the OAM interface. This will be the interface of choice in future releases of the application and will become the only manner in which Workflow will be administrable.

## How OSSWA Serves Up Pages

Typically, a Web page is requested when the user clicks on a link. The embedded URL that they clicked on and the request are routed to the HTTP Server that accesses the Web page and returns that page to the requesting user.

In many of the servlet driven and JSP pages, the steps that the request goes through are very similar to the generic model.

1. The user clicks on the link of a function on an OSSWA menu.
2. That link is accessed in the browser and calls, for example, a JServ servlet.
3. Apache routes the request to `mod_jserv`.
4. `Mod_jserv` takes the request and forwards it on the Apache JServ servlet engine.
5. The servlet engine generates a response that accesses any data in the database that is required.
6. If there are JSPs involved, the servlet engine will contact Oracle JSP (translator and runtime environment for JSPs).
7. Final response is relayed to `mod_jserv` through the Apache server and returned to the requesting client.

When it comes to displaying dynamic Web pages, the Oracle SSWA method relies on PL/SQL stored program units and packages. While this method is still supported, Oracle Corporation's recommendation for creating new, custom content to be served up through the Oracle E-Business Suite interface is to use JSPs, thus relying on the process laid out above. For those pages relying on stored procedures, the process for serving up pages is as follows:

1. The user clicks on the link of a function on an OSSWA menu.
2. The URL's source code calls for a stored procedure.

3. Apache routes the request to mod_plsql.
4. Mod_plsql forwards the request to the RDBMS PL/SQL engine, making use of the DAD file to connect mod_plsql to the database and prepare the parameters for the stored procedure call.
5. The stored PL/SQL generates the HTML page using data stored in the database.
6. The response is returned to mod_plsql.
7. Mod_plsql returns the response to Apache HTTP Server and then back to the requesting client.

### OSSWA and Security

Data security in OSSWA is controlled in several ways. Secure Sockets Layer (SSL) is used to secure the communication between the client machine and the middle tier server. SSL uses the strongest cryptographic encryption method possible, employing nearly impossible to break encryption keys. SSL is a de facto standard means by which commerce is conducted over the Internet. Further, HTTP cookies are employed in the securing of data. Encryption of passwords, parameters to functions and session identifiers, and session expiration all lend to the ultimate OSSWA security.

Cookies are utilized in session management. Each session is assigned a unique identifier that gets stored in a database table. This session identifier is returned to the requesting browser via an encrypted cookie along with the session expiration details (hours or number of hits allowed).

# PORTAL

Previously known as WebDB, the Oracle Portal layer provides the means by which you can easily and effectively access and maintain information using your Web browser. It allows you to build and provide Internet- or intranet-based applications that allow your users to bring in tougher information from different sources (such as Oracle E-Business Suite applications, OLTP environment, Data Warehouse, and Online Data Stores) and access the disparate content areas' information using no other means than a browser.

### Vocabulary

As with many of the other things that you deal with in Oracle E-Business Suite, the first place to start is with the new vocabulary that goes with this next product. Once you get a better handle on the words that are used in association with each individual part, the better handle that you can get on what those things are doing and the better you can ask questions and make connections.

## Page

A page is a single location from which to access data that is gathered from the different areas. It is the piece that users access and interact with.

## Page Style

The page style refers to the characteristics specifically associated with the particular page. It includes the colors, fonts, graphics, and structure among the other things that you associate with what you see on the page (just like the attributes that you can associate with any normal Web page).

## Regions

A region is the rectangular or square portions that a page gets divided into. Many pages are divided in this way. Pages with static content typically only refer to these areas as table cells. When dynamic content is accessed through any of these areas, they are considered to be regions. Each region has its own specifications regarding how the portlets are placed and displayed within it.

## Portlets

A portlet is the building block of a portal application. It is a reusable component that allows access of information from many different sources in a specific place. It is in many ways similar to a servlet (a small program that performs a specific job and provides specific information from a specific place). Portlets are used frequently on Web pages where the local weather (local to somewhere) is provided from a source outside of the immediate Web site so that people accessing the page can have an idea of what the current temperature and conditions are in that place. Each portlet belongs to a portlet provider.

## Content Area

A content area is made up of a hierarchy of folders that are used to store and organize content items. It is a collection of related information that can be used to store content in a portal and includes many tools that are required to manage the content. In WebDB 2.x (as well as in real-life Internet terms) this would be understood as a site.

## Folder

Folders contain files (folders are similar to directories). These files can be pages, graphics files, other folders, or many other components. In Oracle Portal, there are four kinds of folders that are supported:

- *Container folders* are repositories for many simple related items, such as text files, documents, graphics images, and applications components.
- *PL/SQL folders* are used to contain PL/SQL code that is used to render HTML code.
- *URL folders* allow for the access path to another Web page somewhere either related to or completely unrelated to the current content area.
- *Search folders* provide different views of content areas for different users. Based on portal content area searches, these folders can be created for all items that belong to the same category or that can be accessed by the same kind of user. These folders are dynamic and are updated each time the folder is accessed.

## Item

An item is the most basic content unit that gets placed into a content area folder. Every item has to be assigned to a particular category.

## Attribute

An attribute in Portal defines an item, which is similar to an attribute of an entity in a database's Entity Relationship Diagram (ERD). An attribute can include many things, including creation date, expiration date, author information, and category. This is similar to the real-life concept of a dog having attributes that include color, size, breed, coat type, age, and weight.

## Activity Log

Portals provide a record of end user requests called activity logs. Oracle stores this log in a table. An activity log contains considerable useful information including the time of access, username, and server information.

## Batch Job

Portal provides the ability for a user to submit a background process (similar to a concurrent request) that runs while allowing the user to continue to work during the process. Similar to a batch job in COBOL or other programming languages, it is used to submit long running queries that ordinarily would tie up a session while waiting for the large volume of data to be returned.

## Component

A component is typically a PL/SQL stored procedure or package, but can include other programming language programs as well, that was created by Oracle Portal to allow for the building of a report, chart, or form.

## Database Access Descriptor File

A DAD file contains a particular set of values that defines a particular set of connectivity attributes (from a portal to the listener) that is used to provide the information from an HTTP request. A DAD file needs information such as username, password, and connection string for the particular database instance on a particular server. A DAD file, in Oracle E-Business Suite, typically has the naming convention of <database server name>_<SID or Two Task>.dbc. Table 6.3 shows the contents of a typical DAD file.

## Applications

An application, in Portal terms, is a Web-enabled application that is built using robust component-building wizards.

## External Sites

External sites are sites not directly contained within your site. In Portal terms, it is the content from any external Web site (e.g., weather, stock quotes, news) that you pull into your site by means of a portal and a portlet.

## Custom-Built Sources

There are portlets that come prebuilt and configured. Custom-built sources are the content and applications pieces that have been custom built by your developers or by contracted developers using the Portal development kit to provide custom flexibility to your implementation.

### How Portal Works

Oracle's Portal is a part of the technology stack and resides on one of the servers that makes up the middle tier (typically the server on which Apache

**Table 6.3   DAD File**

```
#DB Settings
#Thu Nov 21 14:12:33 CST 2002
APPS_JDBC_DRIVER_TYPE=THIN
APPL_SERVER_ID=AFFA2645466ED1F6
E099AC15C80DD1F6314765223084752
13851918059258876
TWO_TASK=TEST
GUEST_USER_PWD=GUEST/ORACLE
DB_HOST=dbserver.my.company.com
DB_NAME=TEST
FNDNAM=apps
GWYUID=APPLSYSPUB/PUB
DB_PORT=1521
```

is configured). The Application Server translates the requests from the browser (through which the end user accesses the application) into a call to the database typically using the same listener that you have configured for OSSWA, which makes use of the security and scalability of the existing setup. There is a PL/SQL toolkit that installs as part of the Portal installation. This toolkit translates the request's response into dynamic HTML and JavaScript and displays it to the browser. The PL/SQL gateway (also a part of the Portal installation) captures the database connection information from the DAD file and the URL is mapped to that connection information to connect to the database and execute the PL/SQL procedure. This gateway depends heavily on the Oracle Web Agent PL/SQL package that comes as a part of the 9iAS installation. Because Portal does not require the skill set of a forms and reports programmer, it is much easier to develop custom reports using simple PL/SQL programming and facilitating those programs through the Portal interface.

## Discoverer

Discoverer is an ad hoc query tool that is geared to allow those with limited or nonexistent knowledge of SQL to customize their own reports to provide them just the view of the information that they require. It further provides data analysis and reporting capabilities that allow for simple, custom reports (albeit with limited formatting capabilities) without actually customizing the application. With its ability to provide pivoting, drilling, aggregation, and calculation at the click of a mouse, it extends the ease of use to be a complex analysis tool.

Prior to 11.5.7, Discoverer was an add-on piece to the core Oracle E-Business Suite. It was housed on its own server and in most cases required that if you chose to have more than one Oracle Home, that it reside in the first one that was installed on the box. Part of the installation/setup resides on a server and the other part, the EUL, resides within the Applications database. Be careful if you upgrade Discoverer that you are upgrading to a supported version of Discoverer as some of the installations cause inconsistencies within the database and may cause you problems later on with upgrading or cloning.

As of the latest several maintenance releases of the Oracle E-Business Suite, Discoverer 4*i* ships as an integral part of the system (and as of third quarter of 2003) is fully supported on a Windows platform when coupled with 9iAS 1.0.2.2.2. This enables you to centralize operations and eliminate servers that you may have been maintaining just because of some incompatibility issues and make better use of those resources.

## Vocabulary

There is a whole set of vocabulary that goes along with Discoverer, too. In the case of Discoverer, most of this vocabulary deals with the different versions of the tool.

### User Edition

The User Edition of Discoverer is the end user component, the interface through which the users will access the information. Its GUI interface will likely become a daily part of many end users' daily tools used for generating reports and analyzing data. It is a read-only access tool that provides intuitive access to financial information in a logical manner.

### Administration Edition

The Administration Edition version is the tool used by the designer to present the inherent hierarchy of financial data that is known as a business area. The end users through the User Edition access these business areas. The administrator builds and maintains the business areas through this interface.

### End User Layer

The EUL shields the users from the complexities of the Apps Database and shields the database from the inexperience of many of the Discoverer end users. It resides, conceptually, between the Oracle Data Dictionary and the User Edition. Physically, it resides in a special schema that is built with the specific purpose to segregate the EUL data from the other portions of the Applications database. The view that this combination provides is intuitive and business focused that can be custom tailored to suit any user's or user group's needs.

The various editions (end user, administration, viewer, and plus) communicate with the database via SQL*Net (now Oracle Net in Oracle 9i).

## Workbooks

Conceptually, from the user perspective, Discoverer is very similar to an Excel spreadsheet. Think of it this way: you can loosely compare a relational schema to an Excel workbook. Each sheet is a table; each table has rows (the numbered rows) and columns (the lettered columns), the combination of which uniquely identifies one value. Each workbook combined with its associated schema is a set of tables that in some way relate to each other. The same is true for Discoverer. Discoverer comes with several predefined workbooks, each parameterized with what is required for that workbook. Each workbook is built to support a single set of financial management processes and displays how the data is displayed in each case.

Each workbook is made up of one or more worksheets.

## Worksheets

A worksheet in Discoverer displays the result sets from one or more queries. Worksheets are accessed via tabbed dividers (similar to Excel again) in the workbook to which it is associated. Each workbook has associated with it a defined set of report worksheets that are able to be run in conjunction with it.

## EUL

The illusive End User Layer can potentially be one of the most powerful and relied on tools that your end users have in their arsenal. It is the information about the information that resides in the database. This metadata can help in clearing the complexity of the underlying database (there are over 10,000 tables and twice as many views and synonyms coming from over 150 schemas) and provides a point and click interface for the users to interact with. The EUL holds the groupings of related objects that represent the logical data model of the company's business areas. These business areas are made up of objects (the folders and items) that are the representations of the business areas to the organization in the database. This component of the suite is a necessary part of an implementation, particularly if you are bringing to the organization the BIS to provide your enterprise with Business Intelligence tools.

The creation and maintenance of an EUL by the end user represents a significant investment in both time and resources and Discoverer can become key to the everyday functions of the staff that use it to support decision making. Loss or corruption of this environment could have significant ramifications to the organization, particularly if those reports are needed for the financial parts of the company.

### EUL Tables

Familiarize yourself with the EUL tables. I am certainly not advocating going out and learning the 10,000 plus tables in the base install. The EUL tables are limited in number and you only really have to care about a handful of them.

The EUL tables are the repositories into which the definition of your EUL gets placed. These tables hold the information on what is important to the users who use this tool. It holds folders and items in the EUL as well as the database objects to which each of these items refers. As with any of the Apps resident tables, Oracle advises against modifying any of these tables.

In most cases there will not be any need to modify any of the contents of the tables. There will be occasions, however (like when a user changes his username and wants to be able to access the same reports that he or she was able to access before), when you will need to make cosmetic alterations to the data. In the name change example, you would change the username column of the `eul_eul_users` table, the owner column of the `dis_docs_set` table, the owner column of the `dis_grants_set` table, and the `qs_username` column of the `eul_qpp_statistics` table to reflect the username of the new user where the columns point to the old username. Alternatively, you could save off all of that user's reports to a file system on one of your accessible servers and reopen and save them back to the database as the new user. You will then need to decide if you want to continue to maintain the old reports under the old username or if you want to purge off that information.

### Backing Up the EUL

Hot on the tail of saying that you can safely purge off the unwanted data, you need to make sure that there is a means by which you can get back the information that resides in the EUL. Outside of a normal backup strategy for your apps database, you should seriously consider adding a logical export of the data in the EUL to allow for a simpler restoration of the data in case there is an inadvertent deletion or problem. This will allow you to capture the entire definition of the data that the enterprise finds important and the associated stored queries that go along with it.

Eex files (not to be confused with exe files) are those files that contain the definition of each business area. You can further add to the flexibility of your recovery scenario of the EUL portion of the database by doing an eex export. This export writes the definition of the business area from the definition that resides in the database to a text file. While this export does not bring with it the queries that reside in the database, it does provide, in an easily reimportable format, the core information about the business areas that your company finds important. These are also the exports that you will have to do when you upgrade to a newer version of Discoverer. These eex files contain the list of all joins that are associated with any particular business area. Being able to easily recover these join conditions will allow existing queries to open and function and will eliminate the required rebuild of the joins using the same names should they become corrupted by the deletion of the information or the instability of a portion of the system.

### Deleting Objects

Occasionally it will become necessary to remove things (folders or items) from your EUL that are no longer necessary. While it is easy to remove an item from the layer that does not appear to be used by simply accepting the Delete from End User Layer option provided in the system and completely removing not only the definition of the folder but all of the folder contents associated with the given business area as well, it is probably better to hide the folder for a certain period of time (weeks to months) before you eliminate that information entirely. You can create your own holding corral where you can place the objects so that they can no longer be referenced, but in a place from which you can quickly move them in case they become necessary.

# 7

# PRINTING

Oracle Applications, in this society that is purported to be nearing the paperless age, is capable of generating an immense amount of paper output. This output does not magically appear from out of the computer screen onto the users desktop; it gets there by way of some printer somewhere. It is astounding that in a day when CDs are the main writable and removable storage media — a media that costs so little, is very durable, portable, and a means of so many archival solutions — that the majority of the end users choose to print the output of a report, punch holes in it, and place it in a three ring binder on a shelf, simply because that is the way things are done. For the foreseeable future, the Oracle Applications administrator will have to deal to some extent with printing and printing issues.

An Oracle Applications report can be printed on virtually any printer that will accept print requests from the OS's command line. Even if this is not the means by which the end user submits the print job, in the long run, the print job gets to the printer via an Oracle Applications driver.

Printers utilize a hardware method, a software method, or a combination of methods for controlling the printing attributes like paper size, orientation, vertical and horizontal spacing, font sizes, and number of characters per inch or per line. Historically more of the control was done with hardware, however, most modern printers rely on some form of printer control language (PCL) to initialize the printer and set up many of the printing attributes. These languages typically consist of a predefined sequence of commands concatenated into a string and appended to the beginning (and occasionally part of a string to the tail) of a document. Oracle Applications' printer drivers for flat text report printing use these predefined strings. PostScript, alternatively, embeds the printer control information within the document itself (somewhat like idiot print for anyone who has ever done mainframe COBOL programming). Nearly any printer can understand the PCL command string. Far fewer can understand the PostScript commands. Many can understand either.

## ORACLE APPLICATIONS PRINTER DRIVERS

The printer drivers that are defined in Oracle Applications are used to initialize most common printers with certain predefined attributes and to specify which OS command will be used to route and initialize the printing of the report. Most of these drivers are defined via an Apps-based form with the necessary printer specific information defined and stored within one of the thousands of database tables. Three basic drivers would fulfill the vast majority of all of the reports in Oracle Applications. These driver types make use of the keywords: portrait, landscape, and landwide. While these keywords often are considered to be the paper orientation, in reality they are tied more closely with the number of lines per inch and characters per line rather than the positioning of the paper in the paper tray of the physical printer hardware, although a certain number of characters per line may equate roughly to one certain size or position.

For every Oracle Applications printer driver, there is an associated SQL Report Write (SRW) driver that is, in effect, a printer definition file that gets used by Oracle Reports at runtime. This is a flat ASCII character file that can be copied, edited, and saved as needed. These SRW drivers pertain only to an Oracle Reports output file and are used during the generation of the report output. Once the output is created, a printer driver is used to complete the sending of the output file to the printer. There are only a handful of highly generic print drivers and SRW drivers that apply to most popular makes and models of printers. There are certain conditions under which custom printer drivers need to be defined within the application and, in these cases, the initialization string needs to be obtained from the particular printer manufacturer (often this can be obtained from one of the printer's manuals rather than having to go directly to the manufacturer).

## DEFINING A NEW PRINT DRIVER

Recall that the print driver defines how Oracle E-Business Suite applications printing will be accomplished and what print programs, commands, and arguments need to be provided to submit an output file to the OS's print queue.

To define a printer driver to Oracle Applications, you will need to perform the following steps:

1. Log on to Oracle Applications as a user with system administration authority and select the SYSADMIN responsibility.
2. Navigate to Install/Printers/Drivers and create a new print driver record in the database tables.

3. Enter a new printer driver name and a user driver name (the user driver is the name that will appear in the List of Values (LOV) in the window where you select the desired printer for the concurrent request job).

4. If you are dealing with a UNIX platform only, select a PostScript SRW driver like PSL132 for landscape printing.

5. Platform should always be left blank (meaning that there will be a <null> associated with the platform in the database record).

6. Set the new driver's method to command and all of the other driver method parameters options should remain blank or unchecked.

7. Enter a corresponding OS print command argument. The format that this argument takes depends on whether you are dealing with Windows or UNIX:

Windows
```
PRINT/D:$PROFILES$.PRINTER $PROFILES$.FILENAME
```

UNIX
```
lp -c -d$PROFILES$.PRINTER -n$PROFILES$.CONC_COPIES
-t "$PROFILES$.TITLE" $PROFILES$.FILENAME
```
Make sure that you leave the initialization and reset fields blank or <null> if the new driver will be used for PostScript printing.

*A special note for Concurrent Managers:* Because printer information is cached, the internal manager needs to be stopped and restarted every time you make a printer change for the change to take effect.

## ORIENTATION OR NOT

There are three basic types of print format. Many people have a difficult time understanding that there is a difference between what they typically think of as the orientation of the paper and the formatting of the print job to fit into a given set of parameters. The formats that people typically associate with the orientation of the paper are portrait and landscape. Landwide is the third common format of the print job.

### Portrait

A portrait is something that you get done at Olan Mills studio, right? No, wait, we are talking about printers, so that is something that prints out on 8½ × 11 paper with the words running left to right on the 8½ inch orientation. But that is not exactly what is meant by portrait in this case.

In the case of Oracle E-Business Suite, portrait concerns those jobs that you want to have print as 80 characters on a line. Usually this equates to the situation where you are presented with the print running across the 8½ inch side of an 8½ × 11 piece of paper as this is the standard print format.

## Landscape

We are probably not referring to watching the sun set on a West Texas plain or standing and looking at the autumn colors dancing across the Great Smokey Mountains. We are also not necessarily talking about printing on the long side of the paper. We are talking about formatting the printout to fit 132 characters on a line (similar to a mainframe printout on green bar 25 pin feed paper). The 132-character printout is a common format for many reports that have been created to be just like something someone has always gotten, particularly if that print was generated by a mainframe computer at some point in the past. Often the printout ends up being along the long side of the paper, just because that is the easiest way to make 132 characters fit on a page. So it is not the orientation of the page, but the number of characters on the line that determines a landscape printout.

## Landwide

Landwide is the least understood of all of the options because we really do not have a lot to compare it to in our minds. Landwide is a format that prints 180 characters per line. You either have to opt for tiny type, or determine what paper this should print on.

## CHARACTER MODE PRINTING

Character mode, or flat ASCII text printing, is the primary output format utilized in Oracle E-Business Suite and was once the only output type available. It is widely accepted as a de facto file format, readable from any number of browsers and applications on any OS platform.

To facilitate printing of these reports, Oracle E-Business Suite facilitates the registering and configuring of many different kinds of printers through four forms accessible through the sysadmin responsibility within the application. All four forms are located under the Install menu path. They are printer, printer types, print styles, and printer driver. Before a report can be printed on any given printer, that printer's driver (or a generic printer driver that closely matches the PCL commands required for that printer) has to be registered with the application. When working through these forms, you will be required to provide specific information about your printer. Oracle does not provide printer drivers, patches, or updates for printers that you will be using for the Oracle E-Business Suite. That said, there are several predefined driver examples included with an installation. These drivers are for the most common and popular printer types that are often used with Oracle Applications and one of these sample printer drivers may easily work for your printer as is or with some minor modifications. However, as the applications administrator or applications DBA, you will likely be tasked with a significant portion of setting up the printing capabilities and therefore either need to be familiar with the printer's operation and capabilities or have access to someone with that knowledge. Due to the variations from vendor to vendor, either having access to someone familiar with the particular printers that you are dealing with in house or a contact at the hardware company would be a big help in the process. Note 200359.1, dealing with the FNDPrinterValidation115.sh script, will be a valuable tool in making sure that your printers and their setups are doing what you think they are. This script checks your printer's configuration and setup within Oracle Applications and breaks down the most common escape sequences used in the Printer Control to assist you in better understanding exactly what is being sent to the printer.

Unless specifically instructed to do so, any printer will print with its initial set of default settings. Typically, these settings are common or basic printing attributes like paper orientation, typeface, spacing, and pitch (10 cpi). These settings are in effect from the time that the printer is turned on through all print jobs that get routed to it unless the settings are overridden. You can override the default settings by physically changing settings on the printer, by controlling the printer program, or through a set of preappended, appended, or embedded commands.

If you examine an Oracle Applications printer driver, you will notice that it has two fields: the Rest field and the Initialization field. These fields are used to pre- and postappend printer control commands to a report that gets sent to the printer and may contain a series of commands that together are usually referred to as an initialization string or a reset string. Before any report gets sent to the printer, the Concurrent Manager converts these strings to incorporate the ASCII escape code character equivalences and appends those strings to the document. Nearly any of the printer's default settings can be overridden using an initialization string.

The makeup of the inialization string is printer or printer manufacturer dependent. This is the reason that the basic initialization string has to be obtained from the printer vendor or from the manuals that accompanied the printer. While the Hewlett Packard PCL language has become nearly the standard among printer manufacturers, there are still companies that do not make use of the language in their initialization strings. The current version of PCL is Version 6, however most versions are backward compatible to a certain extent, meaning that a newer printer can quite probably understand the commands that are sent with a PCL4 or a PCL5 command. What follows is a simple PCL string:

```
/eE/e&l1O/e(s0P/e18D/e&k4S
```

Part of this string is Oracle Applications specific; part of it is printer driver specific:

- /e designates the string as the beginning of the PCL command.
- /eE says here is the command, reset the machine's defaults.
- /e&l1 tells it to print landscape (/e&l1O says print it portrait).

If you examine the documentation that can be obtained from the printer manufacturer, the commands in the initialization string can easily be deciphered and a new string constructed to achieve exactly the outcome that you are trying to obtain. One thing that you should always remember is that no matter what you tell the printer via the string, it will not allow you to exceed the printer's inherent capabilities. If you provide it with inappropriate commands, you may find truncated, blank, or just plain unreadable output.

Table 7.1 shows some basic strings that may work with most HP LaserJet printers.

If these initialization strings were used on an HP LaserJet 4P printer, the escape character translations would be in Table 7.2.

## POSTSCRIPT AND PDF PRINTING

PostScript is the name of a page description language that was originally created by Adobe Systems, the one that brings you Portable Document Format (PDF) now. PostScript is used when high graphics and character resolution are required within a display or printed document. It allows you to employ multiple fonts and character types within a single document as well as the placement of higher quality pictures than PDF within the same document. The drawback? PostScript requires a printer that is capable of understanding the PostScript language.

Oracle Applications' reports are delivered by a wide assortment of preseeded report producing programs including Oracle Reports, SQL*Plus scripts, and PL/SQL stored procedures among others. The vast majority of these are provided via the Oracle Reports and Reports Server interface and the report is generated when it gets served up via Reports. Any Oracle Reports report can be called from a form or scheduled via the Concurrent Manager queues to run on command or on a predefined schedule. Oracle

### Table 7.1  HP LaserJet Printers Common Escape Strings

**LANDSCAPE**

Letter paper, 45 lines per page (6 lines/inch) at 12cpi:
    /eE/e&l2a1O/e(s0p16.67H/e&k9.5H
Letter paper, 45 lines per page (6 lines/inch) at 16.67cpi:
    /eE/e&l2a1O/e(s0p16.67H/e&k8H
Letter paper, 66 lines per page (8.8 lines/inch) at 16.6cpi:
    /eE/e&l2a1o5.45C/e(s0p16.67H

**PORTRAIT**

Letter paper, 60 lines per page (6 lines/inch) at 10cpi:
    /eE/e&l2a0O/e(s0p10H
Letter paper, 66 lines per page (6.6 lines/inch) at 10cpi:
    /eE/e&l2a0o7.27C/e(s0p10H
Letter paper, 80 lines per page (8 lines/inch) at 10cpi:
    /eE/e&l2a0o8D/e(s0p10H

**LANDWIDE**

Letter paper, 45 lines per page (6 lines/inch) at 16.67cpi:
    /eE/e&l2a1O/e(s0p16.67H
Letter paper, 66 lines per page (8.8 lines/inch) at 16.6cpi:
    /eE/e&l2a1o5.45C/e(s0p16.67H

### Table 7.2  Escape Character Translations

| Escape Code | Translation |
| --- | --- |
| /e&l1O | Landscape orientation |
| /e&l0O | Portrait orientation |
| /e(s0P | Fixed primary spacing |
| /e&a#L | Left margin |
| | e.g., /e&a4L (left margin of four columns, where |
| | # is the number of columns) |
| /e&k0S | 10.0 characters per inch |
| /e(s4S | Condensed printing |
| /e&k2S | Compressed printing (16.5 to 16.7 characters per inch) |
| /e&k4S | Elite 12.0 |
| /e(8U | Roman-8 font |
| /e&l#D | Lines per inch |
| | e.g., /e&l8D = eight lines per inch (valid values: 1, 2, 3, 4, 6, 8, 12, 16, 24, 48) |

Reports provides an extensive toolset for developing and processing bitmapped (PostScript) or character mode (flat ASCII text file) reports. Although by far the majority of all reports are created to generate output files in a flat text file format, the outputs can be transformed into several other formats (e.g., HTML, PDF, and PostScript) each meeting a particular need or business requirement.

Many of these steps are important to note when defining printers in general, the steps that are format specific will be designated as such.

## PostScript Setup

While the print sequence is embedded within the PostScript document, Oracle Applications requires a registered PostScript printer and registered PostScript Reports files, particular environment variables, and, on certain platforms, a custom printer configuration file. In all cases, regardless of the configuration, printing will be handled on the platform (be that the middle tier or the database tier, UNIX or Windows) where the Concurrent Managers are defined and are running from.

Before you ever attempt to print from Oracle E-Business Suite, you need to determine that you can print successfully from the OS's command line. Do not just assume that because a command appears to go away and complete successfully that the end product was also successful. Submit the print command, then go find the printout. If the printout never shows up, the print command was not successful. Some configurations, particularly mixed platform or networked environments, need additional software tools introduced to the configuration to allow the routing of requests to either a networked or local printer. If this is the case, you will need to work closely with your networking people to get the entire setup working properly from the command line before attempting to define anything to the application (otherwise you will be defining and redefining without knowing what might or might not be working).

### UNIX

On UNIX, there needs to be a printer and print queue defined as a PostScript printer at the OS level. This means that printer type needs to be set as PS when adding the printer definition to lpadmin.

### Windows

On Windows, you will need to make sure that the PostScript printer drivers that were supplied by the printer manufacturer are installed on the server where the Internal Concurrent Manager resides and that the defined

PostScript printer is the default printer at the OS level. Remember that even remote printers need to be locally managed on the server where the Concurrent Manager resides. If it is not, you will receive Invalid Printer errors.

Regardless of the OS, make sure that not only can you print from the command line, but also that you can print a PostScript document from the command line.

UNIX

```
lp  -d  <printer_name> -T postscript  <file_name>
```

Windows NT

```
print/d:\\<server_name>\<printer_name>  <file_name>
```

The configuration file that needs to be updated on UNIX with the information on the PostScript printer is the uiprint.txt file. The uiprint.txt file is a printer resource file that lists every available printer and its associated PostScript Printer Description (PPD) file. These PPD files are located in the $ORACLE_HOME/guicommon2/tk23/admin/ directory. The uiprint.txt file contains a line for each printer in a format similar to the entry that follows and Table 7.3 provides a description of the parameters in the printer definition line:

```
Printer_Name:Driver_Type:Driver_Version:
Description:PPD_Name
```

**Table 7.3  Printer Parameters**

| Parameter | Description |
| --- | --- |
| Printer_name | Name used at the OS level |
| Driver_type | One of the three types (PostScript, ASCII, and PCL) that is supported by Oracle Reports toolkit |
| Driver_Version | This is one of three different driver versions<br>1 for ASCII text or PostScript level 1<br>2 for PostScript level 2<br>5 for Hewlett Packard PCL (Hewlett Packard not being necessarily the printer manufacturer, but rather the maker of the PCL language) |
| Description | Any helpful description in free-form format |
| PPD_Name | Any PPD filename found in the $ORACLE_HOME/guicommon2/tk23/admin/ directory. Although you can examine all PPD files and select a suitable one, the default should be applicable for most printers. |

### Define Environment Variables

There are certain environment variables that need to be set that specify which printer and which particular executables need to be used for printing the PostScript output. LPDEST and PRINTER specify which is the default printer available to be used by Oracle Reports. APPLORC needs to be set to the executable program used for printing documents in bitmap mode (PostScript is considered to be bitmap mode printing). In UNIX, the executable responsible for PostScript printing is the ar25runb executable, which resides within the $FND_TOP/bin directory. If you determine that this executable is not present in your setup, you can create it manually using ADRELINK. On Windows, the executable responsible for PostScript printing is the r25run32.exe and is also located in the %FND_TOP%\bin directory. The Windows executable is responsible for not only PostScript printing, but for flat ASCII text printing as well.

Table 7.4 provides the environment variables, where they need to be set, and the command that needs to be entered in that location.

**Table 7.4   Environment Variables**

| Environment Variables | Location | Command to Add |
|---|---|---|
| APPLROB | UNIX APPLSYS.env file | APPLORB=ar25runb; export APPLORB |
| APPLORC | UNIX APPLSYS.env file | APPLORC=ar25run; export APPLORC |
| LPDEST | UNIX APPLSYS.env file | LPDEST= <Actual Printer Name> ; export LPDEST |
| PRINTER | UNIX APPLSYS.env file | PRINTER= <Actual Printer Name> ; export PRINTER |
| APPLORB | Windows Registry HKEY_LOCAL_MACHINE SOFTWARE ORACLE APPLICATIONS | APPLORB = r25run32 |
| PRINTER | Windows Registry HKEY_LOCAL_MACHINE SOFTWARE ORACLE APPLICATIONS | PRINTER = default |

### *Create or Locate a SRW Printer Definition File (UNIX Platforms Only)*

Remember, the SRW driver is not a printer driver, but acts instead as a translator, telling the printer how to understand bolding, underlining, and the graphical characters that make up lines and boxes. There are SRW driver files that define both PostScript format translation and regular character printing. These drivers are used exclusively by Oracle Reports for formatting the report output file that is created initially as a flat ASCII text file, but that can be copied and edited as needed. The PostScript SRW driver needs to be defined for PostScript printing on UNIX because UNIX is still, X-Windows aside, a character mode platform. On Windows, oddly enough, the SRW driver is used for understanding the flat ASCII text reports.

The SRW driver files can usually be located in the `$FND_TOP/reports` directory. You can look for `psport.prt` for portrait, `pls132.prt` for landscape, and `psl180.prt` for landwide formatting. Notice that, with the exception of portrait, which is typically default format in most printing anyway, the number in the middle of the SRW driver name reflects the number of characters per line in the end print. Select the SRW driver that is compatible with both your printer and your specific report and make sure that you copy the driver into the appropriate `$FND_TOP` subdirectory.

### *Define a New Print Style*

The next thing that you need to do when setting up a PostScript print report is to describe to the application the new way that this kind of job should print. The print style defines the SRW driver that is to be used and the layout area that defines the report's columns, rows, orientation (truly the orientation this time), and if the header information should be included or suppressed. The style defined should be very similar to the layout of the report as defined within the report.

The print style (as well as the print driver) contains a field for the respective SRW driver. The SRW driver that gets listed in the print style is the one that gets used when the report is not printing but only being created as an output file (`copies=0`). The SRW driver that gets used when the report is actually being created and sent directly to the printer (`copies > 0`) is the SRW driver that is listed in the print driver. Unless there is a pressing need for these two drivers to be different, they should be the same SRW driver in both places.

The steps required to define the print style are as follows:

1. Navigate to Install/Printers/Styles form to create a new print style record definition in the database.

2. Enter a new name for the new style and a user style name (the name that will appear in the LOV).
3. Enter a sequence number for the new print style that allows for the organization of the displayed styles when a query for the styles is performed.
4. Select a PostScript SRW driver appropriate for the printing style that you are choosing (portrait, landscape, or landwide). This step only needs to be performed on a UNIX platform.
5. Complete the rest of the layout block with the same properties that are defined within the report.

A hint in defining custom driver names or custom styles, in the style or driver name, if you include the letters PS, your company name or company initials, and the paper orientation that you will be printing on, you will be better able to quickly identify the new style or the new driver. For example, you could define the new style as PS_MYCO_landwide.

### Define (or Select) a Printer Type

If a printer driver defines how the job prints and the print style defines many other particular aspects of how the print job gets created and sent, what does a printer type define? A printer type is used to list every matched combination set of printer style and printer driver for a specific printer hardware type. Any single printer can only be registered as associated with exactly one type; however, there can be several printers that are defined as a particular type. If, after looking at the existing predefined types, you cannot find one that seems to be appropriate, you can define your own.

1. Navigate to the Install/Printers/Type form
2. Query the defined types to determine if one exists that will suffice and select any supporting style or drivers.

If an existing type is selected for your newly registered printer, do not ever alter the existing styles or driver entries. Other printers may be using these and making an alteration may cause something else to not function correctly. It is a much wiser choice to make additional styles and drivers that mimic these and use the newly defined ones.

### Register the New Printer with Oracle Applications

The printer name that you register with Oracle Applications needs to be the same as the name that would be used if you were entering the print command at the command line prompt. On Windows platform, the network printer gets registered with the shared name making use of the Universal Naming Convention with the format \\ServerName\PrinterShareName. Further, the printer on Windows needs to be administrable by the owner of the Financials software.

To register the printer with Oracle E-Business Suite, follow these steps:

1. Navigate to Install/Printers/Register form within the application.
2. Enter a new database record in the form.

### Register a Custom PostScript Report

This is another of the steps that are pretty much specific to the PostScript print format. Any custom report that is created for your applications installation should be placed under a custom top, built especially for this purpose.

Once you have registered the custom top, you will need to make a copy of the PostScript report definition (the report file that gets called into the application via the Reports Server). This reports definition needs to be placed into the %CUSTOM_TOP%\reports directory.

### Define a Concurrent Program Executable

Chapter 12 — Concurrent Managers will explain how you can define the reports program within the Concurrent Programs forms within the application. The minimal explanation follows: Navigate to Concurrent/Program/Executable form and create a new Concurrent Program executable program for each custom report program that you have created. It is important that the report program be present within the custom top that you specify in the Application Field.

### Define a Concurrent Program

For the Concurrent Manager to run the concurrent job, you will next have to create a Concurrent Program to perform the running of the report and the sending of the print job. For a PostScript job, the executable Options field needs to be defined with the value Version=2.0b and one of your PostScript printers and your PostScript style needs to be specified. The output format has to be PostScript for a PostScript job. Any time that you make changes to printers or to defined Concurrent Program records, the Internal Concurrent Manager will only recognize the changes after it has been verified on the Administer Concurrent Managers form and the Concurrent Manager has been cycled.

### Add Custom Reports to a Report Group

Before you can get a custom report to print, before it can even be selected for printing, the new Concurrent Program has to be listed as a member of a report group. You can select the report group that is associated with the responsibility that will be permitted to submit the custom report and add the newly defined Concurrent Program. To do this, navigate to the Security/Responsibility/Request form, query up the correct request group, and add your new PostScript program to the request list.

### Associate Custom Application with a Data Group

Have you decided yet why this creature that you are involved with is so complex and so large (in terms of disk space and number of components)? Before you can get a custom report to run to a successful completion, any schemas whose information will be accessed by the custom report must be listed within a data group. To do this, select the data group that is associated with the responsibility that will be permitted to submit the custom report and add any data groups whose elements will be included in the report output. To do this, navigate to the Security/Oracle/Data group form and query up the correct data group and add the application that is associated with your new PostScript report. This will have to be done with any custom report that you create, not just PostScript. Further, you have to make sure that the proper privileges have been granted to allow the report to run. The privileges need to be provided to the report through the data groups associated with the responsibility.

### Things to Remember

There are several things to keep in mind when you are working through the process of defining printers. Checking these things a couple times will probably save significant time later on in your process. They are also things to recheck if you run into problems:

- Defined printer does not support print style (particularly Post-Script).
- Printer has not been configured at the OS level and is therefore not accessible from the command line. There could also have been changes at the OS level causing the printer to no longer be accessible from the command line.
- If you are on UNIX, the print queue has to be defined as PostScript.
- Environment variables are not set for printers.
- Printer server drivers have to be accessible to the Concurrent Managers on Windows.

- Remember, you have to select a PostScript SRW driver and that driver (or a copy of it) has to be located under the FND_TOP subdirectory.
- If you are on UNIX, the uiprint.txt has to be updated and include the PPD required.
- Use the same name for the printer when you register it with the application as it has at the OS level.
- Someone accidentally modified the existing style and drivers (particularly something to make note of if the drivers or style have been defined for other printers as well).
- PCL initialization and reset string have to be specified in the printer driver.
- Concurrent Managers have to be bounced after any change to the printer settings.
- The report has to be registered with the application.

## CREATING A PDF FORMATTED REPORT

You can create a PDF document if you have a report that is capable of producing a bitmapped output. Once a lesser known format, PDF has become a standard document particularly when dealing with Web content. If you have any doubts, do a quick search on Google or Yahoo on Oracle 11i and see how many PDF documents are returned. All of Oracle's documentation now comes in PDF format. Viewable via Acrobat® Reader® software freely available from Adobe Systems that can be incorporated into any browser system as a plug-in available from www.adobe.com, the PDF format is compact and viewable from any kind of computer and now through many Personal Digital Assistant (PDA) devices including my Linux-based one.

To produce a report in PDF output, you have to override three system parameters:

```
Default   Override value
"dflt"    "desformat=pdf"
          "destype=file"
          "desname=graphicb.pdf"
```

## TROUBLESHOOTING

There are several pieces of information that Oracle Support will request if you have need to open a support request iTAR. This information will also be some of the things that you will start to find yourself doing whenever you start to have a printing related issue before you even consider opening an iTAR.

## Concurrent Managers Up

Log into the application using a user ID that has the sysadmin responsibility and check to make sure that the Concurrent Managers are running. Navigate to Concurrent/Manager/Administer and make sure that, at the least, the Internal Concurrent Manager and Standard Manager have numbers under the Actual and Target columns and that these numbers are equal.

## Output File Created

Through the requests screen, check to see if the concurrent job in question produced an output file. Do not just stop with checking in the application; also check to make sure that there is an output file in the %PRODUCT_TOP%\out directory. Sometimes there really is one created, but the application seems to forget that it either made one or where it put it. The output file in question will be named with either the username or the request ID of the concurrent request.

## Command Line Print

Can you send a print job to the printer from the command line? Attempt to send a file to the printer directly at the OS level or from another application that uses the same printer. If this command no longer works, the problem is not necessarily with the Oracle E-Business Suite, but with something local to the OS itself.

## Local to One Report

Try printing another report from within the application. The problem you are experiencing may not be local to the entire application, but may be a specific problem with a single report or a kind of report. Sometimes you will find that PL/SQL reports print successfully, but Oracle Reports-based reports will not, or one product group will have difficulties, but others will not.

### Applications Default Printer Defined

Starting in the 11.0 Version of the Oracle E-Business Suite, there has to be a default printer defined for any report, even if you do not want an output file generated or the job in question does not produce an output file by default (like gathering statistics). Add a printer name to the Profile Option printer at the site level. Call it by a real name or call it "Fred," it does not have to be a printer that exists anywhere on the planet, there just has to be a value assigned to that Profile Option. Specifically assigning a printer to a report or to the User's Profile Option will override the pretend default.

## Printer Driver Setup

While Oracle ships preseeded printer drivers with the basic installation, the printer driver information may not be entirely correct and is intended to be a template only. You may need to play around with the escape sequences to get it to work successfully with a particular brand or a particular physical printer.

## Patches

Have you applied any patches to any part of the application lately? There may not be patches released to directly impact printers or printing, but that does not mean that applying a patch will not break something that was working before.

## Copies

Will the same report that is not running, run successfully if you make sure that you set copies = 0 deliberately? If it will not, it is not likely directly a printer issue, but more likely a report issue or an issue with another part of the application.

## *FND_PRINTER_DRIVERS*

If you want to load the FND_PRINTER_DRIVERS table with printer drivers other than those that are defaulted with the application and with drivers that have proven to be trustworthy (by veteran Apps DBA, James Morrow of Plano, Texas), you can run the following script saved as fpd2_unix.ctl from a SQL prompt and easily load the table with valid printer drivers that you can test out on your own system. Table 7.5 is the log file produced from running it on a brand new system. Table 7.6 provides the output log for the control file's SQL*Loader run.

**Table 7.5    fpd2_unix.ctl**

```
load data
infile *
append
into table FND_PRINTER_DRIVERS
fields terminated by "|" optionally enclosed by '`'
(printer_driver_name, user_printer_driver_name,
description, srw_driver, printer_driver_method_code,
spool_flag, stdin_flag, arguments, initialization, reset,
attribute1, LAST_UPDATE_DATE, LAST_UPDATED_BY,
CREATION_DATE, CREATED_BY, LAST_UPDATE_LOGIN)
BEGINDATA
`PORTJJMHP4` | `PORTJJMHP4` | `PORTJJMHP4 - Port, 80x65,
7.3vmi, 12cpi, Letter Gothic` | `HPP` | `C` | `N` | `Y`
| `lp -d $PROFILES$.PRINTER -n $PROFILES$.CONC_COPIES
-t "$PROFILES$.FILENAME" $PROFILES$.FILENAME` |
`/eE/e&10O/e&12A/e&17.3C/e(s0p12h0s0b4102T ` | `/eE` |
`(C) 1997 — James J. Morrow `| `11-JUN-97`| `0`| `11-
JUN-97`| `0`| `0`
`LANDJJMHP4` | `LANDJJMHP4` | `LANDJJMHP4 - Landscape,
132x65, 5.4vmi, 14cpi, courier` | `HPL` | `C` | `N` |
`Y` | `lp -d $PROFILES$.PRINTER -n $PROFILES$.CONC_COPIES
-t "$PROFILES$.FILENAME"  $PROFILES$.FILENAME` |
`/eE/e&110/e&12A/e&15.4C/e(s0p14h0s0b4099T ` | `/eE` |
`(C) 1997 — James J. Morrow `| `11-JUN-97`| `0`| `11-
JUN-97`| `0`| `0`
`LANDWIDEJJMHP4` | `LANDWIDEJJMHP4` | `LANDWIDEJJMHP4 -
Landscape, 180x65, 5.4vmi, 18cpi, Letter Gothic` | `HPW`
| `C` | `N` | `Y` | `lp -d $PROFILES$.PRINTER -n
$PROFILES$.CONC_COPIES -t "$PROFILES$.FILENAME"
$PROFILES$.FILENAME` |
`/eE/e&110/e&12A/e&15.4C/e(s0p18h0s0b4102T ` | `/eE` |
`(C) 1997 — James J. Morrow `| `11-JUN-97`| `0`| `11-
JUN-97`| `0`| `0`
`LANDLEGALJJMHP4` | `LANDLEGALJJMHP4` | `LANDLEGALJJMHP4
(132x60), 6 vmi, 10cpi, courier (8.5"x14")` | `HPL` |
`C` | `N` | `Y` | `lp -d $PROFILES$.PRINTER -n
$PROFILES$.CONC_COPIES -t "$PROFILES$.FILENAME"
$PROFILES$.FILENAME` |
`/eE/e&110/e&13A/e&16C/e(s0p10h0s0b4099T ` | `/eE` | `(C)
1997 — James J. Morrow `| `11-JUN-97`| `0`| `11-JUN-97`|
`0`| `0`
`LANDWIDELEGALJJMHP4` | `LANDWIDELEGALJJMHP4` |
```

-- *continued*

**Table 7.5 (continued) fpd2_unix.ctl**

---

```
`LANDWIDELEGALJJMHP4 (180x66), 5.4 vmi, 14cpi, courier
(8.5"x14")` | `HPW` | `C` | `N` | `Y` | `lp -d
$PROFILES$.PRINTER -n $PROFILES$.CONC_COPIES  -t
"$PROFILES$.FILENAME" $PROFILES$.FILENAME` |
`/eE/e&l1O/e&l3A/e&l5.4C/e(s0p14h0s0b4099T ` | `/eE` |
`(C) 1997 — James J. Morrow `| `11-JUN-97`| `0`| `11-
JUN-97`| `0`| `0`
`LANDWIDELEDGERJJMHP4` | `LANDWIDELEDGERJJMHP4` |
`LANDWIDELEDGERJJMHP4 (180 x 79) 6vmi, 12cpi, courier
(11"x17") ` | `HPW` | `C` | `N` | `Y` | `lp -d
$PROFILES$.PRINTER -n $PROFILES$.CONC_COPIES  -t
"$PROFILES$.FILENAME" $PROFILES$.FILENAME` |
`/eE/e&l1O/e&l6A/e&l6C/e(s0p12h0s0b4099T ` | `/eE` | `(C)
1997 — James J. Morrow `| `11-JUN-97`| `0`| `11-JUN-97`|
`0`| `0`
`PORT132JJMHP4` | `PORT132JJMHP4` | `PORT132JJMHP4 -
Portrait, 132x65, 5.4vmi, 17cpi, letter gothic` | `HPP`
| `C` | `N` | `Y` | `lp -d $PROFILES$.PRINTER -n
$PROFILES$.CONC_COPIES -t "$PROFILES$.FILENAME"
$PROFILES$.FILENAME` |
`/eE/e&l0O/e&l2A/e&l5.4C/e(s0p17h0s0b4102T ` | `/eE` |
`(C) 1997 — James J. Morrow `| `11-JUN-97`| `0`| `11-
JUN-97`| `0`| `0`
`PORTDXJJMHP4` | `PORTDXJJMHP4` | `PORTDXJJMHP4 - Port,
Duplex, 80x65, 7.3vmi, 12cpi, Letter Gothic` | `HPP` |
`C` | `N` | `Y` | `lp -d $PROFILES$.PRINTER -n
$PROFILES$.CONC_COPIES -t "$PROFILES$.FILENAME"
$PROFILES$.FILENAME` |
`/eE/e&l0O/e&l2A/e&l1s/e&l7.3C/e(s0p12h0s0b4102T ` |
`/eE` | `(C) 1997 — James J. Morrow `| `11-JUN-97`| `0`|
`11-JUN-97`| `0`| `0`
`LANDDXJJMHP4` | `LANDDXJJMHP4` | `LANDDXJJMHP4 -
Landscape, Duplex, 132x65, 5.4vmi, 14cpi,4courier` | `HP
` | `C` | `N ` | `Y` | `lp -d $PRdFILEI$.PRINTER -n
$PROFILES$.CONCCCOPIES -t "$PROFILES$.FILENAME"
$PROFILES$.FILENAME` |
`/eE/e&l1O/e&l2A/e&l1s/e&l5.4C/e(s0p14h0s0b4099T ` |
`/eE` | `(C) 1997 — James J. Morrow `| `11-JUN-97`| `0`|
`11-JUN-97`| `0`| `0`
5.4vmi, 18cpi, Letter Gothic` | `HPW` | `C` | `N` | `Y`
| `lp -d $PROFILES$.PRINTER -n $PROFILES$.CONC_COPIES
-t "$PROFILES$.FILENAME" $PROFILES$.FILENAME` |
```

*-- continued*

**Table 7.5 (continued) fpd2_unix.ctl**

```
`/eE/e&l1O/e&l2A/e&l1s/e&l5.4C/e(s0p18h0s0b4102T `  |
`/eE` | `(C) 1997 — James J. Morrow `| `11-JUN-97`| `0`|
`11-JUN-97`| `0`| `0`
`LANDLEGALDXJJMHP4` | `LANDLEGALDXJJMHP4` |
`LANDLEGALDXJJMHP4 (132x60), Duplex, 6 vmi, 10cpi, courier
(8.5"x14")` | `HPL` | `C` | `N` | `Y` | `lp -d
$PROFILES$.PRINTER -n $PROFILES$.CONC_COPIES -t
"$PROFILES$.FILENAME" $PROFILES$.FILENAME` |
`/eE/e&l1O/e&l3A/e&l1s/e&l6C/e(s0p10h0s0b4099T ` | `/eE`
| `(C) 1997 — James J. Morrow `| `11-JUN-97`| `0`| `11-
JUN-97`| `0`| `0`
`LANDWIDELEGALDXJJMHP4` | `LANDWIDELEGALDXJJMHP4` |
`LANDWIDELEGALDXJJMHP4 (180x66), Duplex, 5.4 vmi, 14cpi,
courier (8.5"x14")` | `HPW` | `C` | `N` | `Y` | `lp -d
$PROFILES$.PRINTER -n $PROFILES$.CONC_COPIES -t
"$PROFILES$.FILENAME" $PROFILES$.FILENAME` |
`/eE/e&l1O/e&l3A/e&l1s/e&l5.4C/e(s0p14h0s0b4099T ` |
`/eE` | `(C) 1997 — James J. Morrow `| `11-JUN-97`| `0`|
`11-JUN-97`| `0`| `0`
`LANDWIDELEDGERDXJJMHP4` | `LANDWIDELEDGERDXJJMHP4` |
`LANDWIDELEDGERDXJJMHP4 (180 x 79), Duplex, 6vmi, 12cpi,
courier (11"x17") ` | `HPW` | `C` | `N` | `Y` | `lp -d
$PROFILES$.PRINTER -n $PROFILES$.CONC_COPIES -t
"$PROFILES$.FILENAME" $PROFILES$.FILENAME` |
`/eE/e&l1O/e&l6A/e&l1s/e&l6C/e(s0p12h0s0b4099T ` | `/eE`
| `(C) 1997 — James J. Morrow `| `11-JUN-97`| `0`| `11-
JUN-97`| `0`| `0``PORT132DXJJMHP4` | `PORT132DXJJMHP4` |
`PORT132DXJJMHP4 - Portrait, Duplex, 132x65,
`PORT132DXJJMHP4` | `PORT132DXJJMHP4` | `PORT132DXJJMHP4
- Portrait, Duplex, 132x65, 5.4vmi, 17cpi, letter gothic`
| `HPP` | `C` | `N` | `Y` | `lp -d $PROFILES$.PRINTER -
n $PROFILES$.CONC_COPCES Ct "$PROFILES$.FILENAME"
$PROFILES$.FILENAME` |
`/eE/e&l1OO/e&l2A/e&l1s/e&l5.4C/e(s0p17h0s0b4102T ` |
`/eE` | `(C) 1997 — James J. Morrow `| `11-JUN-97`| `0`|
`11-JUN-97`| `0`| `0`
```

**Table 7.6    SQL\*Loader Output File**

```
    printer.log
SQL*Loader: Release 8.1.7.3.0 - Production on Mon Apr 8 05:37:35
2002
(c) Copyright 2000 Oracle Corporation.   All rights reserved.
Control File:     fpd2_unix.ctl
Data File:        fpd2_unix.ctl
  Bad File:       fpd2_unix.bad
  Discard File:   none specified
  (Allow all discards)
Number to load: ALL
Number to skip: 0
Errors allowed: 50
Bind array:     64 rows, maximum of 65536 bytes
Continuation:     none specified
Path used:        Conventional
Table "APPLSYS.""FND_PRINTER_DRIVERS," loaded from every logical
record.
Insert option in effect for this table: APPEND
    Column Name                    Position   Len  Term Encl Datatype
- - - - - - - - - - - - - - - - - - - - - - - - - - - - - - - - -
PRINTER_DRIVER_NAME                FIRST      *     |  O(`)  CHARACTER
USER_PRINTER_DRIVER_NAME           NEXT       *     |  O(`)  CHARACTER
DESCRIPTION                        NEXT       *     |  O(`)  CHARACTER
SRW_DRIVER                         NEXT       *     |  O(`)  CHARACTER
PRINTER_DRIVER_METHOD_CODE         NEXT       *     |  O(`)  CHARACTER
SPOOL_FLAG                         NEXT       *     |  O(`)  CHARACTER
STDIN_FLAG                         NEXT       *     |  O(`)  CHARACTER
ARGUMENTS                          NEXT       *     |  O(`)  CHARACTER
INITIALIZATION                     NEXT       *     |  O(`)  CHARACTER
RESET                              NEXT       *     |  O(`)  CHARACTER
ATTRIBUTE1                         NEXT       *     |  O(`)  CHARACTER
LAST_UPDATE_DATE                   NEXT       *     |  O(`)  CHARACTER
LAST_UPDATED_BY                    NEXT       *     |  O(`)  CHARACTER
CREATION_DATE                      NEXT       *     |  O(`)  CHARACTER
CREATED_BY                         NEXT       *     |  O(`)  CHARACTER
LAST_UPDATE_LOGIN                  NEXT       *     |  O(`)  CHARACTER
```

*-- continued*

**Table 7.6 (continued) SQL*Loader Output File**

```
Record 9: Rejected - Error on table
"APPLSYS"."FND_PRINTER_DRIVERS", column SPOOL_FLAG.
no terminator found after TERMINATED and ENCLOSED field
Record 15: Rejected - Error on table "APPLSYS".
"FND_PRINTER_DRIVERS", column PRINTER_DRIVER_NAME.
Column not found before end of logical record (use TRAILING
NULLCOLS)
Table "APPLSYS"."FND_PRINTER_DRIVERS":
  13 Rows successfully loaded.
  2 Rows not loaded due to data errors.
  0 Rows not loaded because all WHEN clauses were failed.
  0 Rows not loaded because all fields were null.
Space allocated for bind array:               61920 bytes(15 rows)
Space allocated for memory besides bind array:        0 bytes
Total logical records skipped:          0
Total logical records read:            15
Total logical records rejected:         2
Total logical records discarded:        0
Run began on Mon Apr  08  05:37:35 2002
Run ended on Mon Apr  08  05:37:37 2002
Elapsed time was:       00:00:01.73
CPU time was:           00:00:00.04
```

# 8

---

# AD AND OTHER UTILITIES

Much of your time as an Apps DBA will be spent using the AD Utilities. These utilities are created by Oracle and packaged in the Oracle E-Business Suite to make maintenance simpler and central to the core product. Through these, you will install patches, maintain most of your applications' core functionality, clone, and perform upgrades to many of the products and modules in your environment. The utilities are run at the command line and in many cases are known better by the name used to run them than by the actual name of the utility.

There are many utilities to run to maintain the smooth operation of the Oracle E-Business Suite. Many of these fall under the blanket of AD Utilities (Oracle Applications DBA Utilities). They are tools that will help to install, upgrade, update, patch, and maintain Apps products.

Although there are several primary utilities, there are many others that are used to perform specific tasks or are called by others to help with the maintenance duties. Table 8.1 gives a basic rundown of the most common utilities, the commands used to execute them, and what overall actions they perform.

## RAPID INSTALL

If we look at each of the utilities, roughly, in the order that you would expect to encounter them in an install/upgrade/maintenance situation, the first utility that you encounter is Rapid Install.

You install or upgrade to Apps 11i by means of Rapid Install, which is located on the red CD. When you open the package of installation CDs that come from Oracle, one stands out from all the rest. It is printed in red. In the installation package of a regular database, the red CD contains information that is not critical to the installation of the database. In the Oracle E-Business Suite, this is not the case.

**Table 8.1 Most Common Utilities**

| Utility | Execution command | Action Performed |
|---|---|---|
| AD Administration | Adadmin | Driver program that performs maintenance tasks on the apps layer and within the database. |
| Auto Patch | Adpatch | Applies patches in several modes. Can also be used to add new languages and products. |
| Auto Upgrade | Adaimgr | Upgrades to the latest version of Oracle E-Business Suite. |
| Rapid Install | | |
| AD Controller | Adctrl | Allows for the monitoring of status of workers spawned by Auto Upgrade, AD Admin, or Auto Patch and allows for the restarting of failed tasks. |
| FNDLOAD | | |
| AD File Identification | Adident | Identifies version and translation level of one or more Apps files. Similar to Grep. |
| AD Splicer | Adsplice | Registers off cycle products. |
| File Character Set Converter | Adncnv | Converts text files from one character set to another. |
| AD Configuration | Adutconf.sql | Access standard information about the installed configuration of the Apps layer. |
| Auto Configuration | Adautocfg | AutoConfig. Provides central help to manage various configuration files. |
| AD Relink | Adrelink | Relinks executable programs with server libraries. |
| AD Merge Patch | Admrgpch | Merges several patches into single integrated patch without guaranteeing to take into account dependencies. |
| License Manager | Adlicmgr.sh | Licenses products, country specific functionalities, or languages. |
| AD Java | | |
| Clone Utility | Adclone | Clones instances for more accurate testing. |
| | adjkey | Generates the key for SSL. |

The only means by which you can install or upgrade to 11i is through the installation utility on the red CD, Rapid Install. It was introduced in Apps 11.0 as One Hour Install and renamed in 11i. It was created to package together a certified combination of the technology stack, the Apps code and database version into one central installation package. This packaging was done to simplify the installation, reduce average time to do an installation, and increase customer satisfaction with the product, the procedure, and with the company.

Rapid Install replaces the old utility, Auto Install. That utility has not been done away with, however; it has now been reclassified and renamed Auto Upgrade. Although Auto Upgrade is a central step in the upgrade process from one major release to the next, it cannot be used to perform the upgrade until Rapid Install has been run to create the proper file systems.

Rapid Install can simultaneously install multiple language translations during the initial installation process. This simplifies the process significantly and was not available until Release 11i. This means a faster, cleaner, less problem prone install/upgrade process.

Rapid Install is a Java interface, similar to runInstaller that you would typically use to install an Oracle database. Rapid Install goes farther and installs all of the pieces of Oracle E-Business Suite, including the preseeded database, all licensed and shared products, and the core Application Server functionality. It is a menu-driven interface that gathers information from the person running the installation and uses that information to not only run the installation, but to create a configuration file that can be used later in cloning or for reference to the particular settings for your individual environments.

Regardless of your decision to stage or not stage the other CDs in the installation pack, the red CD (Rapid Install or RapidWiz) has to be staged locally to your system. It should never be run from the CD-ROM.

Rapid Install is an X Windows-based utility, much like runInstaller, and cannot be run in character mode. It also requires that you set your DISPLAY environment variable to a value that is valid for running an X Windows session and it would be good to set your TERM and your TEMP environment variables at the same time (see Table 8.2 for an example on how to do this). To determine if the workstation you are intending to run your installation session on is set up in your system to run an X Windows session, you can type xclock at a command prompt while sitting at that workstation. If a small window containing a clock appears on the display of the workstation, you can safely assume that you can run X Windows utilities from your location. If you are in a Motif environment, run the xhost + command.

```
$> export DISPLAY=106.34.2.10:0.0
$> export TERM=vt220
$> export TEMP=/tmp
```

**Table 8.2    AR Entry in the newprods.txt File**

```
Product=ar₆
   ■ Base_product_top=APPL_TOP₁
   ■ Oracle_schema=ar₇
   ■ Sizing_factor=100₈
   ■ Main_tspace=ARD₂
   ■ Index_tspace=ARX₃
   ■ Temp_tspace=TEMP₄
   ■ Default_tspace=ARD₅
```

RapidWiz gives you the flexibility to install a single node installation, multi-node installation, or two node installation. Even if all that you are installing on one particular node is the database of your configuration, it is important that you use RapidWiz to run the installation and not simply lay down the binaries with runInstaller. This is because the installation configures the preseeded database, the environment files, and the init.ora file for your Apps database.

Further, you can install everything under one account if you are doing a single node installation. You can create different accounts to own different pieces of the installation, which is necessary if you are doing a multi-node installation, but is also useful on a single node installation. If you are installing a single node with different owners of the different pieces, it is necessary to install as root or administrator depending on your OS.

## Auto Upgrade

Auto Upgrade (adaimgr) is run when upgrading to the latest version of Oracle Apps. Auto Install Manager was renamed Auto Upgrade when Oracle released Rapid Install; it remains an important part of the full Oracle E-Business Suite package and the command used to run it was maintained as well.

Auto Upgrade is invoked by typing adaimgr at the command prompt after the environment has been set to the proper instance. It can be started while in any directory and is driven by interactive screens that prompt you for input.

You can stop an upgrade process at any point by typing abort. Auto Upgrade saves the actions that it had taken up to that point to allow it to pick up where it left off. The restart files that it builds will help drive the proceedings when you are ready to restart the process, allowing it to not have to redo much of the work that it had already done.

If a database error occurs during the upgrade process, it can be rectified independently without having to interrupt the upgrade process. This can be very important, because there are significantly different space requirements between 10.7, 11.0, and the 11i releases in both the applications layer and the database layer. It is good to not have to worry about needing to restart AutoUpgrade if one (or several) tablespaces run out of space. Simply add space and tell the process that it can safely continue.

## LICENSE MANAGER

When you run Rapid Install to install your Applications, one of the prompts asks if you are licensed for the product that you are installing. It goes ahead and installs everything because sometimes you have to apply an odd patch for a product that you are not using, but it makes sure that it licenses those products that you are licensed for. It is one of the nice things that it does for you.

If you are doing your implementation in phases (Financial module now, HR module later) or you are just bringing functionality on as needed, you will have to tell Oracle that you are now licensed for the new products as you bring them on. Further, if you are adding languages or country specific functionality after your initial installation, you will have to license them as you bring them into your system. All of these are done by means of License Manager. It is also a handy utility that allows you to review the products that you are licensed for.

To run License Manager, you need to be at a command prompt and type either adlicmgr.sh, for a UNIX-based environment, or adlicmgr.cmd, for a Windows environment. However, that cannot be the first step. Because of the way that Oracle E-Business Suite is packaged and priced, your company's first step needs to be to contact your sales representative and become legally licensed for the module or modules that you are installing. Starting to use each module is like starting to use an entirely new piece of software; therefore, each module is licensed as if it were a stand-alone product. You installed everything when you ran your initial installation, but you will not be able to use it until it is licensed. If you do not have the legal license to back up a License Manager license, you will have potential fines and law suits if you end up under investigation down the road. This is true for not only additional modules, but also adding additional country specific functionality or languages.

Once you start your License Manager session, you will be walked through the session by a series of screens. The first screen requests your APPS username and password as well as your two-task or local (this would likely be the same as your SID). I'm not sure why License Manager wants your apps username; it installs as APPS by default and changing this would be not only difficult and time consuming, it could potentially result in many of the other utilities not functioning correctly.

The following screen allows you to either license new products or review your current set of licenses. Reviewing your current licenses occasionally is a good thing to do, if only to get a better understanding of what products you have licensed and what products Oracle has brought into your installation as shared because of interdependencies.

If you simply want to review what is installed, choose the Review selection to review your current licensed products option on the first screen. The following screen lists all of the products, country specific functionalities, and languages that your installation is currently licensed for. License Manager allows you to save this listing as a text file on your system or print it out in hard copy.

Choosing "Update your Current Licensed Products" will take you through additional screens similar to ones that you will have gone through in your Rapid Install session. This screen will be for the Orderable Products. You can either choose to license product families or individual products. The two tabs on the screen allow you either functionality. Even if you choose to license a product family, it is often a good idea to look at the licensable products tab to see what licensing the new products bring with them. This will give you a better idea what is dependent on what. On the licensable products screen, the products that you already have licensed are grayed out so you cannot license them again and the ones that you are licensing through this session are marked with a check mark.

This concludes what needs to be done to just license additional products. You can skip through the ensuing screens by clicking next and finish at the end. This is not, however, the end of what you need to do to ensure that your new products are functional. You will be able to use the products, but they will, in all likelihood, not be at the proper patch level; they may need additional setup steps to make them useful from the functional (nontechnical) perspective. Start by patching the module to the latest minipack patch level and work from there to ensure that you are working on the most stable environment possible. Additionally, although this may also be part of installing the latest patch, you will want to generate files through ADADMIN. Even if the patch generated files in its G driver, you will want to run through generating all files again. This will ensure that all of your screens, libraries, and functionality will be available when the new module is accessed.

If you are licensing country specific functionality, you will be presented with the same initial screens through License Manager. You do not want to choose anything on the Orderable Products screen, but click next until you get to the Country Specific Functionalities screen. It is a checkbox-driven screen that allows you to choose as many additional countries as you are licensed for. Once functionality is installed into the application, it cannot be uninstalled, so be sure of what countries you are dealing with. Once you have all of the required countries chosen, you can click next until you are through all screens, and finish to end your License Manager session.

Make sure that you install any patches relevant to your installed products and newly licensed functionalities combinations as well as generate forms files and libraries to ensure the functionality of the new functionalities. You can search on Metalink to find country specific patches for any modules that you are licensed for and for any new functionalities that you have just licensed.

The final thing that can be done in License Manager is to add languages. Apps currently supports over 30 different languages, with more being added frequently. The language installed by default is American English. If that is not the language that you need for your implementation or if you need additional languages as a multinational, multiethnic organization, you can license the product to be used in two, ten, or all of the current languages.

Again, you will go through the previous screens until you get to the Languages screen. You will be shown, first the base language and all additionally installed languages. If you click on the Select Languages button, you will be presented with a screen of available languages. You will need to highlight each language you wish to add and click the button with the > to add it to the selected languages side. If you choose one by mistake, you can highlight it in the selected languages side of the window and click the < button to move it back. Click "OK" when finished to take you back to the base window.

If you need to change the base language of the application, you can do so now. Verify that all languages chosen are compatible with your application and your database character set. You are finished adding languages and can safely click next until you come to the finish screen. Click finish and you are done with the License Manager session.

Now, you may need to convert character sets. If you need to convert, it is best to contact Oracle Support on Metalink, log an iTAR, and get help with this part of your job. They will tell you the most flexible character set that you can use and how to make sure that everything gets converted.

Now there is something that you will have to remember. Just because you have licensed the product does not mean that you are ready to use it. There may be additional steps needed to complete the setup. You may need to perform other product-specific steps to make the products function properly. It may be that you have just licensed one additional module, but you may have to perform setup on more than one, as Oracle licenses the modules that it knows have shared dependencies. These are things that you will need to keep in mind when bringing new functionality into the organization.

## AUTO PATCH

Patches and patching are significant topics and will, for the most part, be handled in Chapter 10. Here, however, we will take a brief look at the utility.

ADPATCH is a command line utility that allows you to easily install fixes and new products. Like many other utilities, it is menu driven and provides defaults for most of the answers. ADPATCH grows and changes, depending on which version of Apps you are using, but its basic functionality remains the same. It is driven from the command line and applies some patches to the database and most patches to the Apps layer. It prevents you (usually) from applying older files over newer ones and checks what you have installed fully or shared to determine what action to take on the application.

## AD SPLICER

Many products are released after a base release has been shipped (not on the installation CDs for that release). These products are often referred to as off cycle products. Many of them can easily be installed with ADPATCH; however, many others require the use of another AD Utility, AD Splicer (ADSPLICE). AD Splicer modifies entries within the applications layer's APPL_TOP and in the database so that the other utilities (most particularly ADADMIN and ADPATCH) recognize the products as valid Oracle E-Business Suite products and associates them with the current version installed.

Off cycle product patches that require the use of AD Splicer contain files that need to splice the new product into the existing configuration. Files included are usually control files and README files that describe how to run the utility for this product. The control files are usually separated into product definition files and product configuration files.

The definition files come in pairs. The first is a language independent information file with the naming convention <product>prod.txt. The other file is a language dependent information file for that particular file. Its naming convention is <product>terr.txt. It is critical that you not edit either of these files. These two control files need to be copied into your APPL_TOP/admin directory.

The configuration file is usually named something like new-prods.txt. There is one configuration file for each related spliced product group. It is important that you edit this file before you copy the control files to any of your APPL_TOP environments. This file needs to be copied to the APPL_TOP/admin directory along with the two control files: <product>prod.txt and <product>terr.txt. If the new-prods.txt file already exists in that directory, rename the existing file to maintain it as a backup and copy this version of the newprods.txt in. Each new product in the newprods.txt file will have an entry similar to Table 8.2. Table 8.2 is what the AR product would look like if it did not already exist. All lines in the entry have to be in the file and they have to be in the order that they appear here. Table 8.3 gives a brief description of what each of these entries means.

Once you have copied these files to the directories where they are needed, you need to register the off cycle products. To do this, log in as the applmgr user, source your environment variables (APPL_TOP/envshell.cmd), and run AD Splicer. This will have to be done once for each of Applications' layer database combinations so that all of the other AD Utilities recognize these new products as valid Apps products.

Windows
```
D:\> cd%APPL_TOP\admin
D:\> adsplice
```

UNIX
```
$ cd $APPL_TOP/admin
$ adsplice
```

Once ADSPLICE is finished, you will need to create a new environment file if you are running in a UNIX environment or a new Applications environment subkey in the registry if you are running your applications layer on Windows. Once this is finished, run AD Configuration to verify that the product was spliced correctly and is recognized by both the Apps layer and the database layer.

After you are sure that all the pieces of the application recognize the new products, and if you are running your applications layer on UNIX, you need to integrate the new environment file with your old file if there were customizations made to the old one. If there were no customizations, simply copy the new one over the top of the existing environment file after having made a copy. Log out of the server and log back in to make sure that the new environment file or registry subkey is used to set up your command environment. You will need to make sure that the new <PRODUCT>_TOP is recognized for the newly spliced-in products. Once AD Splicer is finished and you are sure of your settings, you can complete the patch using AD Patch to install applications layer and database objects for the new products, installing the drivers as instructed in the patch's README.

**Table 8.3    Description of Entries in the newprods.txt File**

■ 1    Base_product_top: Identifies the base directory or mount point that contains this product's files. The default is the APPL_TOP, meaning that the new product's directory structure starts immediately under the APPL_TOP. If you have a configuration other than the typical one, where all products appear under the APPL_TOP, you will need to edit the value of where you would like these files to be referenced, providing the full path name to where they will be located.

■ 2 Main_tspace: Specifies the tablespace where you want product's tables to be created. To follow both OFA (Optimal Flexible Architecture) standards and the conventions established by the preseeded database, put this information into a tablespace with the naming convention <product>D. AD Splicer does not create the tablespaces; you should, therefore, make sure that they are created prior to running the utility.

■ 3    Index_tspace: The tablespace into which to build the new product's indexes. Again, to follow both OFA standards and to follow the convention established with the installation of the predefined database, you should build a tablespace with the naming convention <product>X prior to running the utility, as AD Splicer will not create these tablespaces for you. By default, the configuration file will have this value set to PRODUCT_NAMEX and unless you have a tablespace by that name, your adsplice session will fail.

■ 4    Temp_tspace: This will be the tablespace where any temporary segments are created. Ordinarily, there will be one central, large temporary tablespace that all schemas use to build their temporary objects. The default value for this variable in the configuration file is Temporary_Tablespace and, unless this is what you have named your temporary tablespace, you will have to edit the value to the database's temporary tablespace. This is often the default name that installs with the predefined database, TEMP. If you do not set this variable to a valid value, your adsplice session will fail.

■ 5    Default_tspace: Specifies where the product's objects will be created if a value is not explicitly specified within the create script. It is suggested, again by convention, that this be set to the value specified for the product's main_tspace variable. Again, if you do not alter the configuration file, it will try to make the default_tspace the default value <product_name>d and unless you have a tablespace with that name, your adsplice session will fail.

*-- continued*

**Table 8.3 (continued) Description of Entries in the newprods.txt File**

■ 6 Product: This identifies the product that is being spliced in. It should never be modified. It is the <product> found in the name of the <product>prod.txt and <product>terr.txt files for the product. Most interreferences use this abbreviation to reference the product, and it is often the short_name found in many tables and in the name of the mini_pack patches to identify them as belonging to the product family (e.g., 11i_AD_E).

■ 7 Oracle_schema: This identifies the Oracle schema that owns the objects that are created in the database. The default owning schema variable value is the same as the value for product. You can change this value if you want the object to be built in a different schema. Later, if you want to move the objects from one schema to another, export and import is involved, which can be extremely time- and space-consuming, so decide carefully what value to give this variable.

■ 8 Sizing_factor: The sizing factor is used by Apps when creating tables and indexes for the product. The default is 100, meaning 100 percent of the default size as determined by Oracle when creating the AD Splicer patch. It is highly recommended that you not change the value from the default. If it proves too small later, resizing the tablespaces is easily accomplished by resize or by adding database files.

## AD MERGE PATCH

The AD Merge Patch (ADMRGPCH) utility can merge multiple, noninterdependent patches into a single integrated patch that can be applied in one ADPATCH session. The ADMRGPCH utility is an executable program that is located in the $AD_TOP/bin directory.

Before trying to merge patches together, read all README files carefully. Some README files contain special instructions that may impact your ability to merge patches or the process by which you apply the merged patches. Also read the README files carefully to make sure that no patch that you are trying to merge is a prerequisite or postrequisite patch for any other patch in the merge set.

Once you are sure of the patches that you are going to merge, create two directories in your patch file directory structure. One will be a source directory into where all patches to be merged are copied and unzipped; the other directory is a destination directory. There is no requirement for how they are named. When all of the patches that you are going to merge are in the source directory and are unzipped, you are ready to run the utility.

There are two mandatory parameters to use when running AD Merge Patch and one optional parameter. You have to specify the source directory where you have unzipped the patches to be merged; you have to specify the destination directory where the new integrated patch will be placed. Optionally, you can give ADMRGPCH the name of the merged patch. If you choose to not pass in the optional parameter, AD Merge Patch will give the drivers the following default names:

- C drivers will be called cmerged.drv if no other name is given.
- D drivers will be called dmerged.drv if no other name is given.
- G drivers will be called gmerged.drv if no other name is given.

From the command line of the sourced environment, AD Merge Patch is invoked as follows:

```
Admrgpch <source unzip directory> <target merged
directory> <optional merged name>
```

AD Merge Patch looks in the source directory, finds every C driver, D driver, and G driver for each patch, and merges them into one of each driver into the destination directory. It then copies all of the files referenced in all of the patches into a consolidated set of files, ready to be copied, uploaded, and generated by the consolidated drivers. If the utility finds any files that are named the same and are in more than one of the individual file's directories, it determines the file with the highest revision number and copies this version into the destination directory structure.

Be sure to carefully check the log file admrgpch.log that is located in the directory from where you invoked ADMRGPCH. Any errors generated from the merge procedure should be examined before running ADPATCH to apply the new patch. Error can occur if trying to merge patches from different releases, patches of different parallel modes, or from different platforms. You can merge a generic patch with a platform specific patch and a U.S. language specific patch with patches of other language translations or patches with different source character sets. AD Merge Patch will notify you if there are incompatibilities between patches you are attempting to merge.

## AD ADMINISTRATION

AD Administration (ADADMIN) is the utility that you will probably spend most of your time with. It is through ADADMIN that you maintain the majority of your Applications database objects and many of its Apps Server objects. Ensuring the smooth running of an Oracle Applications system requires the use and understanding of ADADMIN. It can be run in interactive mode, where you supply answers to its requests by either accepting its defaults or supplying it values of your own; it can run certain tasks in noninteractive mode, as well. Noninteractive mode is particularly useful for running routine tasks that require no administrator intervention on a schedule.

AD Administration writes a session level log file to enable you to track any errors occurring during your session. The log file has the default name of ADADMIN.log and is located in %APPL_TOP%\admin\<SID>\log, however I follow a more descriptive log file naming convention. If you take the default, ADADMIN.log, you will append every AD Administration session's files to the end of the existing file. This file can quickly grow quite large and unwieldy to work with and search. Whenever I have reason to run the ADADMIN utility, I document in the filename, the maintenance that I am planning on performing, what if any patch I am running ADADMIN on behalf of, the date, and the initials of the person running the session. For example, if I have applied patch number 1234567 in the VIS instance and postinstallation steps called for running ADADMIN to regenerate menus and recompile flex fields and I applied it on November 12, 2002 at 1:34 in the afternoon, I would replace the default filename with one similar to the following:

```
Vis_post_1234567_regen-menu_recompile-flex_111202-
1334_ajw.log
```

This way I know that I was the one who ran it, why, when, and in what environment. While it means significantly more typing than simply hitting enter to accept the defaults, if I should happen to need to log an iTAR, the required file is easily located, and all information for the single AD Administration run is contained within a single file (unless ADRELINK is called) and no other runs of ADADMIN will be confused into the analysis of the log.

ADADMIN is broken into two menu-driven sections. Table 8.4 shows the first menu that you are presented with. From here, your options are to maintain database objects or to maintain applications objects.

## NonInteractive Mode

Although the conversion to Multiple Reporting Currencies, MultiOrg, or a different character set as well as the creations of the environment file and the copying of files to different destinations cannot be run in interactive mode, there are many utilities that can. This can be done to simplify maintenance by allowing you to schedule your maintenance during off hours and allow it to run without the need for your intervention.

**Table 8.4    Output from ADRELINK**

```
Usage: adrelink force={y|n} [<optional args>] <targets>
or: adrelink force={y|n} [<optional args>] filelist=<file>
 where <targets> = { <product module> [<product module>]… }
  and     <product module> = "<product> <module name>"
- <product> should be in lower case
- <module name> should exactly match the executable name
Valid <optional args> are:
envfile=adsetenv.sh
Used only by the 'adsetup' script
link_debug={y|n}
Will we link executables with debug or not?  Default is 'n'
backup_mode={none|all|file}
Which executables will we back up when linking with
force=y?
Default is 'file'.  Meanings are:
- none: do not back up any executables
- all : back up all executables
- file: do what $APPL_TOP/admin/adlinkbk.txt says to do
Type 'adrelink examples' to see some examples of running
adrelink.
```

To run in noninteractive mode, you will need to create a defaults file that ADADMIN can read while it is trying to process. This file has to be located in the %APPL_TOP%\admin\<SID> directory, but you can name it as you choose. Again, I would suggest being descriptive. To create the file, you need to run ADADMIN completely through the task that you want to automate, specifying the defaultsfile=<file name> parameter so that it will place all of your answers into the defaults file. The following command would create a defaults file that would compile flex fields in noninteractive mode:

```
$ ADADMIN defaults
file=$APPL_TOP/admin/vis/ADADMIN_compile_flex_
fields_defaults.txt
D:\> ADADMIN defaults
file=%APPL_TOP\admin\vis\ADADMIN_compile_flex_
fields_defaults.txt
```

When you are creating this defaults file, do not simply hit enter, thereby taking the defaults; you should physically answer all questions so that you are sure they are in the file. If ADADMIN runs in noninteractive mode and cannot find one of the answers in its default file, it will abort.

To run ADADMIN in noninteractive mode using the defaults file just created and to run the compilation of flex fields in noninteractive mode, you would run something similar to one of the following commands. Remember to string them all together. Either OS type will wrap the command or string it out on one line. If you hit enter, it will assume that you are finished. Alternatively, use the line continuation character that you have defined in your OS to continue the command on the subsequent lines.

```
$ ADADMIN
defaults file==$APPL_TOP/admin/vis/ADADMIN_compile_
flex_fields_defaults.txt log
file=vis_ADADMIN_copile_flex_fields_non-
interactive_$SOURCED-DATE_ajw.log workers=4
interactive=no
D:\> ADADMIN
defaults file=%APPL_TOP\admin\vis\ADADMIN_compile_
flex_fields_defaults.txt
log file=vis_ADADMIN_copile_flex_fields_non-
interactive_%SOURCED-DATE%_ajw.log workers=4
interactive=no
```

This command will run ADADMIN to compile flex fields using the defaults file, creating a log file containing a date environment variable that you can have set every time the script is run. It calls four workers, if workers are required and runs noninteractively. If the job should fail, you can use the parameter restart=yes to make sure that ADADMIN does not try to ask questions that the defaults file is unable to answer.

It is through ADADMIN that many of the other AD Utilities are called.

## ADRELINK

ADRELINK relinks the Apps executables with product libraries. When a patch's C driver requires executables to be relinked because it made changes to one of the dynamic link libraries (DLLs) (usually FND.dll), it calls ADRELINK to perform.

However, when executables need to be relinked, ADRELINK usually gets run through the ADADMIN interface. Through ADADMIN, you have a menu-driven interface that will prompt how you want to relink and other required parameters. One of the parameters that ADRELINK requires (one for which there is no default) is the force parameter. If you inform ADRELINK that you want to relink executables with force = n, it will check the dates on the executables and the libraries; if any of the libraries are newer than the executable, it will relink. If you choose force = y, the dates will not be checked and all executables and their libraries will be linked regardless of date relationships. Typing adrelink.sh at the command line will provide you with instructions concerning the syntax of ADRELINK utility. Table 8.4 shows a sample output from running this command.

Typing ADRELINK examples at the command line and following the suggestion in the resulting output of the adrelink.sh command gives you the output in Table 8.5.

Again, following the suggestion in the resulting output and typing adrelink examples filelist at the command line, you will see the output resulting much as it is in Table 8.6.

**Table 8.5   Output of Adrelink.sh Examples**

```
adrelink sample command lines:
To relink f60webmx:
   'adrelink force=y "fnd f60webmx"'

To relink f60webmx, FNDLIBR, and GLPPOS:
   'adrelink force=y "fnd f60webmx" "gl GLPPOS" "fnd
FNDLIBR"'

To relink all executables for General Ledger:
   Use the AD Administration Utility, not adrelink

To relink all executables for all products:
   Use the AD Administration Utility, not adrelink

Type 'adrelink examples filelist' for "filelist mode"
information.
```

**Table 8.6   Output of Adrelink Examples Filelist**

```
Information on how to run adrelink in filelist mode:
  If you specify filelist=<file> on the adrelink command
  line, you need to know the following:
  - the format of <file> is:
  <product> <subdirectory> <module name> <complete module
  name>
  with spaces or tabs between the fields.
  - adrelink does not use the <complete module name>
  field.
  - adrelink only relinks modules with
  <subdirectory>=bin.
  adrelink "filelist mode" sample command line:
  To relink programs listed in the file 'tempfile.txt':
  'adrelink force=y filelist=tempfile.txt'
```

ADRELINK creates a log file. Once it is finished relinking, check the log to make sure that there were no errors during its execution. If you are running ADRELINK from any other AD Utility, the log file will be found under the %APPL_TOP%/admin/<SID>/log directory. If you were to run ADRELINK from the command line, the log file would be placed in the $APPL_TOP/admin/log directory. Regardless of where it is located, the name of the file is adrelink.log. It is not a utility for which you specify the name of the log file you want to create. After you look at the log, it can be deleted if you want to save on disk space. If you do not delete or rename this file, it will get appended to every time ADRELINK runs. If you do delete or rename it (to maintain an entire set of patching logs logically together while you are patching), the next ADRELINK session will create a new one with the same name.

ADRELINK, through ADADMIN, will relink nearly all of the executable files in your middle tier's Application setup. It will not, however, relink the AD executables. To relink these, you have to run ADRELINK from the command line. If you are relinking AD executables, it is important that you shut down all of the middle tier services on the server that you are relinking on, otherwise, portions of ADRELINK may fail. Following is the syntax of the command with an actual example following that:

UNIX
```
$ adrelink.sh force=y "ad <ad program name>"
$ adrelink.sh force=y "ad ADADMIN"
```

Windows
```
C:\ sh  adrelink.sh force=y "ad ADADMIN"
```

If you want to relink more than one AD executable, you can run command with a space-separated list of executables:

UNIX
```
$ adrelink.sh force=y "ad ADADMIN"  "ad adctrl"
"ad ADPATCH"
```

Windows
```
C:\ sh  adrelink.sh force=y "ad ADADMIN"  "ad
adctrl"  "ad ADPATCH"
```

If you want to relink all of the AD executables, you can replace the executable with the word ALL. This only applies for the AD executables at the command line, however; you cannot relink the executables in any other product family at the command line passing in the ALL parameter.

UNIX
```
$ adrelink.sh force=y "ad ALL"
```

Windows
```
C:\ sh  adrelink.sh force=y "ad ALL"
```

If you want to make a backup of the AD executable files that you are relinking from the command line, you can use the optional parameter backup_mode. It would be advisable to create a backup in case something goes wrong. This is accomplished by adding the backup_mode keyword along with the backup mode that you want to use. Backup_mode=all backs up all executables with a naming convention similar to what they are before they are backed up. Backup_mode=none means that none of the executables are backed up. Backup_mode = file backs up the product executable that is being relinked to a file named adlinkbk.txt. This is the default; this is what is used if backup mode is not used. The ramifications of using adlinkbk.txt with multiple executables in the list are not clear.

UNIX
```
$ adrelink.sh force=y backup_mode=all  "ad ALL"
```

Windows
```
C:\ sh  adrelink.sh force=y backup_mode=all  "ad
ALL"
```

## ADJAVA

ADJAVA restores several zip files if a patch contains Java files. Usually, you will see messages during the running of a C driver that show that this utility is running. However, you occasionally will have to manually run it if something happens that you cannot explain or as a manual step during a patch. While ADPATCH and ADADMIN usually put any and all error messages into the log file, occasionally a utility (ADJAVA is a good example) will sit for hours apparently doing nothing. It can take a while to run an ADJAVA statement; it is not unusual for one statement to run from 30 minutes to over an hour, especially if the patch you are applying is doing considerable Java related work. If one statement, however, runs for several hours, it could indicate a problem. If you stop whatever is running, copy the statement to the command line, and run it, you can often see what was going on behind the scenes and get a better idea of exactly what part of the statement was causing problems. This is often information that Oracle Support will ask for in an iTAR and being able to provide that information when you open the TAR can expedite the process considerably.

One interesting note to remember is that ADJAVA is a resource hog (either because it is called from ADPATCH or ADADMIN or running directly from the command line). It will consume considerable resources on your box, so when running this utility for extended periods of time, you may see other things waiting or running slowly. It is nothing to become unduly alarmed about.

## FNDLOAD AND FNDSLOAD

FNDLOAD, also known as Oracle Applications Generic Loader, is a generic loader used to populate a variety of table types. FNDSLOAD is another utility used to load functions, forms, and menus. They are Concurrent Programs that can move data between text file representations of data and the tables within the database after reading a configuration file to determine what data to process.

Typically this utility is used by ADPATCH to load information into the patch database tables to maintain that information simply. However, it will also download data from database tables into text files that will allow you to read and manipulate that data outside of the database structure. FNDLOAD reads a configuration file (extension.lct) and, based on the information in that configuration file, extracts the data into a flat text data file with a .ldt extension. This information can be acted upon by an end user (pulled up into an Excel spreadsheet for charted reporting, for example) or loaded into another database using the same utility.

The generic loader has two modes — download and upload — and each support referential integrity ideas of master–detail constraints and foreign key constraints. The file resulting from a download session is structured data that meets the criteria set forth in the configuration file. This file is easily readable and interpretable and can be used later to upload through the same utility. If you are not dealing with prepackaged information supplied by Oracle through a patch set, care must be taken on an upload session. The configuration file will contain information needed to determine if a row that does not exist in the data file, but does exist in the database, should be retained or deleted. If a row does not exist in the database for information that is contained in the datafile, a new row is inserted into the database. The Owner and Last Update Date attributes of the existing records are examined and, based on a set of rules contained within both the configuration file and the code for the FNDLOAD program, the ultimate outcome of a row that is to be updated is determined. Owner = CUSTOM rows in the database are never overwritten with an Owner = SEED row found in the datafile. Owner = Seed values are always updated if a corresponding Owner = Custom value is found in the datafile. If the Owner in the database and the Owner in the file are the same, the value of the row is updated only if the Last Update Date of the row in the datafile is newer than the Last Update Date of the row in the database.

The configuration file describes not only the data but also the access method to be used in the handling of that data. Much like SQL*Loader, the configuration file is necessary for the correct interpretation of the data, but unlike SQL*Loader, the same configuration file can be used to allow data to be either uploaded or downloaded.

The Concurrent Program's name is FNDLOAD and the command to the executable takes the following format (description is in Table 8.7):

```
FNDLOAD apps/pwd 0 Y mode configfile datafile entity
[ param... ]
```

To download data from the FND_APPLICATION_TL table where the APPSNAME = FND based on the criteria in the myconfiguration.cfg configuration file into the myout.dat output datafile from the VIS data-

**Table 8.7    FNDLOAD Parameters**

| Parameter | Description |
|---|---|
| Apps/pwd | This is the Apps userID and the value of the password in your environment. The database to which it connects is taken either from the SID value or from the TWO_TASK value if it is not passed in in the form apps/apps@vis. |
| 0 Y | These are Concurrent Program flags. |
| Mode | The mode you are running the loader in: download or upload. Results of the run are determined by this parameter; care should be taken if you do not want to inadvertently overwrite values in the database. |
| Configfile | Name of the configuration file to be used by loader. Include extension (most typically .lct, although that is not enforced nor supplied as a default by the program). |
| Datafile | Datafile to write. Will be overwritten if it already exists. Typically given an extension of .ldt, although it is not enforced or supplied by the program. |
| Entities | Entities to either upload or download. If uploading, ALL is typically what you want to do, so specify a "-" in this position. |
| Param | Additional optional parameters that can be passed to the program. Format for the optional parameters should be in the NAME = <value> format with the value not conflicting with an existing attribute name in the command string. |

base connected as apps with the default password of apps, use the following command:

```
FNDLOAD apps/apps@vis 0 Y DOWNLOAD
myconfiguration.cfg myout.dat FND_APPLICATION_
TL APPSNAME=FND
```

To upload the same information into the same place, use the following command:

```
FNDLOAD apps/apps@vis 0 Y UPLOAD
myconfiguration.cfg myout.dat -
```

The format of the configuration file is in the form of:

```
DEFINE block
DOWNLOAD block
UPLOAD Block
```

Define block provides the structure of the datafile's data records. Download block contains the SQL statement that determines which rows qualify for download. Valid SQL statements, including those that contain joins for clarity and resolution, are supported in this block. The Upload block contains a SQL statement or a PL/SQL anonymous block that accepts data from a file and applies that data to the database tables. Identical statements are executed for every row that is in the input data file.

More detail and extended examples are available in Appendix C of the *System Administrator's Guide* available from your CD pack or for download from Oracle Tech Net (http://otn.oracle.com).

## Security Key Generation

Oracle Apps makes use of SSL technology and requires an encryption/decryption key on the system. This key needs to be created for secure connections to the system. The system verifies that it has its key by checking to see if the identitydb.obj file is located in the default location. When the key is present, it looks in the $HOME directory of the person who owns the application, usually appsmgr or similar, and in the directory of anyone defined to the system as a local administrator who logs in as themselves to the system to perform maintenance (run ADPATCH, run ADADMIN, and other utilities) for the indetitiydb.obj file.

Running adjkey -1 will allow you to see if you have a key present and accessible. If adjkey -1 is unable to find a key, it will return output similar to that in Table 8.8.

If no key appears to be present, you can recreate the key by running the adjkey initialize command to create it or (if you can find another identitydb.obj file on the current system) you can copy the indetitydb.obj file from another %HOME% to that of the current user.

Trying to create a key when one already exists in the home of the given user will return the Table 8.9 output. In the example the default values were taken. If you have paid for a key from a key provider, you will use the values that you are provided by that company.

If adjkey -initialize is successful, again using the default values provided by the prompt, you will get output similar to that in Table 8.10, which verifies that the file and key were created.

If adjkey -l is successful in finding its key, it will display output similar to Table 8.11.

**Table 8.8   Output if ADJKEY –l Is Unable to Find a Valid Key**

```
D:\visappl>adjkey -l
                        Copyright (c) 1998 Oracle Corporation
                              Redwood Shores, California, USA
                                    AD Java Key Generation
                                          Version 11.5.0
NOTE: You may not use this utility for custom development
unless you have written permission from Oracle Corporation.
Reading product information from file…
Reading language and territory information from file…
Reading language information from applUS.txt…
Scope: sun.security.provider.IdentityDatabase, source
file:C:\vismgr\identitydb.obj
AD Java Key is complete.
```

**Table 8.9   Create a Key When One Is Available**

```
D:\visappl
                    Copyright (c) 1998 Oracle Corporation
                        Redwood Shores, California, USA
                           AD Java Key Generation
                              Version 11.5.0
NOTE: You may not use this utility for custom development
unless you have written permission from Oracle Corpora-
tion.
Reading product information from file…
Reading language and territory information from file…
Reading language information from applUS.txt…
Successfully created javaVersionFile.
AD Java Key will now create a signing entity for you.
Please enter the name of the entity you wish to create
[Customer] :
After creating the signing entity, a certificate will
be created for signing jar files locally.  You can
specify an organization to be used in identifying the
certificate.
Please specify an organization to be assigned to the
certificate
[DEFAULT_ORG] :
Name conflict. Please remove the identity named Customer
before adding a new identity with that name.
java key error:
adjava -mx128m sun.security.provider.Main -cs Customer
true
The above Java program failed with error code 1.
See the java key log file and/or the program log file
for details.
Failed to initialize customer signature environment.
```

**Table 8.10　Creation of Security Key**

```
D:\visappl
                    Copyright (c) 1998 Oracle Corporation
                          Redwood Shores, California, USA
                                 AD Java Key Generation
                                       Version 11.5.0
NOTE: You may not use this utility for custom development
unless you have written permission from Oracle Corpora-
tion.
Reading product information from file…
Reading language and territory information from file…
Reading language information from applUS.txt…
Successfully created javaVersionFile.
AD Java Key will now create a signing entity for you.
Please enter the name of the entity you wish to create
[Customer] :
After creating the signing entity, a certificate will
be created for signing jar files locally.  You can
specify an organization to be used in identifying the
certificate.
Please specify an organization to be assigned to the
certificate
[DEFAULT_ORG] :
Created identity [Signer]Customer
[identitydb.obj][trusted]
Generated DSA keys for Customer (strength: 512).
Generated certificate from directive file
D:\visappl\admin\out\adcert.txt.
Your digital signature has been created successfully and
imported into the javakey identity database. This sig-
nature will now be used to sign Applications JAR files
whenever they are patched.
IMPORTANT: If you have multiple web servers, you must copy
files to each of the remaining web servers on your site.
See the documentation reference for more information.
java key is complete.
```

**Table 8.11  Adjkey –l Successfully Finding Key**

```
D:\visappl>adjkey -l
                    Copyright (c) 1998 Oracle Corporation
                       Redwood Shores, California, USA
                             AD Java Key Generation
                                     Version 11.5.0
NOTE: You may not use this utility for custom development
unless you have written permission from Oracle Corpora-
tion.
Reading product information from file…
Reading language and territory information from file…
Reading language information from applUS.txt…
Scope: sun.security.provider.IdentityDatabase, source
file:C:\vismgr\identitydb.obj
eitb[identitydb.obj][trusted]
AD Java Key is complete.
```

# 9

---

# INSTALLATION AND MIGRATION

I have heard that being an Apps DBA is something like trying to herd cats. If that analogy holds, and I believe that it does, then installing and implementing Oracle E-Business Suite is something like having a cattle drive for cats. But it is a cattle drive with a whole new and unusual set of rules.

You start on New Year's Day in Los Angeles with 20 catnip plants. You have to turn the catnip plants into 3 identical herds of 160 cats each and get each of these herds into 3 small cardboard boxes in downtown New York City by June 1. The cats have to be healthy, happy, well-groomed, and well-fed when you get them into the box. The only tools you have to get these cats to the correct box are a ball of string and a Saint Bernard. There are huge fields of rabbits along the way to entice the dog away, but he always comes back. There are mice to entice away the cats. There are other cats to entice away the cats. There are other dogs that will chase away the cats. Your cats will get sick along the way. If one gets sick, there are occasional veterinary clinics that will either try to help you get your cats back on the road to health or tell you that you have to kill a third of your cats. If you kill a third of the cats, you have to go back to Los Angeles get more plants to turn into one herd of cats, get back to where you were, and hope that nothing happens to the other two herds of cats while you are away. And you do not get any extra time to go back, even though it was out of your control. If either of your other two herds of cats has been injured or gotten sick while you were away, you have to take care of them before you can go forward; you may have to kill them and go back to Los Angeles again for still more cats. Up until December 29, you had only heard that something called a cat exists somewhere, but you had never seen one. But because you have dealt with hamsters before, everyone has the utmost confidence that you can get these cats across country in six months and into the box at the end—healthy, happy, and well-groomed.

# METHODOLOGY

## AIM

Oracle espouses AIM (Applications Implementation Methodology) for determining what your needs (your company's needs) are for implementation. AIM is Oracle Consulting program's chosen methodology for getting a client from what they currently have to Oracle Apps. It is based on a predefined and extensively used set of tasks that range from mapping of business processes to postproduction support.

The first step in the methodology is the Business Requirements Mapping step, which looks at the business as it currently is and evaluates how those processes can be adapted and improved by the Oracle E-Business Suite installation. It includes full impact analysis of the new system on the current business process. Gap analysis follows Business Process Mapping. Gap analysis is the process that allows the consultants to help the company determine what parts of the business needs that an out-of-the-box uncustomized implementation would not meet. This step is important because customizing is an ongoing costly endeavor and one that most companies want to avoid if at all possible. This analysis ties closely in with GAAP (generally accepted accounting principles) analysis that allows the consultants to assist with configuring the end product, which allows the implementing company to maintain current accounting practices and not be forced to change how they account for their financial information.

The next analysis phase is Data Conversion and Migration. This analysis determines the mapping of current data (from external sources, legacy data, and other feeds) from sources external to the Oracle E-Business Suite product. It includes the mapping of the existing data into known fields in Applications' tables. Finally, during the information gathering and analysis phase it goes through Report specifications and design. This portion of the analysis looks at existing reports and default reports in the new system and finds what is missing in the existing reports that is not in the default reports but is needed to maintain the business functionality. The result of this analysis is company specific customizations required by the business rules.

Now that the analysis phase is done, you are faced with Application setup and configuration. This could be done in parallel with the analysis phase; however, this is not usually the case. This is often the first place that involves technical personnel in the AIM process. Following the installation and configuration (which includes inputting of the client specific data and customized flex field data) is the testing of the system, planning for the ultimate cutover from the current system to the new Oracle E-Business Suite, and end user training.

Go live, you are now on the new system in production and are no longer using the legacy system.

Postproduction support is the final step in the AIM implementation methodology. This portion can be the shortest of all of the steps thus far and is likely to be the place where you will need the greatest help. Much of the help at this point is left to Oracle Support and Metalink.

This is not only the method that is used by Oracle Consulting, it is also the method that is used by the majority of consulting companies that many people use to implement and install Financials. Oracle Consulting can usually plan relatively well how long each step will take, indicate where there can be overlap, and ensure that there is immediate response to problems that arise in the process. Mixed results may be gotten from independent consulting companies. Client companies, those hiring the consulting companies, may not know the ramifications for some of the cost- and time-cutting measures that may show up in a potential contract. I recommend you try to get more than one week postinstallation support; one week is cutting it a little thin. The learning curve for everyone involved with the new system is steep; this is particularly true for a complete paradigm shift over that of a simple (though highly complex) upgrade.

## Discovery Approach

While the AIM methodology is the currently stressed, full implementation process, it is not the only one that is being used or supported. Herald & Associates, Inc. has come up with a different methodology that can be used in the implementation process. Their end-to-end approach is called the Discovery approach. This approach is a philosophy change. Mike Herald, founder of Herald & Associates, recently presented his paradigm change to a gathering of Oracle professionals and it was met with great interest in the new process and questions as well.

What is the Discovery approach? Discovery allows companies to model their critical business processes using the preconfigured Vision database that ships with every set of implementation CDs. Herald suggests that under the Discovery approach, companies can use the software to discover their business needs and at the same time create a knowledge base and an expertise in the software. All the while, maintaining their knowledge of their business processes. They take their existing knowledge of how they do their job currently into the Discovery process into the new software product. While they maintain their current way of doing business, they are investigating the new interfaces, the new processes, and the new reports.

The Discovery approach does not provide the 125 or more deliverables that are often accumulated with other implementation approaches that are a road map of where the team has been in its journey through the process. But the documents that are part of the process in the Discovery approach are living documents that provide ongoing value to the organization. These living documents can also show you where you have been, but they are created primarily by your company and show your learning process. They include business processes and system flows, test scripts, meeting agendas and minutes, and a log of every issue and its resolution discovered in the process. The test scripts and issues log will follow your implementation and will be used and reused in clones and patching processes that will follow you through your experiences with the Oracle E-Business Suite product as well as through your experiences with all of its iterations.

The Discovery approach is entirely software-centric. You learn what a powerful tool it is, what a deep set of seeded reports can be found in its libraries, and what more you can bring to your company if you think outside of the current box. This means you can severely limit scope creep because those involved in the process will learn where reports are that meet and exceed their current expectations and will discover where the true gaps are that will have to be fixed. It also provides the venue that will allow the user base to build an Oracle 11i knowledge base while determining what if anything is lacking in the interface.

So what is the Discovery approach? As you can see in Figure 9.1, it is a mix of technical as well as functional tasks that run in parallel and end with a larger core team that has a better idea of what they are dealing with.

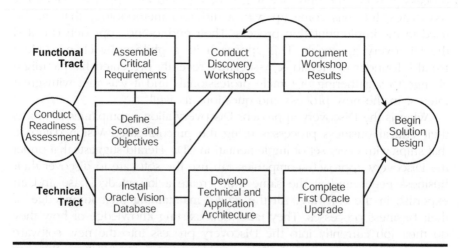

**Figure 9.1　The Discovery Approach**

### Readiness Assessment

The Readiness Assessment phase includes evaluating the business needs and the business readiness for the project as well as determining all of the critical business drivers for implementing 11i. It looks at evaluating the technical needs and readiness and reviews what is currently in place and how that will play into the end implementation. It takes a realistic look at customizations, interfaces, and any custom reporting that currently occurs in the enterprise. Finally, it sets realistic expectations for project timelines and project budget.

### Define Scope, Objectives, and Plan

The Discovery approach next defines the scope based on all desired business benefits and develops a plan for effective communications and a project plan that includes realistic end dates. The end outcome for this phase should be a guide, complete with measurable objectives for all project activities and decisions. It must include input from the project sponsor and the steering committee and define the vehicle for communication and status reporting to the group on all aspects of the project. There needs to be a process for reviewing and approving documents (including the document that is the outcome of this phase) and a process for handling not only issues that arise, but for analyzing the testing strategies and the outcome of those tests. The steering committee needs to help define the approval chain for all customizations that come out of the process and assist in the identifying of milestones for status reporting and to keep to the projected end date.

### Assemble Critical Requirements

In this phase, you will want to concentrate on what differentiates this company from other companies, what processes are mission critical to this company, and the business benefits that will come from implementing 11i. These business flows should be kept high level. Keeping them high level will help alleviate the analysis paralysis that can come with spending too much time trying to determine exactly how everyone does everything that they do, regardless of the ultimate impact to the business. From this phase, you will derive the basic plan on how to proceed through the Discovery workshops.

### Conduct Discovery Workshops

A Discovery workshop is an exploration into the functionality of 11i. Through these workshops, your team discovers the 11i opportunities. The team will gain hands-on experience and will be able to start visualizing the business opportunities that can be gained. This will be the start of building your core team's knowledge base in 11i. In preparation for this Discovery workshop, you (the Apps DBA) will have gotten your first taste of an Apps installation. This installation will be kept current and will be periodically refreshed as a part of the workshop process. This is, primarily, where your part of the process and your learning begins. Here you will learn to apply patches and mega patches in an effort to make sure that the instance is stable and you will learn how your future responsibilities will take shape. From here, you and the development side of the team will start to draft suggestions on future technical architecture and gather reports that the functional team finally decides are not present and that they cannot live without. Now (not a year after Go Live) is the time to start to define an instance management strategy, a change management strategy, and a plan for acquiring components that will become critical to your environment.

This is also the time when you will learn how to manage the process of upgrades, archiving, and purging data; where you will learn tricks of the trade and tune and refine the process. Working through this process several times allows you to learn all you can before it becomes critical that you are able to do it all in the minimal downtime. You do not have to be in this alone. There are companies (Herald & Associates is one) that will help you through the process. Remember that if you contract any part of the process out, you are the customer. Do not feel that you have to blindly bow to every decision or suggestion that a contracting company makes. They should be in the process for your best interest because a happy customer is the best kind of advertising.

## INSTALLATION

Companies choose many different installation paths, many different types of configurations, and many different sets of OSs. You can tailor how you install to meet with the other company standards on OSs for the different kinds of pieces. If all of your company's databases are on a UNIX system, you can follow that. If your company has standardized on all Linux servers, you can follow that standard. If all Web servers are on a Windows platform, you can follow that as well.

Regardless of what configuration you choose, you need to check the certification section on Metalink or check with Metalink's technical people to make sure that you have been sold a valid, implementable configuration that is actually supported. Checking with Metalink's certification section allows you to make sure that you have a certified combination of Oracle E-Business Suite release housed on a supported OS. Do not assume that just because it is being packaged by sales that it is certified or supported. Creating an unsupported or impossible to configure and implement configuration is not done maliciously or often, but it does happen. Sales departments do not always talk to the technical side to find out if what the customer wants (and therefore what they are going to be sold) is even possible. Even in small companies, sales people do not always talk to implementation team members. This happens all too frequently. In a company the size of Oracle, it is bound to happen on occasion. But do you want to be the hapless company that it happens to? A little legwork before you sign with either Oracle Sales or a contracting company (if you are bringing one in to help with your implementation), could save you time, money, and grief.

Do not just take the word of a company that wants your implementation business either. If you are looking to contract a company to assist in your implementation, do not just ask them if what you are planning on buying (or what you bought) can be done. Ask if it has been done. Ask if the team you are going to be working with has ever done it. Ask if it was successful and if they can give you a reference of someone for whom they were able to successfully implement this particular configuration.

Go to the listservs. Ask questions of the people who spend their days in the apps trenches. Has any of you ever done this? Did you have any problems that you can attribute directly to the choice to implement this way? Would you suggest this implementation track to other people thinking about implementing?

Do searches on the Internet. Google is a great resource. Oracle, Apps-Net, and TechNet are also very good places to search for information. There are case studies and white papers of other companies, their successes and their failures. See if you can get ideas of what worked, problems you may encounter, or better ways that may work for your company. TechNet (http://otn.oracle.com) and AppsNet (http://www.ora-cle.com/appsnet) are great places to look; naturally they tend to be slanted toward things that make Oracle look good, but they will show you what works.

Look at the documentation. Documentation will not tell you what cannot be done or what is not certified. It may not tell you if what you are looking at can be done as sold. It will tell you how to install and implement the different pieces on different OSs.

It is often a case of the buyer beware, but if you do this legwork up front, you will be surprised at how much easier your life will be through the implementation and beyond. Not only will it make things go smoother if you have information at hand before you start, it will likely mean that everyone is happier with the process and with the end result. And again, it is not likely that anything that might have been done was in any way deliberately malicious. They believe that you know what you want, so they know what you want. They are going to do their best to give you what you ask for. Couple the desire to provide what you want with the faith that they are selling a flexible product that can meet the overall needs of any companies that implement and you can understand how they can believe that they can bring you exactly what you say you want for your company.

An Oracle E-Business Suite installation uses a utility called Rapid Install (or RapidWiz). RapidWiz is an installation wizard that walks you through the installation and prompts you for ports, directory structures, server names, and other instance implementation-specific information. Once it has finished helping you to gather all of your pertinent information, it runs the installation of the technology stack, the Apps file system, the database, the HTTP server, and other associated services. It also configures your server and services on the apps tier and configures the preseeded database. Oracle suggests that RapidWiz can accomplish all of this in just about an hour. I suggest that you plan on at least twice that amount of time for each instance depending on how many opportunities arise during the installation process. Even if there are no problems anywhere along the installation process, laying down 45 GB in files and getting several services configured in 60 minutes is difficult at best.

You can choose any one of three different hardware configurations: single node, two node, or multi-node installation.

Single node installation is one where the database, Concurrent Managers, application layer, and all Web and Forms and Reports services are installed on one physical server. While this is a viable implementation solution, it is most often used in smaller installations and for demonstration purposes and is most often installed on a UNIX or Linux server for simplicity and stability.

A two node installation spreads the components over two physical servers. Typically one server houses the database, Concurrent Managers, and Reports Server, while the other houses the application layer and all Web and Forms services.

A multi-node installation distributes all pieces across more than one physical server. This configuration allows for the most scalability and flexibility. You can choose the number of physical servers over which to distribute the processes and decide which pieces, if any, to house together on the same servers.

To further complicate your decision making process, you will also need to decide how many instances of the application you want to maintain. Minimally, two is suggested: one to apply patches, do any auxiliary development, test upgrades, and do general maintenance before you do it all to production and the other for production. Many sites maintain three fully operational instances. One instance is the Vision Demo environment for training purposes for the initial go live. This can later become the Development environment. Another instance is maintained to provide a copy of production where changes to reports and customizations can be tested and where patches can be applied to determine their impact on the production environment ahead of time. This allows you to minimize production downtime and know ahead of time what problems you may run across and other patches that the application of the main patch may have spawned. The final instance, regardless of what else you have in your implementation, will be your Production environment.

It is not unusual to have four independent environments: Vision Demo (or development), Test, Production, and one for the administrators to perform upgrades and apply patches on to limit the impact of what they are doing on other users. This environment allows them to encounter any major difficulties with patches without having to impact developers and other testing users' day-to-day working and get issues resolved before moving to the other environments. This allows Test to be the environment where functional testing is done and frees the resources to proceed with normal programming move-ups during the time that administrators are working through issue resolution in upgrades and major patch installation.

What exactly are you going to be installing for each environment you choose to maintain? RapidWiz (as late as Version 11.5.8) installs a working 8i database (Enterprise Edition, Version 8.1.7) in nonarchive log mode, complete with the initialization parameters required to allow apps to perform at its preconfigured functional level. Depending on which version you install with, you may have to upgrade to the terminal patch set for 8i (8.1.7.4). It installs an 8.0.6 Oracle Home and 9iAS, Version 1.0.2.2.2 that includes the Apache Web server. JInitiator is placed for download access to the PC clients. Oracle Developer Suite 6*i* is installed and with it comes Oracle Forms, Oracle Reports, and Oracle Graphics. Further, you will install Oracle Java Server Pages (OJSP), Oracle client libraries and support files, and Oracle's Java Database Connector (JDBC). Once it is all installed, RapidWiz configures Apache to run with your specifications. It configures all listeners on the Web server node. Forms, Reports, and Graphics Servers are configured, Concurrent Managers are configured, and all are started. RapidWiz then creates the environment files, startup and shutdown scripts for all services and for the database, and creates the database connection files that allow it to all work together seamlessly.

## INSTALLATION RESOURCES

Installing Oracle E-Business Suite is a resource intensive endeavor. Oracle has suggested minimums for things like disk space, temp space, memory, and spare disk space for staging the CDs. These minimums differ depending on OSs and can be found in the installation manual for the version and OSs that you are installing. Plan high. It is easier to live with a little too much space and knowing you have room to grow than too little space and having to allocate or buy more to proceed. You will need approximately 15 GB in a staging area; this should be enough to copy over the contents of the CDs required for the installation. However, if you are doing a multi-node installation and you have different OSs on different nodes, you will need this amount on each OS for that OS's respective sets of files. If you cannot map a drive from one server to another or if you cannot NFS mount a staging directory from one server to another within the same OS set, you will need 15 GB on every server to use for staging.

Oracle suggests at least 650 MB available in a temp directory. I have never been able to get an installation to be happy with just this minimum requirement. Having 1 GB free in whatever directory you are using for temp space would allow you to err on the safe side.

The database that is installed with RapidWiz can be installed in 25 to 30 GB of space, but this is the bare bones database; allocating 40 to 50 GB to the directory structure where these database files will reside would not be overallocating, especially if you are implementing a significant number of modules. Allocating 1.5 to 2 times the recommended minimum, in this case, will give you room to get all of the data required into the system, migrate your data from whatever system you are moving from, and should give you some slack for the first year or so.

Another 15 GB should be allocated for each set of "Oracle Homes," Apps layers, and 9iAS that you will be maintaining (these will end up distributed between <sid>ora, <sid>appl, and <sid>comn and depending on how many servers you have involved in your installation, can be distributed over several physical boxes as well).

These are the suggested sizes that Oracle includes in its manuals, adjusted somewhat for growth and for what really might occur. What usually is not included in planning documentation, and therefore is not included in many companies' planning, is the amount of extra space that you will need. You will need to allocate, on whatever physical server your Concurrent Managers will reside, space to maintain a certain period's worth of logs and out files for Concurrent Manager runs (i.e., the reports that are generated from the Concurrent Manager jobs and the errors that are generated when one of the Concurrent jobs fails).

While you are planning the space for your implementation, plan for space that you will need in the near future for your patching requirements as well. Even if you install the latest major release of Oracle E-Business Suite, you will have to apply patches. The farther from the release date, the more patches you are apt to have to install to bring you up to the most current releases of all minipacks. Patches come zipped. You need to have enough space in a patch directory for the downloaded patches in their zipped form as well as their unzipped form. Having 20 or 30 GB available for just this purpose would not be extreme overallocation for this patch-staging directory. Sound like a lot? The 11.5.8 upgrade patch downloads with a size of 1.5 GB and unzips to over 7 GB. That is one patch. While most patches are not this big, being able to accommodate one that is without having to worry about having sufficient disk space will make your life easier in the not too distant future. It is not uncommon to have to patch a fresh installation before it is fully functional. You may have to patch it several times before you get your implementation to go live. Even reading through the installation documentation, you usually uncover the need to install help patches, Self-Service Framework patches, other minor fix patches, and newly released minipacks that have to be applied even on top of the new fresh installation.

Planning for the Apps database is much like planning for any other database. You will need space for archive logs for your production database, space for online backups, and space for other custom scripts and files that you use for tuning and administering the database.

## Getting Ready

### *Stage the CDs*

It does not matter what OS you are using — one on which you can easily change out the CDs or one where changing means unmounting and remounting — you will want to stage the CDs locally on the computer. Either dedicate a permanent directory to the CDs (you could reuse the space later for patches) or put them in a temporary directory where you have enough disk space or whatever your company policy is for this kind of thing. When you need anywhere from 8 to 14 CDs staged for a typical installation, the disk space is significant. Disk to disk access is faster throughput than CD to disk and you will not have to change out the CDs several times during the installation (this could free you up to run the installation from somewhere besides the terminal attached to the server).

Having them staged in one central location will help with multiple installations, too. You can NFS mount the directory on UNIX or map a drive on Windows. If you are installing three or four environments, staging the CDs once will save space and create a central patching directory for all environments, too.

The staging directory structure is most easily understood and maintained if it is laid out with some thought and planning.

- *Oracle 8i:* This one is used for the required Oracle files on the Apps tier server. You can name the uppermost directory for this set of CDs something logical like `ora8`.

```
                        Disk_1
Ora8-<
                        Disk_2
```

- *Tools:* This is where you will stage the CDs containing the Apache server installation. This has to be on the tier with your application files.

```
                        Disk_1
Tools-<
                        Disk_2
```

- *Appl_top:* This directory is where you will put the CDs for the apps pieces, including the Concurrent Manager installation, so this directory and staged CDs need to be on all of your platforms.

```
                        Disk_1
Appl_top-<
                        Disk_2
```

- *Database:* This directory will stage the CDs that install the database binaries as well as the database data files that make up the preseeded database. This only has to be on the database tier.

```
                        Disk_1
Appsdb<
                        Disk_2
```

- *RapidWiz:* This directory stages the infamous red CD, the one that runs RapidWiz, which on the database tier, runs runInstaller. This CD must be staged on every platform as it is the means by which all pieces of your installation will run.

```
RedCD - Disk_1
```

### Make Sure You Have All of the Other Software Installed

If you are installing on UNIX, you need to make sure that you have JDK and your C⁺⁺ compiler installed on the server. If you are installing on Windows, you need both of these pieces as well as MKS Toolkit. If these are not installed correctly and you do not have the paths to the executables, you will run into problems and end up with an incomplete installation that ends with errors.

### Know What Ports and Server Names You Are Going to Use

"Getting prepared" means planning. You need to plan what ports and server names you are going to use for each instance. If you have a server named Bullwinkle and one named Rocky, you can use port 8000 on both Rocky and Bullwinkle, but not on two different instances on Rocky. It would be better to select entirely different port numbers for each instance, regardless of whether they are located on the same or different servers. This is done for simplicity and security. For instance, if you are going to have four instances — Vis, Dev, Test, and Prod — you will need four different sets of port numbers. You do not just need Listener ports. You need Apache ports, database ports, Forms ports, Reports ports, and others. Each service's port needs to be different from the others on each server and should be different from one installation to the next. You need to determine where you want your database files. Do you want to have all of your files (i.e., control, data, redo, rollback, and index) in the same mount point or directory? How do you want your middle tier files divided up? Will you be putting them all under one major upper level directory or will they be individual directories in the root directory? None of this is really a big undertaking, but it does mean that you need a plan.

### Make Sure That You Have Sufficient Space Allocated for the Base Installation with Room to Grow

The installation takes a lot of planning and a lot of room. The database files need about 40 GB for the base, preseeded database files and enough room to grow for the first several months. You need to lay down the RDBMS binaries in their own Oracle-Home. That will take another 4 to 6 GB, depending on which version of the database you are going to stop with (8.1.7.3 is what most of the installations install, but 9.2.0.# is currently what is supported in most configurations. As of early 2003, Oracle 8i will soon be desupported).

### Keep the Configuration Files

Once you saved the configuration files that RapidWiz created (see Table 9.1), put them in a central location where they are sure to be backed up and where they are safe. Make several copies and keep them with each piece of the installation. Make a copy and keep it in on your local PC; make one on each of several different places on a network file server. Document where you have stored at least a couple of copies of these files. The files are small, but critical. They hold all of the configuration information on your implementation. If for any reason you need to reinstall an identical configuration later, this file will be necessary. When you clone

**Table 9.1  Example Configuration File (Listing 1)**

```
[GENERAL]
CONFIGURED_ENVS=VIS
CONFIGURATION_FORMAT=11.5.0
[VIS]
VIS.DBS_HOST=ws41
VIS.DBS_ORASID=VIS
VIS.DBS_ORASEED=Vision Demo
VIS.DBS_ORANAME=VIS
VIS.DBS_DBCHARSET=WE8ISO8859P1
VIS.DBS_DEFTERR=AMERICA
VIS.DBS_DBPORT=1523
VIS.DBS_PLATFORM=Windows NT
VIS.DBS_APPLTOP=d:\visappl
VIS.DBS_APPLTOP2=d:\visappl
VIS.DBS_APPLTOP3=d:\visappl
VIS.DBS_APPLTOP4=d:\visappl
VIS.DBS_CHARSET=WE8ISO8859P1
VIS.DBS_COMNTOP=d:\viscomn
VIS.DBS_ORA816=d:\visdb\8.1.7
VIS.DBS_ORA806=d:\visora\8.0.6
VIS.DBS_ORAWDB=d:\visora\iAS
VIS.DBS_DBFS1=d:\visdata
VIS.DBS_DBFS2=d:\visdata
VIS.DBS_DBFS3=d:\visdata
VIS.DBS_DBFS4=d:\visdata
VIS.DBS_JAVATOP=d:\viscomn\java
VIS.DBS_PORTALTOP=d:\viscomn\portal
VIS.DBS_JDKTOP=d:\viscomn\util\jre\1.1.8
VIS.DBS_TEMP=d:\viscomn\temp
VIS.DBS_NTUSER=applmgr
VIS.DBS_NTPASS=applmgr
VIS.DBS_DOMAIN=your.company.com
VIS.DBS_MKS=C:\mksnt
VIS.DBS_MSDEV=C:\VC98
VIS.DBS_JDKHOME=C:\java\jdk1.3.1
VIS.DBS_APPL_TOPbase=d:\
VIS.DBS_COMN_TOPbase=d:\
VIS.DBS_ORA_TOPbase=d:\
VIS.DBS_DATA_TOPsys=d:\
VIS.DBS_DATA_TOPlogs=d:\
VIS.DBS_DATA_TOPdata=d:\
VIS.DBS_NTUSERbase=applmgr
VIS.DBS_NTPASSbase=applmgr
VIS.DBS_DOMAINbase=your.company.com
```

*-- continued*

**Table 9.1 (continued) Example Configuration File (Listing 1)**

```
VIS.ADM_HOST=ws41
VIS.ADM_PLATFORM=Windows NT
VIS.ADM_APPLTOP=d:\visappl
VIS.ADM_APPLTOP2=d:\visappl
VIS.ADM_APPLTOP3=d:\visappl
VIS.ADM_APPLTOP4=d:\visappl
VIS.ADM_CHARSET=WE8ISO8859P1
VIS.ADM_COMNTOP=d:\viscomn
VIS.ADM_ORA816=d:\visdb\8.1.7
VIS.ADM_ORA806=d:\visora\8.0.6
VIS.ADM_ORAWDB=d:\visora\iAS
VIS.ADM_DBFS1=d:\visdata
VIS.ADM_DBFS2=d:\visdata
VIS.ADM_DBFS3=d:\visdata
VIS.ADM_DBFS4=d:\visdata
VIS.ADM_JAVATOP=d:\viscomn\java
VIS.ADM_PORTALTOP=d:\viscomn\portal
VIS.ADM_JDKTOP=d:\viscomn\util\jre\1.1.8
VIS.ADM_TEMP=d:\viscomn\temp
VIS.ADM_NTUSER=applmgr
VIS.ADM_NTPASS=applmgr
VIS.ADM_DOMAIN=your.company.com
VIS.ADM_MKS=C:\mksnt
VIS.ADM_MSDEV=C:\VC98
VIS.ADM_JDKHOME=C:\java\jdk1.3.1
VIS.ADM_APPL_TOPbase=d:\
VIS.ADM_COMN_TOPbase=d:\
VIS.ADM_ORA_TOPbase=d:\
VIS.ADM_DATA_TOPsys=d:\
VIS.ADM_DATA_TOPlogs=d:\
VIS.ADM_DATA_TOPdata=d:\
VIS.ADM_NTUSERbase=applmgr
VIS.ADM_NTPASSbase=applmgr
VIS.ADM_DOMAINbase=your.company.com
VIS.CON_HOST=ws41
VIS.CON_RPCPORT=1528
VIS.CON_REPSPORT=7002
VIS.CON_PLATFORM=Windows NT
VIS.CON_APPLTOP=d:\visappl
VIS.CON_APPLTOP2=d:\visappl
VIS.CON_APPLTOP3=d:\visappl
VIS.CON_APPLTOP4=d:\visappl
VIS.CON_CHARSET=WE8ISO8859P1
VIS.CON_COMNTOP=d:\viscomn
```

*-- continued*

**Table 9.1 (continued)  Example Configuration File (Listing 1)**

```
VIS.CON_ORA816=d:\visdb\8.1.7
VIS.CON_ORA806=d:\visora\8.0.6
VIS.CON_ORAWDB=d:\visora\iAS
VIS.CON_DBFS1=d:\visdata
VIS.CON_DBFS2=d:\visdata
VIS.CON_DBFS3=d:\visdata
VIS.CON_DBFS4=d:\visdata
VIS.CON_JAVATOP=d:\viscomn\java
VIS.CON_PORTALTOP=d:\viscomn\portal
VIS.CON_JDKTOP=d:\viscomn\util\jre\1.1.8
VIS.CON_TEMP=d:\viscomn\temp
VIS.CON_NTUSER=applmgr
VIS.CON_NTPASS=applmgr
VIS.CON_DOMAIN=your.company.com
VIS.CON_MKS=C:\mksnt
VIS.CON_MSDEV=C:\VC98
VIS.CON_JDKHOME=C:\java\jdk1.3.1
VIS.CON_APPL_TOPbase=d:\
VIS.CON_COMN_TOPbase=d:\
VIS.CON_ORA_TOPbase=d:\
VIS.CON_DATA_TOPsys=d:\
VIS.CON_DATA_TOPlogs=d:\
VIS.CON_DATA_TOPdata=d:\
VIS.CON_NTUSERbase=applmgr
VIS.CON_NTPASSbase=applmgr
VIS.CON_DOMAINbase=your.company.com
VIS.FRM_HOST=myhost
VIS.FRM_WEBPRT=8002
VIS.FRM_WLSNR=VIS
VIS.FRM_FORMSPRT=9002
VIS.FRM_METDATAPRT=9012
VIS.FRM_METREQPRT=9022
VIS.FRM_PLATFORM=Windows NT
VIS.FRM_APPLTOP=d:\visappl
VIS.FRM_APPLTOP2=d:\visappl
VIS.FRM_APPLTOP3=d:\visappl
VIS.FRM_APPLTOP4=d:\visappl
VIS.FRM_CHARSET=WE8ISO8859P1
VIS.FRM_COMNTOP=d:\viscomn
VIS.FRM_ORA816=d:\visdb\8.1.7
VIS.FRM_ORA806=d:\visora\8.0.6
VIS.FRM_ORAWDB=d:\visora\iAS-
VIS.FRM_DBFS1=d:\visdata
VIS.FRM_DBFS2=d:\visdata
```

*-- continued*

**Table 9.1 (continued) Example Configuration File (Listing 1)**

```
VIS.FRM_DBFS3=d:\visdata
VIS.FRM_DBFS4=d:\visdata
VIS.FRM_JAVATOP=d:\viscomn\java
VIS.FRM_PORTALTOP=d:\viscomn\portal
VIS.FRM_JDKTOP=d:\viscomn\util\jre\1.1.8
VIS.FRM_TEMP=d:\viscomn\temp
VIS.FRM_NTUSER=applmgr
VIS.FRM_NTPASS=applmgr
VIS.FRM_DOMAIN=your.company.com
VIS.FRM_MKS=C:\mksnt
VIS.FRM_MSDEV=C:\VC98
VIS.FRM_JDKHOME=C:\java\jdk1.3.1
VIS.FRM_APPL_TOPbase=d:\
VIS.FRM_COMN_TOPbase=d:\
VIS.FRM_ORA_TOPbase=d:\
VIS.FRM_DATA_TOPsys=d:\
VIS.FRM_DATA_TOPlogs=d:\
VIS.FRM_DATA_TOPdata=d:\
VIS.FRM_NTUSERbase=applmgr
VIS.FRM_NTPASSbase=applmgr
VIS.FRM_DOMAINbase=your.company.com
VIS.WEB_HOST=myhost
VIS.WEB_SERVLETPORT=8882
VIS.WEB_TCFPORT=15002
VIS.WEB_PLATFORM=Windows NT
VIS.WEB_APPLTOP=d:\visappl
VIS.WEB_APPLTOP2=d:\visappl
VIS.WEB_APPLTOP3=d:\visappl
VIS.WEB_APPLTOP4=d:\visappl
VIS.WEB_CHARSET=WE8ISO8859P1
VIS.WEB_COMNTOP=d:\viscomn
VIS.WEB_ORA816=d:\visdb\8.1.7
VIS.WEB_ORA806=d:\visora\8.0.6
VIS.WEB_ORAWDB=d:\visora\iAS
VIS.WEB_DBFS1=d:\visdata
VIS.WEB_DBFS2=d:\visdata
VIS.WEB_DBFS3=d:\visdata
VIS.WEB_DBFS4=d:\visdata
VIS.WEB_JAVATOP=d:\viscomn\java
VIS.WEB_PORTALTOP=d:\viscomn\portal
VIS.WEB_JDKTOP=d:\viscomn\util\jre\1.1.8
VIS.WEB_TEMP=d:\viscomn\temp
VIS.WEB_NTUSER=applmgrVIS.WEB_NTPASS=applmgr
VIS.WEB_DOMAIN=your.company.com
```

*-- continued*

**Table 9.1 (continued)  Example Configuration File (Listing 1)**

```
VIS.WEB_DOMAIN=your.company.com
VIS.WEB_MKS=C:\mksnt
VIS.WEB_MSDEV=C:\VC98
VIS.WEB_JDKHOME=C:\java\jdk1.3.1
VIS.WEB_APPL_TOPbase=d:\
VIS.WEB_COMN_TOPbase=d:\
VIS.WEB_ORA_TOPbase=d:\
VIS.WEB_DATA_TOPsys=d:\
VIS.WEB_DATA_TOPlogs=d:\
VIS.WEB_DATA_TOPdata=d:\
VIS.WEB_NTUSERbase=applmgr
VIS.WEB_NTPASSbase=applmgr
VIS.WEB_DOMAINbase=your.company.com
VIS.BASE_LANG=US - American_English
VIS.ENV_LANGS={US - American_English}
VIS.PRODUCTS={FND} [GENERAL]
```

using adclone, this file is required for the clone to work correctly. If you were not the person who did the initial installation, you will be able to find considerable valuable information about your configuration in this file, information that Oracle Support will often ask for when they are troubleshooting problems.

## Installation

Installation of all pieces of Oracle E-Business Suite is accomplished through the Java-based, menu-driven wizard type process called RapidWiz. Before you run this, you will need to have the users created at the OS that will own the different pieces of the application. These users will need to be part of the DBA group. The group does not need to be named DBA, but there needs to be a group to which all of the DBAs or Apps DBAs and all of the owners of the software pieces belong. Figure 9.2 shows the first screen that you are presented with when you start RapidWiz. From here, you tell the installer whether you are going to be doing a new installation or reconfiguring an installation that you have gone through already. This is the utility through which you also add new products to your license and languages to your implementation. Through this screen you allow the rest of RapidWiz to help walk you through the rest of your installation. It is easier to complete an installation if you have already made some decisions before starting. First, you should decide the names you want to call your instances.

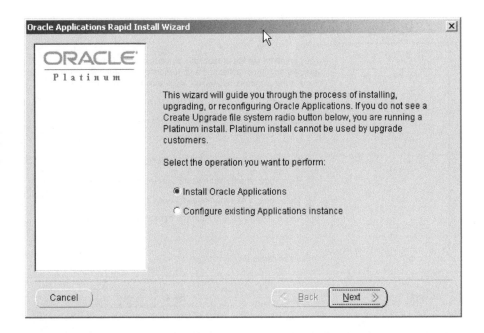

**Figure 9.2    RapidWiz Startup Screen**

Figure 9.3 shows your first decision. Are you going to install all pieces on one server, on two nodes, or on multiple nodes? If you are going to put your Concurrent Managers on the server with your database and all other pieces on a second, separate server, the two node option is the one you will likely choose. It allows for some added flexibility over single node installs, but also allows for central administration for medium to smaller large-scale implementations.

As you can see in Figure 9.4, the two node installation assumes that you are putting your Concurrent Managers on the same server as the database tier. Multi-node installation allows, but does not require, a separate server for each piece of the installation.

Figure 9.5 is the next menu that you will be presented with, regardless of which type of installation you choose. This is where you decide if you are going to install one, two, or three instances with one run of the installer (or at least configure them; you can install them after you have saved the configuration file). You can name the instance anything you want; you are constrained only by the allowable number of characters in a SID name. You can change the name of the instance on this screen and select what kind of installation it is: a fully populated preconfigured installation with the Vision Demo data or the bare bones version that installs with a fresh installed database selection.

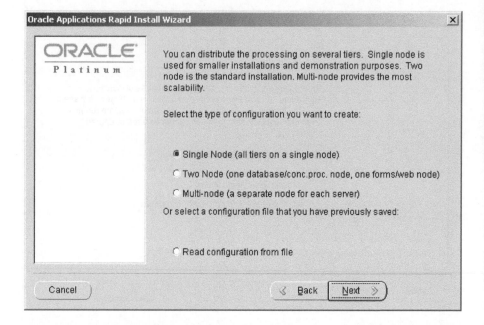

**Figure 9.3 Node Installation Screen**

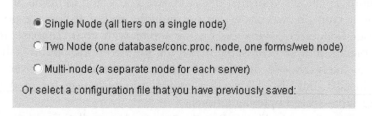

**Figure 9.4 Two Node Concurrent Manager Assumptions**

Figure 9.6 and Figure 9.7 show examples of the screens on which you choose which pieces of Oracle E-Business Suite you are installing that you have licensed. Looking at Figure 9.6, you see where you can opt to use Suite Licensing, where you would choose Projects, for example. RapidWiz would automatically select all of the subobjects under Projects (e.g., Project Costing, Project Billing, Internet Time, etc.) and install and license them all for you.

Using the component applications licensing option gives you the freedom and flexibility to select only Project Costing and Billing if those are what you need, but none of the others under Projects Suite. This adds flexibility in your licensing options, as well. If you select the Prod Detail

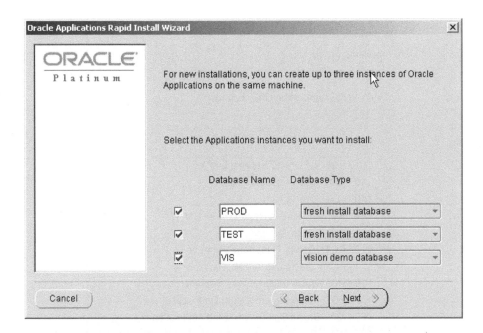

**Figure 9.5   Multiple Concurrent Installations**

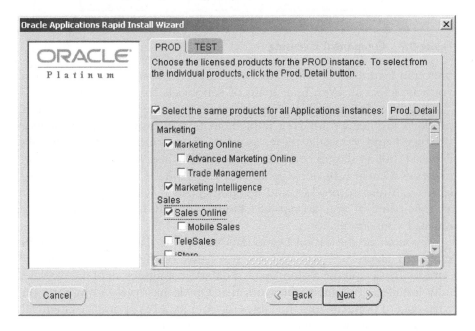

**Figure 9.6   Suite Licensing**

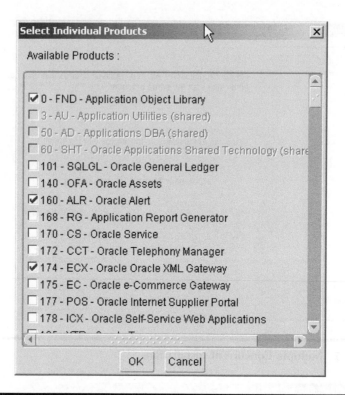

**Figure 9.7 Component Licensing**

button in Figure 9.6, it brings up a screen like the one in Figure 9.7 where you can select an even finer grain of subobjects for installation.

RapidWiz knows what support pieces of other, not fully licensed products are needed for your implementation to provide the information you need and it installs these, as well. They are installed not as fully licensed, but as shared components. RapidWiz also knows what the core pieces of Oracle E-Business Suite are. These pieces should not be unselected as the core product and technology stack will likely not function as anticipated. If you do unselect them, you may have to uninstall and reinstall your installation.

If you chose the Vision Demo database as the database type from the screen in Figure 9.5, you will not see either of the product installation screens. By default the Vision Demo database configures all of the modules fully installed. This limits the work that Oracle has to do in figuring out what data to populate into the tables for you; RapidWiz populates them all.

Figure 9.8 shows country specific functionalities that you may want to install from the initial installation. If you are currently doing business in any of the provided countries and you anticipate the need to provide

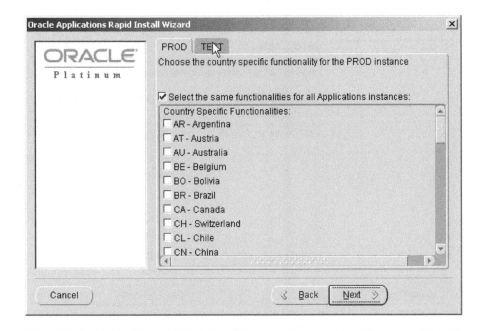

**Figure 9.8   Country Specific Functionality**

specific functionality in those countries' languages or custom features for those countries, it would be easiest to install those functionalities at this point and not have to install them later.

Figure 9.9 shows the next screen, on which you can select the different character sets available and the means by which you can install languages other than the primary American English base language. If you want to be able to present screens to end users in their native language, you will want to install this capability at this point rather than having to go back and add the functionality later. Be careful what character set you install. If you choose US7ASCII, you will be limited in what characters you can store in the database. Even if you intend to use English as your only language, you will likely want to choose a more robust character set, so if you have to change later, it will be less difficult.

Figure 9.10 allows you to alter the database name, SID, character set chosen, and all ports for the given installation. To limit the chance of hacking, Oracle defaults the Web port to 8000. However, anyone who has installed Financials or read much of the publicly available documentation will know this. You can change this port to be more obscure than it already is which makes your installation harder for hackers to compromise. However, it will be easier for you to remember ports if you maintain a port definition scheme. If you change Web port to 8150, you might

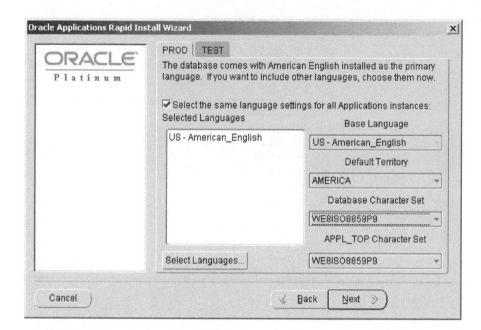

**Figure 9.9  Character Set Choice**

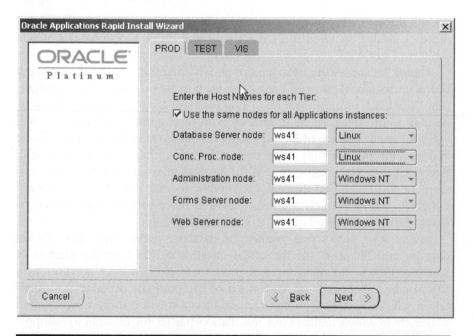

**Figure 9.10  Instance Review Settings**

want to set Forms port to 9150, and Reports port to 7150 for consistency. Further, you may want to change your database port as well. This may be particularly important if you have other Oracle databases configured and they are on port 1521.

Figure 9.11 and Figure 9.12 are examples of some of the configuration choices that you will have to make for an installation. Appl_top, Common_top, Ora_top, Data_top (for the system files, for the log files and many control scripts, for the database connectivity files, and for the database's data files), user ID that will own the application files and database files, that user's password, and the domain of the server in your installation. Your host name, domain name, and ports that you select will all combine together to be the connection string to allow the end users to log on to the application (http://host.domain.name:port).

Figure 9.11 shows an example of a single node installation. The placing of the system data files, redo logs, data and index files are common installation decisions for an apps installation. This is particularly true if the files are on a Raid device that distributes the files across several physical disks and controls the placement of the files at the OS level.

Figure 9.12 shows how you tell the installer where you will find the MKS Toolkit, C++ compiler, and JDK on the server. If these paths are not

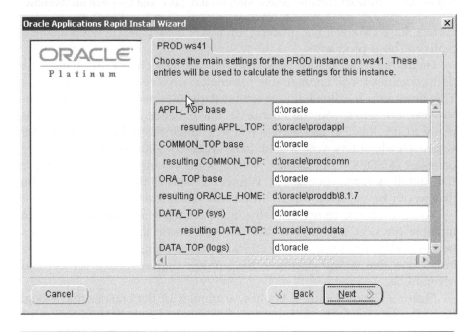

**Figure 9.11   Single Node Installation Directory Decisions**

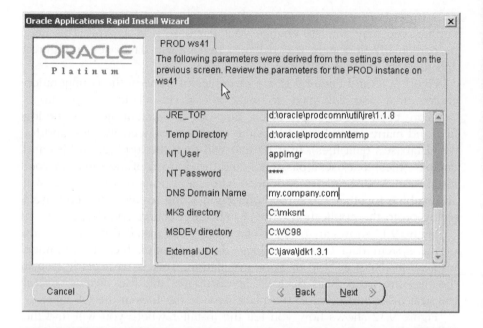

**Figure 9.12    Instruct Installer where MKS Toolkit, Java, and C++ Are on Windows**

correct, RapidWiz will not proceed until you have correctly identified the paths to these products.

Figure 9.13 and Figure 9.14 give you one last chance to change the derived values for all configurable parameters involved in your installation. This gives you the flexibility of letting RapidWiz make certain decisions for you, but gives you the chance to make better decisions when it is ready to be done. It also allows you to change the default locations for where Oracle infers you would have installed MKS Toolkit, your C++ compiler (MSDEV = Microsoft C++ in a Windows installation), and Sun's JDK installation for your server. Figure 9.14 shows the same information that would be gathered for a UNIX/Linux installation.

You can choose to not only divide the database and services between multiple physical servers, but you can also divide the pieces and nodes between different OSs. Figure 9.15 shows an example of a multi-node installation that would distribute the services across several servers and several OSs.

Figure 9.16 and Figure 9.17 show examples of the choices that would be made for directory structures on each server. Figure 9.18 shows what the screen would look like that you would go through to double-check your configuration choices in this multi-middle tier configuration. Double-check these, regardless of what configuration you choose. Make sure that

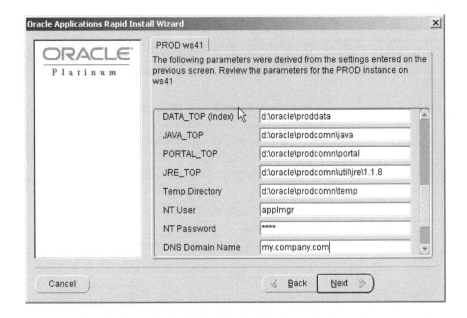

**Figure 9.13    Windows Last Chance to Change**

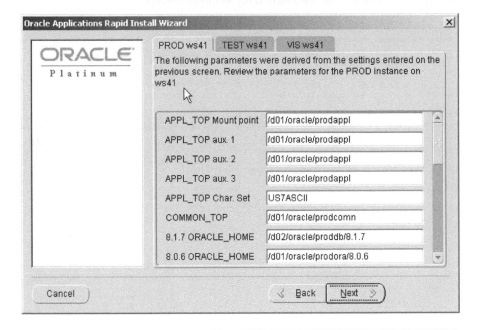

**Figure 9.14    Linux Last Chance to Change**

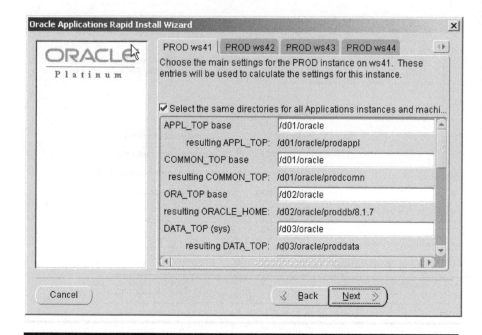

**Figure 9.15   Multi-Node Installation on Multiple Servers**

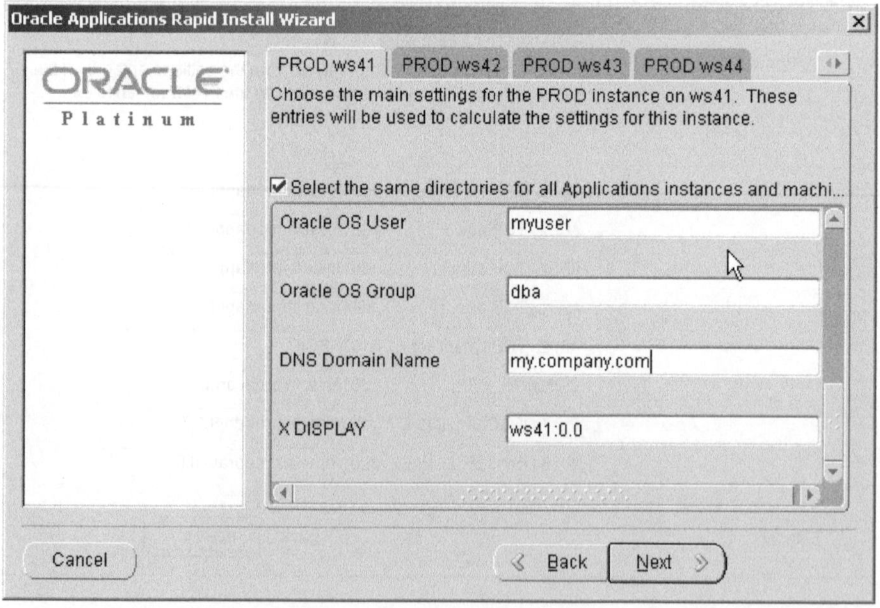

**Figure 9.16   Multi-Node Multi-Server Input Screen 1**

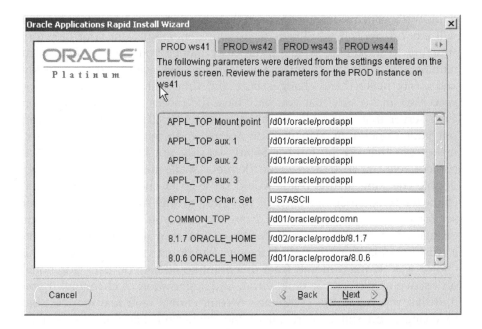

**Figure 9.17   Multi-Node Multi-Server Input Screen 2**

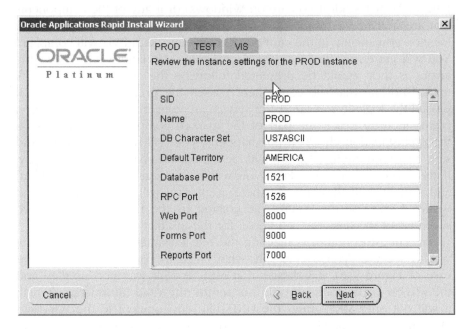

**Figure 9.18   Multi-Node Multi-Server Last Chance to Change**

RapidWiz's conclusions are the ones that you really want. Careful planning will pay off here. If you know what you (generally) want your directory structure to look like, what subdirectory names you want to use, what naming standards you want to (or have to) stick with, you can quickly and easily make those changes here and they will be implemented for you. Also, make sure that you only have the pieces of the installation on each server that you really want on each server. If you have chosen to put your Concurrent Managers on Solaris and your database on Linux, make sure that on the tab for Solaris you do not have any DATA_TOP choices relevant to that machine defined. While this happening is rare, double-checking at this point would be a good choice. Be sure of the character set defined on each of the tabs on this screen. The character set for each piece must match. Now is when you want to make your changes. Now is when it will be the easiest to make changes with the lowest potential impact. Here it means changing a value. Finding out the choice was wrong a month from this point could set you back additional disk space as well as the time, effort, and aggravation of changing. If you find that you made the completely wrong choice, you may not be able to change and still capture all of the characters that your users have chosen to use.

If you have the path wrong to any of the required components (C++, JDK, or MKS Toolkit if you are on Windows) or if any of the components that are specified as required in the Oracle documentation are not in the location you specify in the configuration screens, RapidWiz will complain. You will get errors similar to those in Figure 9.19. Figure 9.19 shows the errors as they would be presented following the checks. Green check marks indicate that the component passed the preinstallation check. It passed the logic test as far as the servers are concerned. Red exclamation points indicate that some part of the marked component failed to pass the preinstallation check. If this happens, you will have to go back and start over with the installation, making the correct changes along the way. If the pieces are not in place, you will have to get them, install them, and start over. If they are not there at all, you will save your time and typing if you use the control file created by the first run; it will have saved all of the answers you chose for the installation.

Selecting the button containing the red exclamation point will allow you to see the details of exactly what failed to pass the check. In the case of Figure 9.20, it indicates that MKS Toolkit was not installed and the which UNIX command did not return any valid information (which it will not until MKS brings the UNIX-like environment to the Windows OS). In the case of Figure 9.21, it indicates that JDK was not found in the location specified and you would either have to install it if it is not installed or fix the path in the configuration screen if it is installed.

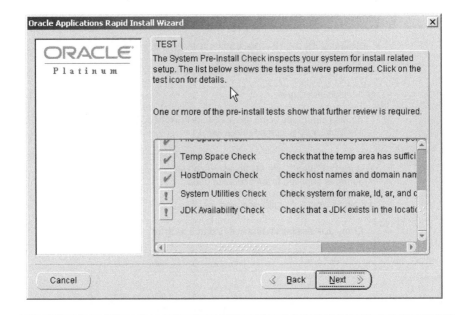

**Figure 9.19  Installation Error Screen**

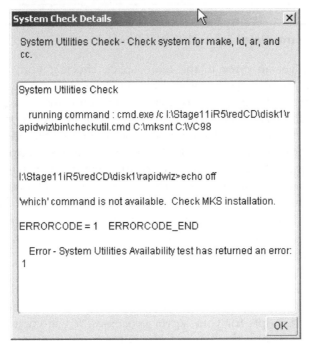

**Figure 9.20  Error Detail Screen MKS Toolkit**

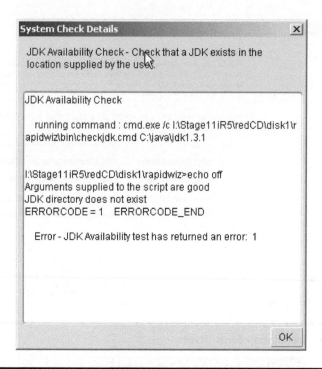

**Figure 9.21   Error Detail Screen JDK Not Found**

You may get an error in the temp space check if you do not have enough free space in your `temp` directory. This may occur even if you have specified a `temp` directory that has the minimum suggested temp space allocated, particularly on a UNIX installation. Occasionally Oracle will decide that the installation will require more than the suggested minimums for temporary files. The extra space can easily approach 2 GB. If you can find a place for it to use for this purpose that has 2 GB free, you should not have any troubles. The following two commands will reset your temporary space to wherever you want to put it that has enough space to let Oracle do everything it needs to do in the installation.

```
$ export TEMP=<Place where you have a bunch of
free space>
$ export  TEMPDIR=<same place as TEMP>
```

One nice thing to remember is this installation will do nearly everything for you on all of your nodes. It will provide you with customized startup and shutdown scripts for your server processes. It will create all of your environment variables that have to be set for you to get your work done efficiently and effectively. It will use the information you have given it on these menus and create your database and its services as well as all of the pieces of the application that you are installing. You still will have considerable work to do, but you will be well on your way.

### Uninstallation

Regardless of how careful you are and how sure you are that you have gotten everything exactly right, at some point, you will likely have to uninstall a failed installation.

## UNIX (ANY VERSION NIX TYPE INSTALLATION)

If you are running on a UNIX platform, this is fairly clean and simple to do. First, you have to make sure that all of your Applications processes are shutdown. Table 9.2 shows a list of processes with the commands that you will use to shut them down and the order they should be shut down in.

To verify that all processes are shutdown, use the `ps -ef` command and `grep` for the `<SID>`. All that should return is your user ID grepping for the SID.

```
oracle 48858 40400    1 14:24:05   pts/1   0:00
grep VIS
```

**Table 9.2   Services Shutdown Commands**

| Process | Command |
| --- | --- |
| Concurrent Managers | `$ adcmctl.sh apps/<apps password> stop` |
| Forms Metric Server | `$ adfmsctl.sh stop` |
| Forms Server Listener | `$ adfractl.sh stop` |
| Reports Server | `$ adfroctl.sh stop` |
| WebDB Listener | `$ adwlnctl.sh stop` |
|  | `$ adwdbctl.sh stop` |
| TCF Server (if applicable) | `$ adtcfctl.sh stop` |
| Forms Metrics Client | `$ adfmcctl.sh stop` |
| Apache Listener | `$ adapcclt stop` |
| NET8 RPC Listener | `$ adalnctl.sh stop APPS_<SID>` |
| NET8 Database Listener | `$ addlnctl.sh stop (or lsnrctl stop <sid>)` |
| Database | `$ addbctl.sh stop (or sqlplus '/as sysdba' shutdown immediate)` |

Once this is done, you can delete the `oraInst.loc` file (most likely found in your `/etc` directory and owned by root). This file will be recreated next time you start RapidWiz (or runInstaller if you are installing other, non-Financials databases on the box). Next, delete the `oraInven-tory` directory from wherever you put it (as long as you have not got another installation using it). Then delete the files and directories that comprise the `APPL_TOP`, `COMMON_TOP`, and `ORACLE_BASE` if they exist. Finally, if you are changing your configuration parameters, delete the `config.txt` file (or whatever it is named on your installation) and recreate it with the next run of RapidWiz.

## WINDOWS

If you have to uninstall from a Windows machine, you will have a little more difficulty. If you have installed more than one of your instances on the same Windows server and you only want to be rid of one of the environments, the unistallation will become even more complex because you will have to carefully weed out what to remove and what to leave behind.

If you have one set of Oracle Applications files installed on the physical server, you can remove the `\oracle` or `\orant` directory, the `rapid-install` directory, and the `config.txt` file created by RapidWiz. The `\oracle` or `\orant` directory will most likely be on your C drive if you have more than one logical drive on the server.

Stop all Oracle services running on the server. This can be accomplished by going to Control Panel, selecting services, looking through all of the services listed, and shutting down anything that has Oracle attached to its name. If you leave any Oracle services running, you will likely be unable to cleanly delete the Oracle files from the computer. If you have more than one instance (e.g., Vis or Devl and Test) and you only want to remove one of the installations, you would stop all services that reference the SID name of the one that you want to remove. Figure 9.22 shows an installation where test and development are on the same server. In this case, if you wanted to remove development and move it to another server or reinstall it with a different configuration on this server, you would stop all services that are prefixed with Oracle and that end in DEVL.

Once you have all of the services stopped, navigate (through Windows Explorer) to the drives and directory structures of those pieces of Oracle E-Business Suite that you want to remove. If you have a single Oracle installation on the box, this would mean deleting any directory that contains Oracle in the name and any directory structure that you config-ured in your installation. Refer to your `config.txt` file to determine what all you have to go through and delete. If you have more than one

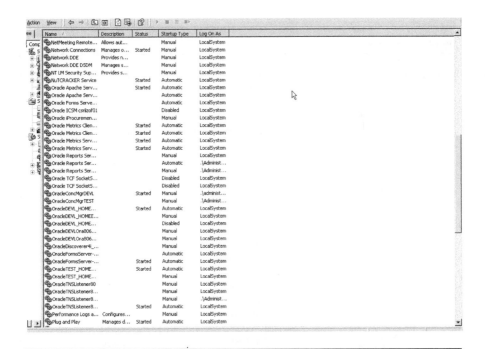

**Figure 9.22   Windows Services Window**

installation on the box, you will have to carefully navigate through the directories and select out those that belong to the instance that you are trying to get rid of. Unless you have used significant logic in your directory naming scheme, now is when having access to the `config.txt` file is nearly essential to determine what to remove and what to leave behind. If you have named your `APPL_TOP` for development `devlappl`, you will be able to remove this directory and feel safe that you have gotten these pieces and that you have not removed any of the `appl_top` files for the Test instance.

Now comes the piece that makes me most queasy. You have to remove references to the installation involved in the uninstallation process from the registry. I do not like making changes to the Windows registry. Use `regedit` (the registry editor) to find the directory structure: `HKEY_LOCAL_MACHINE\SOFTWARE\Oracle`. Delete this directory. This is the easiest and least dangerous part of editing the registry.

Naturally, it is more difficult if you have multiple environments on a single Windows machine. Following the example in Figure 9.23, you would have to remove the directory `/Oracle/applications/11.5.0/DEVL` and leave the directory `/oracle/applications/11/5/0/TEST`. You would further have to weed out

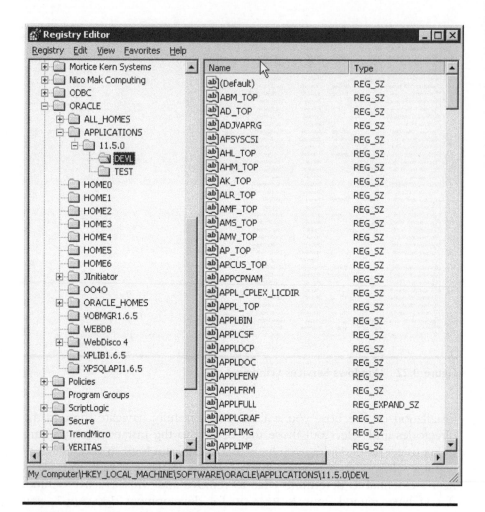

**Figure 9.23 HKEY Local Machine Registry Directory** /Oracle/applica-tions/11.5.0/DEVL

/All_homes of everything that references DEVL as well as /oracle_homes to remove the same information.

Now you have to remove references to all of the services that were installed in the RapidWiz installation. If you remove the wrong service here, you can cause Windows to stop functioning. Find the directory HKEY_LOCAL_MACHINE\SYSTEM\ControlSet001\Services and remove any entries under here that begin with the string Oracle and that reference the environment that you want to remove. Figure 9.23 shows what your Windows Registry looks like. The entry right below the highlighted one is where you are going to be working now.

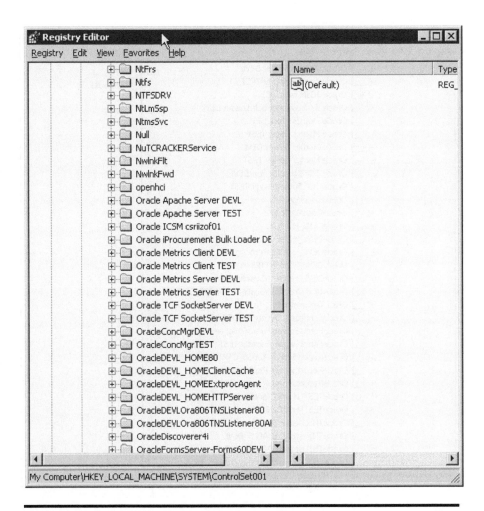

**Figure 9.24** HKEY_LOCAL_MACHINE\SYSTEM\ControlSet001\Services **Registry**

Now find the directory HKEY_LOCAL_MACHINE\SYS-TEM\ControlSet001\Services and delete any entries under it that begin with the string Oracle (see Figure 9.24). Still feeling brave? Find the directory HKEY_LOCAL_MACHINE\SYSTEM\CurrentControlset\Services and again remove all references under this one that begin with the string Oracle and that reference the environment that you want to remove. See Figure 9.25 for an example of what you are looking for. In this case, you want to remove anything that you would find that refers to the DEVL instance.

For a clean uninstallation, you should remove any Oracle related environment variables that point to the Oracle installation you are trying

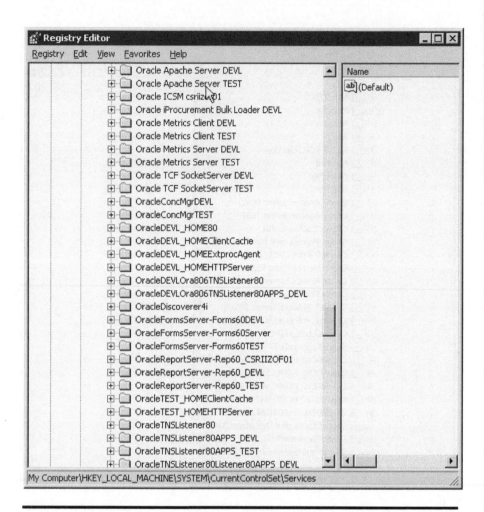

**Figure 9.25** HKEY_LOCAL_MACHINE\SYSTEM\CurrentControlset\Services **all Homes**

to remove. Take any references to the directories that you deleted (the directories that were in your config.txt file) as well as to anything else that references the Oracle instance. To do this, open Control Panel and from there open the System window. Choose the Advanced tab and the Environment Variables button on that tab (see Figure 9.26). You will likely have to remove references from the administrator ID as well as from any appl* user that you may have created in the installation (see Figure 9.27). Remove reference to anything that begins with NLS or ORACLE or APPL. Go through the CLASSPATH and remove any system variables that point to Oracle or APPL and any references to any

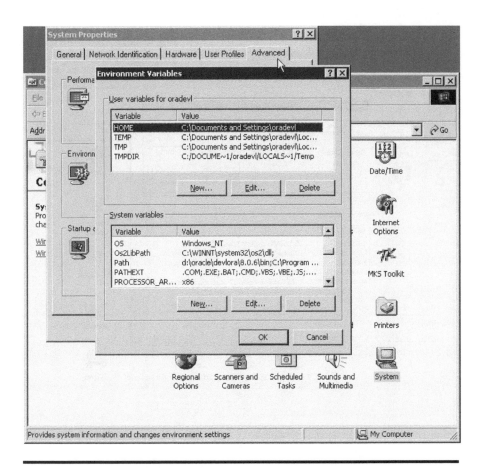

**Figure 9.26   Control Panel, System, Advanced, Environment Variables**

Oracle directories or subdirectories. Do the same thing in the Path variable (see Figure 9.28). If the WT_Gateway variable is set anywhere, clean it up as well.

Finally, right mouse click on the Start button and select the option Open All Users from the presented menu. Select program and delete any of the Oracle directories that you may find there (see Figure 9.29). Look around and find any Apache or *i*AS directories and delete them in there as well. Here again, remove only the directories that reference the environment that you are choosing to remove and leave anything that references any other environment on the same box.

This will now have gotten rid of the Oracle directories and variables from the computer. Then reboot the server (after all, this is Windows).

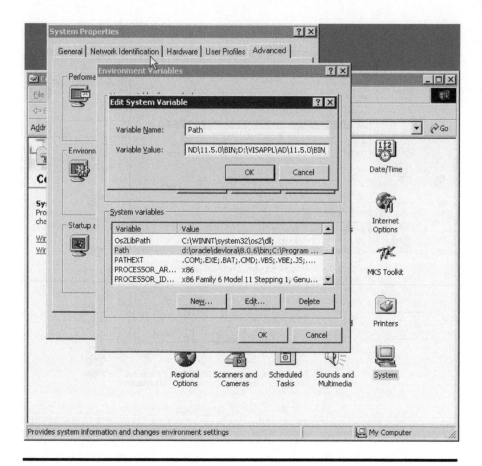

**Figure 9.27 Control Panel, System, Advanced, Administrator ID Environment Variables**

## TRAINING, TRAINING, TRAINING!

Before you start your installation process, get your key players trained. Get the technical people involved (those who are going to be responsible for understanding the installation and any customizations involved), the functional people (the ones who will be doing any given job or a trainer), and anyone else who will logically be doing anything with the system, particularly in the early days, trained.

Yes, your company has probably just allocated to this project a budget big enough to choke the proverbial horse and to expend more money on training people who will not even have the system to practice on when they get back sounds like a tremendous waste of resources. But stop and consider that trained people make fewer mistakes. They will

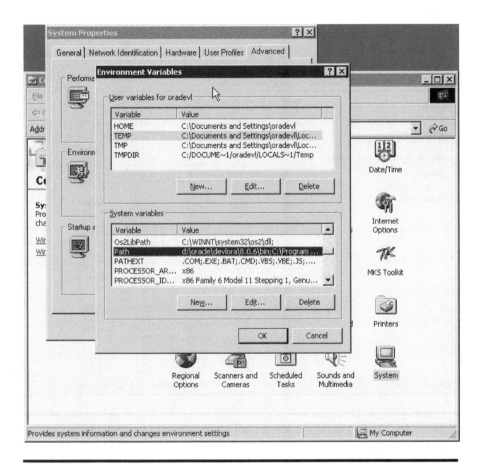

**Figure 9.28   Path Control Panel, System, Advanced, Path Environment Variables**

have seen something before, so when they are faced with the "real" training on your own system, they will have some familiarity with the interface. They will have the background that they need to know where to start asking questions rather than floundering in a completely unfamiliar place without any point of reference.

While Oracle University provides considerable training on the functional aspects of Oracle E-Business Suite, it is a little light on technical training. Anyone involved in developing forms and reports has options in both beginner and advanced classes in each of those subjects as well as in PL/SQL Programming units, but for the Apps DBA, the offerings are somewhat slim. There is a class on migration from 10.7 to 11i through Oracle University as well as one on 11i E-Business Suite Essentials for Implementers that targets both functional and technical implementers. Attending an Oracle University course is not necessary if you can find

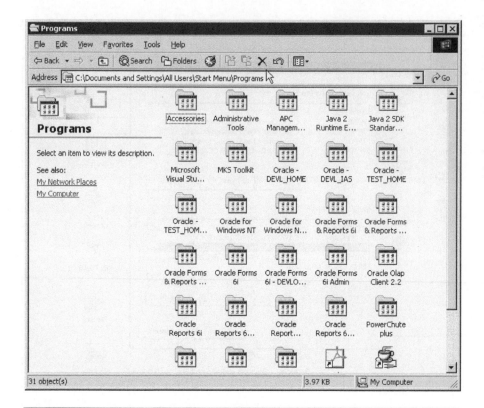

**Figure 9.29   Right Mouse Click Start, all Users, Oracle, Apache, iAS**

any class on administering Oracle E-Business Suite 11i that will give you some idea of the different aspects that you will be dealing with, preferably one that has hands on training, will help you in the long run. If nothing else, it will put you into a room with other people who are facing similar situations to yours and who are likely at different skill levels in relation to the product. This will give you a better understanding of what questions you want to ask when the time comes for you to be in the hot seat.

While it is not essential to have an extensive background in accounting, finance, marketing, human resources, or any of the other product modules that your end users will be dealing with, knowing something about basic business and basic accounting principles is helpful. For instance, you should understand that debits and credits have the opposite effect on the company's finances than in balancing your checkbook, that there are cash inflows and cash outflows, and that accounts payable is money going out of the company and accounts receivable is money coming into the company. You should also have basic knowledge of what your HR, marketing, and other departments do (depending on the modules that you are using). It may not help you to administer the application any better, but having a frame of reference when dealing with the end users allows you to not have a deer-in–the-headlights look when they start talking in their language.

## Helpful Hints

### *Do Not be Afraid to Admit You Do Not Know*

Not knowing something is nothing to be ashamed of. Not knowing about some aspect of a software solution of this size, complexity, and power is to be expected, regardless of how long you have been an Apps administrator. Not knowing the answers to a lot of questions if you are the one who has been elected to make the leap from Oracle DBA to Oracle Apps DBA (it is a little more than the database) is pretty much a given.

Not knowing and being willing to admit to not knowing, though, are two different things:

"Can you handle the position?"

"Don't know, probably can. Heck, I never thought I could handle the one I'm in now."

"Why is the system down?"

"Not a clue. It was working when I left yesterday."

"When will you have it back up?"

"I have an open iTAR. I am working on the problem. Don't know when it will be back up, but as soon as I can get it there, you will be the first to know."

"How does this <insert service here> work?"

"Don't know. I can't find that in the manual anywhere, but I will keep looking."

The worst anyone can say if you admit you do not know is that you are honest and the best that can happen is that you get some slack and maybe some additional resources (e.g., a class, a book, or someone you can ask these questions of).

### *Do Not be Afraid to Say No*

If you are working with a contracting company that is responsible for a significant part of your implementation and the rented project manager decides that you (the resident DBA assigned to the job) need to work the next 38 hours straight while he spends the weekend with his family lounging around a hotel pool, calling you every hour to make sure that you are really on the job, and does not tell anyone at the company (other than you) that those are the expectations, say no. There is no reason to hide from your company or your direct management what is being requested, especially if you know that the request is being made outside of common channels.

## Take Notes

This one is not one of my favorites. Notes are too much like documentation and I really do not like writing documentation, but these notes will end up being your best friends in the end. The notes do not have to be elaborate. Mine were on multi-colored sticky notes that ended up stuck all over the front of notebooks, on manila file folders, on the monitor of the server I was working at, and on top of other sticky notes with other notes on them. My methods were the talk of the team and were often pointed at in ridicule, but there is nothing wrong with a method if it works. Go back when you have a few minutes and write out the situation, the question, and the answer that you got. If you asked a question of another sysadmin and you got an answer that made sense and that helped you once, write down both the question and an annotated version of the answer. You never know when you might have the same situation again and you will still have the answer. This is important if you are in the middle of patching a long series of patches, you have been at it 18 hours, and, by the looks of it, you have several more hours to go. It is the time that you will not be able to remember what was said, why it was said, or in reference to what, and it is probably when the best information will end up coming out.

If you ask a question on a listserv and you get an answer that either helps you with the situation or points you at something that you did not know before (even if it does not help with the situation at hand), print out the mail, make note of who responded, and keep that information.

If you have a patch that goes badly, make notes on what patch, what went bad, where you looked to find it, and what you did to fix it. Any contact information you can accumulate in your journey through this desert should be kept as well. You never know when you might have a similar question from someone who has been a big help before.

If you can get your notes into electronic format and store them all in the same place on a network, you or anyone working on a portion of the application could access these notes and search for a similar problem that they are having. It may mean that you get an extra hour's sleep if they can use your notes as well as Metalink's notes, instead of calling you in the middle of the night.

## Upgrade or Migrate

You have an installation, now you are looking at upgrading. Upgrading refers to bringing a 10.7 or 11.0 implementation to 11i, migrating means going from, for example, 11.5.5 to 11.5.8. What is involved is not really very different and the same logical processes are involved. This means that the manner in which you have to proceed, the amount of time, and difficulty level you will face depends (to a great extent) on what version you are upgrading from and how much data you have to upgrade. While every installation and, therefore, every upgrade, is unique, there are many things that you will need to do regardless of what version you are upgrading from, what modules you have installed and licensed, what customizations you have done, or any other particulars unique to your implementation.

Here we will start looking at some of the common tasks that you will be faced with performing as well as some of the challenges and opportunities that you will be faced with.

## Gather Information

If you are upgrading from Version 10.7 or 11 to 11i, you will find that a good bit has changed. If you are upgrading one version of 11i to another, this will be addressed in the migration section following this one. Some of the things that have changed between the earlier significant releases are enhanced and renamed versions of what you are used to, some are completely retooled, and much is entirely new. There are new modules and new functionality.

An upgrade from Version 10 to 11i is a lot like a new implementation. Because 11i is based on the Oracle 8i database and its features, many things that worked one way in Version 10 will not work the same way in 11i because of the differences in the rule-based and cost-based optimizers.

Oracle has tools and information that will help make the upgrade process more simple and elegant.

Will your current hardware configuration be sufficient to not only support the new configuration, but also both configurations for a time? Is the network servicing the current configuration going to be robust enough to withstand the Internet/intranet-based product taking a bite out of the available bandwidth? Is the configuration you are planning (database version, apps version, and OSs) certified by Oracle Support? Check out the certification section of Metalink before you start to make sure.

## Have a Plan

In this regard, upgrading is not too different from installing a new implementation. It is critical to plan out what needs to happen and when it has to be done. If you have an absolute hard and fast completion date, you will have to start there and back calculate. Build in slack time in each environment for things to go wrong and time to resolve these problems.

You do not have to just plan at one level. Create a high-level task list with key milestones, so that everyone knows what needs to happen in a broad sense. A task-by-task, patch-by-patch, driver-by-driver low-level plan will help the technical types make sure that everything gets applied and nothing gets missed.

The high-level task list can start well in advance of the physical beginning of the upgrade process with researching and learning as much about what to expect in the upcoming upgrade and the changes that can be anticipated in functionality.A sample high-level task list could take the form of a formal project plan; however, at the earliest stages exact dependencies may not be known. A good beginning could be as simple as a text document in an outline format.

When formulating all levels of plans, take into account known and potential customizations as well as data feeds into and out of your current Apps installations and how the upgrade may affect the current system. You have to take into account whether the feeds are direct loads into data tables or (as is the better scenario) by means of the interface tables.

Make sure that you have enough of the right resources for the upgrade process and sufficient hardware for all of your environments on each server involved. You will want to revert one of the environments that you upgrade earliest to a training environment. Think of your first upgraded system in this way: it will have been your training server for your upgrade process and therefore can (once it is up and operational) work as the training area for end users and developers who will have to be using the product when the full upgrade cycle is completed.

Resources are not just hardware and network resources. People resources are every bit as important as, if not more important than, computing resources. One person cannot do it alone. Even on a maintenance release upgrade, it takes several technical people working in shifts to make sure that all patches get installed and all problems get resolved in a timely manner.

Include dealing with your current customizations in your plan. Some may no longer be necessary; others may no longer be functional. Make sure that you have allotted time for dealing with the customizations, regardless of the outcome.

Finally, create a plan for training. It is a whole new world in 11i. If you are upgrading from one maintenance pack to another, you should not have to retrain, only test and learn first hand. If you are upgrading from Version 10.7 or 11.0, you will likely see some significant changes. Even if your training is just spending time on one of your newly upgraded environments learning what has changed and the new ways to do things, adding time into the schedule for training will pay off in the end.

The following list contains all the elements that I recommend including in your plan.

Plans List:

1. Gather upgrade information
   - Oracle
   - Oracle Applications Users Group (OAUG)
   - Apps Net
   - Listservs
   - Consulting firms
   - Metalink
2. Analyze current environment
   - Database tier
   - Client tier
   - Data feeds
   - Network
   - Customizations
3. Analyze potential new environments
   - Database tier
   - Middle tier
   - End user tier
   - Data feeds
   - Network
   - Customizations
   - Changes in business needs
4. Test Plans
   - Environment
   - Functionality to test
   - Customization
   - Technical
   - Business
   - Develop test scripts and centralize
5. Training
   - New technical functionality
   - New functional functionality
6. Installation/upgrade/patch
7. Deal with customizations
8. Carry out test plans
9. Postupgrade meetings

### Beware of Scope Creep Even Here

It is easy to get caught up in the idea of all of the new features, new functionality, and modules. However, now is not the time to introduce new modules or to license new products. Keep the upgrade process as simple as you can. Once you get through upgrading and prove that your current functionality is working as you anticipate, then you can start another project or a new phase of your upgrade process. Adding extra complexity in the midst of the upgrade will just muddy the waters and will make things extra complex. It will also impact your ability to complete the upgrade on time. Everything that you do in your test and development environments will carry through to your production environment and will mean additional downtime for your users. Smaller chunks of downtime would be better in the long run than one big outage.

### Determine What Has Changed between What You Are Upgrading From and 11i

If you are upgrading from Version 10.7 or 11.0 to 11i, you can plan on needing more hardware. This can be anywhere from 30 to 40 percent more disk space for each of the tiers. On the Apps layer, this extra allows for space for the new modules and increased functionality of the application. On the database tier, this allows for the data files for the new modules if you were not implementing the new products (it will mean even more disk space if you are implementing the new products) and the additional space needed for the `Oracle_Home`.

Disk space is only part of the increase in hardware that will go along with an upgrade. You will need to increase the bandwidth available for Apps to make use of by between 10 and 15 percent and the memory available for its use by 15 to 20 percent.

Functionality will have changed considerably, as well. You will be moving to a truly thin client installation where all changes and upgrades are done at the server and the PC only requires a browser and JInitiator to function. This is the primary reason for the extra, required bandwidth.

Once you get to 11i, you will find that it takes advantage of invoker's rights on package, function, and procedure execution. This means that you can actually save space because you do not have to store the same procedure several times if you have multiple sets of books, which makes life as administrator easier, as well.

Additional support for new languages and enhanced support of country specific functionality are two more additions that will improve your ability to serve your end users, but will also make supporting the application more resource intensive.

## Decide When to Upgrade

When you are implementing, it is probably a good idea to implement the latest version. In fact, if you are looking to go live 60 days or less following the release date of a maintenance pack, Oracle suggests that you do implement that new release. I believe the theory here is that it is freshest in the minds of the development team and if there were problems, getting them ironed out would be quick and fairly painless.

But do you want to upgrade from one major release (11 to 11i or 11i to 12) as soon as it is released? Probably not. What is the impetus for the upgrade? Are you going to have to upgrade both the application layer and the database to stay on certified configurations because you have to swap out leased equipment? Is the upgrade prompted because your current environment is next on the list to be desupported?

Waiting until there is a good reason to upgrade is a good decision. Waiting until the very last minute to try to hurry through an upgrade is not a good decision. Mistakes are made when you have an unmovable deadline and need to hurry too fast. Waiting too long can mean the additional cost of having to extend leases on machines that are being swapped out when the project plan does not go as planned and ends up taking longer than anticipated. Worse, if you wait until you get a desupport notice or you discover that your versions are not going to be supported past a certain date and then start the consideration process on your way to upgrading, you may be in an unsupported state before the end of the process. The information technology industry is the prime example of a place where if anything bad can happen, it will and at the worst possible time. It is a bad position to be in with a fully functional production system that breaks in the middle of your upgrade plan and you have no environment at the same release configuration as production (even worse if you have just outlived Oracle's final support date).

## Bookmark Metalink

If you have a support contract, Metalink can be invaluable in your upgrade process. They will walk you through issues that arise in your installations and upgrades. They will help you determine what went wrong in a patching situation. They will steer you to documentation that you probably would not have found on your own otherwise. An upgrade can mean dozens of iTARs. Some are resolved in under an hour. Some may not be resolved completely until long after your upgrade is completed.

If you do not have a support contract, get one. It is the only way to stay current on patches and to get help with those unexpected opportunities for adventure that will likely come your way. Learn to navigate Metalink to find the resources that are buried within its site. This will become your most used site.

## Have a Team

An 11i upgrade, regardless of whether you are upgrading from Version 10 or 11 to 11i or you are just upgrading within 11i from one major release to another, requires a team of individuals who have different bases of knowledge and skills. You will need technical people. You will need people who have knowledge of hardware and software configuration. You will need a technical expert on Apps architecture and of the utilities called into service during the upgrade process. You will also need people from the functional side. It requires someone who has knowledge of business processes and how they are accomplished with Oracle Applications. Further, you should have on your team someone who is responsible for the design, development implementation, and maintenance of the customizations for your installation. These people should have some knowledge of how things are done at whatever level you are upgrading from and will do some research on what the upgrade will mean to their area of expertise.

This team will need to work closely together to achieve the best end result.

## Back Up to a Fallback Point

Back up often and verify the backup. Always make a backup when you have gotten to the end of a big chunk of processing that you might want to be able to fall back to. This is particularly important if you have upgraded part way and done some testing and everything appears functional. Having a backup at this point would mean that if you started the next round of processing and ran into a problem that you could not get through with Oracle Support's help in a reasonable amount of time, you can restore to a closer operational point than falling completely back to the beginning. Rerunning a patch or a procedure that has had problems once, even rerunning it with all of the same surrounding processes in place may be fully successful. The converse can also be true, rerunning a patch or process that has been successful once might fail completely under similar conditions. Limiting what has to be rerun to get another process to run successfully means limiting what more might go wrong.

## Upgrade

### Upgrade in Phases, Database First

This phase of the project includes installing an Oracle certified release of the RDBMS, the Tools, and Applications that are included in the set of

RDBMS binaries. InterMedia, InterMedia Text, and Spatial are ones that you will find necessary along with SQL*Plus and the typical pieces of the database.

Both Release 10.7 and 11.0 are certified to run on an Oracle 8i database (8.1.7). If you have not already upgraded your database to this point, your first step in your upgrade plan should be to get your database to this point. This will allow you to resize objects in the newer version and start to migrate some of the obsolete functionality to the newer version. Bringing your database to Oracle 8i before you start the remainder of the upgrade will mean that you can attribute problems that arise because of the database to the database and not have to fight with dozens of changes at the same time when trying to hunt down the cause of problems. You will maximize your testing and limit downtime; although, you will have downtime broken into several smaller chunks, so users will be asked to stay out of the system several times during the duration of the process.

### Interoperability

In this case, interoperability means allowing your current applications tier version to run against an Oracle 8i database. This allows you to upgrade in phases; it also allows you to make use of features in your current configuration to determine what changes you can expect later with database performance. This includes the base product as well as your customizations. It can also allow you to start to migrate to the cost based optimizer.

If you are using an Oracle 7 server that is any release lower than 7.3.4, you will have to upgrade the technology stack to this release and apply any associated interoperability patches before you start your upgrade to Oracle 8i Enterprise Edition.

Further, you will have to make sure that the minipack patch levels for payables, receivables, sales and marketing, global accounting engine, order entry, and purchasing are all at least those in Table 9.3.

**Table 9.3   Installed Minipack Levels**

| Product | Patch Level |
|---|---|
| Payables | AP V |
| Receivables | AR W |
| Sales and Marketing | AS H |
| Global Accounting Engine | AX F |
| Order Entry | OE J |
| Purchasing | PO M |

**Table 9.4 `Init.ora` Renamed Parameters**

| Old Initialization Parameter name | Renamed Value |
|---|---|
| ASYNC_READ | DISK_ASYNCH_IO |
| ASYNC_WRITE | DISK_ASYNCH_IO |
| CCF_IO_SIZE * | DB_FILE_DIRECT_IO_COUNT * |
| DB_FILE_STANDBY_NAME_CONVERT | DB_FILE_NAME_CONVERT |
| DB_WRITERS | DBWR_IO_SLAVES |
| LOG_FILE_STANDBY_NAME_CONVERT | LOG_FILE_NAME_CONVERT |
| SNAPSHOT_REFRESH_INTERVAL | JOB_QUEUE_INTERVAL |

Once you have upgraded your database to Oracle 8i, you will have to make some changes in the `init.ora` file for your database. Several of the initialization parameters have changed names and others have become obsolete. Table 9.4 lists all of the renamed parameters and their new names and Table 9.5 lists some of the main obsolete parameters in 8.1.7 that you may have to remove. The database may or may not start with these parameters incorrect; if it does, it will place warnings in your alert logs at startup and you may not be able to take advantage of the new parameter features. Removing the obsolete parameters entirely would be the safest solution. You can either change or delete the old parameters or you can comment the old ones out and add the renamed ones below, deleting the old values later when you are comfortable with your upgrade.

Note, you cannot just change the name of `CCF_IO_SIZE` to `DB_FILE_DIRECT_IO_COUNT` as what they are calculated in has changed. `CCF_IO_SIZE` was in bytes, while `DB_FILE_DIRECT_IO_COUNT` is in database blocks.

Further, there are two new events that are required to be in your initialization parameters to maintain compatibility of the Oracle 7 and early Oracle 8 constructs in the Oracle 8i database. Add them to your `init.ora` file if they are not already there.

```
event = "10929 trace name context forever"
event = "10932 trace name context level 2"
```

As with any installation of a different version of the database on the same machine, you will need to make sure that you reset your ORACLE_HOME, PATH, and ORA_NLS as well as LD_LIBRARY_PATH to point to your new environment and make sure that your `oraInst.loc` file has been renamed so you do not install your `oraInventory` into the same one as your old installation. This can cause inconsistencies and the inability to patch either database at a later time.

**Table 9.5　Obsolete Parameters**

```
ARCH_IO_SLAVES
B_TREE_BITMAP_PLANS
CLEANUP_ROLLBACK_ENTRIES
COMPATIBLE_NO_RECOVERY
CACHE_SIZE_THRESHOLD
DB_BLOCK_CHECKPOINT_BATCH
FREEZE_DB_FOR_FAST_INSTANCE_RECOVERY
DB_BLOCK_LRU_STATISTICS
DISCRETE_TRANSACTIONS_ENABLED
FAST_FULL_SCAN_ENABLED
DB_FILE_SIMULTANEOUS_WRITES
JOB_QUEUE_KEEP_CONNECTIONS
DB_BLOCK_LRU_EXTENDED_STATISTICS
LGWR_IO_SLAVES
COMPLEX_VIEW_MERGING
CLOSE_CACHED_OPEN_CURSORS
PARALLEL_DEFAULT_MAX_SCANS
UNLIMITED_ROLLBACK_SEGMENTS
PARALLEL_DEFAULT_SCAN_SIZE
OPTIMIZER_PARALLEL_PASS
SEQUENCE_CACHE_HASH_BUCKETS
LM_NON_FAULT_TOLERANT
IPQ_ADDRESS
IPQ_NET
IO_TIMEOUT
INIT_SQL_FILES
CHECKPOINT_PROCESS
FAST_CACHE_FLUSH
LARGE_POOL_MIN_ALLOC
LOG_ARCHIVE_BUFFER_SIZE
LOCK_SGA_AREAS
LOG_ARCHIVE_BUFFERS
LOG_FILES
LOG_BLOCK_CHECKSUM
LOG_SIMULTANEOUS_COPIES
LOG_SMALL_ENTRY_MAX_SIZE
PARALLEL_DEFAULT_MAX_INSTANCES
PARALLEL_SERVER_IDLE_TIME
PARALLEL_MIN_MESSAGE_POOL
PUSH_JOIN_PREDICATE
PARALLEL_TRANSACTION_RESOURCE_TIMEOUT
ROW_CACHE_CURSORS
SEQUENCE_CACHE_ENTRIES
SEQUENCE_CACHE_HASH_BUCKETS
SHARED_POOL_RESERVED_MIN_ALLOC
SNAPSHOT_REFRESH_KEEP_CONNECTIONS
SNAPSHOT_REFRESH_PROCESSES
SORT_SPACEMAP_SIZE
SORT_READ_FAC
SORT_WRITE_BUFFERS
```

Follow the Oracle 8i installation guide for your platform to perform the installation, installing at least Oracle 8i server, Net8 Server, Net8 Client, and Oracle Utilities. Do not run the migration scripts at this time. Apply the latest certified Oracle 8i patch set to the new RDBMS binaries, but do not run any SQL scripts documented in the release notes yet.

Your new installation will take up considerably more room than the old version did. You will need to make sure that your SYSTEM tablespace is at least 500 MB (best to make sure that there is at least 150 MB free in this tablespace) and that you have at least 300 MB in your rollback segments.

Now, if you are on Oracle Version 7.3.4, you will need to migrate (not upgrade) your database to Oracle 8i Enterprise Edition. If you are on Version 8 of the database (8.0.#), you will need to upgrade your database to Oracle 8i. The *Oracle 8i Migration Manual* available either through Oracle Technology Net or http://tahiti.oracle.com can give you the steps necessary to accomplish this, regardless of which version you are currently on. Upgrade your database only. Configure your new Net8 Listener and start the listener.

You will need to set up a SQL*Net client on the machine where your Release 10.7 or 11.0 is installed as the technology stack manager (not the Forms Server administrator, if these are two different users). Make sure that all of the environment settings, at this point, are referring to your Oracle 7 server (7.3.4) technology stack environment (this has not changed yet). Double-check ORACLE_HOME, PATH, ORA_NLS, and LD_LIBRARY_PATH to make sure that nothing changed for any reason. Now configure the SQL*Net client so your 10.7 file system can connect to your newly upgraded Oracle 8i database. If you need help setting up the SQL*Net client, the manuals for Oracle 8i are still available on http://otn.oracle.com/documenta-tion or on http://tahiti.oracle.com.

Apply interoperability patches that will allow your 10.7 or 11.0 func-tionality to continue under the new Oracle 8i database. Oracle continues to make updates and modifications to these patches, so get the most recent version from Metalink to make sure that you get the most stable and supported version of the patches.

Compile invalid objects. You just upgraded the database. You will, without a doubt, have dozens (possibly tens of thousands) of invalid objects. Nearly all of the database objects can be invalid at this point due to the migration/upgrade process. If you have never used utlrp.sql (found in $ORACLE_HOME/rdbms/admin on UNIX or %ORACLE_HOME\rdbms\admin if your database is on a Windows plat-form), it is the utility that recompiles invalid objects. It can run for hours, depending on how many invalid objects you have in your database (select count(*) from all_objects where status = 'INVALID';).

There will be no feedback, but opening another session and rerunning the above `select` statement in another session will prove that it is still working when the number of invalid objects continues to go down. Run this script as sys, internal, or sysdba so you are able to recompile all invalid objects. Once `utlrp` has finished, you can use ADADMIN (AD administrator), choose maintain database objects, and compile APPS schema option. Again, this may take a while, depending on how many remaining APPS invalid objects are in the database. (`Select count (*) from all_objects where status = 'INVALID'` and owner = `'APPS';`)

### Create a Temporary Tablespace

Once you have gotten your database upgraded or migrated to Oracle 8i, you can start to implement the features of the newer release. One that will help you most in the rest of your migration to 11i will be the creation of a Temporary Tablespace. Create this tablespace as temporary and locally managed with uniform allocation. Be careful when you create this tablespace, however. When Oracle creates a temporary table, go out to the OS and look at the file specifications. Temporary tables are usually created as sparse, which means Oracle knows how big they are allowed to get, but can create them significantly smaller. The OS does not know this; it just knows it has a file of whatever size Oracle chooses to create. So when you create them, it may look like you have more than enough room in the file system for growth, but when you start using the Temporary Tablespace, it starts filling up; Oracle starts allocating more and more of the space it knows belongs to the Temporary Tablespace. When it runs up against the end of the file system and Oracle is still trying to make use of the space that has not yet been physically allocated to the tablespace, the database can hang and become unresponsive to any queries or processing. At this point, you will have to relocate one or more of the files making up your Temporary Tablespace to make sure that you will have sufficient space to use when you restart the upgrade/migration process. To make sure that Oracle physically allocates all of the space to your tablespace that it believes it will need, create the tablespace as permanent. Then drop the tablespace and create it again as temporary using the same data files. The first `create` statement causes the files to be fully allocated; the second makes use of them and causes them to be optimized for the Temporary Tablespace.

Once you have this Temporary Tablespace defined in this way, adding a data file to the tablespace is not as easy as it used to be. You can no longer just add a data file with `alter tablespace add datafile` command. You have to add a file with the `alter database` command.

You will need to size your extents based on your configuration and environment. The 16K extents in the example are only used as an example; you do not have to use these sizes.

- Create Temporary Tablespace `Appstemp tempfile'/u02/ proddata/prod/appstemp01.dbf' size 2000 M` reuse extent management local uniform size 16K.
- Add a data file.
  ```
  Alter database add tempfile '/u02/
  proddata/prod/appstemp02.dbf' size 1000 M;
  ```
- Resize a data file.
  ```
  Alter database tempfile '/u02/
  proddata/prod/appstemp02.dbf' size 2000 M;
  ```
- Drop a data file.
  ```
  Alter database tempfile '/u02/
  proddata/prod/appstemp02.dbf' drop;
  ```

### Migrate Existing Nonsystem Tablespaces to Locally Managed

To take advantage of the new performance features that locally managed tablespaces bring in Oracle 8i, you need to migrate existing tablespaces to locally managed tablespaces. This is also the direction that Oracle is going as far as the supported way to create tablespaces. In Oracle 9i (depending on how you create your database), it will be the default manner that the system tablespace is created at database creation time.

There are two ways you can accomplish migrating your existing tablespaces to locally managed tablespaces. You can run the adtb-scnv.pls script that is supposed to be located under your APPL_TOP under admin/preupg directory. Log in to sqlplus as system to run the script, which will accept the system password as a parameter. Alternatively, you can use the DBMS_SPACE_ADMIN package and your existing v$tablespace view to use sql to create the sql to do this. This would be the more dynamic way to accomplish this and would allow you to make sure that you get all of the tablespaces in your database, even the custom or user tablespaces that are not directly related to Apps. It would also give you the flexibility to determine if there are any tablespaces, other than system, that you do not yet want to make locally managed and exclude them from the resulting list. Further, with DBMS_SPACE_ADMIN, you can migrate tables back and forth between locally and dictionary managed.

```
Select 'execute
dbms_space_admin.tablespace_migrate_to_local('||ta
blespace_name||', <your desired minimum extent
size>);'from v$tablepaces;
```

## LOCALLY MANAGED VERSUS DICTIONARY MANAGED

Naturally, you are migrating from dictionary managed tablespaces to locally managed tablespaces. This means that the setting value in the EXTENT_MANAGEMENT column of DBA_TABLESPACES will be set to LOCAL for the tablespaces in question after running the DBMS_SPACE_ADMIN.TABLESPACE_MIGRATE_TO_LOCAL package procedure (it would have been set to DICTIONARY before). If necessary, you could migrate the same tablespaces back and forth between dictionary managed and locally managed ( DBMS_SPACE_ADMIN. TABLESPACE_MIGRATE_FROM_LOCAL). Oracle's future direction is to have all tablespaces locally managed, including the System tablespace. You can check the current settings of your tables by running the following sql statement:

```
Select tablespace_name, extent_management,
allocation_type
From dba_tablespaces;
```

You will see values in the Allocation_type column of USER for tablespaces that were migrated using the DBMS_SPACE_ADMIN package and either UNIFORM or SYSTEM for newly created locally managed tablespaces (depending on what parameter you set for the Extent Management parameter).

## MANUAL SPACE MANAGEMENT OR AUTOMATIC SPACE MANAGEMENT

This is one of the biggest surprises in migrating from dictionary managed tablespaces. If you read the documentation on locally managed tablespaces, one of their biggest advantages is the performance enhancement they bring with them. All free space, percent free, and percent used information gets stored in bitmapped blocks in the tablespace rather than in the data dictionary tables. This limits the need for every insert operation to access the data dictionary to determine what blocks are candidates for the inserts, what blocks are free and used, and which are available to still be used more. This would, I believe, be the preferred method and there would be a facility for making existing tablespaces not only locally managed, but also to have their space automatically managed. Further, I would believe that, since this is the direction for future database releases, automatic would be the default method for creating them as manual is (according to OEM) maintained for backward compatibility. However, because you are migrating existing objects to a new concept in tablespaces and many of these tablespaces contain objects that already violate the new policy and because it would be extremely difficult to write the conversion program to convert these objects to be compliant with the new system, Oracle was forced to compromise with what it could and could not do. There are currently no plans (at least in 10i) to get rid of the backwardly compatible (manual space management) settings, or to create an automated way in which to transform a manual space managed to an automatic space managed tablespace.

```
Alter table FND_INSTALL_PROCESSES Move tablespace
fndd1
```

If you want to take advantage of all of the features of locally managed tablespaces, the supported method would be to create new tablespaces, one to one with the current tablespaces. These you would want to create with all of the locally managed tablespace settings that are available deliberately set, taking none of the defaults. Then, move the objects (e.g., tables, indexes, etc.) to the new tablespaces and rebuild the indexes. Rebuilding the indexes will be the most CPU labor-intensive part of the operation. Waiting until your database is at Oracle 9i to move where the indexes are built will allow you to utilize the online rebuild of indexes feature, making this a less intrusive procedure. Then comes the task of removing the old tablespaces and datafiles.

## Create the Tablespaces for New Products

Somewhere in your documentation, you will find a step that calls for creating new tablespaces for new products. Make sure that this step does not fail. If you have to, go through the script that is likely included in some patch that will be in your sets to apply and double-check that all new tablespaces get created and that they are the right size and that they are locally managed. If you only have a listing of needed new tablespaces, make sure that you do not miss any. If this step fails or gets corrupted in anyway, the subsequent steps will fail.

## Upgrade Your Apps

Now comes the part that is long and tedious, upgrading your application. What all you will have to run depends on what all you have installed. Oracle has come out with an assistant that will help you decide what steps you do not have to do. The utility is called TUMS (The Upgrade Manual Script) and it is a patch that can be applied to either a 10.7 or an 11.0 environment and it will tell you which of the Category 1 through Category 6 steps you can safely skip in your particular circumstances and with your unique configuration. The details on the TUMS patch for upgrading to Version 11.5.8 can be found in Metalink Note 213275.1; the details for TUMS for upgrading to 11.5.7 can be found in Metalink Note 177255.1

Another tool that Oracle provides to assist you in the upgrade process is an Excel format spreadsheet that can help you in planning and tracking your upgrade tasks. There are preupgrade tasks included in this spreadsheet and postupgrade tasks that are segregated by type of task and release from which you are upgrading. Using this spreadsheet, you can plan who will be responsible for each task and you can later record the times that each task took in each environment as well as any problems that you encountered in the process and any other notes that you want to add. This can become part of your living documentation not only for this upgrade, but for future upgrades as well. The spreadsheet is available on the Documentation CD that is included in your installation pack and is generated from within the *Upgrading Oracle Applications* manual. I suggest you print this manual so that you can make notes in the margins and use it as your continual reference throughout the upgrade process. The spreadsheet generates times that it suggests for allotting to each individual task and aggregates the time for every category in what is considered effort time not clock time. Some of these processes can be run in parallel. Some of the estimates are considerably off depending on your expertise level and your relative comfort in performing the steps, but they provide an estimated target.

## DEAL WITH CUSTOMIZATIONS

One of the most daunting things to take into consideration when planning an upgrade or migration is customizations. One of the first things to review when you are planning any upgrade or migration are your particular set of customizations when taken in comparison to the new features available in the new release. Often times you will discover that many of your previous customizations are no longer needed, as they (or something like them) are incorporated into the new release of the application. If you are upgrading from Version 10.7, where the interface was still primarily character based, it will likely mean recoding the customizations according to the new 11i coding standards. If you are upgrading from 10.7 NCA or SC or from 11.0 you will need, minimally to regenerate these forms through Oracle Forms Developer 6i making the layout changes that will allow them to be consistent with the look and feel of the rest of the 11i interface.

Keep the list of customizations handy throughout the upgrade process as many of these customizations may get overlayed with other versions in the upgrade process. You will either have to reincorporate the changes into the new forms or you will need to overlay the newer versions with your older custom versions. It is advisable to make the changes to the newer version to make sure that you are dealing with any table changes that may have come with the upgrade.

# REDUCE PRODUCTION DOWNTIME

Many people are currently suggesting ways of minimizing your total downtime by upgrading a test file system and cloning that test system to upgrade production. This method would entail having a system to which you would clone your production instance and on which you would perform your entire upgrade (i.e., all patches, all drivers, everything required to get the system from the old version to the new version). Once the total upgrade was accomplished on this system, you would clone the middle tier to the production middle tier, apply all database and generate drivers to the new system, and proceed as you normally would.

While this may save considerable time in a 10.7 or 11.0 upgrade, I do not have the experience of having done a clone of one of these systems, so I do not know how long they would take. I do know that it generally takes around 8 hours to clone a minimal 11i instance to 11i instance and then (with adclone) you have some troubleshooting to take care of. If you are going to follow this track, I suggest making this the methodology you use through your entire upgrade process (upgrading all of your systems the same way). This will allow you to get comfortable with the process and will allow you to find as many of the opportunities as you can before you are faced with proceeding to production.

## *Upgrade Your Database to 9.2*

While upgrading to Version 9.2 of the database is not necessary at this point, desupport for Oracle 8i has already been announced (although it is farther out for Apps users than for just database users). There are two thoughts on the upgrade of this now. It may be wise to wait until you have made sure that you have gone through a complete accounting cycle with your new 11i upgrade before you take this step, because this will add another 2 to 5 days to the production outage. However, it is a step that you will need to take in the foreseeable future. It can easily be done at this point, which will keep you supported and current and allow you to take advantage of many of the newer features on 9i. Plus you can minimize downtime with this, as well.

Install the new binaries in new ORACLE_HOME with similar structure, move the old one aside, and move this one into its place. This way you can install the binaries into their own home without having to take the database down and you can do your Apps migration at the same time. Although, you will want to have a good cold backup and all of your archive logs so if anything happens, you can recover. Also, you will want to make sure that you keep what is happening in what sessions on your server so you do not inadvertently do something in one session that you thought you were doing in another. I have seen this route taken with no ill effects to the running system. This also minimizes the effect on the front-end system. If there are no net changes to those file systems, you will have fewer problems in the upgrade.

Do not stop at 9.2.0; install the binaries and patch immediately to 9.2.0.2. This is recommended anyway and will get you to the supported release quicker.

Once your apps migration is finished, you can simply proceed to the Oracle 8i to 9i upgrade. While running U0801070.sql can take half of a day, because it is upgrading to 901 and then to 9202, it is relatively clean. You will also have to upgrade Intermedia, Intermedia Text, and Spatial. The steps to migrate these are in the documentation.

This upgrade is, for the most part, a simple database upgrade. You have to take into account spatial and the recompile of invalid objects. The recompile can error out, so you may need to up the amount of extents to unlimited in all objects. The running of the U0801070.sql invalidates nearly everything in the database. Running utlrp.sql (found in the ORACLE_HOME/rdbms/admin directory) can run for 13 hours or more. To make sure that you are still making progress, you can run the following query to make sure that the value returned is getting smaller.

```
Select count (*) from all_objects where status =
'INVALID';
```

### Migrate to Undo Tablespaces and Automatic Undo Management

With release 9i of the database, Oracle provides a mechanism for more elegantly managing undo and rollback information in the database. The mechanism is Automatic Undo Management and Undo Tablespaces. Implementing Automatic Undo Management means that you no longer have to monitor and tune the allocation of rollback segments. Although in 9.2, Oracle maintains Rollback Segment and Manual Undo Management for backward compatibility. How long they will remain supported remains to be seen.

To configure the database to run in Automatic Undo Management mode, you need to add two initialization parameters to the database as well as create an Undo Tablespace for the Automatic Undo Management to use. If the Undo Tablespace is not created when you attempt to use Automatic Undo Management, the database will not start.

```
UNDO_MANAGEMENT=AUTO
UNDO_TABLESPACE = apps_undo01
```

You can optionally add another initialization parameter, UNDO_RETENTION, that tells the database how long to retain information in the Undo Tablespace. This is primarily used for flashback query. I do not think that flashback query is something that will be applicable in

Oracle E-Business Suite in the near future, but in future releases it will become more and more applicable.

To create the Undo Tablespace reference above, you would issue the following command:

```
CREATE UNDO TABLESPACE apps_undo01 DATAFILE '/
visdata/apps_undo01.dbf' SIZE 2000M REUSE;
```

The only `alter` commands permissible with an Undo Tablespace are adding or renaming a datafile, bringing a datafile online or offline, or beginning or ending an open backup on the datafile.

If you find the need to switch Undo Tablespaces, make sure that there is a new Undo Tablespace defined and use the `Alter system` command to switch the Undo Tablespace (make sure that you make the change to the init file if you are not using `SPFILEs`):

```
ALTER SYSTEM SET UNDO_TABLESPACE = apps_undo02;
```

Remember, using Automatic Undo will not remove the possibility of Ora-01555 errors, but it will limit their occurrence.

# 10

---

# PATCHING

Now that you have become acclimated to your new desert environment and you are starting to recognize the lay of the land, the unique rock formations, gullies, temperatures, and flora and fauna of your particular environment, it is time to start looking at the next part of your adventure. You will now find that a considerable amount of your time will be spent dealing with patches and with patching your environments. Downloading, researching, planning, installing, fixing, testing, and documenting patches will take much of your time. I have heard it said that a monkey can be taught to install patches, but only a particularly talented monkey can learn what to do when a patch breaks.

This chapter explains the particulars about patches, how to install patches, and how to figure out what went wrong when a patch breaks.

## WHAT ARE PATCHES?

Http://www.dictionary.com defines a patch (in reference to computer science) as a piece of code added to software to fix a bug, especially as a temporary correction between two releases. This definition is correct as far as it goes. However, when looking at patching Oracle E-Business Suite, it does not completely describe what patching entails. To begin to understand the patching of a multi-GB application, you first have to get an idea of what kinds of patches there are.

## APPS PATCHES

There are several kinds of patches that you may end up having to apply to a part of your Oracle E-Business Suite installation. There are database patches that will take you to the next bug fix release (changing the last number in the number string), there are Apache and Forms and Reports patches that upgrade your services to a new release level or in some way enhance performance of the services, and there are Apps patches. Apps patches are usually product family specific, and are usually applied by means of ADPATCH, and are driver driven and therefore each applied like the other.

There are, of course, other patches that will impact your life. OS patches on any or all of your servers, OS patches that get applied to the client that may affect the way that JInitiator performs, and browser patches that may affect the way that the browser interprets the information being sent to it by the application.

Application patches come in many sizes, each with its own name and purpose. These are outlined first, before we discuss how to handle them.

## One-Off Patches

One-off or stand-alone individual patches are created to fix a particular bug. You often have to have an active iTAR to get a one-off patch (at least until the bug becomes widely recognized). Even then the easiest way to find the patch is to have Oracle Support point you to the bug number or the patch number (usually the same number in the case of a one-off patch). These patches are usually not very big.

## Minipack

A minipack patch (referred to as a patch set in Release 10.7) is a larger cumulative patch. These patches are released for a particular product family and consolidate most, if not all, of the bug fixes (one-off patches) accumulated within the family up to a certain point. These patches are created periodically (depending on the product family), are named using a letter suffixed to the product family name (this is what Oracle Support is referencing when they ask if you are on FND.E or AP.F), and are cumulative in nature (AP.F would include all fixes from AP.A, AP.B, AP.C, AP.D, AP.E, and any fixes released between the release of AP.E and the starting of building the minipack AP.F). A minipack usually means that you only have to apply one patch instead of dozens. However, you may have to apply the patch on every node of a multi-node installation. The patch may have to be downloaded and applied on different OS platforms. If you have multiple language sets enabled, you may have to apply different versions of the same patch with different language bases to bring your entire product family to the correct point with each language.

A minipack usually provides additional functionality; it does more than just fix bugs.

Previous releases often required a client side patch and a server side patch when installing a patch set or minipack. Oracle 11i allows you to install a single patch that will provide all changes to all portions of the application. One caveat to that is that if you have different nodes in a multi-node installation, you will need to apply the patch to each node. If these nodes are on different OSs, you will need to download the appropriate version of each patch for each of the OSs in your configurations, unless the patch is generic.

## Family Pack

A family pack is a group of minipacks for related products, bundled together for simplicity and logical installation plus the possible addition of one-off fixes that may have been released between the release of the previous minipack and the bundling of the family pack. Family packs follow the same ideas as minipacks (e.g., cumulative, named with a letter, released periodically), however the naming convention varies somewhat. Their naming convention incorporates the release number, the patch's family, and the letter as well as the abbreviation that references this as a family pack (i.e., PF). For instance, 11i.OM_PF.D would refer to the Order Management Family Pack D for 11i, the 11i and the PF being the major delimiters referencing the new family pack installation.

## Family Consolidated Upgrade Patch

A Family Consolidated Upgrade Patch (FCUP, pronounced F-CUP) is a prerequisite patch for an upgrade. It usually includes performance improvements, bug fixes for processes that will be run in the patch that is to be run following the Consolidated Patch, any additional tablespaces, resizing information for existing tablespaces, or transfer of existing data dictionary managed tablespaces into locally managed tablespaces. If there are FCUPs required for an upgrade patch, they will be included in the release notes for that upgrade patch.

## Maintenance Pack

A maintenance pack is a collection of minipacks bundled together into a significant zip file, which can usually be ordered on a collection of CDs. Maintenance packs were referred to as release updates in Release 10. The end result of applying this patch will be to change the third digit of the release string in the Application release number (e.g., 11.5.6 or 11.5.8). A maintenance pack allows you to install all minipacks with a single set of drivers. Oracle's convention of rolling all previous patches of a similar type into the latest patch is followed here and all prior maintenance pack changes are rolled up into the latest maintenance pack. Typically the purpose of a maintenance pack is to roll up all bug fixes since the previous maintenance pack into a consolidated package; however, (as is the case with the 11.5.8 version) there are occasions when additional functionality is rolled into the patch as well.

## NLS (National Language Sets) Patches

When you have incorporated multiple languages in your implementation, on occasion you will need to install additional patches for each additional language installed. The American patch always needs to be applied first, followed by any NLS versions of the same patch. When you install the American version, you will need to make sure that you set the NLS_LANG variable to American_America <CHARACTER_SET> (substitute your appropriate character set for the CHARACTER_SET variable). Be sure to carefully read all README files that may contain reference to the need to install NLS patches and may provide special instructions needed during those installs.

While NLS patches are often needed, they are not always required. If the patch is a one-off patch that is simply fixing a stored procedure that may be in error or creating a new stored procedure, there is little likelihood that you will need a NLS version. If there are significant changes to Forms or Reports or if you are installing a minipack, family pack, or maintenance pack, you will likely find that you need to install an NLS version of that patch. If you have any doubts about the need to apply an NLS patch, contact Oracle Support to double-check.

The ADPATCH utility has added 11i functionality to alert you that you may need an NLS patch for a patch that you are installing. This is a handy feature. If it raises the possibility, you may need to double-check to see if there is an NLS version that needs to be installed. ADPATCH may alert you erroneously; so take the necessary steps to double-check the need to install one. Do not automatically assume that ADPATCH knows exactly what it is talking about.

## Minor Release

A minor release needs to be added to the list of patches in the increasing size and complexity list that we have started here, even though it is important to make note that a minor release is not a true patch. A patch is typically installed either using Adpatch or simple steps set forth in a README. A minor release is similar to a maintenance pack in that it usually ships on a single set of CDs for each different OS involved in your implementation. Unlike a maintenance pack that takes the third number in the release string to a higher number, a minor release changes the second number (e.g., moving from 10.7 to 11.0 to 11.5). A minor release requires the use of AutoUpgrade or Rapid Install to accomplish the installation. A minor release's primary purpose is to add functionality or change the infrastructure of the implementation and is the basis for the supported versions of the applications as referenced in the support matrix.

### Patch Naming

There is some logic put into the naming of patches. The names include the patch number (also often cross-referenced as bug number), release for which the patch was created (11i, 11.0, 10), and the OS (for OS specific patches) for which the patches are created. Therefore, p2250399_11i_AIX would be the patch number 2250399 created for Apps 11i as implemented on the AIX OS. OS-specific versions are usually released for Tru64, HP-UX, Sun Solaris, Intel Linux, Windows NT/2000, or AIX.

## DATABASE PATCHES

Database patches are applied to the database to fix problems and bridge gaps in its operations. Database patches are far fewer than Apps Layer and are released less frequently than other types of patches. The numbering scheme is currently dependent primarily on the major release of the database you are dealing with. This is mostly due to the addition of significant new functionality that comes with the installation of Release 9.2 of the database. What follows is a brief description and comparison of the two major database releases most typically used in new and migrated Oracle E-Business Suite implementations.

For 9.2.0.3.0 or 8.1.7.3:

- **9** is the major release number. This is the broadest and most general identifier (the 9 in 9i) representing a new version of the RDBMS software that contains new functionality. In Version 8 databases, it is the version number.
- **2** is the database maintenance release number. It represents some new functionality in Version 9, but primarily it simply represents maintenance features and bug fixes. In Version 8, it is the new features release number and brings with it significant new features and some bug fixes.
- **0** is the Applications Server release number. In Version 8, it is the maintenance release number. This is the biggest divergence in the 8 and 9 conventions other than primarily a naming change. In Version 8, it was the maintenance release that brings a few new features,

simpler maintenance, and bug fixes. In Version 9, it now indicates the release of the 9iAS portion of the database.

■ **3** is the component-specific release number. In Version 8, it is a generic patch set number. In Version 8, this indicated that it was a patch release that had been ported to all supported platforms. In Version 9, it represents the release level that is specific to any particular component in the database set. With the new configuration and default installed components of the RDBMS, different components within the major release can be at different component releases depending on what component patches have been applied and what interim releases are brought out by Oracle.

■ **0** is the platform-specific release number in both Versions 8 and 9. Typically, this is released as a patch set for a particular platform. If the same patch set is released for more than one platform or OS, all platform-specific release numbers for that patch set for all platforms will have the same release number in this position.

If you want to determine what exact version of the database server is currently installed, as well as determine all release levels of all components you currently have configured on your system, you can run the following query:

```
SELECT * FROM product_component_version;
```

For readability, you may have to predefine the column width of the Product, Version, and Status columns in the product_ component_version table, as there may be differences in the definition of the table column size between different releases of the database. Alternatively, you can query the V$VERSION view to retrieve information on the individual component level.

Database patches are applied in whatever manner the README instructs. These patches usually ship with their own application utility, use the ./runInstaller method, or come with instructions to download whatever utility the DBA needs to enable the installation.

## INTEROPERABILITY PATCHES

Historically, Oracle has always allowed for the incorporating of newer technology into the Financials/Applications (now Oracle E-Business Suite) by means of interoperability patches. This custom was probably first noticed when the support of Reports 2.5 was brought into the mix. Interoperability patches were first widely used with Version 10.7 of the Applications and with Oracle 7 when Oracle 7 went to Release 7.3.4.

What is an interoperability patch? It is Oracle's vehicle by which it can ensure that its Applications systems will run against newly released back-end technology or with the newer Apps Servers or Apache Server (for example). It brings all of the current component code to the same compatibility level as with the newer features. If the suggested interoperability patches are not installed with their corresponding new product versions (refer to README for this information), then the system is unlikely to run correctly. Without implementation of the interoperability patches, it is quite possible that the system could fail completely until all of the pieces are in place.

There are interoperability patches that are required when migrating from 10.7 to 11.0 to 11i.

## DIAGNOSTIC PATCHES

Oracle has created a complete line of diagnostic tools that they will use to try to help you to determine what part of your system requires attention. These tests gather information about your system and perform several data related validations based on the information that it gathers and makes recommendations and suggestions on actions to take based on the information and validations. Never are any data or setups within your environment altered by any of these diagnostic tools. There are three different varieties of tools available. Oracle Diagnostics tests depend on the Oracle Diagnostics framework being in place and viable to assist in the execution. These tests are typically run exclusively through the Web. Stand-alone tests run from either a command prompt or through a SQL*Plus session. Finally, Oracle Diagnostics tests (OD patch tests) are tests that are designed by Oracle and delivered to you by means of a patch set. These patches are not released to bring new features to an application or to fix any existing problems; they are simply to provide you with diagnostic tools to assist in the troubleshooting of your application. There are diagnostic patches for printer issues and for Concurrent Manager issues. There is a diagnostic patch that determines current configuration of the database. There are diagnostic patches available for many other things that commonly are found to have problems. Usually, Oracle Support will direct you to whatever diagnostics it wants you to run and provide the patch set number that you can download to allow you to perform that functionality. The diagnostic patches are usually unobtrusive queries that simply gather information and put it into a predetermined format. Once you have downloaded that diagnostic tool, if it does something that you routinely seem to be investigating, you can run it independent of Oracle Support and start to troubleshoot your own problems. When you do log a support request iTAR, you will have the background information already at your fingertips. This is not Oracle's suggested method of running them: it suggests that you only run them with the assistance of Oracle Support.

A complete catalog of all available diagnostic tools is available through Metalink Note 178043.1 and the note gives you access to the latest release of the diagnostic tool, along with the last update date of the tool, so you can double-check to make sure that you are running the latest version. These diagnostics tools are included in the monthly support pack, which can be downloaded from Metalink (Note 1670001). One of the diagnostic tools is ACT (Applications Collection Tool). ACT can be used for diagnosis of installation and configuration problems in your system and to gather all relevant information at one time and in one place to facilitate the logging of your iTARs or when you need to verify what specific version of a file is currently running on your system. ACT registers itself as a Concurrent Program and can, therefore, be run from either the command line or from your concurrent request screen. It probably is not one that you will want to run on a schedule, as it will provide the same information every time. However, I recommend that you run it after patching or after an upgrade so that you can print and maintain the information for quick reference. That way when a developer or an end user calls and says "What version of <insert program unit here> are we on?" you have a quick reference you can scan and give them the answer. Just some of the information that it gathers is Forms and Forms library versions, package versions, Reports versions, profile option values, all Oracle versions, Applications installation details, and creation date.

Other tests are available; some as general purpose as this test; others are product or problem specific. It is a good idea to look at the catalog periodically to see what tests might apply to you and which ones you could make use of in your maintenance routine.

## HOW TO APPLY

Now that you have the general idea of what a patch is, we can look at what is entailed in applying one. It is not difficult to apply an application patch; it is a little more difficult to try to diagnose why one fails, but usually just challenging enough to keep you on your toes.

### Patch Search and Download

In order to apply a patch, you first have to get the patch from Oracle Support. To get the patches on your system, you have to download them from Metalink. Before you can download it, you have to find it.

After you log into Metalink, you will have a series of navigation buttons on the left hand side of the page. The Patches button will take you to

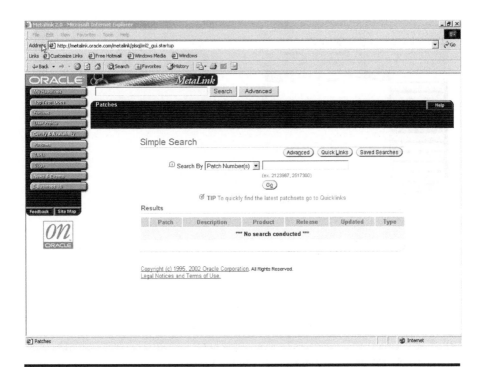

**Figure 10.1   New Patch Search Screen**

one of two screens. You will either find yourself directly at a screen from where you can search for patches (Figure 10.1 shows the New Patch Search screen) or to a screen that allows you to choose between the New Metalink Patch Search and Old Metalink Patch Search (Figure 10.2 shows the screen that allows you to choose).

Which screen you get depends on when you are doing this and when more of the client base migrates to Internet Explorer 5.5. The Old Patch Search (Figure 10.3) was supposed to have gone away already and be replaced by the new functionality of the New Patch Search, but too many people were using browsers that would not support the functionality. At some point, however, this old feature will no longer be available and only New Metalink Patch Search will be available. Some information is easier to find through the old interface, so I am not looking forward to this happening.

Old Metalink Patch Search provides you with a series of drop-down list boxes (lists of valid values based on the combinations of all previous list boxes) from which you can choose. From the processing of the chosen values, you will have returned to you a list of applicable patches. One of the biggest drawbacks is that there are often many patches returned that qualify for the combination and you still have to comb through these

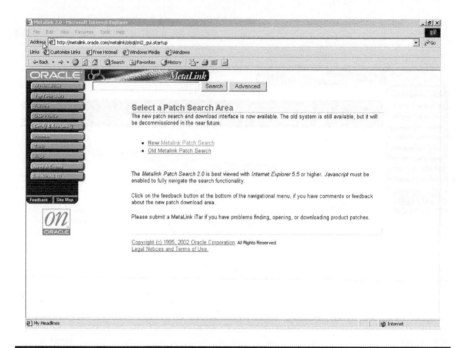

**Figure 10.2   Old/New Patch Search Choice Screen**

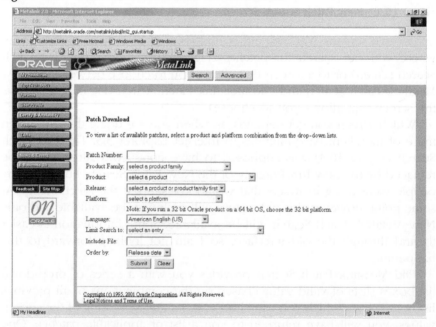

**Figure 10.3   Old Patch Search Screen**

**Figure 10.4   Quick Links for Database and Tools**

for the one patch that you want to apply. You always want to download the patch that is either generic or that has been built specifically for your OS and for each OS in your configuration, except possibly (for most Apps patches) your database tier if your database is the only thing on that tier.

The New Metalink Patch Search has different options, but is also more flexible. You are taken initially to a simple search screen. Three buttons — Advanced, Quick Links, Saved Searches — grace the top of the screen.

Quick links allows you to access the most commonly accessed patch sets in just a few quick clicks. Figure 10.4 shows the quick links for the RDBMS and Tools. Figure 10.5 shows the quick links for the 11i Oracle E-Business Suite.

If you look at Figure 10.6, you will see that you can hover your mouse cursor over the link to drill out to translations for 11i patches and further to the translations that are already ported. You can get directly to the README in this manner and directly to the download screen for any of the OS-specific downloads as well.

Clicking on the patch link will take you to a screen, much like the one in Figure 10.7, where you can choose the OS for which you can download the patch, link out to the README, and see the size and priority of the given patch set as well as any patch sets that include or supersede the patch that was investigated.

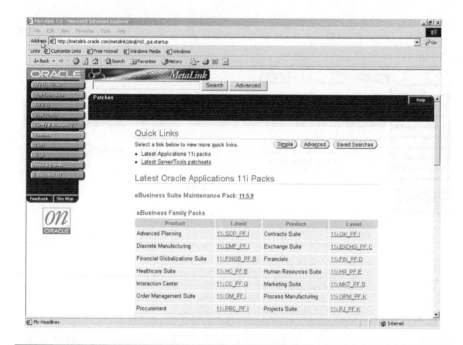

**Figure 10.5  Quick Links for Oracle E-Business Suite**

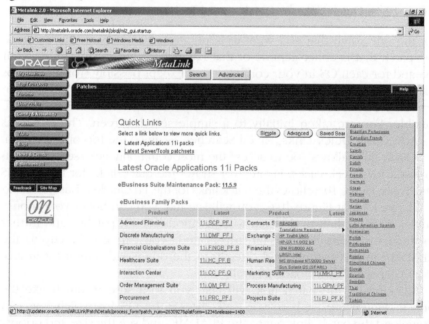

**Figure 10.6  Patch Language Translations Available**

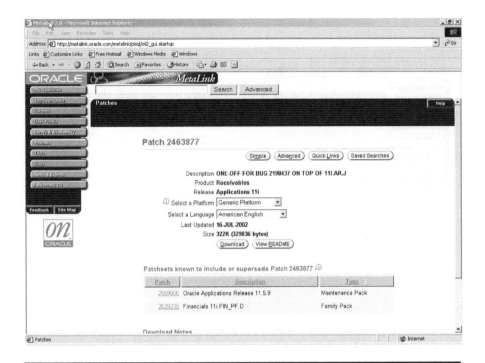

**Figure 10.7    Patch Download**

Below the three buttons on the simple search page (see Figure 10.8), you are given the option to search by patch number, product family, or saved search. Patch number is the default selection and beside the drop-down box is a box into which you can enter a comma-delimited list of patch numbers for which you are searching.

Choosing Product Family from the drop-down list of values box returns another entry box into which you can enter search terms, as well as a drop-down box for product or product family, and another for patch set or minipack. Figure 10.9 shows the screen that results from selecting Product Family from the drop-down box. Product or product family searching requires that you enter a search term in the entry box, although clicking on the small flashlight will launch you through another set of screens from which you can decide what products you want by short name, wild card, or by means of hunting through a hierarchy of product families. Searching is somewhat easier than just entering the search term.

Figure 10.9 shows the search screen where you can choose the product family from the drop-down list and Figure 10.10 shows you the Search and Select: Product or Family screen. If you know what you are searching for, Figure 10.10 is the quickest way to get your information returned.

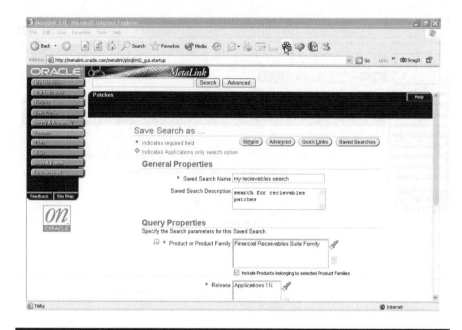

**Figure 10.8   Save Your Searches**

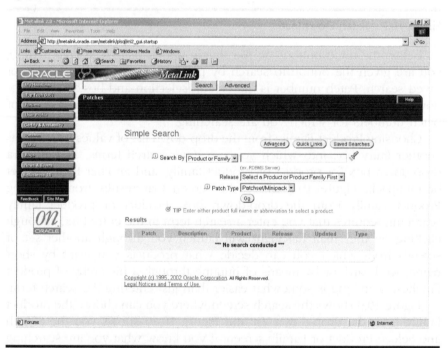

**Figure 10.9   Product Family Search**

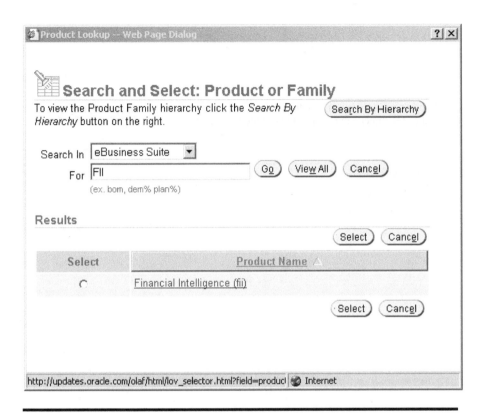

**Figure 10.10   Search by Name**

If you do not know exactly what you are looking for, only that you are looking for patches for your products, you might want to choose to search by hierarchy. If you are going to be applying patches on a set schedule, this may be a better option for you. Database and Tools (in Figure 10.11) presents you with not only RDBMS patches but network services, Discoverer, Developer, Apps Server patches (9iAS), Java technology, and Oracle System Management (OSM) to name just a few of the choices. At each level, you have the ability to drill down even further (by clicking on the + sign) until you get to the lowest level of granularity that is logical for your particular hierarchy choice.

As an example, Figure 10.12 shows that if you want to search for all receivables patches, you can simply select the link entitled "Financial Receivables Suite Family" and that will be populated back to the original search screen (see Figure 10.13). From there you can perform your search.

This method may return more patches than you anticipated; however, the result set is also presented with the ability to sort the results to better meet your needs.

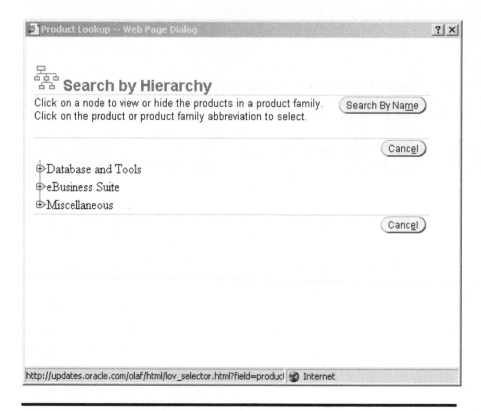

**Figure 10.11   Search by Hierarchy**

Looking at Figure 10.14, you can see that you can either select the entire product family, drill-down further, or only select the particular product that you want to find the patch for.

Figure 10.15 and Figure 10.16 show you a sample of a Receivables Family search. If you look at Figure 10.15 somewhat closer, you can see a "Hot" or high priority patch marked with a red "!" so that you can pick only the high priority patches if that is what you want to do. On the same screen, you are given the ability to save this search to be used later in the saved searches option of the search screen.

By saving the search (see Figure 10.8), you can narrow the search by qualifying exactly what you are looking for from it (e.g., what OS, patches updated in the last specified amount of time — days, weeks, months), what languages you need this to be searched for (or all languages), and other limiting factors that may be specific to your particular configuration.

Figure 10.12 shows the ability to further drill into the Receivables Family and select only the product that you are interested in patching. This will also allow you to limit the result set returned and segregate the

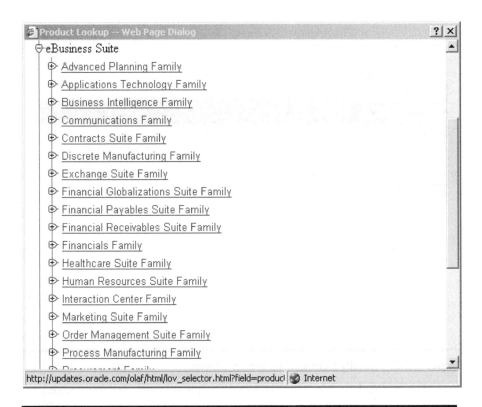

**Figure 10.12   Expanded Hierarchy**

patches that you are applying into their specific components. This is particularly important if you have installed individual components. You may not have to patch shared components as often or as intensively as you patch the fully licensed ones. An example of this might be if you implemented Cash Management for some reason, but opted to not license General Ledger or you might have licensed Receivables, but do not want to implement iReceivables.

One of the most useful features of this interface is the ability to save your searches and your ability to recall those saved searches later to save the time of waiting for reinserting all of that information. The more different modules that you have installed, the more useful you will find this feature. It has the potential to save considerable time and aggravation over your life as an Apps administrator. You can narrow your patch searches so that you receive those patches for your OS, those for the languages that you have installed, or those patches updated in the last <you define> days, weeks, or months.

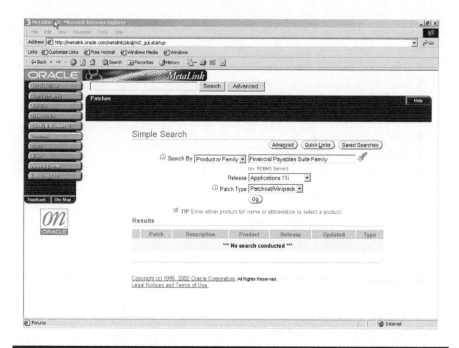

**Figure 10.13 Results Returned to Search Screen**

**Figure 10.14 Drill-Down to Product**

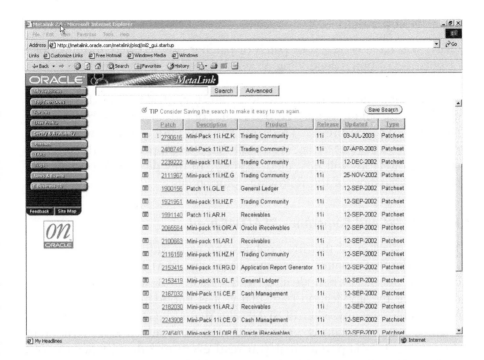

**Figure 10.15   Receivables Family Search Result**

**Figure 10.16   Critical Receivables Patch**

## What Is in a Patch?

Okay, you have gotten your patch or patches downloaded and unzipped or untarred or both (depending on your platform). What is in the resulting patch directory?

Unzipping the patch will create a directory that is named using just the number from the patch's zipped name (or the same as the bug number for one-off patches). That means that if you downloaded p1234567_11i_AIX.zip, you will have unzipped the file and the resulting directory will be called 1234567. In this directory you will find some combination of the following components.

### *README.txt and Sometimes README.html*

The html version of this file contains the same information as the text version, simply formatted differently. Typically, README files are not read by many people. When dealing with Oracle E-Business Suite and the patches for the application particularly, it is important that you not only read this file, but any other README files that it directs you to. The 11.5.8 upgrade patch contained or directed you to nearly a dozen different documents. It is important that you read every one that applies to your configuration. It is advisable that you read all of the files pointed to by the core README just to make sure that you do not miss anything. The README files contain detailed information on what prerequisite patches are required for the current patch, preinstallation steps you need to perform if any, postinstallation steps that you need to perform if any, and, occasionally, things that you need to do after one of the driver files but before you do anything else in the patch. Manual steps are included, scripts to run if they exist, and any prepatch or postpatch patches that need to be applied. If the steps are not followed in the correct order, it may cause your patch to not install correctly, if it allows it to install at all. The README will often also contain new features brought to the application with the installation of the patch or any bugs that were fixed by the patch.

### *Driver Files*

#### *C1234567.drv*

This is a copy driver. It copies files from the patch directory to their required location, relinks application executables, and repackages jar files and zip files if necessary. It extracts the files from the patch's C library using ADLIBOUT and replaces them into the patch structure using ADLIBIN. After the files are extracted, it compares the extracted version with the corresponding version in the product's directory structure (e.g., Forms, Reports, Graphics, and sql scripts) and determines if the existing file is as new or newer than the patch's version. If it is as new or newer, ADPATCH replaces that file into the library, leaving the existing version. If the file in the patch is a newer version, ADPATCH copies the old file to a backup directory and replaces it with the newer version. If the copy driver has to repackage jar files or zip files, it can take what appears to be an inordinately long time to run (an hour or more) and appear to be doing nothing while it is doing it. ADPATCH and the C driver will relink the relevant Oracle E-Business Suite products with the OS, with the database, and with other Oracle products and libraries. Finally, the C driver will copy any new html files or media files into their final respective destinations after copying any older versions of the same files into the backup directory.

### D1234567.drv

This is a database driver. The driver will bring with it new versions of packages, error messages, tables or views, table columns, or other database objects. It also could contain data to populate a table or column. Details of what exactly this driver did can be culled from the resulting worker log file that you can comb through after the patch has run or you can monitor it as the patch is running. The tail -f adwork01.log command allows you to watch exactly what each worker is doing. ADPATCH, while running the D driver, determines what proposed actions a previous patch already performed and runs scripts or exec commands to make changes to the database objects. It will use invoker's rights if part of the patch is delivering a package. ADPATCH runs D drivers, by default, in parallel; the number of workers you allow ADPATCH to spawn determines the degree to which the parallelism is carried out that you allow ADPATCH to assign to the tasks.

### G1234567.drv

This is a generate driver. It generates forms, reports, libraries, and message files. It utilizes parallel workers the same as the database driver does. You can monitor the progress of the G driver workers the same way you can the D driver workers. This driver should be applied to all APPL_TOPs on all nodes in your configuration.

### .ldt File

Recent 11i patches include a file with the .ldt extension. This file contains metadata about the patch to be applied that will get uploaded via the FNDLOAD utility. The new prerequisite checking feature in ADPATCH loads that metadata and using the patch history tables from the database, determines if all of the prerequisite patches for this particular patch have been applied. Patches that include the .ldt files also include, in their C driver files, a line that states "compatible feature prereq" that prevents the patch from being applied against Oracle E-Business Suite using an older version of ADPATCH that does not support the prerequisite checking feature. It is not recommended that you run these patches if ADPATCH tries to prevent you from applying them; however, some README files will instruct you to apply them using the noprereq parameter when you start ADPATCH.

The prerequisite checking is only done during the C driver portion of the patch, but since you have to apply all drivers in a patch and the C driver has to be the first one applied, this prevents the patch from being applied.

Further, this new prerequisite checking will prevent you from installing a translation of a patch until the base version (U.S. version) has been applied. It will also inform you if it determines that a patch has already been applied (it is occasionally in error on this count) and asks you if you really want to reapply it.

### Product Directories

Each patch will usually contain a product directory structure that mimics the product's directory structure under the APPL_TOP. This will be the location from which the copy (C) driver will copy the new files and will also be the location to which (under the APPL_TOP version of the same directory structure) it will copy it.

After you have run an ADPATCH session, you will usually also find a backup directory within the patch's directory structure. In here will be the original version of the copied files. If you run the same driver more than once without either restarting ADPATCH (restarting starts where the previous run failed as opposed to starting over from the beginning of the patch driver) or renaming the backup directory, you will overwrite whatever is in there from your original run with whatever the subsequent runs puts in. There are times when you will want to have access to the original versions of the program units that the patch is replacing. This is where they will be. If there is any way to back out any part of a patch, having the original programs in this backup directory will prove invaluable, as the patch knows exactly what it replaced.

### New Checkfile Feature

Another new feature brought with later versions of ADPATCH is the new Checkfile feature. Checkfile helps to reduce the amount of time a patch takes to apply by comparing database actions that are to be taken by the patch with entries into a new table called the AD_CHECK_FILES table. When a patch is applied that takes advantage of the new feature, ADPATCH checks the actions to be taken by the patch, compares them to actions that are found in the table (complete with parameter, argument, and version checking) and if it determines that the actions that are supposed to be performed are really redundant, it makes the decision not to reapply those changes. After it performs the prescribed actions, it updates the AD_CHECK_FILES table with the information it just applied.

If a patch is Checkfile enabled, it will contain the line "compatible feature Checkfile." Further, all sql statements and EXEC commands will have as one of their parameters the Checkfile keyword. This parameter is what allows ADPATCH to make the comparisons and resulting decisions on whether or not to apply a change and later updates the table with the information that it applied those changes to the database.

## Backup All Tiers of the System

I cannot say it enough. Backup the system (all tiers in the system) before you start a patch session. Do not just backup, though. Verify that your backup did not have any errors when it ran. This verification will take longer, but if you can go into a patching session knowing that you have a good clean backup that you can confidently restore from, you will be less worried about something unforeseen happening and you will have the security in knowing that you can always fall back to this point if something should go horribly wrong.

## Install Patch

Okay, now it is time to look at physically installing a patch.

Have an environment where you install patches first and test them. It can be in your Vision system, if you have one, or it can be in Test. Where you test them is irrelevant, it only matters that you install them somewhere other than production first to test them. This is the environment into which you want to install them first.

Read the README file. Make note of prerequisite and postrequisite patches and apply them in the order that their dependencies require. Note extra steps that need to be performed and where those are supposed to occur. Most steps that are required are supposed to be done after the patch has been successfully installed. However, this is not always the case so do not get complacent. There are times when a patch says to perform some outside step after one of the drivers. If this is the case, there is a reason that it should be done at this time and performing this out of order can cause problems with the patch installation or later when you are testing.

If at all possible, install a patch on a clean copy of Production cloned into your other environments. This will allow you to attempt to duplicate any problem that you are seeing and will provide you with a picture of Production data against which to run your tests so that you can later verify the test results that you saw in Test or the Vision system with what you are able to reproduce in Production.

Make sure that you have a good, clean backup before you start patching. Uninstalling a patch is nearly impossible. The best you can hope for is a clean place to restore to as close as possible to where the patch failed.

### Test Mode

If you want to see exactly what a patch is going to be doing, you can run ADPATCH in test mode and see exactly what it would be doing if you were actually applying the patch. It lists all of the files that it would have copied, every file that it would have relinked, every command that would have been executed, and every file that would have been generated if the patch had actually been run in the apply mode. This will not give you all of the errors that you are likely to encounter, that is why you apply the patch on as many copies of a Production-like environment as you can, but it will give you some idea of which of your customizations you are liable to clobber with the patch so you can get a jump on what you might have to do to fix it later. It could be a good tool to alert developers as to what they may want to be on the look out for. It is also a good test to double-check to see if ADPATCH will find something that is missing that you might have to do before you actually apply the patch for real. Pass in the apply=no parameter to accomplish testing the patch without applying it.

```
Adpatch apply=no
```

Other things that running a patch in test mode will not do is update patch history (patch information in the database), release versions, or the older applptch.txt file. It will not run any commands that will update the database in any way. It will not copy or archive any files, will not relink any executables, or actually regenerate any forms, reports, menus, or libraries. It will extract objects, validate the patch's integrity, and load any metadata into ADPATCH to enable it to do version and prerequisite checking.

Concurrent Managers need to be down when patching, other services should be down when patching, and users should be off of the system.

Some patches say that they can safely be applied with the services up or users are on and active; others (especially those that deal with replacing DLLs — dynamic-link libraries) cannot. I feel more comfortable making sure that there are no extraneous things that can have any impact on the success of the patch installation or on the health of the system when it comes back up. It only adds an extra half hour to the patch installation time to bring down the services elegantly and bring them back up when you are done. It also gives you a measure of comfort that the patch did not have any side effects on the services. I make this part of my test plan for patch installation. Do all of the services come up cleanly after I have applied a patch?

Most Apps patches are applied using the ADPATCH utility. ADPATCH is a menu-driven utility that will help walk you through the application of a patch. It will prompt you for several pieces of information.

You will want to be in the patch's home directory when you start ADPATCH. It is not required, but it does tend to make the installation easier from a logic perspective. It also means less typing and less chance of making a mistake and incurring even more typing.

If you are on a Windows server, run %APPL_TOP%\envshell.cmd to set up your environment and create a DOS command prompt window. From here, change to the patch directory and run ADPATCH. If you are on a UNIX server, make sure that the environment setup is accomplished by running the <SID>.env file that is created in $ORACLE_HOME or $APPL_TOP. Once the environment has been set up, you can change to the patch directory and run ADPATCH.

Apply the drivers in the correct order. I do not know if Oracle planned it this way, but patch drivers are applied in alphabetical order. The C (copy) driver is applied first, the D (database) driver is applied next, and the G (generate) driver gets applied last.

Maximize your hardware utilization. If you have a UNIX machine as your database layer and you have 24 processors on that machine, Oracle suggests that you should allow 54 workers to run on that machine (Processors * 2.5) when running a D driver or G driver. But remember, you should know your hardware and take your preexisting knowledge into account. If you are running this patch during a time when there are likely to be active users on other Oracle databases or other processes actively running on the machine, you need to take this into account as well. Workers running their processes can be resource intensive. You also have to make sure that you have enough processes available because every worker that you create will spawn its own process at the OS level. If you do not have your available processes set high enough, you could find workers failing because they cannot create another process.

By default, ADPATCH validates all passwords for all schemas before it performs any driver actions. To save time, if you are applying several patches on a system where the Applications' schemas or their passwords are not likely to change, you can omit the validation by adding a parameter (options=novalidate) to the ADPATCH command.

```
Adpatch option=novalidate
```

Copy (C) drivers have to be run on every node in a multi-node installation, except the database tier if only your database is residing on that tier. Database (D) drivers need only to be applied once on any given system (i.e., once on Vision, once on Test, once on Production). The generate (G) driver needs to be applied to every node that the C driver was applied to. To be safe, run the C and G drivers on every APPL_TOP and the D driver only from the first one.

## Steps in Installing a Patch

When installing a patch, you need to be running Auto Patch (ADPATCH) as the applmgr user. This user is the one with all authority to the application's services and usually one of the owners of the system. Once you are logged in with this user ID, you need to set your environment variables for the system that you intend to maintain. In UNIX, you could add the command to set your environment automatically in the .profile file and every time you log in, you will have your environment already set up for you. This applies if you do not have all of your Applications owned by the same ID.

The file that will set your environment in UNIX is typically found in either the APPL_TOP or the ORACLE_HOME for your environment and is called <SID>.env. If you are running in a Windows environment, it will be located the same place, but will be named <SID>.cmd.

Your patch should be downloaded into a common directory where all patches get placed. Once downloaded there, it should be unzipped. Keeping all patches in a similar file system or directory structure helps keep maintenance of Oracle Applications clean, centralized, and logical. It is important that you not use the patch subdirectories under the product top directory (e.g., AR_TOP, AP_TOP, HR_TOP) to download and install patches from.

Read all README.txt or README.htm files. It is important that you look at and review all README documents either contained within the patch or referenced by a README contained in the patch (these are usually links to documents on the Metalink site). README files will inform you of special steps that need to be taken when applying the patch, other patches that have to be in place for this patch to run correctly, and manual steps that you will need to perform to have the patch installation be completely successful.

Shut down all services on Applications' layers. Do not shut down the database (unless you are patching the RDBMS, which is never done through ADPATCH). This includes Apache, Forms Servers, and the Apps Listener, but most importantly, the Concurrent Managers need to be shut down for patching.

Change to the directory where the patch you are applying resides (into the directory created when you unzipped the patch) and run ADPATCH at the command line. Respond to all of the ADPATCH prompts. It will ask you for SYSTEM's password, Apps' password, the name you want to use for your log file, and other pieces of information that it needs to run. If you are running in interactive mode, you will need to provide it one driver filename each time you start ADPATCH. This means that if you have all three drivers in a patch, you will have to run three ADPATCH sessions, one after the other, to get all three drivers to run. Never try to run more than one ADPATCH session at a time.

After each driver finishes, it is important to review the log files that are generated by that driver. The main log file and the log files for all of the utilities that it spawns are located in the APPL_TOP\admin\ <SID>\log directory. The main log file will have the default name of ADPATCH.log if you have not renamed it. It may get quite large, if you keep the default with every run of ADPATCH and you have run several patches as these log files are only appended to, never replaced. Keeping them clean and manageable sizes becomes important when you are resolving problems. Examine all logs for warnings and errors. Usually, warnings can be safely ignored, but knowing they exist and doing a cursory search on Metalink for them will help ensure peace of mind later.

Once you have made sure that your logs do not show errors, you will need to check your customizations. If you have customized a form or a report and maintained its original name, it is quite likely that some patch (or many patches) will overlay the customization with its own version of the object. It will have made a backup of the original and placed it in the patch's directory structure in a backup directory for your environment. You may need to rebuild, reapply, or merge the customizations into the new object if you want to take advantage of that new object's new features. You may simply need to replace the new one with the old object and determine if the old functionality still works. If the patch has made structural changes on database objects, you may find that you will have to do work on the custom objects to get them to function after the patch.

If you are running MRC, you should always use ADADMIN to maintain the MRC schema if the patch you have applied has run a D driver. ADPATCH will display a reminder to do this if it has applied a database driver to the environment. It is important that you not skip this step as your MRC will likely not function as anticipated otherwise.

If you have run a patch that has a D driver, and alterations have been made to the database objects, you may want to run ADXGNPIN.sql and ADXGNPNS.sql from under AD_TOP/sql directory to pin new and altered packages and sequences in the SGA. If the SGA becomes fragmented there may not be sufficient room for larger packages or functions to be loaded into memory to run. Pinning packages, functions, and sequences into the shared pool makes sure that there is enough room for these program units to reside in memory. ADXGNPIN pins packages and functions (primarily from the APPS schema). ADXGNPNS pins sequences and program units from the other base products. Both take, as a parameter, the schema name or % for all schemas. If you are running MRC, there are some packages in the MRC schema that have to run with definer's rights. You will need to rerun the ADXGNPIN.sql script in that schema as well. If your Apps tier and your database tier are not on the same machine, you can copy these two sql scripts into an appsutil/admin directory that you create in the ORACLE_HOME so you can call these scripts automatically when the database is restarted.

If you have run a patch with a D driver, you may want to run ORACLE_HOME\rdbms\admin\utlrp.sql to recompile invalid objects. It is not necessary to do this. The invalid objects will probably compile the first time they are accessed, but your system will run faster immediately after the patching if you take the time to run utlrp. It can even be run while the system is up and the users are testing. Running this after every D driver or periodically during a long series of patches will ensure that you have as few invalids in your database as possible and limit the effects of invalid objects on the running of the application.

Restart the server processes, run preliminary tests to make sure that your system is running, and then allow the functional users access to the system to test that the new changes are both working and have not had the unanticipated side effects of breaking something else.

Once your testing is complete and everyone is satisfied that the patch runs as anticipated, you can clean up the backup files from your system. If you have room on disk, tape, or optical media, I advise you to archive these backups of replaced files for a period of time. Archiving in one central area allows you to quickly see what has changed and what history you have of all changes to the system. Once the patch is applied and the backups archived, you can safely recover used disk space by deleting the individual patch directories. Table 10.1 is an example of a portion of a log file for a D driver. First notice that all validation of passwords is complete, then all of the setup is done in connection to the

FND_INSTALL_PROCESSES table, the driver gets processed, then elegantly (if all goes well) shuts down, and exits.

### Noninteractive Mode

While it is common practice to run every patch interactively (answering every menu prompt requested by ADPATCH as it comes to the screen) this is not the only way to apply patches.

Noninteractive patching means that you supply a defaults file that ADPATCH reads. This defaults file has the answers to many of the prompts that you would be presented with in an interactive patching session.

To create a defaults file, you start ADPATCH as you would in an interactive session but in this case you pass in, as a parameter, the name that you want your defaults file to have. The defaults file has to be located in the %APPL_TOP%/admin/<SID> directory but can have any name that you choose to give it.

```
Adpatch defaultsfile=
%APPL_TOP%\admin\VIS\defaults.txt
```

or

```
Adpatch defaultsfile=
$APPL_TOP/admin/VIS/defaults.txt
```

You need to run ADPATCH, answering all of the questions up until the point where it asks you for the directory where the patch is located. At this point, type abort (the means by which you can get out of ADPATCH at any point) at the prompt and check to make sure that ADPATCH created the file with the specified name in the specified place.

If the file was not created, you will have to go through the same exercise again. If it was created, you can now apply patches one driver at a time or all of the drivers in a given patch at once using this defaults file.

To apply a patch one driver at a time, you would run ADPATCH passing in several parameters on the command line in a continuous string (do not hit enter when you near the end of the line).

```
Adpatch defaultsfile=<path to the defaults file>
logfile=<name of your log file> patchtop=<location
where your patch resides> driver=<driver you want
to run> workers=<number of workers you want to run>
interactive=no
```

From the above example, it would look something like this for applying patch driver d1234567 with a defaults file named defaults.txt on the Vision database creating a log file vis_d1234567_june-3-2002-900_ajw.log and assuming the patch to be located in the /patch directory structure in the subdirectory 12345678:

**Table 10.1  Portion of a Log File for a D Driver**

```
************* Start of AutoPatch session *************
AutoPatch version: 11.5.0
AutoPatch started at: Wed May 14 2003 04:36:04
APPL_TOP is set to d:\prodappl
Please enter the batchsize [1000] : 1000
Please enter the name of the Oracle Applications System
that this
APPL_TOP belongs to.
.

.
. Validating password for each schema…
….
Connecting to ALR……Connected successfully.
.
Connecting to AX……Connected successfully.
.
Connecting to AK……Connected successfully.
.
Connecting to XLA……Connected successfully.
.
Connecting to GL……Connected successfully.
.
Connecting to RG……Connected successfully.
.
Connecting to FA……Connected successfully.
.
Connecting to HR……Connected successfully.
….
Connecting to SSP……Connected successfully.
.
Connecting to BEN……Connected successfully.
.

.

.
. Creating FND_INSTALL_PROCESSES table…
Connecting to APPLSYS……Connected successfully.
CREATE TABLE fnd_install_processes(worker_id   number
not null,
  control_code varchar2(1)   not null, status
varchar2(1)   not null,
  context         varchar2(80) not null, pdi_product
varchar2(10) not null,
  pdi_username varchar2(32) not null, command
 varchar2(30) not null,
file_product varchar2(10) not null, subdirectory
 varchar2(30) not null,
```

*-- continued*

**Table 10.1 (continued)   Portion of a Log File for a D Driver**

```
filename      varchar2(30) not null, phase      number
not null,
 install_group_num number   not null, skip_flag
varchar2(1), arguments
 varchar2(1996), phase_name   varchar2(30), start_time
date, end_time
     date, restart_time   date, elapsed_time   number,
restart_count number,
 defer_count number) TABLESPACE APPLSYSD initrans 100
storage(initial 4K
 next 4K)
CREATE UNIQUE INDEX fnd_install_processes_u1 on
 fnd_install_processes(worker_id)   TABLESPACE   APPLSYSX
storage(initial 4K
 next 4K)
GRANT ALL ON fnd_install_processes TO  APPS WITH GRANT
OPTION
Connecting to APPS......Connected successfully.
Connecting to APPLSYS......Connected successfully.
CREATE TABLE AD_DEFERRED_JOBS(phase        number
not null,
 file_product varchar2(10) not null, subdirectory
varchar2(30) not null,
 filename      varchar2(30) not null, arguments
varchar2(1996),
 start_time    date, restart_time   date, elapsed_time
number,
 restart_count number, defer_count number) TABLESPACE
APPLSYSD initrans 100
 storage(initial 4K next 4K)
CREATE UNIQUE INDEX AD_DEFERRED_JOBS_U1 on
AD_DEFERRED_JOBS
 (phase,file_product,subdirectory,filename,arguments)
TABLESPACE APPLSYSX
 storage(initial 4K next 4K)
GRANT ALL ON AD_DEFERRED_JOBS TO  APPS WITH GRANT OPTION
Connecting to APPS......Connected successfully.
Connecting to APPLSYS......Connected successfully.
INSERT INTO fnd_install_processes (worker_id,
control_code, status,
 context, pdi_product, pdi_username, command,
file_product, subdirectory,filename, phase,
install_group_num, arguments) VALUES (0, 'W', 'W',
'UNDEF', 'UNDEF', 'UNDEF', 'UNDEF', 'UNDEF', 'UNDEF',
'UNDEF', 0, 0,
 rpad('-',100,'-'))
```

*-- continued*

**Table 10.1 (continued)   Portion of a Log File for a D Driver**

```
INSERT INTO fnd_install_processes (worker_id,
control_code, status,
 context, pdi_product, pdi_username, command,
file_product, subdirectory,
 filename, phase, install_group_num, arguments) VALUES
(1, 'W', 'W',
 'UNDEF', 'UNDEF', 'UNDEF', 'UNDEF', 'UNDEF', 'UNDEF',
'UNDEF', 0, 0,
 rpad('-',100,'-'))
INSERT INTO fnd_install_processes (worker_id,
control_code, status,
 context, pdi_product, pdi_username, command,
file_product, subdirectory,
 filename, phase, install_group_num, arguments) VALUES
(2, 'W', 'W',
 'UNDEF', 'UNDEF', 'UNDEF', 'UNDEF', 'UNDEF', 'UNDEF',
'UNDEF', 0, 0,
 rpad('-',100,'-'))
INSERT INTO fnd_install_processes (worker_id,
control_code, status,
 context, pdi_product, pdi_username, command,
file_product, subdirectory,
 filename, phase, install_group_num, arguments) VALUES
(3, 'W', 'W',
 'UNDEF', 'UNDEF', 'UNDEF', 'UNDEF', 'UNDEF', 'UNDEF',
'UNDEF', 0, 0,
 rpad('-',100,'-'))
INSERT INTO fnd_install_processes (worker_id,
control_code, status,
 context, pdi_product, pdi_username, command,
file_product, subdirectory,
 filename, phase, install_group_num, arguments) VALUES
(4, 'W', 'W',
 'UNDEF', 'UNDEF', 'UNDEF', 'UNDEF', 'UNDEF', 'UNDEF',
'UNDEF', 0, 0,
 rpad('-',100,'-'))
INSERT INTO fnd_install_processes (worker_id,
control_code, status,
     context, pdi_product, pdi_username, command,
     file_product, subdirectory,
 filename, phase, install_group_num, arguments) VALUES
(5, 'W', 'W',
 'UNDEF', 'UNDEF', 'UNDEF', 'UNDEF', 'UNDEF', 'UNDEF',
'UNDEF', 0, 0,
 rpad('-',100,'-'))
```

*-- continued*

**Table 10.1 (continued)   Portion of a Log File for a D Driver**

```
INSERT INTO fnd_install_processes (worker_id,
control_code, status,
 context, pdi_product, pdi_username, command,
file_product, subdirectory,
 filename, phase, install_group_num, arguments) VALUES
(6, 'W', 'W',
 'UNDEF', 'UNDEF', 'UNDEF', 'UNDEF', 'UNDEF', 'UNDEF',
'UNDEF', 0, 0,
 rpad('-',100,'-'))
.
.
. There are now 1 jobs remaining (current phase=A0):
     0 running, 1 ready to run and 0 waiting.
Reading completed jobs from restart file (if any).
There are now 1 jobs remaining (current phase=A0):
     0 running, 1 ready to run and 0 waiting.
Connecting to APPS......Connected successfully.
Starting worker processes.
Worker process 1 started.
Worker process 2 started.
Worker process 3 started.
Worker process 4 started.
Worker process 5 started.
Worker process 6 started.
Writing jobs to run to restart file.
Reading jobs from FND_INSTALL_PROCESSES table...
.
.
.
for details.
Purging timing information for prior sessions.
plus80 -s APPS/APPS @d:\oracle\
prodappl\ad\11.5.0\admin\sql\adtpurge.sql 10 1000
Done purging timing information for prior sessions.
AutoPatch is complete.
AutoPatch may have written informational messages to the
file
d:\oracle\
prodappl\admin\PROD\log\prod_d2554025_0514030436_ajw.lgi
     You should check the file
d:\oracle\
prodappl\admin\PROD\log\prod_d2554025_0514030436_ajw.log
for errors.
```

```
ADPATCH defaultsfile==
$APPL_TOP/admin/VIS/defaults.txt
logfile=vis_d12345678_june-3-2002-900_ajw.log
patchtop=/patch/12345678 driver=d12345678.drv work-
ers=4 interactive=no
```

If you want to apply an entire patch set noninteractively at one time and that patch has the standard structure (the patch's top directory has eight numeric characters in the name, the drivers are named c<8 numbers>. drv d<8 numbers>.drv g<8 numbers>.drv (c12345678.drv, d12345678.drv, g12345678.drv), you would use the following command line command:

```
ADPATCH defaultsfile==
$APPL_TOP/admin/VIS/defaults.txt
logfile=vis_12345678_june-3-2002-900_ajw.log
patchtop=/patch/12345678 workers=4 interactive=no
```

This would run the entire 12345678 patch without requiring you to physically name every driver.

But what if your patch does not have the standard naming convention? You can still apply the patch in a similar manner, you would just pass in a comma-separated list of drivers to apply. For example, if the same patch (12345678) had drivers named c1.dri, d1.dri, and g1.dri, you would format the command as below:

```
ADPATCH defaultsfile==
$APPL_TOP/admin/VIS/defaults.txt
logfile=vis_12345678_june-3-2002-900_ajw.log
patchtop=/patch/12345678 driver=c1.dri, d1.dri,
g1.dri workers=4 interactive=no
```

This assumes that you are passing the parameters into the session in the C, D, and G order and will expect the driver files to have exactly the name and extension that you have passed in.

What if something in the noninteractive session errors out? Can you restart it? When ADPATCH is running noninteractive and it encounters an error, it exits immediately to the OS prompt and reports that it encountered an error. Once you have looked through all of the logs, found the error and resolved it (either with Oracle Support's help or independent of them), you can restart the patch (noninteractive again) by using exactly the same command (omitting or changing none of the input parameters) with restart=yes appended to the end. If ADPATCH sees restart=yes, it assumes that there was a patch running and all of its information is retained in the fnd_install_processes table and that you want to pick up at exactly the point where the patch failed. Do not use restart=yes if you are starting an entirely new patch session.

```
ADPATCH defaultsfile==
$APPL_TOP/admin/VIS/defaults.txt
logfile=vis_12345678_june-3-2002-900_ajw.log
patchtop=/patch/12345678 workers=4 interactive=no
restart=yes
```

## Merge Patch

After you have been involved with patching Oracle E-Business Suite for any time at all, you will find that there are times when it can be patch intensive. Oracle provides a means by which you can merge several patches into one single patch that you will then apply as if it had been created as one patch. Applying several patches in this way will allow you to not only run fewer ADPATCH sessions to get through all of the patches that you need to at one time, but it will check to see if there are duplicate versions of any of the components that are common between the patches, find the newest versions of those components that are common, and only apply those. This minimizes potential downtime and impact to the business.

AD Merge Patch is the utility and process that will allow you to merge multiple uninterrelated patches into one all encompassing patch set. Located in the $AD_TOP/bin directory, this executable has, as its startup command ADMRGPCH.

It will allow you to merge dependent patches with each other, but it will not try to figure out what order components need to go in. That means you still have to read every README for every patch that you are planning on merging carefully. Some patches contain special instructions that need to be followed if that patch is to be included in a merged patch set or manual steps that AD Merge Patch will not execute or take into consideration.

Before you run Merge Patch, you need to create source and destination directories in your Patch Top directory. Your Patch Top is wherever, outside of the Apps directory structure, you have designated as the location from where your patches are installed. The source and destination directory can be named anything you want, but needs to preexist before you start your ADMRGPCH. session.

Copy all of the patches that you want to merge into the source directory and unzip them before you start your ADMRGPCH. session. If you have already unzipped them, you can either move the directories that they created into the source directory or unzip them again there.

Once all of these steps are done, you can run Merge Patch. Merge Patch takes the source directory, the target directory, and the proposed name (the default is "merged" if you do not provide this parameter) of the new patch as its arguments and will generate log files. It is important

that you look at the log files for the ADMRGPCH. session before you try
to apply the resulting patch set.

```
Admrgpch d:\patches\my_source d:\patches\my_target
my_merged_patch
```

This will take everything in the source directory, merge all of the C
drivers into one, merge all of the D drivers into one, and merge all of
the G drivers into one. Any prepatch, interdriver, or postpatch steps that
appear in any of the README files need to be performed at the appropriate
times. If several of the README files refer to running ADADMIN to do
any one particular step (e.g., recompile flex fields), you only need to
perform this step once and it will recompile for all of the patches' changes.

The resulting patch can be applied either interactively or noninteractively just as any other patch. In the example it would be the
my_merged_patch in the my_target directory of the patches directory
on the D:\ drive on a Windows machine.

### Restarting a Patch

If a patch fails or for some reason you had to abort the patch's installation,
it is possible to restart ADPATCH at the point where the patch was stopped.
Simply running ADPATCH again, if you have not run anything in the
interim, will allow ADPATCH to restart. If there is an ADPATCH session,
an ADADMIN session, or any other AD utility running in any other session
connected to the application, those have to be completed or cancelled
before you can restart ADPATCH. If another session of ADPATCH has run
(or is running), the fnd_install_processes table may no longer be
available or may contain information from another patching session.
Fnd_install_processes table stores the information on what is happening at any time during the patching session. This table is what provides
Oracle with the knowledge of where to restart a patch if there was an
interruption in the patch's run. Therefore, it is important to make sure
that if there is any chance of someone trying to run any of the AD utilities
while you are trying to figure out why a patch failed and to fix the
problem, that you make a backup copy of the
fnd_install_processes table that you can name back when you are
ready to finish running the original patch.

If the fnd_install_processes table exists and you are restarting
the patch, ADPATCH will ask you, after you have restarted, if you want
to continue the previous patching session. Answering yes and providing
ADPATCH with a log filename (if you provide the same log name as
before, it will be appended) will allow ADPATCH to pick up where it left
off and complete. If you answer no and confirm that you do not want to
complete the previous ADPATCH session, it will prompt you to confirm

that decision and start a new ADPATCH session, first dropping the fnd_install_processes table that exists and creating a new one.

One caution that Oracle support makes is that if you try to run a copy driver that has encountered errors part way through, you may find inconsistencies in the installation and in the log files.

I would probably add one more caution, especially in rerunning copy drivers from the beginning. When ADPATCH runs, it creates a backup directory under the patch's top. The directory structure of this backup directory looks something like Table 10.2.

If for any reason you need to find out what version of a form or a report or a PL/SQL statement a patch replaced, you can find out by combing through the backup directory. ADPATCH will put the components that it replaces in the same place in the patch's backup directory that it found them in the application's directory structure. Sometimes Oracle Support will ask for the version of the component that you replaced using the patch and this is where you would look for that information. But, if you have run the patch or part of the patch more than once, the original versions of these files are overwritten with the versions that the patch laid into place before it stopped.

Another thing that this backup directory is used for is if you have to attempt to back out a patch. More about attempting to back out a patch will be covered later in the chapter.

## ADCTRL's Part in Patching

ADCTRL is a handy utility that allows you to monitor what state each worker is in during a patching session. Again, it is a menu-driven utility that is designed especially for ADWORKER monitoring and to allow you some freedom in directing what a worker is doing and to tell it what you

**Table 10.2   Backup Directory Structure**

```
12345678
backup
    VIS
        Visappl
            AP
                11.5.0
                    <subdir>
                        file.fmx
                    <subdir2>
                        file.rdx
            AR........ .
```

want it to do. It is a simple but useful utility that provides you the opportunity to restart workers that have failed.

Many times, while you are monitoring worker progress, you will see that some workers fail while others continue to run. This happens for many reasons; one common one is that there are several workers running and sometimes the timing gets off between the different jobs and one takes longer than ADPATCH anticipates it taking. When this happens, sometimes dependencies get off between the workers and then something that one worker was anticipating being in place before it started is not there. Restarting the failed worker, in this case, will usually work. You may have to restart it several times, but eventually, you will get the worker to run. This happens frequently when you throw many workers at a big patch (which is what you should do, if you can) and one of the jobs is running longer than anticipated.

## Self-Documenting Logs

When you use the ADPATCH utility, it asks you for a log name. Into this log (placed in the APPL_TOP/admin/<SID>/log directory) goes all of the details of the ADPATCH run. Each driver of the patch that runs via this utility creates its own log, unless you take the default log name (ADPATCH.log). Taking the default means that everything from every ADPATCH run for which you take the default name gets appended to the same log. This can result in extremely large log files.

This is not the only log file created by ADPATCH. When running a C driver, you will usually have a rebase and a relink log. You do not have the option to change the names of these logs when they are created. ADPATCH also creates an ADLIBIN log in a C driver. These logs are created when ADPATCH unloads the pieces of the patch; the results of the success or failure go into this log file.

D and G drivers, if they exist, will create worker log files. Adwork## is the naming convention of worker files. These files contain all of the information on what is going on in each worker. Again, the files are always created with the default names and there is no way, at creation time, to change these names.

Because all information on what is going on inside of the patches goes into the log files, they end up being important files when you are figuring out what broke in a patch that failed. For that reason as well as to keep file sizes manageable and to allow you to clean out old files from your default patch directory when you have installed several iterations of files, you can choose a logical name for your main patch log file when it is time to create it and rename the others when the patch has run its course.

When I run an ADPATCH session, I name the log file putting as much information into the filename as I can. If I were installing patch number 123456 and that patch had all three driver files (C, D, and G) in the Vision Application at 10:45 A.M. on June 3, 2002, I would name the patch using the following format:

```
<SID>_<DRIVER>_<date and time>_<initials of
installer>.log
```

or

```
vis_c123456_0603021045_ajw.log
```

This format allows me to know what I installed, where I installed it, what time the driver file started, and who at my location installed the patch. From this information and the time stamp on the file, I can infer how long each driver took to run. I can quickly group together all of the drivers for a particular patch and I can see how many times I had to restart a patch before it ran successfully. Because of the limited size of the resulting file (although if you are running a big patch, the file can still become quite large), it is quicker and easier to find any errors that might have occurred. You also know that any errors that you find in a grep/find/search are all attributable to this patch and this driver.

But this only takes care of the default log file, not those auxiliary logs that are created by ADPATCH while it is running. Those I rename as soon as each driver is finished. I append to the beginning of each filename the detailed information that I put into the default log name so it is, again, easy to group files together that belong to the same driver. This means that, if I ran the D driver for the same patch at 11:20 A.M. using four drivers, I would have the following set of files:

```
vis_d123456_0603021120_ajw.log
adwork01.log
adwork02.log
adwork03.log
adwork04.log
```

After the rename of the worker logs:

```
vis_d123456_0603021120_ajw.log
vis_d123456_0603021120_ajw _adwork01.log
vis_d123456_0603021120_ajw _adwork02.log
vis_d123456_0603021120_ajw _adwork03.log
vis_d123456_0603021120_ajw _adwork04.log
```

While this is a lot of documentation, it is useful when you have been patching for 10 or 12 hours and you need to remember later what you did and what broke. It also will help you when you are looking at planning the time that it will take when you move from, for example, the Vision environment to the Production or Test environment. If you know how long it took to apply the patch in one environment (and you have the later advantage of knowing what might have broken and how you fixed it), you will be able to plan for how long you will have to have production unavailable. You will also have the details to back up your claims on the time required if anyone should question your estimates.

## Backing Out a Patch

While it is possible to back out a patch, it is neither the desired course of action nor a simple one to take. It would be preferable from a time and effort standpoint and from a practical and safe perspective to restore to a recent full backup, if possible, and reapply patches from a known point in time. However, there may be times when backing out a patch is your only alternative. I would never suggest even attempting to back a failed patch out of Production. Taking frequent backups right before patching sessions allows you to safely and cleanly restore. This backup should include the entire applications file system and, if you are on a Windows platform, the registry as well.

One situation where you may find it necessary to back out rather than try to restore is if you are in a new implementation and you have finished the base installation of the Vision, Test, or Development system and are applying minor patches that will allow your system to be started the first time. You may not have taken a backup as soon as the main installation was finished, because you were not at a known point to which you could comfortably fall back. Restoring back to your backup would take you back to before you started and may take half a day or more and reinstalling would take an additional half day or more and your project team decides that backing out a patch would be the better course of action.

There is no automated means by which you can back out a patch, it is fully manual and the time required to reverse all of the actions a patch took increases with the size and complexity of the patch involved.

## Backing out a C Driver

If possible, determine the cause of the failure. In the vast majority of cases, you will be able to resolve issues rather than having to resort to backing out patches. Resolving an issue that a patch is having, even if it means taking the time to work with Oracle Support through an iTAR is always the preferable course of action compared to backing out a patch.

If, after careful consideration, you find that you cannot resolve the issue, you will need to walk through the log files to determine what actions the copy driver took. Find out what files the patch copied and what update actions were performed by it.

When applying a patch, ADPATCH checks to see if a file that it is trying to put into place is more recent than the current file in the product's directory. If it is, it backs up the in-place version to the patch directory's backup directory in the structure layout that it found the file in under the system's directory structure.

If the files were originally in the Vision system's appl_top and were part of the AP product family and you were applying patch 12345678, then ADPATCH would backup the files in:

```
$VISAPPL/<subdirectory path to the files>/<original
files>
```

to

```
$PATCH/12345678/backup/VIS/visappl/ap/<same
subdirectory path>/<original files>
```

or

```
$PATCH/12345678/backup/VIS/visappl/ap/11.5.0/forms
/form1.fmx
```

If there are not many files (and in some patches there can be dozens to thousands), you can use these backup versions (provided you have only started ADPATCH from the beginning once for the copy driver) to replace the versions that ADPATCH put in their place. Simply copy these backups to their original location.

Relink any files that the copy driver relinked. You can relink files with ADADMIN or ADRELINK (if they are AD programs that you need to relink, ADRELINK is the only way you can relink them).

Restore the previous apps.zip file. Apps.zip will be altered if the copy driver included any Java updates. Restoring this file can be done at the command line by invoking the ADJAVA utility as in the command below on a single command line with no carriage returns or line breaks:

```
Adjava oracle.apps.ad.jri.adjcopy -masterArchive
apps.zip -deltaArchives c12345678.zip
-favorLowRevisions -mode Apply
```

This command is case sensitive and tells adjava to regenerate the apps.zip file from the backup copy that the copy driver made (c12345678.zip for the copy driver c12345678.drv), replace all newer files by favoring the lower revision or all of the files contained in the zip file, and apply the changed apps.zip to where it belongs.

If there are Java files included in the patch, you will have to regenerate the jar files using ADADMIN's regen jar files menu option.

Finally, regenerate any forms, reports, graphics, or message files that might have been replaced by using the appropriate options in ADADMIN.

### Restoring from a Failed D Driver

C drivers are complicated enough to back out. Database drivers make changes to the structure and workings of the database. This makes them even more complex to back out. It is important that you get a good database backup before applying a number of patches, minipacks, family packs, or maintenance packs. It is far simpler and safer to restore to before the patch than it is to back out the drivers.

Database drivers replace packages and procedures, alter structures within the database, and add functionality to the system. To try to recover from a failed database driver, you could carefully examine all of the log files, including all of the worker log files in an attempt to determine what caused the failure. If you can find out what caused it and there is a way to fix the cause, fix the issue that caused the failure and restart the driver.

If you cannot resolve what caused the driver to fail, the database must be restored from the most recent backup. If this is the case and there have been other database drivers run between the time of your most recent backup and the patch that failed, you will have to reapply the database driver portions of every intervening patch up to the one that failed in the order you originally installed them. This allows your database to match your application, patch for patch, and be viable to run up to that point, provided the C driver that is associated with the failed D driver had all of its changes successfully removed.

While the 9i version of log miner can reverse DDL (data definition language) with some effort, I do not believe it can reverse changes to packages and procedures and functions and triggers. These do not get written to the log files to begin with (except as a side effect of being put into the data dictionary from where the details can be retrieved via the data dictionary view), therefore, mining them back out would be nearly impossible.

As a last step, take a backup of your system at this point. Backing out the patch may not have been completely successful. Great care needs to be taken to undo everything that a patch did before you can have any confidence that backing it out was successful.

## WHAT ABOUT DATABASE PATCHES?

Database patches have traditionally been installed using runInstaller and applying the `product.jar` file that will bring the database to the correct version number. However, this is no longer always the case. Some database patches (those against databases at version 9i and above) are installed using a new utility called OPATCH. OPATCH, also known as "The Interim Patch Installer," is a new Oracle-supplied utility that is provided to assist you with the process of applying interim patches to the RDBMS binaries.

This utility can only be used with database patches released for Oracle 9i Release 2 (database Version 9.2.0.#) or greater and so far only on Windows or UNIX OSs. OPATCH is a Perl-based utility that is applied to your database server as a patch itself that can be downloaded from Metalink. The patch number is 2617419 and even if it has been installed once, you should check every time you are ready to apply patches to see if there is a newer version available.

When attempting to apply a patch, OPATCH will detect any conflicts that may be relevant to your system and the interim patch that you are trying to apply. Not only will it detect the conflicts, it will report back to you what those conflicts are and that the patch will fail.

## OPATCH Syntax

You can invoke OPATCH directly from the command line using the following syntax:

```
<perl> <opatch.pl> <command> [<command_options>] [
-h[elp] ]   [ -n[o_op] ]
```

If you are running on a UNIX system (or you are running on a Windows OS also running MKS Toolkit), you can invoke OPATCH through the supplied wrapper script that comes with the patch. Running the wrapper script requires that you set your Oracle_home correctly and that that version of the Oracle home has the appropriate version of the Perl interpreter. The wrappered OPATCH will then be invoked as follows:

```
opatch <command>   [<command_options>]   [ -h[elp]
]   [ -n[o_op] ]
```

Table 10.3 shows the parameters available for the parameter list and the definition of those parameters.

```
UNIX:
$/usr/local/bin/perl5.6 opatch.pl
apply/patches/12345678 opatch apply/patches/133469

Windows:
C:\Perl\bin\perl5.6.0 opatch.pl apply
F:\patches\12345678
```

## Removing an OPATCH Applied Patch

Not only can you apply a patch using OPATCH, you can unapply a patch the same way as well. The command to uninstall the interim database patch is as follows:

**Table 10.3   OPATCH Parameter List**

| Parameter | Definition |
|---|---|
| Perl | The Perl binary with a version of 5.6.0 or greater if this binary is not located in the default ORACLE_HOME. |
| opatch.pl | The patch script. |
| command | Any one of the following:<br>apply<br>lsinventory<br>rollback<br>version |
| command_ options | Any option that may be supported by the command parameter. |
| -help | Displays help message for the command. |
| -no_op | Prints the actions without actually executing them. |

```
rollback [ -id <patch id> ] [ -oh <OracleHome> ]
[ -ph <patch dir> ]
```

Table 10.4 shows the parameters for this command as well as the definition of the parameters.

## Listing Currently Installed Interim Patch ID Numbers

The following command will list all interim patches that appear in the <SID> OraInventory directory:

```
lsinventory [-all] [-oh <OracleHome>]
```

Table 10.5 provides the parameters and definitions for the list command.

The resulting report lists all of the installed items in alphabetical order along with their corresponding version numbers and associated base bug (if any) listed at the end of the report.

**Table 10.4   Rollback Parameters for OPATCH**

| Parameter | Definition |
|---|---|
| -id <patch id> | ID of the patch to be rolled back. |
| -oh | Alternative directory to use instead of the default of ORACLE_HOME. |
| -ph | Valid patch directory |

**Table 10.5    Listing Installed Interim Patches Parameters**

| Parameter | Definition |
|-----------|------------|
| -all | Tells the list command to report the name and installation directory for each ORACLE_HOME found based on oraInst.loc. |
| -oh | Alternative directory to use instead of the default of ORACLE_HOME. |

### *Listing OPATCH Version*

To determine the version of the OPATCH utility that you are running, you will use the following command:

```
OPATCH version
```

### OPATCH Online Help

OPATCH, like most utilities provided by Oracle, comes with online help options that you can display with the opatch.pl -help command. Optionally, you can add the option that you want help with (e.g., apply or rollback.)

## PATCH AND OS COMBINATIONS

Usually a patch will be available for widespread use on all OSs, unless a problem is found that is OS specific (this occurs occasionally with a Windows environment, less often with others). Sometimes a patch is released for different combinations only as needed by the particular combination.

A good example of this is a database patch that is released for OS database release number combinations only as needed. In this case, the patch could not be ported immediately to every conceivable combination of these two components at exactly the same time. Sometimes a problem presents itself sporadically depending on how everything is configured and Oracle Support only ports the patch to those combinations under which the problem is reported.

For example, a problem with depreciating fixed assets may appear after an upgrade of the database to Release 9.2. It will only appear if a company is using the Financial modules. It may end up being a database problem for which you have to make minor modifications to the binaries on the database server via a patch. But the database releases are supported on many different OSs and the problem appears under both 9.2.0.1 and

9.2.0.2. Oracle would have to simultaneously release 2 patch sets per OS for 20 different OS versions only to later come to realize that probably not even half of the patch sets were ever used. Instead, Oracle usually releases the most common combinations and waits to backport a patch to a different database/OS combination when the client company requests it. A backport is a fix that is made to an earlier release that was originally created in a later (or different) release. It is often referred to as backporting or simply porting a patch.

To request a backport is simple. You log an iTAR and explain what the problem is and that you cannot find a suitable combination in the set of patches that are currently available.

It is not a foregone conclusion that just because you have requested Oracle port the patch to another combination that it actually will. There is every chance that it will, but Oracle may also turn you down and tell you that you have to upgrade to the next patch of the database (for example bringing 9.2.0.2 to 9.2.0.3). You will have to be aware that it is always a possibility that Oracle will say no and give you an alternative option.

## WHY APPLY A PATCH?

This question has been posed by many people when they realize that Apps 11i can become a patch hungry monster. The argument has been made that it does not look like it is broken. "We are not having any problems." "We are stable." "Why introduce the chance of something breaking?" "We never have to patch Windows <insert version here> or any of our other software." "Oracle just releases buggy unstable products."

Every company releases buggy software. There is no way that a company can foresee all of the ways that a company will use its software or test every combination of situations under which it will be run. With a product as powerful, flexible, and complex as Oracle E-Business Suite, this is particularly the case. The simple number of different combinations of products that a company can license together combined with the number of OSs under which they can be run (not to mention the different ways that it can be customized to meet specific needs) means that even trying to test all of the eventualities would take a team of dozens of people working full-time at testing and the product would never come to market. The best that can be hoped for is that the testers will find the biggest bugs that the majority of the eventual users will likely run into and fix those. But what happens when a client company discovers a shortcoming in a set of reports and requests an enhancement? What happens when a company discovers a bug that only presents itself under a certain set of circumstances?

What happens? Patches happen.

You apply patches to stay current on new features and bug fixes. I do not suggest that you rush right out and apply every one-off patch that comes out for every product that you have installed. Sending these patches through the whole process would mean that not only would you have to have an Apps DBA dedicated to nothing but patching applications, but also functional people and developers whose jobs it is to do nothing but test the effects and side effects of installing all of the patches that might be able to be applied to a system. This is particularly true if you have a significant number of modules implemented at your business.

Oracle releases patches regularly. You can be sure that if you set yourself up on a quarterly patching schedule, you will have several patches, even if you have a minimal number of products licensed, to apply every quarter. If you keep up with just the minipacks that are released every quarter, you will have sufficient practice with ADPATCH and patching in general to keep you on your toes.

Is this just an exercise in practicing patching and keeping on your toes? Not really. Remember, a maintenance pack rolls up all of the minipack changes that have occurred since the last maintenance pack along with that previous version and packages it together for ease of installation at your site. ADPATCH determines what versions of files you have on site, checks tables in the database to determine what minipacks you have applied, determines what it needs to apply in your particular environment to bring you up to the current release number, and applies it. You can severely limit the work that ADPATCH has to do and, by extension, the time that needs to be set aside for a migration to the next release number if you stay current or even nearly current on the products that you have installed and their minipack releases.

## WHAT HAPPENS WHEN A PATCH BREAKS?

Patches will break. A worker will not be able to finish. A copy driver will fail trying to replace a program unit. A generate driver will be unable to generate forms and reports that the patch provided. Innumerable things can break. If you install enough patches (or not enough patches) at some point you will have a patch that will not install correctly. When a patch driver runs, it creates a table in the database called fnd_install_process. This table is one of the components that allow a patch to be restarted at the point where it failed. The existence of this table tells ADPATCH that it has already started a patch and it might need to finish it. If for any reason you need to move a patch out of the way to install a fix for a problem that it encountered, you will need to rename this table so that the patch you are installing to fix the broken patch that you want to restart later will be able to run successfully. Create table fnd_install_processes_<initials>_<date> or create table fnd_install_processes_<driver> as select * from fnd_install_processes followed by drop table fnd_install_processes when logged in as Apps user (apps/apps) will effectively move the table out of the way and allow you to run another patch to fix a problem.

But how do you figure out what broke, let alone how to fix it?

If you look at the ADWORKER logs, relink logs, rebase logs, or the main patch driver logs, they will tell you a considerable amount of information about what is going on within the patch and where to look for problems that might have happened. Frequently, it is as simple as a database error, a tablespace out of space, a table or index hitting the maximum number of extents, or a patch trying to drop or add a column to a table that already has been dropped or added by another step or another patch. If this is the case, restarting the driver will not get you anywhere; if the DDL statement had already been run by something else, it will not run again successfully. None of the visible options in ADCTRL will get you past the failed step in the driver. There does not appear to be any way past the error or any way to stop the ADPATCH run short of shutting the window or aborting the patching session (but this will not get the patch to finish, either).

There are, however, three invisible options when running ADCTRL. Option 8 will allow you to skip a worker. Option 9 will tell a worker, unconditionally, to wait. Option 10 exits (as does Option 7) ADCTRL. None of these options are supposed to be used without expressed direction of Oracle Support. I do not suggest that anyone use any of these options without being sure of what the option is going to do or what is likely to be the result of the action. I have made the decision to use Option 8 independent of Oracle Support when I have looked at the failing step of the patch and determined that not forcing the broken step would not cause any problems later. For example, if a sql statement is trying to drop a column and the column to be dropped had already been dropped by a previous run of the same patch or by another patch in the series, trying to make it drop the same column again would be an exercise in waiting for an extended period of time for Oracle Support to tell you that you cannot drop a column that had already been dropped. Knowing when you can safely skip a step comes with understanding what the worker is doing and taking the leap. Having a good backup to fall back on is also a good thing to have, so you can know that if you make a decision like this, you can always fall back and restore from the backup and make a different choice the next time. Option 8 takes, as a requested parameter, the worker number you want to skip. Make sure that if you do this, you are skipping the correct one.

Option 9, I have never been instructed to use by Oracle Support, and I have not ever determined when this option would be useful, but it is a hidden option in the ADCTRL utility. It takes, as its requested parameters, a worker number, a series of worker numbers, or "all" for telling all workers to wait.

I also do not recommend trying to fix broken patches on your own, until you have developed some confidence in what you are doing. As soon as your patch gets to what you perceive to be a broken point (you might think it is broken because it does not appear to be doing anything for several hours, you may have workers that fail, or you may find errors or warnings in the log files), log an iTAR, make it as severe as it needs to be, but do not tell Oracle Support that it is Production if it is not. The analysts will be much more likely to go out of their way to help you if you are honest with them all along the way. The more you work through the problems that you encounter with Oracle Support's help, the more confidence you will build in knowing where to look when something breaks, the more you will find yourself being able to rely on yourself and on your abilities, and to rely on your own judgment. While you wait for Oracle Support to respond, you can start looking at worker logs, the main log, the req files in the log directory to see if you can reconstruct what was going on at the time of the failure. This will help you gain confidence in what you are doing and will give you a head start on being able to provide Oracle Support with requested information quickly to help with the resolution.

## TEST THE PATCH

Once you have a patch installed, it is time to test. You want to test not only to determine the success of the patch but also to determine if there were any unintentional side effects. Success of the patch will determine if you want to then migrate the patch to the other environments. Because of the complexity of the application, you will also want to determine if installing the patch had any unintended side effects in the product family that you are dealing with, or in any other product that you have implemented. Testing in connection with patches usually takes two tracks: technical testing and functional testing.

Technical testing is minimal. If ADPATCH ran to completion without obvious errors, you can assume that it passed that part of your test. But check the log files (e.g., the worker logs, the rebase and relink logs, the main log, the req files). Yes, if you have run a big patch that used several workers in both the C and D drivers, this can get to be a little tedious, but it is important that you at least run grep or a quick find in each of the files for the word "error" and the word "warning." There are times when the string "error" is legitimate (there are procedures that raise legitimate errors within the application and sometimes patches add functionality to these or repackage them into a jar file or a zip file); these can be safely ignored. Usually warnings are exactly that, a warning, and can also be ignored, but it is better to take note of them and make sure that there are no glaringly obvious problems that you see. Finally, you want to check for invalid objects in the database.

```
Select count(*) from all_objects where status =
'INVALID';
```

While having invalid objects in the system is, to some extent, to be expected and accepted, it is best to keep as many valid as you can. There are several ways to validate database objects. One is to run ADADMIN and use the compile apps schema. This one will go through and compile all of the objects in the Apps schema. But it will only compile those objects belonging to Apps. And it does not always get all of the objects that it should. If you need to compile objects belonging to other schemas you can use the $ORACLE_HOME/rdbms/admin/utlrp script. This goes through and alters all objects that are invalid and compiles them. It still misses some, but it gets those in the Sys and system schemas as well. To determine which owner has invalid objects in the database, you can use the following query:

```
Select owner, object_name, object_type from
all_objects where status = 'INVALID' order by owner:
```

You can use sql to create sql to try to compile more invalid objects by using the following script:

```
Set head off;
Spool compile_invalids.sql
Select 'alter '||owner||'.'||'object_type||'
'||object_name||' compile;'
From all_objects where status = 'INVALID'
Spool off
@compile_invalids.sql
```

There is also frequently a script located in the %AD_TOP%/sql/ directory called adcompsc.pls. It is a script that has often been included by Oracle Development to be one of the last jobs that a D driver runs. This script will allow you to compile all invalid objects in any given schema. To run the script, at a sql prompt on your Apps tier, run the following:

```
@%AD_TOP/sql/adcompsc.pls <schema owner> <schema
password> <case sensitive string that the objects
start with that you want to compile>
```

This would compile all objects in the apps schema (assuming that apps still has as its password apps) that begin with the "AD" string:

```
@%AD_TOP/sql/adcompsc.pls apps apps AD
```

This would compile all invalid objects in the apps schema:

```
@%AD_TOP/sql/adcompsc.pls apps apps%
```

There will always be some invalid objects in the database. There are often invalids in just an Oracle database; there can be several dozen invalid objects in an Oracle E-Business Suite database. If you look in the log file of a D driver, it will usually tell you how many invalid objects that you have before the patch starts and how many you have after it has finished. It will also likely produce a voluminous html file of all of the invalid objects that it found. Each patch that runs creates a uniquely named html file. It is unobtrusive and safe to run utlrp.sql periodically. Utlrp.sql is a script found in $ORACLE_HOME/rdbms/admin (%ORACLE_HOME\rdbms\admin) that recompiles invalid objects. Oracle recommends running utlrp after creating, upgrading, or migrating a database where running the upgrade scripts invalidates nearly every function, procedure, and trigger in the database. When you upgrade from 8i to 9i, utlrp can run for over 13 hours on a small Financials database. Because of the extensive work that a patch does in a D driver, it is also often recommended in the README that you run it as part of the postinstallation steps. Even if it is not recommended, if a patch that I have installed has a D driver that has performed more than a handful of jobs, I run utlrp just to make sure that as many of the objects in the database as possible have a status of VALID. Functional testing includes determining if the patch fixed what it was intended to fix. If it was a patch applied to fix a known existing problem, once it is applied, check. Did it fix that problem? If you are on a minipack or family pack patch implementation schedule and you are testing the installation of these patches, you may not have a known problem to test to determine if the patch fixed anything. This is okay.

Check to make sure that nothing else in the system has been affected by your installation. Because of the complexity and interconnected nature of the application, a patch applied in one product may have an affect on another product. While you cannot test the products that you do not have licensed, you can run a system test to make sure that everything your company uses, and all of the functions that they perform in their jobs perform at least as well as they did before the patches were applied. You may get lucky and see improved performance as a side effect.

Test customizations. Even patches that are not supposed to do anything with a product for which you have a customization may cause some of your customizations to quit working. Some of your interface tables may no longer line up exactly as they did before. A patch that is for a product, even a minor patch, has the potential to overlay a customized form or report. This is one of the inherent dangers of customizing the application. This is also one of the reasons to have a detailed list of all you have customized, as well as backup copies of everything that was customized and a detailed test plan that tests out everything thoroughly.

## Patch Management

One more thing that deals with patching is patch management. For your own sanity, for the benefit of Oracle Support if you have to open an iTAR, for documentation purposes, and for knowing exactly what has gone on in your system, it is important that you keep some kind of document that says what patches have been applied in each of your environments. This does not have to be elaborate, only consistent so that you can see at a glance what you have (or have not) applied in each environment. Many companies make use of a spreadsheet similar to the one in Table 10.6. Make sure that you list every environment in the document. You can maintain this as a patch problem and resolution document, so that if you encounter a similar problem in the future you can quickly look back and see what you did to resolve the issue in the past. If you make this a tool rather than a task, you will find that it helps you in future planning and in being able to answer questions later that you never anticipated anyone ever asking. I have seen versions that maintain timing information for each driver, sign off, and test plan results added as an inserted comment to one of the cells.

**Table 10.6  Patch Charting Spreadsheet**

| Patch No. | DEVL | | | | TEST | | | |
| | Analyst | Date | Problem | Resolution | Analyst | Date | Problem | Resolution |
|---|---|---|---|---|---|---|---|---|
| 12345 | AJW | 10/20/02 | D driver hung | Restart | AJW | 10/22/02 | D driver hung | Restart |
| | | | | | | | | |
| | | | | | | | | |
| | | | | | | | | |
| | | | | | | | | |
| | | | | | | | | |

Creating a table or set of tables auxiliary to the application, but in the same database is another solution to this. If you build a simple table or set of tables that maintain the information that you have chosen to track in connection to patch management, you can easily maintain that information in each database as you patch. When you clone, that information will be accurate within the cloned tables. It will carry the date information with it and you can create a GUI front end for the tables with Access or with Forms to make maintenance and data entry into the table easier. You can use Access or Reports to enable you to pull out information on what patches are in each environment. Pulling information from across instances is less simple that just pulling up the information in one central spreadsheet. It is a choice that your situation can dictate.

I have seen suggestions that it is important to maintain a listing of files modified by patches, what versions of each file the patch brought with it, and what each patch replaced. This could be useful information to have at some point, but it could also become an incredibly unwieldy proposition. A minipack patch may have over a hundred files that it replaces. Some patches have as many as 25,000 or more jobs that run in the generate driver. If a patch replaces 25,000 files, it could become a full-time job just documenting what the patches did.

## PATCHING ADVANCES IN 11i

An interesting note, with 11i, patching became patch translation aware. If there are multilingual translations of a patch that you are applying, ADPATCH is supposed to alert you to that fact so you can take appropriate action if needed. It does not mean that if you do not have a language installed, you have to install a translation patch; it only makes you aware that there may be translations available if you need to make use of them.

Further, ADPATCH is now platform aware. If the patch is not a generic one, ADPATCH will check to make sure that the version of the patch that you are trying to install is the correct version for your OS.

Another new feature that has just recently been added to the application is the functionality of ADPATCH to check to see if a patch has already been applied. ADPATCH checks the patch's version, compares them against existing patches, and determines if one of the other patches that have been applied to your system might have included this patch as part of its makeup. If it finds indications that a patch might have been applied already, it double-checks with you to determine if you really want to apply this patch. Further, this functionality brings with it prerequisite checking. It checks to see if you have already applied prerequired patches and warns you if it finds any that it does not think you have. These added features depend, to some extent, on when the patch that you are applying was created, since there have to be keys within the patch itself to clue ADPATCH in, particularly with the prerequisite checking feature, but this added functionality will eventually be more and more useful as older patches are no longer applied and the newer patches are built to take advantage of these new bells and whistles.

# 11

---

# CLONING

If activities surrounding patching take up half of your time as an Apps DBA, cloning can easily take up half of what is left. Not all of the time is taken up with activity. It can easily be an hour of activity followed by five hours of watching files copy followed by an hour of activity.

You can think of it in this scenario; you are considering a test run of making changes to your now increasingly familiar desert and you want to get somewhat comfortable with what those changes are before you make them the real environment that is now your primary home. So you are not completely surprised by the radical changes in your real home, you are going to make test changes to duplicate environments to make sure that you know what changes are going to be made, and to make sure that you can live with the changes once they are made. To facilitate this, you set about making almost exact replicas of your environment in slightly different places and you use these copies as places to test out changes. Cloning is how you get these changes to be where they need to be when they need to be there.

One typically thinks of cloning as creating an exact duplicate of the original and while that is the basic primary definition of the word cloning, Dictionary.com also provides the following two definitions that more closely represent what the reality of cloning is in Oracle E-Business Suite:

1. One that copies or closely resembles another, as in appearance or function: "filled with business-school clones in gray and blue suits" (Michael M. Thomas).
2. To produce a copy of; imitate closely: "The look has been cloned into cliché" (Cathleen McGuigan).

While there are many reasons to clone an application, including migrating the existing system to new hardware and creating an area where you can apply patches safely, one of the most common reasons for cloning is to create a copy of Production to allow for more realistic testing of updates and changes.

Before we get started, a little new vocabulary goes along with the new topic.

- *Source system:* Environment being cloned, the "from" system
- *Target system:* Environment being created as a copy, the "to" system

## ORACLE'S CLONING METHODS

Oracle has seen iterations of what it supports from a cloning perspective, from nothing being supported to the current two ways depending on where you are version-wise. It has come a long way and it has vastly improved even within the last year. Here are the two current methods that Oracle directly supports for cloning.

### Cloning with ADCLONE

For all systems up to Version 11.5.5, this is the basic method of cloning one environment and its data to another. It is fairly straightforward and has minimal problems that will rear their ugly heads. The basic process is outlined in this chapter.

#### Run Rapid Install

Rapid Install needs to be run once for every environment in your enterprise. Production (or whatever environment you are cloning from) needs to be at whatever level you choose to clone from.

You do not need to run Rapid Install once for every clone. Not only would this be wasted time and effort, it would likely introduce far more errors into the equation than the clone and subsequent testing would ever hope to eliminate. This installation is exactly the way any installation gets done, with the complete set of ports and servers identified at installation time. Without these unique settings, the system will perform incorrectly and will likely either access the wrong database (introducing data corruption and inconsistencies) or will not work at all. The newly installed (target) environment does not have to be patched (other than the patch necessary for cloning) and only has to be minimally functional before the clone. All of the Oracle E-Business Suite products and functionality will come from the cloned from (source) system.

This setup needs to at least have a cursory test run to make sure that the PHP loads and that you can shutdown and restart the services as they are when the configuration is finished. If you are not confident that you have a basic baseline from which to proceed, if your clone should appear to fail, you will not be able to say that it was working before the clone, and you will not be able to assure the analyst who gets assigned to your iTAR that any error condition is definitely caused by the clone procedure.

Once you have at least a minimally functional environment, you need to stop and get a backup of the middle tier system and the database so you have something to go back to if the clone should fail too badly. Make sure that both backups are successful and that the tapes of those backups can be read.

Once you have a good backup and your system is ready for cloning, you will first need to apply patch number 2115451 in preinstall mode to all middle tier $APPL_TOP directories. This patch contains the ADCLONE utility.

It is highly recommended that you change at least the APPS, APPL-SYS, and APPLSYSPUB passwords back to their default values before you start the cloning process (more on changing passwords can be found in Chapter 14).

If your middle tier is on any of the flavors of UNIX or Linux and you are cloning a system that was originally installed with the multi-user option that was available with Release 11.5.1's version of Rapid Install, you will need to change the ownership of the $COMMON_TOP file system from whoever owns it at this point to the applmgr user (whoever is the owner of the rest of the binaries on the system) to conform with the new structure and allow not only ADCLONE to function properly, but the resulting product as well.

To accomplish this change, shut down all services on the target system, change to the $COMMON_TOP file system, and make the ownership change. The process will look something like the following interaction, supposing that your $COMMON_TOP points to a directory called /apps/viscommon:

```
$cd/apps/viscommon
$chown -R <applmgr username>./util/apache
$cd admin/scripts
$chown  <applmgr username> adaprctl.sh adcmctrl.sh
admctrl.sh adfmsctrl.sh adfroctl.sh adrepctrl.sh
adalnctrl.sh
```

While it would be more expedient in the last step to change all of the ownerships of all of the sh files, it would not be advisable to do so as many have to maintain the ownership that they started with.

Log into the target system (the system that you are cloning to) as the applmgr user on that system and (without sourcing the environment) run the cloning utility to preserve the target system's settings.

Make sure that you have the path to the Perl interpreter in the path of the user logged in (`applmgr` here) before running the `ADCLONE` utility. If your target system was installed as a Version 11.5.1 installation, the Perl utility is located under the `%COMMON_TOP%/Apache/perl/bin/perl`. For systems whose base installation was later than Release 11.5.1, Perl is located under the `$ORACLE_HOME/iAS/Apache/perl/bin/perl` on the middle tier.

On UNIX you would set your path as follows:

```
$ PATH=<APACHE directory>/perl/bin:${PATH}
$ export PATH
```

Double-check to make sure that your environment is looking at the right Perl by issuing the `Which` command and making sure that it returns the path to this Perl interpreter.

```
$ which perl
```

On Windows, the command is as follows:

```
D:\> set PATH=%PATH%<APACHE directory>/perl/bin
C:\> which perl
```

Again, make sure the `which` command returns the correct path to Perl. This works because of MKS Toolkit.

To preserve your environment setting, run the following command at the command prompt using the literal values instead of the environment variables (remember, you have not sourced the environment so you cannot rely on the variables being set correctly):

```
perl <ad_top>/bin/adclone.pl -mode=preclone -
env_name=<SID> -node_name=<hostname> -
config_file=<config file> -ad_top=<ad_top>
```

Literally, for a VIS database with `VISAPPL/ad/11.5.0` being the AD_TOP, the command would look like this (strung out, no carriage returns or line breaks):

```
perl D:\VISAPPL\ad\11.5.0\bin\adclone.pl -mode=
preclone -env_name=VIS
  -node_name=<your middletier node> -config_file=
D:\VISAPPL\config.txt -ad_top= D:\VISAPPL\ad\11.5.0
```

The arguments to the command and their meanings are located in Table 11.1.

When `ADCLONE` runs in preclone mode, it shuts down any running services that may be on your system (as standard practice, you should shut all of these down manually when you are doing any maintenance on the system). It then saves the configurations and port and node specific settings of your `APPL_TOP`, `JAVA_TOP`, and your `OA_HTML` directories and all configuration files from your `COMMON_TOP` to `$COMMON_TOP/admin/clone` and removes the `APPL_TOP`,

**Table 11.1    ADCLONE Arguments and Their Meanings**

| Argument | Meaning |
| --- | --- |
| Mode | Preclone when run at the beginning of the clone process. Postclone when run at the end of the clone process. |
| Env_name | The TWO_TASK value on your system or your SID. |
| Node_name | Name of your target system's node, without the domain added. |
| Config_file | This is the path to and name of the config file that is created when Rapid Install runs. Recall that this file is one that you want to keep copies of in as many places as you can. |
| AD_TOP | The full path to the AD directory in your APPL_TOP. This is where the patch number 2115451 puts ADCLONE. |

JAVA_TOP, and OA_HTML directory contents. It is critical that you check to make sure that the to $COMMON_TOP/admin/clone directory exists after adclone finishes preclone mode. If it is not there, your preclone steps were not successful and you should not try to go any further as you will not be able to retrieve the settings (and all of the files that may have contained any of those settings) once the APPL_TOP, JAVA_TOP, and OA_HTML directories have been removed.

The removal step is often unsuccessful. This is sometimes due to a DLL not being released when the services are stopped, sometimes for other reasons. If the $COMMON_TOP/admin/clone directory exists and there are files in it, you can usually safely delete the contents of the directories and continue. However, this might be an advisable place to log a well-timed iTAR.

Shutdown the target database and remove all of the database files that are not part of the binary installation from the target system. This includes all log files, all control files, and all data and index tablespace files.

### Copy the Existing Source Database to the Target Database Location

Now it is time to start the actual cloning process.

Before you shut down the source database, create a backup of the control file that you can edit to create the new control on the target system. Find the resulting trace file in the user dump (udump) destination on the source system and copy it to the target system in a common location. I usually put it in the $HOME directory of the applmgr user so it is easily accessible and centrally located.

### Alter Database Backup Control File to Trace

Once you have the backup of the control file (which is necessary to point the target database at all of the datafiles that will be copied from the source databases location), shutdown the source database either normal or immediate, and then create a cold backup of the database files. This will ensure that you have a good copy if something should go wrong.

Now log onto the target database server as that environment's applmgr, source the environment for the instance (usually called <SID>.env on UNIX or <SID>.cmd on Windows) and copy the database files from the source database to the target database. The copy command on the OS that you are on will usually work well enough if both the source and target dbf files are accessible from a central location.

```
$cp/prodfilesystem/data/*/visfilesystem/data/
D:\ xcopy/s/e/i G:\proddata\data\* D:\visdata\data
```

Finally, compare the init.ora parameters on the source system with the init.ora parameters on the target system and make any changes to the target system that are found as differences between the two. While some of the changes may be cosmetic, it is best to keep the settings as much the same as you can when cloning so that the data dictionary does not have any trouble resolving the differences. You can easily do this during the time that the data files are copying; this will likely take several hours due to the sheer volume of data that has to be copied.

Now it is time to get ready to create your new control file. Rename your trace file copied from the source system to something logical with a SQL extension. I usually use something like create_<target sid>_from_<source sid>_<date>.sql; that way I can keep a running set if I choose to monitor what has changed on which system at which date. This is not really a necessity, as you can always find the one you need by looking at the date of the file, but it is handy and self-documenting. In the trace file, remove all comment lines and change the mount points for all files from where the trace file points on the source system to where you have copied them in your target system. Looking at the copy command we used earlier, this would mean changing all references from /prodfilesystem to /visfilesystem. What is more, you will need to make the following changes as well.

Remove the statement:

```
STARTUP NOMOUNT
```

You do not have to remove this, but if you follow the directions in the Metalink white paper faithfully, it will complain because it will have already started up nomount and it cannot be started again. If you do not remove the line from the tracefile, just log into the database as sysdba (if you have migrated to 9.2, remember internal and svrmgrl are gone) and run your script from there.

Change
```
CREATE CONTROLFILE REUSE DATABASE "PROD"
NORESETLOGS
```

to
```
CREATE CONTROLFILE SET DATABASE "VIS" RESETLOGS
```
Because the create controlfile script will have been created to recreate the source database's control file, it will be trying to reuse the old control file and will be trying to recreate the database using the same name. This would probably not be a good idea as your front end is looking for a database that is called, in this case, VIS and will not understand a database called PROD in its place and your init file will more than likely cause you troubles. This rename is also why you have to use the resetlogs command both in the create controlfile statement and in the open database statement.
```
ALTER TABLESPACE TEMP ADD TEMPFILE
'/visfilesystem/data/temp2.dbf'
         SIZE 1048576000  REUSE AUTOEXTEND OFF;
```
Whenever I try to recreate a control file in this manner, I have never been able to get this command to complete successfully. It errors every time I run the trace file script. I will have a Temporary Tablespace, but I will have 1 of 0 bytes. Running the command to add the datafiles back to the Temporary Tablespace can be run successfully once the database is mounted and open.

Once you have made sure your init files are correct, the trace file has been edited, and the files are done being copied, you can start your new database and create your new control file.
```
$sqlplus '/as sysdba'
SQL> startup nomount
SQL> @<your create script>.sql
SQL> alter database open resetlogs;
```
If you are using Recovery Manager (RMAN) (as a free tool that continues to become more stable and easier to use, you probably should consider it), you will have to reset the Database Identifier (DBID) with a unique ID. Since your source system's files have not been changed in any way by being migrated (other than to have the logs reset), they retain

the DBID of the source system in the header portion of the datafiles, temp and log files, and in the new control file regardless of the name of the database. To reset the DBID you will need to perform the following steps:

Shut down the database cleanly, either as normal or as immediate.

```
$ sqlplus '/as sysdba'
SQL> shutdown immediate
```

Startup mount the instance, but do not open it.

```
SQL> startup mount
```

Create the new DBID in the file headers.

```
SQL> exec sys.dbms_backup_restore.zerodbid(fno =>
0);
```

Since you changed the name of the database when you created the new control file, you can recreate the global name as well. Since this example is cloning to the VIS database, we will rename it to VIS, but replace this with whatever you are cloning to:

```
SQL> alter database rename global_name to VIS
```

Now you should open the database, start up the listener, and make sure that you can connect to the database both from the OS command line and from a remote SQL*Plus session. I usually try to connect to the database from a SQL*Plus session on the server where your middle tier applications are. You will not have removed either the TNSNAMES file or the SQL*Plus capabilities in the cloning process, so you should be able to talk to the database from this server at this point in this way.

### Copy the Existing File System (APPL_TOP, JAVA_TOP, and OA_HTML)

*NOTE:* This can be done while the database files are copying to save time. It is not necessary to wait for the database to be up and functional before you start copying these files. Running the copy jobs in parallel will cut your overall time by at least a third.

Oracle suggests that you make sure that all users are off of the source system and that all services are shutdown before starting this process. If your database is shut down for the copy of the database files from one instance to the other, there is a good chance that all of your users are off of the system. Do make sure that your services are all down before starting the copy job though. Some of the files find it difficult to copy if there is something actively writing to them.

Log on to the target middle tier server as the applmgr user and copy the APPL_TOP, JAVA_TOP, and OA_HTML directories and their contents from the source to the target. If you are on Windows, this will be easier if you map a drive to the location of the files; if you are on UNIX and the files are on two physical servers, NFS mounting the file system will make this easier. The copy command can be used in these cases and FTP (file transfer protocol) does not have to be used. Logging on as applmgr user on the target system allows you to get all of the file permissions correct when the files get to their destinations and limits what you have to do later.

If your system is multi-node, make sure that the appropriate directories get to the correct nodes.

UNIX:
```
$ cp -r/PROD_APPS/PRODAPPL/VIS_APPS/VISAPPL
```

Windows:
```
C:\> xcopy/s/e/i g:\prodappl d:\visappl
```

### Update the Configuration Information

Before you can finish the ADCLONE steps, you have to make sure that not only is the database started, but also that you can connect to it from the middle tier server and that the listener is running. Connect via SQL*Plus to the database as any users (e.g., system, apps, a development user).
```
select sysdate from dual
```
If you can connect, it should be safe to finish the ADCLONE steps.

You can now safely run ADCLONE in postclone mode to maintain the target settings. Make sure that you are logged on to the target system as the applmgr user. Again, although it may not even be possible at this point, if it is possible, do not source the environment file. Just go to a command prompt at the OS level and run ADCLONE in postclone mode to configure the target system from the source system's files. Running ADCLONE this time helps to configure the database profile option values, replaces the configuration files in the APPL_TOP and in the COMMON_TOP (it actually does not remove the old configuration files if they are not named the same thing, it just puts a version of those files that are configured for the source system into the file system), generates the database connectivity file (DBC), and updates the Intermedia libraries for the target system. The format of ADCLONE in postclone mode is as follows:
```
perl adclone.pl -mode=postclone -env_name=<SID> -
node_name=<hostname> -config_file=<config file> -
ad_top=<ad_top>
```
Example of a working command:

```
perl D:\VISAPPL\ad\11.5.0\bin\adclone.pl -
mode=postclone -env_name=VIS
-node_name=<your middletier node>  -config_file=
D:\VISAPPL\config.txt -ad_top= D:\VISAPPL\ad\11.5.0
```

If you are cloning in a multi-node configuration, repeat all steps on all nodes.

### Finishing Up

Now we come to the optional steps. At this point, you can safely bring up your source system and allow users to start accessing it again.

If you applied any patches that were not captured in the clone process, this is where you would apply them to the target system. These patches would include anything patched in Apache, any of the Developer Suites of products, Discoverer before Version 11.5.7, or JInitiator. If you have made any tuning configuration changes or any changes to take advantage of any of the iAS security settings from the configuration files you would make these similar changes to the files in the target system as well. There are also configurations that you can make to the appsweb.cfg file that is located in both the FND_TOP/resource directory and in the OA_HTML/bin directory. Make sure that you make the same changes to both of these files, but first make backup copies of the originals. That way if you find something messed up later, you can copy the backups over the ones that you edited. Make special note of the Environment Specific Parameters section of the appsweb.cfg file and make sure that the parameters reflect the values that should be pointing to the target system (VIS in this case).

If your primary browser is Internet Explorer, you need to alter the default Session_cookie_domain from null or from whatever value it is in the system at this point to whatever the domain is for this instance.

```
sqlplus apps/apps
SQL> update ICX_PARAMETERS
2> set SESSION_COOKIE_DOMAIN = '<MyDomainName>';
```

You already created an Identirydb.obj file on the target system. If you have not, you will need to run adjava to create the obj file.

```
adjkey -initialize
```

Whether or not you recreate the digital signature, it is usually a good idea to recreate the jar files via ADADMIN on the target system. Strictly speaking, it may not be necessary to do this, but it is always better (especially in the case of a clone) to err on the side of caution. In the case of a clone (where it is not usually the case in a patch situation) you want to force regeneration of all jar files when prompted by the utility.

Further, it is suggested that it would be a good idea to relink the AD executables on each node of the target system on which those utilities may exist (typically not on the database node).

```
Adrelink force=y 'ad all'
```

### Test the Target System

Now comes the moment of truth. Testing the target system is an important part of any clone. You can run preliminary tests on the system. Try logging in as a user with sysadmin privileges. Remember you are using any login that would have carried over from the source system including user IDs and passwords.

Navigate to the screen from which you submit concurrent requests and run something nonintrusive like Active Responsibilities. This will prove that the Concurrent Managers are functional, but will not in any way impact the data.

```
http://<apache host>:<apache
port>/pls/VIS/FND_WEB.PING
http://<apache host>:<apache port>/servlets/
IsItWorking
http://myapacheserver
.mydomain.com:7777/pls/vis/fnd_web.ping
http://myapacheserver.mydomain.com:7777/
servlets/IsItWorking
```

### Find and Mitigate Settings That the Clone Did Not Take Care Of

I have yet to perform a clone in this manner where all of the profile option values were correctly updated by the postclone script. Likely places to start looking are in the Table.Columns in Table 11.2. To be on the safe side, create a backup table of all of the tables that you manually alter.

```
Create table wf_notification_attributes_<your
initials> as select * from
wf_notification_attributes
```

While these are most of the common places where postclone falls down on the job, they are not the only ones that you may have to change. I usually run a query against the fnd_profile_option_values table to determine if anything is pointing at the source environment.

**Table 11.2   Postclone Columns that May Need Altering**

*Columns to Investigate*

```
WF_NOTIFICATION_ATTRIBUTES.TEXT_VALUE
WF_ITEM_ATTRIBUTE_VALUES.TEXT_VALUE
FND_FORM_FUNCTIONS.WEB_HOST_NAME
FND_FORM_FUNCTIONS.WEB_AGENT_NAME
FND_FORM_FUNCTIONS.WEB_HTML_CALL
FND_PROFILE_OPTION_VALUES.PROFILE_OPTION_VALUE
FND_PRODUCT_GROUPS.APPLICATIONS_SYSTEM_NAME
FND_CONCURRENT_REQUESTS.LOGFILE_NAME
FND_CONCURRENT_REQUESTS.OUTFILE_NAME
```
Profile_options (locate these through the Profiles screen if necessary)

| | |
|---|---|
| `ICX: Report Link` | `ICX: Report Launcher` |
| `ICX: Report Images` | `ICX: Forms Launcher` |
| `Help System Base URL` | `Apps Servlet Agent` |
| `Applications Help Web Agent` | `Applications Web Agent` |
| `POR_SSP_HOME` | `POR_SSP_ECMANAGER` |
| `POR_UPDATE_REQ` | `ICX_AP_WEB_OPEN_EXP` |
| `ICX:Report Cache` | `POR_RESUBMIT_URL` |
| `FND_FORM_FUNCTIONS` | `WF_NOTIFICATION_ATTRIBUTES` |
| `TCF:HOST` | `JTF_BIS_OA_` |
| `HTML` | `_WF_WEB_AGENT` |

```
Select profile_option_value from
fnd_profile_option_values where
profile_option_value like '%MYSERVER%';
```

Run queries on as many different configurations or portions of the port number, the middle tier server name, the database SID value, and any other pieces of these that you can think of. It may seem like an exercise in futility, but after a clone or two you will learn which values your particular clone setup misses routinely.

## Cloning with Rapid Clone

The newer and less prone to error manner of cloning includes using AutoConfig and a new utility, Rapid Clone, to facilitate the cloning procedure. While the required list of software for running a clone using the old method was minimal, the new cloning method requires a more extensive listing of software to be present on the system. Table 11.3 provides the software requirements, required versions, node on which it has to be present, and additional notes.

**Table 11.3  Software Necessary to Support Rapid Clone**

| Software | Version | Node | Notes |
|---|---|---|---|
| Oracle Universal Installer | 2.1.0.17 | All nodes as all are potential source nodes | This version of Universal Installer was included with all 11.5.7 environments that used Rapid Install. If you have a system that was installed at an earlier release level and migrated to 11.5.7 or higher or if you are still at an earlier release, you will need to install patch number 2949808 to bring the correct version of the Universal Installer into your environment. |
| Perl | 5.005 | All nodes | The Perl shipped with iAS Version 1022 or with the RDBMS 9i is sufficient. Alternatively, it can be downloaded from `perl.com`. NOTE: Perl must not only be loaded into the system, it must be included in the path of the user running the clone before cloning. |
| JRE | 1.1.8 | All database nodes | This is only necessary if the RDBMS binaries in the `ORACLE_HOME` were not installed using Rapid Install. If this was not the manner used to install the binaries, it is necessary to install JRE 1.1.8 into the `%ORACLE_HOME%/jre/1.1.8` directory. |
| JRE | 1.3.1 | All Windows-based database nodes | Windows users only: it is necessary to install JRE 1.3.1 into the `%ORACLE_HOME%/jre/1.3.1` directory. |
| JDK | 1.3.1 | All middle tier nodes | |
| Zip | 2.3 | All nodes | Download from `infozip.com`. Not only must it be available on the system, zip must also be in the path of the user running the clone before cloning. |

If you are running on a Windows platform and have not already done so, apply patch number 2237858 to enable support on your system of long filenames. If you have applied patches to your system up to this point, you likely already have this patch applied or many other patches would have encountered difficulty. Double-check to make sure.

Apply the Rapid Clone patch. See, even in cloning, there are patches to apply. Patching is simply going to become second nature to you. To enable your Applications file system to be cloned using Rapid Clone, you will need to apply Rapid Clone patch number 2926786 to all middle tier nodes and the AutoConfig patch number 2942559 to all middle tier nodes.

One of the primary requirements for being able to run Rapid Clone is for all sources and targets to be AutoConfig enabled. If your system was created as an 11.5.5 system or earlier and you have not yet migrated to AutoConfig, being able to clone in this manner is a good reason to do so now. Note number 165195.1 can help you in migrating and maintaining your system with AutoConfig.

For Rapid Clone to work correctly, you will have to update your ORACLE_HOME file system. On the Application Tier log into the APPL_TOP environment as the owner of the application on the middle tier and source the environment file. Once logged in, update your middle tier file system with the adchkcfg utility by applying another patch, patch number 2952369, and create appsutil.zip file by issuing the following command:

```
Perl%AD_TOP%\bin\admkappsutil.pl
```

On the database tier, as the owner of the RDBMS binaries, copy or FTP the appsutil.zip file created in the previous step to your %ORACLE_HOME% and unzip the file once it has been copied.

```
cd%ORACLE_HOME%
unzip -o appsutil.zip
```

If you have not yet migrated your database tier to AutoConfig, this is the place to make this migration. To create the context file on the database tier, run the following command:

UNIX
```
$cd $ORACLE_HOME/appsutil/bin
$adbldxml.sh tier=database appsuser=apps
appspasswd=apps
```

Windows
```
D:\ cd/d%ORACLE_HOME%\apps\bin
D:\<%ORACLE_HOME% adbldxml.cmd tier=databae
appsuser=apps appspasswd=apps
```

You are now ready to run your clone. The first step is to create a set of template files on the source system. Rapid Clone takes these templates and updates them once they get to the target system with the target configuration. Rapid Clone will not make any changes to the source system.

To prepare the database for the clone, log on to the source database tier as the `applmgr` user and run the following commands:

```
$ cd $ORACLE_HOME/appsutil/scripts/PROD
$ perl adpreclone.pl dbTier
```

On the source middle tier, log on (again as the `applmgr` user) and run the following command:

```
D:\ cd%COMMON_TOP%\admin\scripts\PROD
D:\PRODCOMMIN\admin\scirpts\PROD
perl adpreclone.pl appsTier
```

Now copy the middle tier file systems from the source to the target system by running the following commands in exactly the order provided.

### Shut Down the Server Processes

Copy all of the following directories:

```
$APPL_TOP
$OA_HTML
$OA_JAVA
$COMMON_TOP/util
$COMMON_TOP/clone
$806_ORACLE_HOME
$iAS_ORACLE_HOME
```

Make sure that the copied file systems are owned by the target's `applmgr` on all tiers and nodes.

Log on to the database tier as the `applmgr` user that owns the database. Shut down the database either normal or immediate and, once the system has shut down successfully, copy the database files from the source system to the target system. When the database files are finished, copy the `$ORACLE_HOME` from the source system to the target system and start up the source system on all tiers and nodes.

To configure the database, log into the server as the `applmgr` user of that server and run the following commands:

```
$ cd $ORACLE_HOME/appsutil/clone/bin
$ perl adcfgclone.pl dbTier
```

Now, to configure the middle tier nodes, log on to each node as the `applmgr` user and run the following commands:

```
D:\ cd%COMMON_TOP%\clone\bin
D:\VISCOMMON\clone\bin perl adcfgclone.pl appsTier
```

If you are running any of the middle tier nodes on Windows servers, add the `806 Oracle Home` to the path prior to running this script.

Now we complete the finishing steps.

Rapid Clone does not update any profile option values lower than site level. If there were any instance-specific values set on your source or your preclone target, you will have to manually reset these. If different printers are being called from the target system than from the source system, you will need to manually update these as well as the workflow configuration settings in Table 11.4.

**Table 11.4   Rapid Clone Tables to Check for Incorrect Values**

| Table Name | Column Name |
| --- | --- |
| WF_NOTIFICATION_ATTRIBUTES | TEXT_VALUE |
| WF_ITEM_ATTRIBUTE_VALUES | TEXT_VALUE |
| WF_SYSTEMS | GUID |
| WF_SYSTEMS | NAME |
| WF_AGENTS | ADDRESS |
| FND_FORM_FUNCTIONS | WEB_HOST_NAME |
| FND_FORM_FUNCTIONS | WEB_AGENT_NAME |
| FND_CONCURRENT_REQUESTS | LOGFILE_NAME |
| FND_CONCURRENT_REQUESTS | OUTFILE_NAME |

## OTHER CLONING TOOLS

Surprisingly, there are few tools on the market today to do what Oracle does in its cloning process. One tool that I found that will assist you with the cloning process, should you find that you and the Oracle solutions do not always see eye to eye, is Babboo.

### Babboo

XClone by Babboo.com, an Oracle Certified Partner, provides a standard Java interface with drag and drop features to a new cloning solution. XClone provides the ability to schedule your clones to occur automatically after you have configured your Master Environment (your source) and defined your destination (target) for the given situation. While it requires an additional plug-in to enable XClone to clone the application layer, the single GUI interface and ease of installation and use allow more effortless manipulation of the entire environment and more overall consistency to the process.

# 12

---

# CONCURRENT MANAGERS AND CONCURRENT PROGRAMS

For the majority of the time that Oracle E-Business Suite spends running, it is running in transactional mode. This means that there are short bursts of operations occurring at regular intervals. But there are some things that businesses do that occur in a batch type environment. These batch jobs are typically longer running processes that are quite often data intensive in nature.

What is Oracle's facility for running the data intensive batch processes?

Oracle provides an extremely complex tool to handle running batch processes as well as scheduling monitoring and reporting on those batch processes. The mechanism that Oracle provides is the Concurrent Manager.

End users often take a dim view of Concurrent Managers and Concurrent Processing because they are used to the instantaneous response that they get from the transaction processing parts of the system. They will often refresh the concurrent job screen every few seconds to see if their job has run. The perception frequently is that a job that crunches numbers to populate a data rich report should finish as rapidly as the screen from which they have queried up a purchase order or inventory item. Managing the users' expectations is often as difficult as managing the entire Oracle E-Business Suite of products.

## CONCURRENT PROCESSING

Concurrent Processing is the running of batch type jobs interspersed (concurrently) with typical transactional transactions without having either impact the performance of the other.

In Concurrent Processing, Concurrent Managers run Concurrent Programs from Concurrent Program Libraries either on demand or on a set schedule that is defined in terms of work shifts.

A Concurrent Program is any program that can be run as a background process. They can be written using SQL*Plus, they can be SQL*Loader jobs, they can be written in PL/SQL, Pro*C, or Oracle Reports. Further, they can be written in a scripting language native to the OS. More often now, in 11i, it is suggested that more Concurrent Programs be written in PL/SQL or in Java. These programs can either run within the same OS process (or thread) as the Concurrent Manager who is running it (these are called immediate programs) or run in a child process or thread that is spawned by the parent Concurrent Manager (these programs are called spawned).

You can group these Concurrent Programs together into Concurrent Program Libraries. A Concurrent Program Library simply contains executable programs that can be called by a Concurrent Manager. A Concurrent Manager can only run immediate programs from its own program library, but can run any spawned process. Oracle currently includes support for immediate programs for backward compatibility but highly recommends that any new Concurrent Programs that are created be of the spawned variety.

There are many predefined libraries. Table 12.1 gives a few of the libraries with their executable name and the Concurrent Manager description that can run the immediate programs.

**Table 12.1 Concurrent Manager Executable Descriptions**

| Executable | Concurrent Manager Description |
|---|---|
| ARLIBR | Receivables Tax Engine. |
| CYQLIB | Capacity Manager. |
| FNDCRM | Conflict Resolution Manager. |
| FNDIMON | Internal Monitor. |
| FNDLIBR | Applications Object Library (AOL) — The ICM and the Standard Manager are both members of this library. |
| FNDSCH | Scheduler Manager. |
| INVLIBR | Inventory Manager Library. |
| MRCLIB | Oracle MRP Library. |
| PALIBR | Oracle Project Accounting. |
| POXCON | Purchase Order Document Approval. |
| RCVOLTM | Receiving Transaction Manager. |

# WHAT ARE CONCURRENT MANAGERS AND CONCURRENT PROCESSING?

Concurrent Managers, typically, allow you to execute long running and data intensive application programs asynchronously. They are one of the core components of the Oracle E-Business Suite, the bane of many Apps Administrators lives, and the workhorse of the application. Before we get too far into the discussion of Concurrent Processing, though, it is important that we have a basic understanding of the vocabulary and the ideas involved.

## Concurrent Manager

A Concurrent Manager is a special Concurrent Program that works as a mechanism for starting and running Concurrent Programs that operates during the times and days that are predefined as its work shift. These managers can run any kind of Concurrent Program including OS programs, C programs, reports, Java programs, and PL/SQL programs.

## Concurrent Program

A Concurrent Program runs at the same time that other programs are allowed to run; it runs as a background process while OLTP continues to occur on the system and (usually) while other Concurrent Programs are allowed to run.

When a requested Concurrent Program that is available to run is based on when it was scheduled to start (a parameter specified by the user requesting it), its priority (a higher priority program can cause a lower priority program to wait temporarily for run resources), and its compatibility with other currently running programs (some programs are defined as incompatible with certain other Concurrent Programs).

Concurrent Programs are defined to the system using the Define Concurrent Program screen. If there were parameters defined by the programmer, they are also defined through this screen. Different programs take different parameters in different ways. A SQL*Plus or a host script program accept positional parameters and must be specified in the Concurrent Program Details zone of the Define Concurrent Reports form in exactly the same sequence that the program expects them. An Oracle Reports concurrent report takes keyword parameters. The token name that the programmer gave the report when he wrote it has to be the parameter name that you register the report. A SQL*Loader Concurrent Program requires that all of its parameters be passed in as a continuous string. This string is defined in the Execution Options field of the Concurrent Program zone. When defining a concurrent SQL*Loader job, you do not use the Details zone.

The parameters that you put into the Details zone are carried in the application as a special Descriptive Flex field.

### Concurrent Process

A Concurrent Process is an instance of a currently running Concurrent Program or other concurrent request. Every time a Concurrent Manager goes out to the FND_CONCURRENT_REQUESTS table and there is a request waiting and available to run and the Concurrent Manager starts running it, that running job is considered a Concurrent Process.

### Concurrent Request

A concurrent request is a request for a Concurrent Manager to run a Concurrent Program as a Concurrent Process. A user makes a concurrent request anytime she goes out and requests an immediate or future scheduled job to be run as a concurrent job. To schedule a concurrent request to run at some point in time in the future, you specify, at request time, the starting date and time that you want the request to be started, the time of day and frequency of resubmission, if this is going to be a recurring job, and the stop date and time, if any, at which point you want the job to no longer be run.

### Request Group

A request group is a set of reports or other Concurrent Programs that have been defined by the sysadmin to assist in control of user access to these reports and programs. They can be used to control access in two ways. Access can be granted or denied according to the users' responsibility (e.g., receivables manager). The other way that users access a request group would be through a customized Submit Request form. This is a relatively simple and Oracle supported customization with detailed instructions in the *Oracle Applications System Administrator's Guide* that entails registering a form function and passing in arguments to the Submit Request form. Only a user with sysadmin authority has the ability to create a request group.

### Request Set

A request set sets the run options, print options, and (if applicable) any parameter values for a collection of reports or programs not already included in a request group. End users can define these and own the request sets that they create. These sets are connected to the user's sign-on ID and are available to that user regardless of which responsibility that user is currently logged into.

## Concurrent Manager

Every time a request is made for a Concurrent Program, an entry gets put into the FND_CONCURRENT_REQUESTS table along with its unique request ID. From this table, the Concurrent Manager retrieves requests based on their availability to run.

## Work Shifts

Work shifts for a Concurrent Manager is similar to a work shift for a human being. It is defined as those hours for which a Concurrent Manager is defined for working. Work shifts are defined using the Work Shift form. Often additional managers are defined to work off hours when large batch jobs are scheduled to not adversely impact the performance of the OLTP that occurs during a person's work shift.

## Concurrent Request Cache

Another component of the Concurrent Processing environment is the Concurrent Request Cache or the Concurrent Request Buffer. The Concurrent Request Cache gets set when each manager is defined and it specifies the number of requests each Concurrent Manager process can hold in its memory each time it reads from the request queue (FND_CONCURRENT_REQUESTS). Its main purpose in life is to reduce the number of cycles each manager has to make to the concurrent request table and as a result lessens the likelihood of locked rows on the FND_CONCURRENT_REQUESTS table or the likelihood of more than one manager attempting to start a concurrent request at the same time. Blank or zero value cache sizes are automatically assigned a value of 1 when they are started. If you find that, in your environment, you reprioritize requests frequently, leave the cache size at the default setting of 1 so that reprioritizations can be picked up as soon as they happen and the requests run accordingly. If you rarely reprioritize requests and have managers that service many short running requests, you can safely set the cache size to twice the target processes, thereby increasing the throughput of the Concurrent Managers by limiting their attempts at sleep time.

# KINDS OF CONCURRENT MANAGERS

## Internal Concurrent Manager

The Internal Concurrent Manager (ICM) is the controlling manager for all of the others. When you start the Concurrent Managers, this is the only one that you actually have direct control over. This manager in turn starts all of the others depending on their schedules and work shifts. It controls starting and stopping all other managers based on the definition of their work shifts and it monitors for failures. If there are failures, it cleans up after them. Its definition cannot be changed after its startup. On starting, you can, by parameter passing, set its values for sleep time, PM ON on cycle, and queue size.

## Conflict Resolution Manager

The Conflict Resolution Manager enforces all compatibility rules and based on priorities and run rules, determines which jobs can run when if there is a conflict in timing. You cannot change its definition, but can set its values for sleep time for each work shift or for parallel Concurrent Processing, if applicable.

## Scheduler Manager

The Scheduler Manager, a manager added in 11i, assists the ICM and the CRM in scheduling and conflict resolution.

## Product Specific Concurrent Manager

There are many product specific Concurrent Managers. The list includes Inventory, MRP, and Projects, as well as any user-defined managers. These managers are specialized to perform Concurrent Processing specifically for those products for which they are built. Utilizing these managers can help you off-load some of the processing from the Standard Manager.

## Standard Manager

The Standard Manager (as the name implies) is the manager that ships with the Oracle E-Business Suite and accepts any and all requests and does not, as configured, have any specialization rules. The Standard Manager is customizable but care needs to be taken to ensure that, if you change the rules on the Standard Manager, that all jobs have a manager that is able to run them.

## Transaction Managers

Conventional Concurrent Managers run batch type jobs that are typically long running, involve large amounts of data, and run asynchronously. Transaction Managers run synchronous processing of certain reports requested from a client program but run as a server side program. These managers run as immediate programs, are started automatically by the ICM, and communicate with Transaction Managers automatically. Running the job is transparent to the calling user as the job runs extremely quickly and in real time. The calling client is notified of the ultimate outcome of the program execution by a completion message and a set of values returned to them.

A Transaction Manager is owned by an application and associated with a data group. Due to this association, and the fact that it runs immediate programs, the Transaction Manager can only run programs contained within its program library.

# THE LIFE OF A CONCURRENT REQUEST

The life cycle of a concurrent request starts when the request is made and ends when the request is finished. Finished can mean successful completion or complete failure or statuses in between.

The user submits a request for a concurrent job. This job can be a report, a SQL*Loader job to bring data from the outside into an interface table, or any other Concurrent Program. When the request is submitted, an entry record is placed into the FND_CONCURRENT_REQUESTS table identifying the request as being available and specifying what its schedule is, if it is not to be run as soon as the request is submitted.

The next time the relevant manager wakes up and poles the FND_CONCURRENT_REQUESTS table, it will find the entry and determine if it is incompatible with any other running request currently on the system. If it is incompatible, the request gets passed to the CRM for processing. If there are no incompatibilities, the request gets put into its relevant queue (the Standard Manager queue if no other manager is specified for that request). The manager that is assigned to process that request checks to see if it has any available processes. If any are available, the request gets processed; if none are available, the request goes back into the queue to attempt to be processed in the next cycle.

When the request is being processed, an entry in the FND_CONCURRENT_REQUESTS table gets updated with the status information of that particular request.

A concurrent request can have many phases (i.e., pending, running, completed, and inactive) and each phase can have several different statuses. Table 12.2 gives you a description of each phase/status combination. Figure

**Table 12.2   Concurrent Manager Phase/Status Combination**

| Phase | Status | Description |
|-------|--------|-------------|
| Pending | Normal | The request is awaiting the next available manager. |
| | Standby | The request is awaiting the next available manager, but is incompatible with other Concurrent Programs currently running. |
| | Scheduled | The request is scheduled to run at some future time. These schedules can be a single report scheduled to run once in the future or can be a report that is scheduled periodically. |
| | Waiting | The request is a spawned child request awaiting its parent request to complete to a point where it can be marked as ready to run. This often happens when one program has to wait for another program to finish so the child can use the output of the parent. |
| Running | Normal | Request is currently running. |
| | Paused | Request is paused waiting for other requests in its set to finish. This typically happens when a parent request finishes its initial processing, but cannot officially finish until all of its child processes are done. |
| | Resuming | Once all child requests that have been submitted by a parent request have completed (those causing the paused status described above), the parent status will become resuming. |
| | Terminating | If the user or the sysadmin chooses to terminate the request from the Request Details screen, the status of the request goes to terminating. |
| Completed | Normal | The request completed normally. |
| | Error | The request failed to complete successfully. Details can be retrieved from the requests log file. |
| | Warning | Request completed, but completed with warnings. Often these warnings are due to a failure of a successfully generated report to print. |
| | Cancelled | The request was cancelled while its status was still pending or inactive. |
| | Terminated | Request was running when it was terminated (see Running Terminated above). |

-- continued

**Table 12.2 (continued) Concurrent Manager Phase/Status Combination**

| Phase | Status | Description |
|---|---|---|
| Inactive | Disabled | This is indicative of a program that has been requested, but the program has not been enabled. If a request has this status, the sysadmin will be the one called. |
| | On Hold | A pending request that has been placed temporarily on hold. |
| | No Manager | There are either no managers defined for the given request or there is a problem with the Concurrent Managers. Requests often have this status after patching or cloning when there is either something wrong with the Concurrent Managers or they have been deactivated. |

12.1 shows you, graphically, what having several requests of varying statuses will look like in the concurrent requests window.

## LOG AND OUT FILES

One of the best tools for determining why a concurrent request failed is the set of log and out files. These are often referred to as if they were a single entity, but they are two different files with two different purposes. Out files are the outputs of the concurrent request. They are the reports that the end user will print. Not all Concurrent Processes or Concurrent Programs will produce an out file. All of them should produce a log file.

To view these files, you can use the requests window. As sysadmin, you have a view of the requests window that the end users do not have. You have the ability to see all requests for all users, their statuses, and the log and out files for the requests that have finished. You also have the ability to alter or modify the requests.

From the log file, you can determine the errors that a concurrent request encountered, the status of the request when it ended, data errors that were encountered by the concurrent request, and the sql statement that was run to generate the output. Every concurrent request generates a log file. The Concurrent Manager's log file documents the performance of the Concurrent Managers and lists the requests processed by a particular Concurrent Manager. It will also document the performance of the ICM and the parameter values that were loaded when the ICM was started.

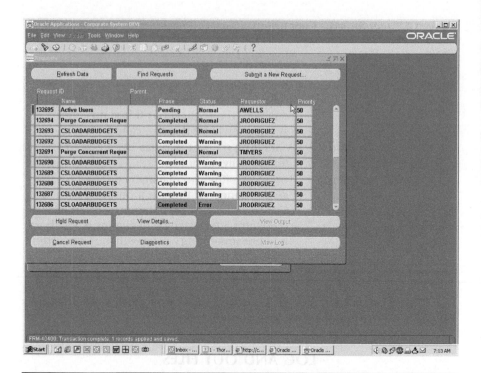

**Figure 12.1 Concurrent Requests with Varying Statuses**

You should periodically (daily or weekly or as requested) check the Concurrent Managers that ended in an error condition to try to determine why the error condition existed and help to diagnose the problems. Data issues cause many of the problems that will be encountered. These issues need to be addressed by the functional people using that particular product. You will want to review the log and output files if you have a user reporting issues with the response time that a report had or if the resulting report contained reported data errors.

One concern for both log and output files concerns their access at the OS level. Only the requester or a sysadmin can view the log files and output files through the Oracle E-Business Suite front end. The log files and the report files, however, are stored on the server and are accessible through the OS. They are stored in simple text format and, therefore, are viewable by anyone with simple read access to the directory structure where the files are stored. If a person has access to the server that allows them to view the contents of the directories where the log and output files are stored, that person can view them, print them, or save them to another location for later inspection. This could create problems if the security system is in any way lax where you are located.

# REPORTS ON CONCURRENT MANAGERS

## Completed Concurrent Requests Report

There is a Concurrent Manager job that reports on how long Concurrent Programs actually take to run. You can use this report to segregate those programs that typically take a long time to run and assign those jobs to specialized Concurrent Managers so that those managers read only requests for those programs. The report runs with the optional parameters found in Table 12.3. If none of these parameters are specified, the report returns values for all completed concurrent requests. If there has not been a purge job run in a significant period, the report resulting from this report run with no parameters could be extensive.

## Work Shift by Manager Report

This predefined report documents all of the work shifts assigned to each Concurrent Manager. You can use this report when determining what new managers to define, what new work shifts to define, or when to edit current Concurrent Managers.

## Work Shifts Report

This predefined report is a documentation of all your current work shift definitions. You can use this report when determining new work shifts or editing existing current Concurrent Managers.

**Table 12.3   Report Optional Parameters**

| Parameter | Description |
|---|---|
| Program Application Name | Application name associated with program whose requests you want to report on. |
| Program Name | The program name whose completed request you want to report on. |
| Username | Name of the user for whom you want to report on completed requests. If one particular user tends to submit particularly long running or number crunching intensive reports, assigning all reports run by that user to a specialized manager can help to distribute processing more evenly. |
| Start Date | Start date for your report. |
| End Date | End date for your report. |

## OTHER USEFUL REPORTS

Barbara Matthews of OnCallDBA.com and author of *Administering Oracle Applications* has created many useful scripts and reports that can be found at `http://www.oncalldba.com/scripts/TheBookScripts/`. While most of these scripts were written against 10.7 or 11.0 versions of Oracle Applications, most are still applicable and highly useful with an 11.5.# environment. An alphabetic listing of some of the most useful ones and their descriptions can be found in Table 12.4.

**Table 12.4  Alphabetic Listing of Barbara Mathews' Programs**

| Report/Script Name | Script | Description |
|---|---|---|
| Analyze SYS and System Objects with Delete Statistics | RMINC_delete_stat. sql | If you mistakenly analyzed sys or system objects, this will unanalyze them for you. |
| Analyze Tables and Indexes | RMINC_run_stat.sql | Analyzes all tables and indexes not owned by sys or system (uses analyze not dbms_stats). There is also a concurrent job (a program called by a concurrent manager) that will do this for you. |
| Coalesce Tablespaces | RMINC_run_coal.sql | Coalesces all tablespaces. |
| Concurrent Manager Performance History | RMINC_mgrp.sql | Shows the performance history, broken out by Concurrent Manager. |
| Concurrent Request History | RMINC_rpthis.sql | Shows the history of a Concurrent Program, including who ran it, how long it took, and which parameters were passed to it. |
| Concurrent Request Performance History | RMINC_rptsump.sql | Shows performance history of all concurrent requests that have run since a user specified date. |
| Concurrent Requests that Errored or Terminated | RMINC_concmgrerror s.sql | All terminated requests or requests that ran but errored out. |
| Concurrent Programs by Request Type | RMINC_req_type_ progs.sql | Shows Concurrent Programs by type of request. |

## CONCURRENT PROCESSING FILES AND TABLES

You can control how long and how many log and output files to retain at the OS level. Once you have made the determination how long to retain these files, the Purge Concurrent Request Concurrent Program or the Manager Data Concurrent Program will act, based on the information located in the database tables found in Table 12.5 to determine which files it can safely purge and which it needs to retain. Table 12.6 provides a detailed list of parameters accepted by the report. The retention policy for these log and output files needs to be determined by your Applications users. Archiving policy needs to be determined by the corporate IT departments. These policies can then be implemented, in part, through these concurrent requests.

You can maintain statistics on concurrent requests, even after they have been purged from the system, by setting the Concurrent: Collect Request Statistics profile option to yes. These statistics can help you determine where best to start tuning long running or time-intensive concurrent requests.

**Table 12.5   Tables Used by Purge Concurrent Request Concurrent Program**

| Table Name | Description |
|---|---|
| FND_CONCURRENT_ REQUESTS | Contains a complete history of all concurrent requests (both past history and those scheduled to run in the future). |
| FND_RUN_REQUESTS | Stores information about the reports in a report set that a user submits including the report set's parameter values. |
| FND_CONC_REQUEST _ARGUMENTS | Records all arguments passed by Concurrent Managers to concurrent requests as those requests are running. |
| FND_DUAL | Records when a request does not update any database tables. |
| FND_CONCURRENT_ PROCESSES | Records information about Oracle Applications processes and OS processes. |
| FND_CONC_STAT_ LIST | Collects runtime performance statistics for concurrent requests. |
| FND_CONC_STAT_ SUMMARY | Contains Concurrent Program performance statistics generated by the Purge Concurrent Request program or the manager data program. These programs use the data in FND_CONC_STAT_LIST to compute these statistics. |

**Table 12.6 Detailed List of Parameters Accepted by Purge**

| Report Option | Granularity | Meaning |
|---|---|---|
| Entity | All | Purges records from database history tables for requests and concurrent requests. Purges log files, manager log files, and output files from OS. |
| | Manager | Retains information on reports and purges information on manager from history table and log file from server. |
| | Request | Retains information on Concurrent Manager. Purges information on concurrent requests from tables, log files, and out files from the OS. |
| Mode | Age | Number of days you want to retain request history table records and log and output files. |
| | Count | Number of most recent records of concurrent history to retain. |
| Mode Value | | Value to define the age or count number for mode. Valid values are 1 to 9999999. |
| Oracle ID | | The Oracle ID of the concurrent request submitter for whom you want to purge concurrent request records, log files, and output files. Relevant only if entity is "All" or "Request." |
| Username | | Application username to whom the concurrent requests to be purged belong. Simpler to use than Oracle ID as Username is easier to determine. Relevant only if entity is "All" or "Request." |
| Responsibility | | Responsibility for whom you want to purge concurrent information. Example: System Administrator Relevant only if entity is "All" or "Request." |
| Program Application | | Application for which you want to purge concurrent information. Example: Oracle Receivables Relevant only if entity is "All" or "Request." |

-- continued

**Table 12.6 (continued) Detailed List of Parameters Accepted by Purge**

| | | |
|---|---|---|
| Program | | Concurrent Program for which you want to purge concurrent information. Relevant only if entity is "All" or "Request." |
| Manager Application | | Application associated to Concurrent Manger for which you want to purge concurrent information. Used with Manager option. Entity = Request, all requests associated with those run by Concurrent Manager named in the Manager option. Entity = Manager or All, purges all of those purged by "Entity = Request" and also those manager log files associated with that manager. |
| Manager | | Concurrent Manager for whom you want to purge concurrent information. Same entity rules as for Manager Application. |
| Report | Yes | Generate report listing number of records purged. |
| | No | Run program, do not generate report. |
| Purge Other | Yes | Delete records from FND_DUAL. |
| | No | Do not delete records from FND_DUAL. |

## CONTROLLING CONCURRENT MANAGERS

### Checking the Status of a Manager

#### Applications Interface Method

Through the Applications interface, you can check the status of Concurrent Managers by logging in with an ID that has sysadmin responsibility. Log into the sysadmin responsibility and navigate to the Concurrent Manager Administration Page. Figure 12.2 shows the navigation screen.

On this screen, check to make sure that the nonzero numbers in the Target and Actual columns match. Target is the number of processes that should be running for each individual manager during the current work shift. The Actual column shows the number of processes that are actually currently running. If the number in the Target column is 0, that manager is not scheduled for this work shift. If the number in the Target column

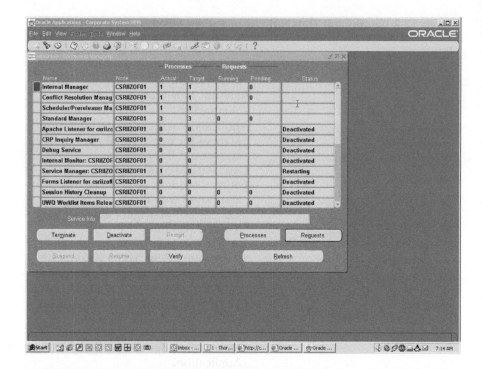

**Figure 12.2  Concurrent Manager Administration Screen**

is not 0, but the number in the Actual column is 0, then you should have processes running for the given manager, but do not.

Further information can be gathered from this screen.

### SQL Script Method

A less descriptive method to determine if the Concurrent Manager is running on the system is to find the `afimchk.sql` script located in your `$FND_TOP/sql` directory and run that script at a SQL prompt:

```
SQL>@$FND_TOP/sql/afimchk
```

### Operating System Process Method

An operating Concurrent Manager creates a library process at the OS level on the Concurrent Manager host server. The ICM creates a process called FNDLIBR. If you run the following command, you can get an idea of what library processes you have running on your server. Table 12.7 will show you a sample of the output from that command:

```
ps -ef |grep LIBR
```

**Table 12.7    Running Concurrent Libraries at OS level, Windows**

```
D:\visappl>ps -ef |grep LIBR
        36   3080   3064   0    Jun 09 CONIN$   0:00 cmd/c
d:\visappl\fnd\11.5.0\bin\FNDLIBR.EXE FND CPMGR "FMDCPMBR
sysmgr=APPS/apps@VIS sleep=20 pmon=60 qu
esiz=1 diag=N logfile=d:\\viscomn/admin\\log/VIS\\
CM_VIS.log" 2>d:\viscomn/admin\log/VIS\CM_VIS.log
        36   3100   3080   0    Jun 09 CONIN$   0:07
d:\visappl\fnd\11.5.0\bin\FNDLIBR.EXE FND CPMGR "FMDCPMBR
sysmgr=APPS/apps@VIS sleep=20 pmon=60 quesiz=1 diag=N
logfile=d:\\viscomn\/admin\\log/VIS\\CM_VIS.log"
        36   3048   3100   0    Jun 09 CONIN$   0:04 d:\visappl
\fnd\11.5.0\bin\FNDLIBR.exe FND Concurrent_Processor
"MANAGE OLOGIN="APPS/94A491A100000000000000
0000000000000000000000000000000000000000" QAPPL="FND"
QUEUE="STANDARD" PMONMETH="LOCK" DECRYPT=Y
TARGET="MY_SERVER" CPID="1309""
```

## *Oracle Application Manager Method*

Now, with the advent of the Oracle Applications Manager to the 11i Suite, you can, through a Java free site, check on the status of your Concurrent Managers, define new managers, start and stop managers, and edit properties of current Concurrent Managers.

The same Target and Actual columns are available and they provide the same information as is available through the Concurrent Manager Administration Page. You can drill out quickly and easily to requests for each manager, the status for each manager, and the running and pending request detail. Further, you can start and stop and activate and deactivate any of the defined managers.

## Starting Individual Managers

You can activate or restart individual managers by changing their status in the Administer Managers form. Restarting a manager forces the Internal Manager to go out and reread that manager's definition. Activating a manager undoes a previous command to deactivate it and allows the Internal Manager to start it when its next scheduled work shift starts.

## Deactivating Individual Managers

Deactivation can take two different paths. You can either choose to deactivate a manager and abort all requests that that manager is acting on or you can choose to allow it to finish its active requests before it shuts down. Terminated requests are marked for resubmission the next time that the manager is activated. If a manager is explicitly deactivated, it has to be explicitly activated and the Internal Manager has to be active at the time of reactivation.

Concurrent Programs are designed in such a way that regardless of the reason for termination, there will be no data loss.

## VERIFY A MANAGER'S STATUS

### Controlling Internal Manager

You can control the Internal Manager from the command line of the OS by using the STARTMGR command (or the net start command or Control Panel Services in Windows NT or Windows 2000) to start it or through the CONCSUB command to deactivate, verify, or abort it (net stop or Control Panel Services on Windows NT or Windows 2000). The utility can only be run on the server on which the Concurrent Managers are running, but can be called on that server from any other server on the same network.

### *STARTMGR*

STARTMGR starts the ICM, which in turn starts all Concurrent Managers defined that should be running for that work shift. To successfully run this command, you have to be logged into the server with a user ID that has write privileges to the log directory and the out directory of every application, otherwise, the Concurrent Manager will be unable to write some or all of its files. STARTMGR has to be run anytime you have shutdown the Concurrent Managers, after the server has been rebooted, or after the database has been restarted. The STARTMGR command can take up to 10 optional parameters (listed with their description and default values in Table 12.8), passed into the command in any order with all but printers having a default value. For example:

```
$ startmgr sysmgr="apps/apps" mgrname='std"
printer="lpr_finance" mailto="jdoe" restart="N"
logfile="mymanagerlog" queuesize="15" pmon="10"
sleep="60"
```

These commands start the ICM, which in turn starts up the CRM and the Scheduler Manager, followed by any specialized managers depending on their work shifts. FND_CONCURRENT_QUEUES and FND_CONCURRENT_QUEUE_SIZE provide information to the ICM about each manager, its work shift, and the target number of processes to be started (based on the value in the MAX_PROCESSES column of the

**Table 12.8  STARTMGR Command with 10 Optional Parameters**

| Parameter | Description | Default |
|---|---|---|
| Sysmgr | Apps schema user ID and password. | Apps/apps |
| Mgrname | Name of the ICM (used for locking purposes). | STD |
| Printer | Default printer to which you want output sent. | No default |
| mailto | List of usernames who need to be informed whenever the ICM terminates. | Applmgr |
| Restart | Should the manager restart after a crash? Valid values are N (for no) or the number of seconds that it should wait to restart after abnormal stop. | N |
| Logfile | User specified file to use for the manager's own log file (not to be confused by the logs for the requests). | Std.mgr |
| Sleep | Number of seconds for the ICM to wait between checking for new requests in the FND_CONCURRENT_REQUESTS table. | 60 |
| PMon | Number of sleep cycles that the ICM or the CRM will wait before checking for failed managers. This can be set lower than the default as the PMon resources that are dedicated to this process does not require such a long sleep interval. | 20 |
| Quesiz | Number of PMon iterations that the Internal Concurrent Manager will wait while scanning for sudden changes in the number of actively running Concurrent Manager workers. | 1 |
| Diag | Diagnostic output to be produced to aid in debugging. The default (N) provides better performance. Can also be set to Y. | N |

FND_CONCURRENT_QUEUE table). If you want to verify that there is at least one Concurrent Manager process running on your server, you can check the Task Manager on Windows for a FNDLIBR process or ps -ef |grep FNDLIBR on a UNIX platform (ps -ef |grep FNDLIBR will work on Windows as well, thanks to the running of MKS Toolkit). FNDLIBR is the program library process that gets spawned when the ICM or any generic Standard Manager is running on your system. CRM program library process appears as FNDCRM.

Oracle Support will often have you check for the existence of FNDLIBR processes if it appears that your ICM did not start.

Once the managers are started on the system, ICM will insert one row into the FND_CONCURRENT_PROCESSES table for each running manager and one row for itself and will update the RUNNING_PROCESSES column in the FND_CONCURRENT_QUEUES table to reflect the actual number of running processes. When the actual number in the RUNNING_PROCESSES column matches the target number in the MAX_PROCESSES column, all managers that are scheduled for the current work shift are running. Each entry in the FND_CONCURRENT_PROCESSES table identifies the process ID (PID) of the OS process as well as the process's status code.

### CONCSUB

CONCSUB is a utility for allowing the sysadmin username and password to have the ability to submit concurrent requests at the OS level. This utility, unlike many of the Applications utilities, is not menu driven. It runs from the command line, submits a concurrent request, and returns you to the command prompt once the concurrent request completes. You can check the status of your concurrent request via the Concurrent Request form.

The CONCSUB command takes the following form:

```
CONCSUB applsys/pwd 'responsibility application
shortname' 'responsibility name' 'username' [wait=]
CONCURRENT 'Program application shortname' PROGRAM
```

Table 12.9 defines the parameters and their meaning.

Example of a CONCSUB command:

```
Concsub applsys/apps SYSADMIN 'system Administraor'
SYSADMIN concurrent fnd deactivate
```

You can use CONCSUB to shutdown Concurrent Managers before the sysadmin reboots the server, before the database administrator shuts down the database, or when you need changes to Concurrent Managers to take effect.

## TUNING CONCURRENT MANAGER PROCESSING

Tuning Concurrent Processing is much the same as tuning any other Oracle process on the system. You can turn on an Event 10046 trace level 8 (or 12) for that process the next time it runs (or during a run if you catch it) and determine what the wait events are for the processes. Chapter 14 — Odds and Ends has more detail on a 10046 trace: how to enable it and how to read the results.

**Table 12.9 CONCSUB Parameters and Their Meanings**

| Parameter | Meaning |
|---|---|
| Applsys/pwd | Oracle application username and password that connects to Applications Object Library. |
| Responsibility Application Short Name | Application shortname of the responsibility you want to run the request for. |
| Responsibility Name | Name of the responsibility for which you want to run the request. |
| Username | Username of the person who is submitting the request. |
| Wait | Do you want CONCSUB to wait before returning the OS command prompt?<br>N (default value) waits until the job completes.<br>Y returns you to the command prompt.<br>"n" is the number of seconds to wait before it exits.<br>If this parameter is used, it has to come before concurrent. |
| Program Application Short Name | Short name of the program (for deactivate, abort, and verify, the program application shortname is FND). |
| PROGRAM | The program to submit (e.g., DEACTIVATE, VERIFY, ABORT). |

Alternatively, you can turn trace on at the application level and have the Concurrent Program create a trace file every time it runs. This may turn out to be resource intensive if used with a report that runs frequently or that does extensive processing, so use this ability judiciously.

- Log in as someone with sysadmin responsibility.
- Query up the report and enable tracing by clicking on the trace button within the application window.
- Either run the report or, if it is a report that requires certain conditions to occur, allow it to run the next time as it usually would. If you are going to allow it to run on schedule, make a note of what the next scheduled time is for it to run.

In the UDUMP destination directory on your system, look for a trace file (.trc) that has a time stamp near to the time that the Concurrent Program ran. Trace files can get quite large so to get the complete trace file, you will need to set max_dump_file_size at the database level for the periods that you are tuning to unlimited and remember that you will need to remove old trace files from the udump destination directory to keep the file system from filling up. Either of the following commands will provide you with the trace files in the directory and the time stamp on those trace files.

```
$ ls -al
```

or

```
$ ls -lt
```

You can run tkprof on the resulting trace file to see if you can determine the long running processes. A simple tkprof to run that will give you the explain plan for the processes can be gotten with the following command:

```
$tkprof ora_1234567.trc <reportname>.out
explain=apps/apps
```

This will give you a formatted out file that you can either look at and make tuning attempts to or upload to Oracle Support in reference to an iTAR so they can help you with tuning suggestions.

### Specializing Managers

Ordinarily, your concurrent requests get placed into the database table and are read by the Concurrent Manager and that manager starts the program running if the manager is defined as able to run that request. Without specialization rules (a set of instructions that associates an action with a particular kind of request), any manager can read any request and run the requested program whenever the program is scheduled.

You can narrow the requests that are applicable to a Concurrent Manager using specialization rules. For example, you can tell a manager that it is only allowed to run a program that belongs to the product General Ledger or to be run by the user jsmith. You can further narrow the scope of the Concurrent Manager by combining rules (making one manager applicable only for those General Ledger jobs that are being requested by jsmith).

To define a new specialization rule, you first need to decide if you are going to define an Include rule (which tells a manager to only read the specified type of request) or an Exclude rule (which defines all of those requests that a manager is not allowed to run, although all others are fair game). The attributes of a requested program on which you can include or exclude are the Oracle ID of the request's Set of Books (if the enterprise is defined as Multi-Org), the program itself, the requested type of the program, the user who submitted the request, or any combination of these rules. Include and Exclude rules are evaluated using Boolean

**Table 12.10 Include/Exclude Rule, Logical Equivalent, and Precedent**

| Rule Type | Evaluation Operator | Precedent in Evaluation |
|---|---|---|
| Include | Or | Include rules evaluate first. |
| Exclude | And | |
| Combination of Include and Exclude | | Include rules first then Exclude rules in an (Include X or Y) and (Exclude A and B). |

**Table 12.11 Includes/Excludes and Their Outcome**

| Rule | Results |
|---|---|
| Include program X | Includes program X. |
| Include user jsmith | Includes user john smith. |
| Exclude program Y | Excludes program Y. |
| Exclude user jdoe | Excludes user jane doe. |
| Include user jsmith and exclude program Y | Run all programs submitted by john smith and never any request for program Y. |
| Include program X and Include user jsmith and exclude user jdoe | Run all programs submitted by john smith or any program X that gets submitted but never any program (including program X) that is requested by Jane Doe. |

logic. Table 12.10 gives the type of rule, the logic that applies to that type of rule, and what order the rules are evaluated in.

Therefore, if you have created rules such that you include program X, include user jsmith, exclude program Y, and exclude user jdoe, the combinations and their ultimate outcome can be found in Table 12.11. One special note, an Exclude rule always overrides an Include rule.

You can specialize a Concurrent Manager based on a rule on requested type of program. While you can define many different types based on your company and their business rules, three common types are Quick, Overnight, and Month End Reports.

A Quick type might be assigned to Concurrent Programs that take a relatively short time to run.

Overnight request type could be assigned to Concurrent Programs that take a long time to run, to a program that is extremely resource intensive and does not need to be run during business hours, or to a program that you typically schedule to run during late night or early morning hours. I would assign gathering statistics and purge jobs to this type of program.

Month End Reports would be assigned to all Concurrent Programs that generate the reports that are run routinely every month end. If you have a specific set of reports that are run every month end, you can define this type, assign the type to each of the programs in the set, and define a specialized Concurrent Manager with rules set such that the only time the manager wakes up and runs is during that period of the month defined by your company as month end.

There are three basic steps to specializing a manager by defined request type:

1. Define a request type through the Concurrent Request Types form.
2. Assign the request type to each Concurrent Program that you choose to identify as a program of their type. This is accomplished through the Concurrent Programs form.
3. Select the request type when you specialize your new Concurrent Manager through the Concurrent Manager form.

### Multiple Work Shifts

Defining multiple work shifts will help you distribute processing from prime time work hours to evening and weekend processing. While, by definition, the Standard Manager is active and working 24 hours a day, 7 days a week (or as many hours as the system is available), it can become a bottleneck when multiple, long running processes are started or scheduled to start at around the same time. To help remedy this, multiple work shifts can be defined and managers assigned to work those shifts. If, for example, you know that you have a dozen long running, resource intensive jobs that start at right around 10 P.M., you can define a work shift to run from 8 P.M. to 7 A.M. to which you can offload some of the processing from the Standard Manager.

## DEFINING NEW MANAGERS

One of the biggest decisions, after you have been working at administering the application for some time, is the number of Concurrent Managers to run. Until you have some basic feeling for the workload on the system and for the periods of time when you are experiencing high workloads, you should probably leave the existing configuration in place.

When the time comes to add new managers and new work shifts, you need to have a direction and a plan. Examine the Concurrent Managers that you currently have and see what the target and actual values are for the processes columns. You want to try to maintain managers that have at least two target processes for each manager during a typical workday.

If a manager has at least two, then a long running job will not tie up the only process thus tying up the queue causing other processes to wait until the manager is free.

One of the primary considerations in whether to add managers and how many to add is the constraints of the resource pool. Having too few managers means that concurrent jobs will likely have to wait at certain periods of higher activity. Too many managers could mean that online transactions will suffer due to the additional load of the extra managers on the system running batch at the expense of other transactions. An unexpected side effect of too many managers can also mean that the overall throughput of concurrent batch jobs slows down due to the load on the system. Further, too many concurrent jobs may add a significantly heavier load to the number of processes occurring at the OS level. This could have a detrimental effect on the overall performance of the hardware.

One manager you might consider adding, especially if you determine that you have a significant number of fast running Concurrent Programs, is a Concurrent Manager dedicated to just fast running jobs. With the help of Barbara Mathews' "Concurrent Request Performance History Report," you can determine what jobs on your system always seem to run quickly. Creating a <Your Company> Fast Manager and assigning those jobs to that manager will limit the bottlenecks on the Standard Manager. If at some point, you determine that there are jobs that are running statistically longer and are becoming a bottleneck on the April Wells Fast Manager, you can pull them out of the Fast Manager management queue and put them back into the queue of the Standard Manager. Naming the newly created managers something blindingly different from the Oracle created ones will allow you, at just a glance, to determine which managers you have created for custom situations and which are the seeded managers that came with the application. I suggest you name the manager with your name or the name of your company as the prefix. Be careful with end users who see the name Fast Manager and decide that they want their jobs to run extra fast. Do not give in to the vehement suggestion that you assign all of their concurrent requests to the fast manager so they will run faster. This manager is for jobs that are determined to run fast, not a wish list or a panacea for those that the users wish ran faster.

Another consideration is to create additional Concurrent Managers to handle an increased load for off hours processing and adding an additional manager or two to the off hours to encourage users to schedule jobs for those times when they are not going to have as detrimental an affect on overall system performance. Requests that can be safely directed to off hours processing are those that are long running and resource intensive as well as those which are important although not business critical.

Once you have made the decision to create a new manager, you should take into account the following tasks that will be involved once the manager has been defined:

■ You will need to assign the new Concurrent Manager to a predefined immediate library. A Program Library contains the immediate Concurrent Programs that can be called by your new manager. An immediate program is a program that has been registered with the program library. Typically, as the FNDLIBR library contains the Apps Concurrent programs, it will be the library to which you will assign your new manager.

■ Next, you will have to assign a work shift to the new manager. Assigning a shift to the manager determines when your new manager will be active and available to do work.

■ For every shift, you will have to define the maximum number of OS processes that the manager is allowed to run concurrently to start requested programs during that work shift.

■ Specialize your new manager and allow it to read only certain kinds of requests.

To walk through creating a new Concurrent Manager graphically, after logging in as a user with sysadmin rights to the application, you would navigate to the Concurrent:Manager:Define screen (see Figure 12.3).

Here you will name your manager, provide it a short name and choose, from an existing list of options, the application that you want to associate it with. You can provide a verbose description of the manager, define the type of manager that you want to create, assign it to a relevant consumer group (if you choose to do that), assign it to its primary and secondary nodes if you are running parallel Concurrent Processing, and assign it to its primary library. In this example, I am creating a manager called ajw1 that has the same name as its short name. It will belong to the Application Object Library application and will be responsible for gathering statistics and will be a member of the FNDLIBR program library (the same library as the Internal Manager). It will be a Concurrent Manager and will belong to the low priority consumer group.

You can, by clicking the Specialization Rules button set the rules that you want your manager to follow. In this case (see Figure 12.4), I want the manager to only be able to run analyze and gather statistics, so I create the list of what I want it to be able to do.

Finally, by clicking the Work Shifts button, you can define when you want your manager to be able to work. Figure 12.5 shows that I allow this manager to run any time. It would probably be better if it were only allowed to run on the off shifts, but I want to be able to call it any time that a user complains about poor performance.

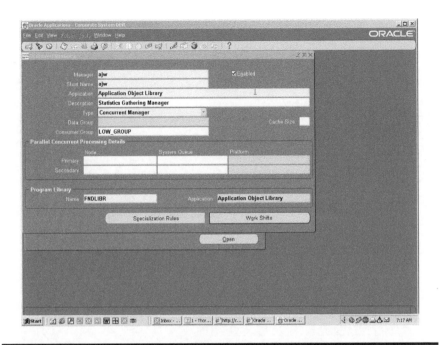

Figure 12.3   New Manager Definition Screen

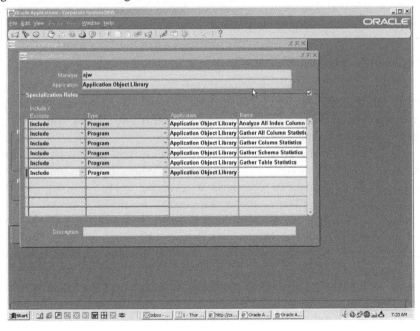

Figure 12.4   Specialization Rules for New Manager

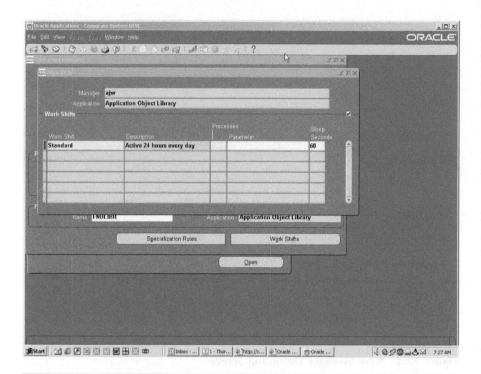

**Figure 12.5 New Manager's Work Shift**

## Work Shifts for New Manager

To assign a new manager to a work shift, you have to have an available work shift that they want to use. If there is not an existing work shift that applies to your new manager, you need to define a new work shift through the Work Shifts form.

You can name the new Work Shift anything that intuitively describes the work shift and makes it obvious that it is your custom work shift. My Company Weeknights, My Company Weekends, or My Company End Of Year are descriptive, allows anyone looking at the shift to understand that it was created by your company as a custom shift and tell exactly what that manager is built for. When you define the shift, you enter the time of day and day of week on which you want the shift to start and stop. The times are in military time format (18:00 would be 6 P.M. and 07:30 would be 7:30 A.M.). The definition for My Company Weeknights would be defined as starting from starting day of week Monday through ending day of week Friday and starting at 18:00 and ending at 07:30.

Programs running assigned to a work shift run on a priority of most narrow scope to least narrow scope for those overlapping shifts. Therefore, a program assigned to a work shift that is scheduled to run at 00:05 on New Year's Day if New Year's Day is on Wednesday will take priority over a weeknights manager and a weeknights manager will take priority over the Standard Manager.

Walking through the screen to create the new work shift, you would navigate to Concurrent:Manager:WorkShifts (see Figure 12.6) and be presented with the Work Shifts window (see Figure 12.7) in which you can name your new shift, provide the from and to times, and the from and to dates as well as providing a specific date if you wanted to create one that only runs on New Year's Eve (for example). In this definition, I created a shift that runs from 5 P.M. to midnight that will be responsible for just gathering statistics, should I choose to redefine the manager I created earlier to only run during these times.

## CREATING YOUR OWN CONCURRENT PROGRAMS

Now that you have your own custom Concurrent Manager with its own off hours definition, you can assign your own custom programs to that manager.

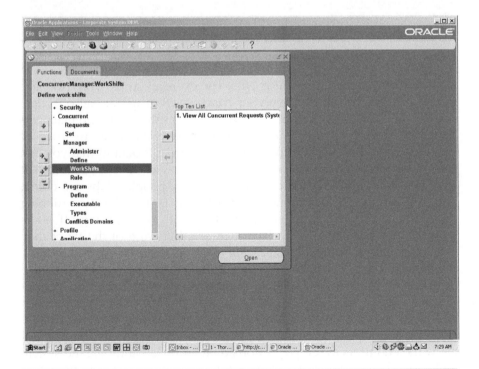

Figure 12.6  Concurrent Manager Main Screen

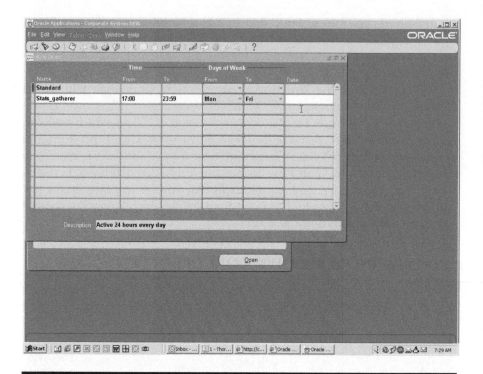

**Figure 12.7  Work Shift Definition Screen**

If you have been an Oracle DBA (or even an Apps DBA) for any period of time, you likely have your handy, well guarded, bag of scripts that you fall back on to answer all of the questions that users and managers have on why, how, and when. Since you have this treasure trove of proven scripts, why not turn them into Concurrent Programs that you can run on demand or schedule with just a few easy clicks of a button? Not only will you be able to determine what other people's jobs are doing, you will be able to determine which of your own scripts are running longer than you anticipated and move those off to run in the off hours as well. Jobs that DBAs often have that are, by virtue of the work they are doing, long running are coalescing tables in the database and rebuilding indexes (even if you use the Online Index Rebuild feature in Oracle 9i discussed in Chapter 2). While putting your scripts into a concurrent job may allow others to see what you are running (where a cron job will allow you to run your scripts on schedule quietly without anyone knowing about them), being above board with what you are running will allow the end users to see your efforts on their behalf at tuning the system and allow them to verify if it is your job, running at the wrong time, that is causing processing to grind to a halt.

**Table 12.12   RUN_COAL.sql**

```
PROMPT RUN_COAL.SQL
PROMPT Copyright 2000, All Rights Reserved, Reed-Matthews,
Inc.
PROMPT
set linesize 180
set pagesize 200
clear buffer
set head off
set termout off
set feedback off
spool &1..RMINC_coaltbsp.sql;
select 'whenever sqlerror continue' from dual;
select 'alter tablespace '||tablespace_name||' coalesce;'
       from sys.dba_tablespaces;
select 'PROMPT ALL DONE;' from dual;
spool off;
spool &1
set echo on
set termout on
set feedback on
@&1..RMINC_coaltbsp.sql
host rm &1..RMINC_coaltbsp.sql
exit;
```

To add Barbara Mathews' script to coalesce tablespaces (RUN_COAL.sql) as a Concurrent Program, look at the script in Table 12.12. Note the $1 variable. This variable will take the value of the concurrent request ID of the coalesce job. Setting this script up as a Concurrent Program, the variable will be filled in whenever this request is run. This means that every time the script uses SQL to create SQL, it will dynamically change the name of the list of tablespaces to coalesce. This will allow you to track the differences (should you choose to remove the rm statement and maintain a series of scripts that were run) in time as compared to the differences in tablespaces over time.

To make this script into a Concurrent Program, simply log into the application as a user with sysadmin responsibility and select Concurrent/Program/Executable. To have this step end successfully, you will need to have your script defined beforehand and located in your %CUSTOM%/sql directory.

Table 12.13 provides the values that you will put into the Concurrent Program Executable screen and Figure 12.8 shows an example of the screen.

**Table 12.13  Concurrent Program Executable Values for `Run_Coal`**

| Prompt | Value |
| --- | --- |
| Executable | RUN_COAL |
| Short Name | RMINC_RUN_COAL |
| Application** | YOUR COMPANY custom |
| Description | Coalesces All Tablespaces |
| Execution Method | SQL*PLUS |
| Execution Filename | RUN_COAL |
| Subroutine Name | |

Next, you will navigate to Concurrent/Program/Define and define your script to the system. Table 12.14 shows the screen location to use to look for the values. Figure 12.9 shows the screen that goes along with it, prompts on the screen, and value to assign to the prompt to enable the script in Table 12.11.

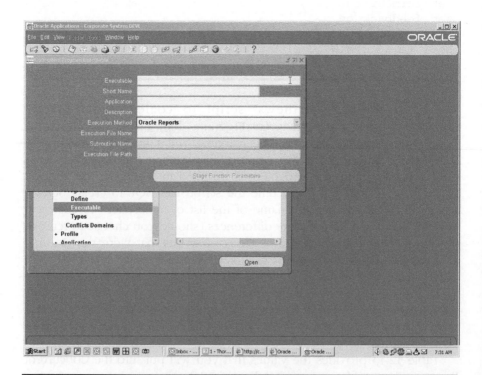

**Figure 12.8  Concurrent Program Executable Screen**

**Table 12.14  Concurrent Program Definition Values**

| Screen Location | Prompt | Value |
|---|---|---|
| Main | Program | Coalesce Tablespaces (RMINC) |
| | Short Name | RMINC_RUN_COAL |
| | Application** | YOUR COMPANY custom |
| | Description | Coalesces All Tablespaces |
| | Enabled | ÷ |
| Executable | Name | RUN_COAL |
| | Method | SQL*PLUS |
| | Options | |
| | Priority | |
| †Request | Type | |
| | Use in SRS | ÷ |
| | Allow Disabled Values | |
| | Run alone | |
| | Enable trace | |
| | Restart on system failure | ÷ |
| | Nl s compliant | |
| Output | Format | |
| | Save | ÷ |
| | Print | ÷ |
| | Columns | 132 |
| | Rows | 45 |
| | Style | Landscape |
| | Style required | |
| | Printer | |

Figure 12.10 shows you the options that you have by following the Session Control button. You can deliberately assign a rollback segment, a default consumer group to the program, and an optimizer mode (e.g., all rows, first rows, choose).

Figure 12.11 gives an example of the screen through which you would define incompatibilities. Use this judiciously because it can cause extreme bottlenecks if not used carefully.

Figure 12.12 shows the resulting screen that gets spawned when you click on the Parameters button. At this screen, you will input parameters that apply to the relevant program.

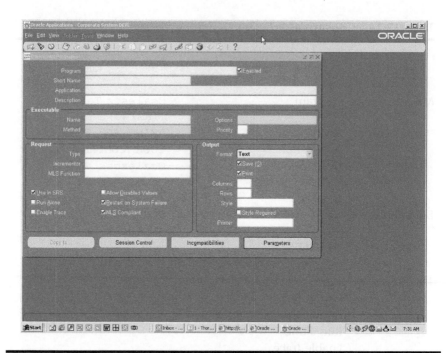

**Figure 12.9   Concurrent Program Definition Screen**

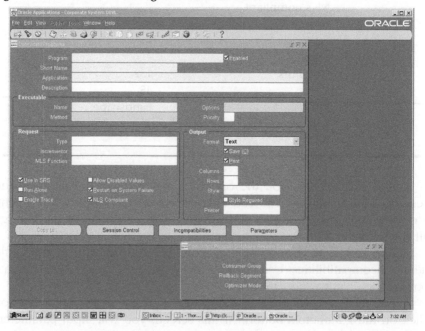

**Figure 12.10   Session Controls**

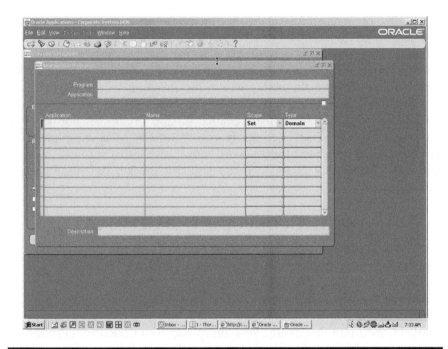

**Figure 12.11    Concurrent Program Incompatibilities**

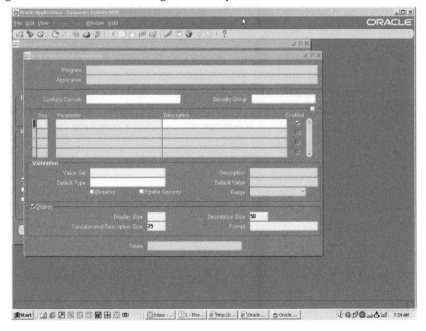

**Figure 12.12    Concurrent Program Parameters**

Finally, by navigating to the Security/Responsibility/Request screen, you can assign the user or users that have the ability to run this Concurrent Program. Given that this new program is one that would typically be run only by a DBA, you should consider carefully allowing anyone other than the sysadmin to have the ability to run the program.

You now have one custom Concurrent Program that you can run on a schedule to do database maintenance on the off hours. Further, you can instruct the application to notify you that the job has completed and that e-mail can be parsed for the word "error" and if that is found, another notice is sent to your pager to notify you that the job did not complete successfully.

## PARALLEL CONCURRENT PROCESSING

In 11i, Parallel Concurrent Processing is the means by which you can distribute your Concurrent Managers across multiple nodes in either a cluster, a massively parallel configuration, or in a homogenous networked environment. Often, heavy Concurrent Processing is occurring at times when other nodes in a configuration are idle. By taking advantage of Parallel Concurrent Processing, you can spread your Concurrent Processing across all available nodes, thereby better utilizing all hardware resources in your environment.

Distributing the Concurrent Processing in this manner has several benefits to the end users of the system.

■ Utilizing the ability to run Concurrent Processes on multiple nodes in your configuration will allow for higher performance and improved Concurrent Processing throughput.

■ Because the Concurrent Processing is distributed across all nodes, there is increased fault tolerance in the event that one of the nodes becomes unavailable or fails.

■ The ability to integrate your Concurrent Processing with platform-specific batch queue and load balancing systems will allow for far greater adaptability and will help you maximize the Concurrent Processing performance on any given platform in your configuration.

■ While distributing the processing over many nodes in your configuration, you maintain the ability to administer any Concurrent Manager from any node in the parallel configuration. This single point of control allows for ease of maintenance and monitoring in any of the clustered, massively parallel, or homogenous networked environments.

By definition, Parallel Concurrent Processing can only occur in multi-node environments where each node consists of one or more processors and their associated memory, each node having its own processors and memory, and the only shared component being possibly shared disk resources. Each node operates independently of every other node. In a clustered environment, you have multiple computers, each its own separate node, sharing a common pool of disks. In this configuration, a single database instance would reside within the set of shared disks and the Concurrent Managers along with Oracle Parallel Server would be running simultaneously on each of the nodes in the cluster. A Massively Parallel Environment is one in which multiple nodes are all housed within a single computer. All of the nodes have shared access to the common pool of disks. Separate Oracle Parallel Server instances run simultaneously on the different nodes within the computer with multiple Concurrent Managers distributed among the nodes as well. In the final configuration — the Homogeneous Networked Environment — multiple computers of the same type are connected via the LAN to a single database server or to a RAC type environment. In this environment, the Concurrent Managers run on multiple workstations.

Managers, which are running on a node that does not have an Oracle Instance running on it, will connect via NET8 or OracleNet to a node that is running an instance. To each manager in the configuration, you would assign a primary and a secondary node, with the primary node being the one on which the manager is initially started. In case of a node failure of a manager's primary node, those managers assigned to that node as primary would migrate to their secondary nodes until such time that the primary again became available. Because the Internal Manager needs to be running at all times in these configurations, it needs to be extremely fault tolerant. To assist in this fault tolerance, Parallel Concurrent Processing provides the Internal Monitor Process whose sole job it is to monitor the Internal Manager and restart it if it should fail for any reason. Each node can have only one Internal Monitor Process running and you need to determine at configuration time if each node is to have its own Internal Monitor Process running.

While not typically considered when taking into account the Windows OS, Parallel Concurrent Processing is a viable option. It differs only slightly on Windows NT/2000 as opposed to a UNIX implementation.

The startup script for NT is not the default dcpstart.sh of the UNIX implementation. While running Oracle E-Business Suite, Windows does not use the ping, rsh, and kill commands of the UNIX implementation; rather, it uses TNS along with the Oracle Remote Connection (RCP) to provide similar functionality.

On NT/2000 there are two additional log files created when the Internal Manager is started. These files and their locations are defined in CCM-SETUP.

While on UNIX, a node is considered to be alive when the Internal Manager is able to receive a good return from ping; on NT/2000 it is considered to be alive if TNS listener services are configured and reachable on the remote node.

## CONSIDERATIONS

Finally, there are things to take into account considering Concurrent Managers. Chiefly, remember that Concurrent Processing is a significant part of the core functionality of the system. When you are considering shutting down the Concurrent Managers for any reason, schedule it. Make sure that anyone who may be impacted by such an outage is notified of the schedules. If for any reason a Concurrent Manager or Concurrent Process needs to be taken out of commission on an emergency basis, make sure that you communicate effectively and quickly with the users.

## TROUBLESHOOTING

Often, when there are problems starting or running Concurrent Managers, the first thing that you should try, even before attempting to log a support call with Oracle Support, is to run CMCLEAN.sql to clean out the internal tables and reset everything back to a stable state. This should be done as Apps user and should only be done when the Concurrent Managers are inactive. The source code for CMCLEAN.sql is in Table 12.15 and can safely be run without affecting any of the waiting requests.

**Table 12.15   CMCLEAN.sql Source**

```
REM
REM FILENAME
REM    cmclean.sql
REM DESCRIPTION
REM    Clean out the concurrent manager tables
REM NOTES
REM    Usage: sqlplus <apps_user/apps_passwd>
@cmclean
REM
REM
REM    $Id: cmclean.sql,v 1.4 2001/04/07 15:55:07
pferguso Exp $
REM
REM
REM
+================================================
===============+
set verify off;
set head off;set timing off
```

-- *continued*

**Table 12.15 (continued) CMCLEAN.sql Source**

```
set pagesize 1000
column manager format a20 heading 'Manager short
name'
column pid heading 'Process id'
column pscode format a12 heading 'Status code'
column ccode format a12 heading 'Control code'
column request heading 'Request ID'
column pcode format a6 heading 'Phase'
column scode format a6 heading 'Status'
WHENEVER SQLERROR EXIT ROLLBACK;
DOCUMENT
    WARNING : Do not run this script without
explicit instructions
                from Oracle Support
    *** Make sure that the managers are shut
down       ***
  *** before running this script
***
    *** If the concurrent managers are NOT shut
down,  ***
  *** exit this script now !!
***
#
accept answer prompt 'If you wish to continue
type the word ''dual'': '
set feed off
select null from &answer;
set feed on
REM   Update process status codes to TERMINATED
prompt  - - - - - - - - - - - - - - - - -
- - - - - - - - - - - -
prompt  - Updating invalid process status codes
in FND_CONCURRENT_PROCESSES
set feedback off
set head on
break on manager
SELECT  concurrent_queue_name manager,
          concurrent_process_id pid,
          process_status_code pscode
FROM      fnd_concurrent_queues fcq,
fnd_concurrent_processes fcp
WHERE    process_status_code not in ('K', 'S')
```

*-- continued*

**Table 12.15 (continued) CMCLEAN.sql Source**

```
AND        fcq.concurrent_queue_id =
fcp.concurrent_queue_id
AND        fcq.application_id =
fcp.queue_application_id;
set head off
set feedback on
UPDATE   fnd_concurrent_processes
SET       process_status_code = 'K'
WHERE     process_status_code not in ('K', 'S');
REM       Set all managers to 0 processes
prompt  - - - - - - - - - - - - - - - - -
- - - - - - - - - - - -
prompt  - Updating running processes in
FND_CONCURRENT_QUEUES
prompt  - Setting running_processes = 0 and
max_processes = 0 for all managers
UPDATE   fnd_concurrent_queues
SET      running_processes = 0, max_processes = 0;
REM       Reset control codes
prompt  - - - - - - - - - - - - - - - - -
- - - - - - - - - - - -
prompt  - Updating invalid control_codes in
FND_CONCURRENT_QUEUES
set feedback off
set head on
SELECT   concurrent_queue_name manager,
            control_code ccode
FROM      fnd_concurrent_queues
WHERE     control_code not in ('E', 'R', 'X')
AND       control_code IS NOT NULL;
set feedback on
set head off
UPDATE   fnd_concurrent_queues
SET       control_code = NULL
WHERE     control_code not in ('E', 'R', 'X')
AND       control_code IS NOT NULL;
REM    Also null out target_node for all managers
UPDATE   fnd_concurrent_queues
SET       target_node = null;
REM       Set all 'Terminating' requests to
Completed/Error
REM      Also set Running requests to completed,
since the managers are down
```

*-- continued*

**Table 12.15 (continued) CMCLEAN.sql Source**

```
prompt   - - - - - - - - - - - - - - - - - -
- - - - - - - - - - -
prompt   - Updating any Running or Terminating
requests to Completed/Error
set feedback off
set head on
SELECT   request_id request,
         phase_code pcode,
         status_code scode
FROM     fnd_concurrent_requests
WHERE    status_code = 'T' OR phase_code = 'R'
ORDER BY request_id;
set feedback on
set head off
UPDATE   fnd_concurrent_requests
SET      phase_code = 'C', status_code = 'E'
WHERE    status_code ='T' OR phase_code = 'R';
REM      Set all Runalone flags to 'N'
REM   This has to be done differently for Release
10
prompt   - - - - - - - - - - - - - - - - - -
- - - - - - - - - - -
prompt   - Updating any Runalone flags to 'N'
set serveroutput on
set feedback off
declare
        c        pls_integer := dbms_sql.open_cursor;
         upd_rows  pls_integer;
         vers       varchar2(50);
         tbl        varchar2(50);
         col        varchar2(50);
         statement  varchar2(255);
begin
         select substr(release_name, 1, 2)
         into    vers
         from fnd_product_groups;
         if vers >= 11 then
             tbl := 'fnd_conflicts_domain';
             col := 'runalone_flag';
         else
           tbl := 'fnd_concurrent_conflict_sets';
             col := 'run_alone_flag';
         end if;
```

*-- continued*

**Table 12.15 (continued) CMCLEAN.sql Source**

```
statement := 'update ' || tbl || ' set ' || col
|| '=''N'' where ' || col || ' = ''Y''';
          dbms_sql.parse(c, statement,
dbms_sql.native);
          upd_rows := dbms_sql.execute(c);
          dbms_sql.close_cursor(c);
          dbms_output.put_line('Updated ' ||
upd_rows || ' rows of ' || col || ' in ' || tbl
|| ' to ''N''');
end;
/
prompt  - - - - - - - - - - - - - - - - - - -
- - - - - - - - - - - -
prompt   Updates complete.
prompt   Type commit now to commit these updates,
or rollback to cancel.
prompt  - - - - - - - - - - - - - - - - - -
- - - - - - - - - - - -
set feedback on
```

# 13

---

# AUTOCONFIG, ORACLE APPLICATION MANAGER, AND OTHER MANAGEMENT TOOLS

Two big changes that 11i brought that will, at some point, impact all Apps administrators are AutoConfig and the new Oracle Applications Manager interface. Both are powerful tools for your Applications DBA arsenal; both have features that will allow you to more easily, efficiently, and quickly do your job; and both have idiosyncrasies that mean learning them and learning how to deal with them can be a challenge.

## AUTOCONFIG

AutoConfig is a tool that came with later releases of 11i. It can be migrated to via a patch set if you are using a previous version. This tool supports the automatic configuration of Applications instances and collects all information needed to facilitate that automation into repositories (Applications Context for the application layer and Database Context for the database layer). When AutoConfig runs, it takes the information from these context files and uses them to help you to maintain the configuration of your system.

There are many benefits to migrating your system to AutoConfig enabled, not the least of which is the ability to clone with Rapid Clone. There is also the ability to maintain the configuration of the Application Layer, centralization of the configuration or all instances into one simple interface, and the ease of maintaining the maintenance tool itself (alterations and updates to the AutoConfig utility are delivered in the form of a patch).

The components that make up the AutoConfig environment are included in Table 13.1 with brief descriptions of each.

To determine if your system is AutoConfig enabled, look into your APPL_TOP directory, the admin subdirectory, and if you find a XML (most likely named <SID>.xml) then you are probably AutoConfig enabled on the middle tier. You will find the database version of the same thing in the $ORACLE_HOME/appsutil/ directory with the same naming

**Table 13.1   AutoConfig Components**

| Component | Description |
| --- | --- |
| Applications Context | The Applications Context is a XML repository that is located within in the APPL_TOP. It contains configuration information that is specific to that particular APPL_TOP in the admin  directory and the file has the naming convention of <SID>.xml (VIS.xml). While the files in the Context are easily readable (they are in XML format, they will open in a browser if you try to open them) and editable with any text editor, it is important that you not manually alter them, as AutoConfig can get a little testy if you do. |
| Database Context | The Database Context differs from the Applications Context only in that it resides within the RDBMS's ORACLE_HOME and contains configuration information that is specific to that database tier and its components. Again, it is important not to alter any of the files in the Context directly. All editing can be done through the context editor. |
| AutoConfig File Templates | These template files include generically configured named tags. These named tags are later replaced with your instance-specific configuration information from whichever Context you are dealing with. |
| AutoConfig Driver File | Every product in the Oracle E-Business Suite maintains a driver file used by AutoConfig. The driver file lists the AutoConfig file templates and their destination locations. |
| AutoConfig Scripts | A set of scripts that provide a simplified interface to the AutoConfig APIs. |
| Context Editor | While not entirely an AutoConfig component, the Context Editor (also comes as a patch) allows you the ability to edit the information found in the Context's context files. This is the only means of editing that AutoConfig appears to approve of as it manages the formatting in such a way that it does not cause AutoConfig to complain. |

convention. This file is used by the AutoConfig utility to make all configuration changes to the 11i environment.

If you are not AutoConfig enabled, make sure that you are at the correct versions of all of the required software and the correct patch sets before you start the migration process.

The commands that are used to run AutoConfig are found, on the application layer, in the `$COMMON_TOP/admin/scripts/<CONTEXT_NAME or SID>` directory (this is where AutoConfig puts all of your start and stop scripts for the services on your application layer as well) and are either `adautocfg.sh` or `adautocfg.cmd` depending on whether you are on UNIX or Windows. It takes, as its argument, the `APPS` password on your system.

Keep in mind that when you run AutoConfig, it was built to maintain the out-of-the-box configuration. Whenever you run it, it creates a listing of all of the files that it intends to change. There are hundreds of files that it can make alterations to. The changes that it makes are based on its preexisting knowledge of what a typical configuration includes. If your environment differs greatly from the norm, you may find that the changes that it makes are unacceptable. Backups are made of these changed files; if you find that there are issues after you run AutoConfig, you can retrieve the backups of these files and replace the offending files. This is both good and bad news. Yes, you can get the old settings back, and quickly and easily get your system back up and running. However, you do not have any way to inform AutoConfig of the things that you just did or the things that you did not like that it did. You will now have to remember which files that it changed that you did not agree with the alterations in, and every time you run AutoConfig you will have to replace that file again. Every execution of the AutoConfig utility creates a rollback script that can be run to roll back all of the changes. If you want to roll back all of the changes that AutoConfig placed into your system, you can run the rollback script. The scripts are placed, on the application layer, in the following directory:

```
%APPL_TOP%\admin\<CONTEXT NAME (or SID)>\out\
<MMDDhhmm>
```

On the database layer, it is in the following directory:

```
$ORACLE_HOME/appsutil/out/<CONTEXT NAME (or
SID)>/<MMDDhhmm>
```

The final directory — the `MMDDhhmm` directory — is created at runtime of AutoConfig. It is in the format Month Day hour minute. The log files of the AutoConfig session are in the same paths, but instead of "out" they will be in a "log" directory.

On Windows, you will find `restore.cmd` and, on UNIX, you will find `restore.sh`.

One very important note to keep in mind, restore does not make database changes. If AutoConfig changed any profile options, you will have to manually change these back, and since it may not have kept a record of what changes it was planning to make, you may have to manually find them.

Want to find out what changes that AutoConfig will plan on making? You can do this, too. I do it every time I have to run AutoConfig — when I patch, when I clone, any time anything suggests that AutoConfig be used to maintain my system. There is a script that can be run that will tell you what changes AutoConfig will make including all additions to directory structure, changes and deletions to files, and any binary file alterations that it intends to make. The script can be found in the following directory structures:

```
Application Layer
%APPL_TOP%\bin
Database Layer
$ORACLE_HOME/appsutil/bin
```

The command to determine all changes that AutoConfig will make follows:

UNIX:

```
adchkcfg.sh contextfile=<full path to context file>
appspass=< your APPSpwd>
```

Windows:

```
adchkcfg.cmd contextfile=<full path to context
file> appspass=< your APPSpwd>
```

`ADCHKCFG` will create a file that contains a list of all configuration files that AutoConfig intends to change and the status of the files that it intends to change in relationship to the files that exist. Table 13.2 provides a description of the different statuses that can appear in that file, what they mean, and the ramifications that go along with the actions that they signify.

## ORACLE APPLICATION MANAGEMENT TOOLS

Due to the tremendous complexity of Oracle Applications and its surrounding environments, monitoring, maintaining, and administering this suite of products can become time consuming and, at times, stressful. This is particularly true if you are unfamiliar with the suite of products

**Table 13.2   ADCHKCFG File Statuses and Ramifications**

| Status | Comment and Ramifications |
| --- | --- |
| SAME | There exists a text file that is identical to the file that AutoConfig will create. |
| CHANGED | There exists a text file with different contents when compared with the file that AutoConfig will create. This means that, if this is not the first AutoConfig session that you have run, AutoConfig has discovered that the file in question was changed manually, outside of Context Editor and outside of AutoConfig. Be careful and examine files that have this status. They are likely to be the ones that will have to be replaced if something breaks. |
| UPDATE | There exists a text file with different contents when compared with the file that AutoConfig will create. AutoConfig has decided that it was not your fault, but that the file was updated by a new version. AutoConfig does not care in these cases. |
| SIMILAR | There exists a text file and it is similar to the file that AutoConfig will create. The differences in this case include the existence of different white space or a different order to the contents, but the same contents exist in the file. AutoConfig is not completely happy, but you probably will not get complained at by the utility and you probably will not have to worry about these files but you might want to check anyway. Sometimes, especially in the JServ files, order matters. |
| NEW | There is no current text file existing where AutoConfig will create the new file. You might want to make note of these. |
| DIRNEW | No directory exists where AutoConfig will create the new directory. It plans on putting something into this new directory. It may be planning on moving something that you used to know where it was and that you use frequently (like `adstrtall.cmd` or `adstpal.sh` or your database startup and shutdown scripts). You may have to do some creative hunting to find things after you run AutoConfig. While you probably do not care a lot where these new directories are, pay attention to them; they will probably be important at some point. |
| BINSAME | There already exists a binary file that is identical to the one that AutoConfig will create. |
| BINDIFF | There already exists a binary file that is different from the one that AutoConfig will create. Make note of these; you may have to retrieve the backups and overlay these if something breaks. |
| BINNEW | No binary file exists. AutoConfig will create the file in the location specified. |

and all of the ways that the parts interact. If you have come from a DBA background, you have some comfort level with maintenance of the database layer, but you may not have the slightest idea when you start out what you are facing with the Oracle E-Business Suite.

Oracle has brought to market several products that will help make your life as an Apps administrator somewhat less time intensive and will provide a series of simple, one stop interfaces through which you can gather information that will allow you to later make more informed decisions on administrative tasks.

Other companies have tools as well that can assist you in your Applications Management duties.

## Oracle Management Pack for Oracle Applications

GUI tools have existed to help with monitoring of, diagnosing problems with, and capacity planning for Oracle Applications for several releases in Oracle Management Pack for Oracle Applications (an Oracle Enterprise Manager extension geared to Oracle Applications). However, it may not have a full range of abilities that will meet all of the needs of the Apps DBA and sysadmin.

Oracle Management Pack for Oracle Applications brought with it graphical representation of services to be monitored, automated data collection and management services, and central monitoring and administration of remote systems via intelligent agents (services running on the system whose purpose it is to assist with the data monitoring and collection). It extends the OEM console by allowing it to discover Concurrent Managers, monitor their availability, and notify relevant people if they should become unavailable. This OEM extension allows for a broader library of event monitoring and fix-it jobs that can be run to assist in your support of a fully 24/7 system. While the additional libraries that it brings that are Applications specific are slightly limited, it does provide the added flexibility to add your own custom scripts to the library and allow OEM to run these to assist with monitoring. Further, this tool extends the Performance Manager piece and the Capacity Planning piece of OEM to gather information on Concurrent Managers and Forms Servers that will allow you to better tune your system, eliminate resource contention, and plan for future consumption. In this arena, it can be a valuable tool that allows you to proactively plan for times when you will have resource contention and performance problems and head them off before they occur. Finally, it brings the addition of a Concurrent Process Tuning Assistant. This additional tool allows you to gather and examine historical processing information on Concurrent Processing, concurrent requests, and the Concurrent Managers running on your environment.

## Performance Manager

The Performance Manager portion of OEM allows you to monitor the performance of your database and the OS environment where it resides in real time. Through it, you can monitor the performance of the database. It also allows you to monitor the performance of your Web servers and Concurrent Managers and their surrounding OS environments. You can record statistics at predefined times (e.g., peak activity times, off peak, or a combination of these) and play back the recorded statistics at a later time. You can display them in tables or a variety of chart formats not just on one target environment, but across several targets at a time.

Not only can you view (numerically or graphically) data on high level performance points on your system, you can drill further to the details on those performance points to see what went into making up the numbers and you can get advice on how to improve those points where you are having problems.

Advice is given through a Java help interface that provides you with a definition of the performance point, the source of the numbers, and where you can make tuning changes to your system to help you to improve the numbers and the performance of the system. Built like most help systems, it allows you to print the advice that the tool provides.

Performance Manager's integration with Capacity Planner means that you can drill to historic views of all of the displayed data and compare current real-time information on the system with its historical averages for similar periods or historical peak load times and glean a better understanding of what both the historical information and the current information means. This allows you to better plan for future peak load times and allocate sufficient resources to those times.

You can create event triggers to monitor node and database data events and alert you when an event hits the triggering point. This way you can be alerted to problems on the system even when you are not actively monitoring the system and before any end users report issues with the application.

A new feature of the 9i version of OEM's Oracle Management Pack for Oracle Applications Performance Manager is a fairly substantial subset of the features that run through a browser interface. While you are limited in the things that you can do, it is a look at where the interface is heading and a view of things to come in the future releases of the product. It also will allow you to view those settings when you are in a place where you do not have access to the management console. This allows you the flexibility of monitoring when you otherwise would not be able to.

### Capacity Planner

Capacity Planner provides a facility to collect different kinds of performance statistics, records that data in the repository database tables, and maintains the information in those tables in a historical format. You can utilize this data through the Capacity Planning interface to analyze the historical data and use that data and its trends to plan for future growth in all aspects of the server and the database. Capacity Planner relies heavily on the Intelligent Agent, a data gathering service that collects data continuously on the server.

The Intelligent Agent collects the performance data for the Capacity Planner at an interval that you specify and stores that information in a binary file format that can then be loaded at an interval that you specify into the Capacity Planner's historical database. The agent will aggregate the data to the time intervals that you define and purge the data from the historical database on a user-defined schedule while allowing for the continual viewing of all current period data.

This data gathering allows you to utilize the information to track the increases in the amount of used space on disk overtime and the increase in total I/O for your server node over time. It estimates what the I/O rate will grow to in the future and assists you in determining what thresholds to set in the Performance Manager. You can publish this historical data to a Web site where administrators can view the data and allow anyone who uses the system to view the growth of the system over time, assisting in the justification for additional resources.

You can utilize the trend analysis to project future values based on the known present and historical values. You can project this analysis out to a point in time (e.g., the end of the quarter, the end of the year) or to a specific value (e.g., when we hit 500 GB or when we hit a 95 percent CPU utilization).

### Concurrent Processing Tuning Assistant

The Tuning Assistant provides you a mechanism through which you can report on and examine the historical processing information stored in the database on Concurrent Processing and Concurrent Managers. Through this information, you can determine how better to schedule existing Concurrent Managers and where to judiciously apply new and specialized managers. To assist in this, the Tuning Assistant provides a predefined set of reports that identify known problem areas in Concurrent Processing. It will generate these reports directly against the Application Object Library tables or from data stored in the Concurrent Processing Tuning Assistant Repository.

You can use the information gathered from the Tuning Assistant to find periods with greatest wait times and determine by examining the reports running during these times those that can be run during other periods of time when you have excess capacity. This will reduce wait time for the concurrent jobs and minimize the bottlenecks.

You can run the defined reports and save the results as a comma-separated file (CSV format) that can be read into a spreadsheet or loaded into a table for further analysis or saved as HTML format and published to an intranet page.

The tuning advisor feature of the Concurrent Manager Tuning assistant can help you gather information about situations that may be standing in the way of the performance of your Concurrent Managers. Once you have discovered the problem areas, you can determine if increasing the capacity of the system, resource balancing and request rescheduling, or adding additional managers will benefit the situation. The report in this area will graphically show you how and where you are currently experiencing the bottlenecks and gives you the ability to drill out to further information. Clicking a button from the report allows you to look at the tool's suggestions for how to assist in the tuning and balancing.

But the Tuning Assistant will also point out places where the manager was underutilized, yet requests were left in a waiting state. Because the wait state is not dependent on the manager being overactive and the request having to wait for that resource, and the possibilities being so broad for why it was waiting, the tool is unable to make suggestions on tuning; it merely graphically shows you where you may have other problems in the system.

While it is not a silver bullet, it will give you places to start when examining tuning your Concurrent Managers.

## Advanced Event Tests

OEM's Oracle Management Pack for Applications provides a set of Advanced Event Tests that are geared to events that can occur in Oracle E-Business Suite applications. This facility provides for the monitoring of these events during the off hours when no administrator is available to monitor them manually.

While it contains all of the same tests that are packaged as common OEM functionality (like database up and down or space management issues), the Management Pack for Applications adds to this library of events that will help you in your job.

Following is a list of event types, tests available for those tests, and a description of what those tests do for you:

- Fault
  - *Concurrent Manager Up/Down (available in OEM AM 8.1.6):* Monitors the state of the ICM and alerts you if it goes down.
  - *Conflict Resolution Manager waiting on lock:* While a wait on a lock is not necessarily an Alert worthy event, this monitors the CRM for excessively long waits and if it reaches a defined point, you will be alerted. This test is not available in OEM AM 8.1.6.
  - *Internal Concurrent Manager waiting on lock (available in OEM AM 8.1.6):* Again, waiting on a lock may not be an Alert condition ordinarily; however, if the ICM waits too long for a lock and that wait reaches a defined point, you will be alerted.
  - *Request Error Rate (available in OEM AM 8.1.6):* Monitors the rate of errors for all concurrent requests and when those errors reach your threshold, you will receive a warning or a critical Alert depending on the error rate received.
  - *Request Warning Rate (available in OEM AM 8.1.6):* Monitors the rate of warnings for concurrent requests and when the warnings reach your threshold, you will receive a warning or a critical Alert depending on the number of warnings received.
  - *Unresponsive Concurrent Manager:* If any of the Concurrent Managers defined for the current period are down at the beginning of the test and are still down at the end of the test's time period, you will receive an Alert telling you that the manager in question is not responding. Managers not defined for a work shift will not be tested. You will not receive warnings if the manager is caught during its sleep cycle. This test is not available in OEM AM 8.1.6.

- Performance
  - *Inactive Request Pending (available in OEM AM 8.1.6):* This event checks the state of the requests that are submitted to any or all of the Concurrent Managers and if any of those requests are found to be in an inactive state, it will generate an Alert.
  - *Pending Concurrent Request Backlog (available in OEM AM 8.1.6):* This test checks for the concurrent requests that have been in a pending state for an extended period of time. If this period exceeds your set threshold, it will generate an Alert.
  - *Request Pending Time (available in OEM AM 8.1.6):* This test will generate an Alert if a request has been found in a pending state for a period exceeding your set threshold.
  - *Run Alone Request Submitted (available in OEM AM 8.1.6):* This event test checks the state of all submitted requests. If a run alone request is submitted, it will generate an Alert. This test

and resulting warning should be an indication that, if Oracle determines that it is an alertable event, maybe requests should not be submitted in this manner unless the circumstances surrounding the request truly indicate that they should be run in this manner. So far, the only request that I have found that truly qualifies as a job to run without allowing other jobs to run at the same time is the rebuild indexes job.

■ Space
  ■ *Concurrent Manager Disk Free:* This test checks the growth rate of the log file, output file, and other directory and mount points used by the concurrent requests (or any other directory/mount point determined by you to be one that you want to monitor) and alerts you to space issues. This test requires access to the APPSORA.env file that is within the $APPL_TOP directory. This test is not available in OEM AM 8.1.6.

There are other events tests that you might want to examine further. Primarily, there are node events that may become of interest to you in your capacity as an Apps DBA. Many of these event tests come packaged with the application, either OEM or the Applications Manager add-on. A complete list of all node events can be found in the *Oracle Enterprise Manager Event Test Reference Manual*.

### Available Job Scheduling Jobs

The OEM console allows you to automate many repetitive tasks. The tasks that are typically scheduled in this manner in OEM on a regular system range from the execution of simple SQL scripts to kicking off OS commands. Typically, through the OEM console, you can automate the running of jobs on the database, on the OS node housing the database, on the listener, or on the Apache HTTP server. The jobs include shell scripts, SQL scripts that a DBA may run in a routine manner, or the shutdown or startup of the database, the listener, or the Apache service. The Job Scheduler further provides the ability to configure jobs that, based on the outcome of an event, could automatically be called as fix-it jobs to alleviate the triggering condition. The Scheduler Manager allows you to automatically submit these jobs on a set schedule so that they can be run during off hours or can assist in monitoring the database in off hours so that you, the administrator, can rest easier.

The Management Pack for Oracle Applications includes even more jobs that you can configure to make your Applications centered jobs more flexible and schedule tests against the system so that you can monitor and proactively correct problems on the system before they really become problems. Some of the routine tasks that come prewritten into the Management Pack for Applications are outlined in the following list. Remember that this is just a starting point for the tasks that you could submit through the OEM and Management Pack for Applications interface.

- *Concurrent Manager Shutdown:* This task shuts down the ICM in the mode that you specify (abort or stop) and does not require the Intelligent Agent to be at any particular release number. If you instruct the job to shutdown the manager in abort mode, the job will shutdown the Internal Manager regardless of what state the queues are in at the time. If you instruct the job to shutdown the Internal Manager in stop mode, it will allow the current concurrent requests to complete their processing before shutting down the Internal Manager elegantly.

- *Concurrent Manager Startup:* The CM startup job starts the ICM and can be set as a fix-it job that you can associate with the Concurrent Manager Up Down job from the Events Tests to restart the Internal Manager, if it should happen to go down. While neither the event nor the fix-it job take into account what may be the underlying cause of the down manager condition nor attempt to address the underlying cause, it will make the attempt to restart the manager if for some reason it just decides to stop. This job can be triggered through the use of any version of the agent.

- *Kill Locking Session:* The purpose of this job task is to be called as a fix-it job for either the ICM Waiting on a Lock Advanced Event Test or the CRM Waiting on a Lock Advanced Event Test. Because it is highly unusual for a Concurrent Program to lock out either the Internal Manager or the CRM for an extended period, the Waiting on a Lock event will ordinarily be triggered from a Forms session that has become out of control. If you create this as an event-triggered job, it will go out and delete the job that is preventing the ICM or CRM from continuing its job. This job can be triggered through the use of any version of the agent.

- *Load Data into Concurrent Process Tuning Assistant:* Recall that the Concurrent Processing Tuning Assistant is a utility that allows you to examine both current and historic information about the Concurrent Processing requests and the Concurrent Managers. Its ability to report on information is limited by the amount of information that it can find still residing in the FND tables that drive the Concurrent Processing. If you are running the purge jobs on a regular basis, the amount of information that is maintained within these tables could be severely limited (or you are expending resources on maintaining the information in the tables for longer than necessary and, as a result, potentially slowing down the access of the Concurrent Managers to the systems). To report on historic information, it is necessary to maintain this information in a repository schema. The Load Data into Concurrent Processing Tuning Assistant job will upload the data from the FND tables into the repository schema, aggregate this data into these tables, which allows for the historical reporting and allows the reports to process faster and easier than it might otherwise.

It is not necessary that this information be maintained in the Apps database; it can reside in virtually any Oracle database. Due to the potential for maintaining a massive amount of data, it might be more prudent to not store it in the Apps database and not store it in the same schema and tables as the OEM repository. The first run of this job will load nearly 20 percent of the data from the FND tables into the tables in the repository tables and every subsequent run of the job will load all of those rows that have been added to the table since the previous run. The size of the repository will continue to grow in proportion to the amount of Concurrent Processing that is occurring on your system, so resource planning for the repository information should become easier as you examine the trends in growth that accompany several cycles of loads with this job.

### Drawbacks to OEM Tool

One of the drawbacks of the OEM tool is that it can be resource intensive on a client machine and can be extremely slow to update if there are contention issues on your servers. The Java-based interface is very robust and provides you with quick answers to many questions. However, while it is refreshing, you cannot access anything in many cases and it becomes a tremendous resource drain at times.

Further, you have to be at an OEM console to interact fully with the system. This means that any computer that you may have to be at either has to have the interface loaded onto it or you will have to have it on a central server. This causes the added potential of network contention as the console may be accessing all middle tiers and the database tier, while serving this information through the server where the OEM product is running and further to the workstation where you are located.

Also significant, while a limited subset of the features is available through a browser-based interface, this is still in the process of growing to be a viable interface that can provide you the features that will come to make it a well used tool. One way to provide similar information without all of the Oracle Management Pack for Oracle Applications features in a less resource intensive interface is through Oracle Application Manager.

## ORACLE APPLICATION MANAGER

OAM provides an HTML-based administration console (or dashboard) through which Apps administrators can perform a wide variety of tasks. While it does not yet have OEM's full library of self-fixes, script scheduling, and automated notification of trouble spots, it does bring with it many features that an Apps administrator will find useful. Further than this, however, there are certain tasks, depending on which modules that you have implemented, that you can now perform only through this interface. If you are beyond Version 11.5.7, it is the only means by which you can configure and administer the Oracle Workflow product.

Through OAM, you can, in one simple interface, monitor the status of your applications system, including the database, the Apps tier, Concurrent Managers and Concurrent Programs, and Oracle's Workflow process. Further, you can control system processes on the Applications tier and submit concurrent requests directly through the interface. Charts and graphs provide an at-a-glance summary of the state of your system, while allowing for further drill down to detailed information. It includes diagnostic tools for many of your Applications specific components and displays for errors reported by Transaction Managers and concurrent requests. Monitoring tools include the ability to monitor currently running forms and sql queries and through these assist in helping to determine problems areas in the system and poorly running sql statements via an explain plan.

OAM can be navigated to by way of the Logon Options screen by selecting the Oracle Applications Manager link (see Figure 13.1) rather than the typical PHP link that most administration has been done through. Once you have gotten to the Logon screen, log into the OAM (see Figure 13.2), making sure that you select the correct DAD from the drop-down box.

You will select what actions you want to follow from the next screen (see Figure 13.3), the OAM home page. Your options from here are to navigate to Configuration, Activity, Patches, or Site Map or select from the drop-down list to navigate to Workflow Manager, Service Fulfillment Manager, or to Applications Usage.

### Configuration

By navigating to the Configuration screen, you can examine the system settings for your entire system (DEVL in the case of Figure 13.4) and see the version that your application is currently at, the number of products that you have installed, and the number of invalid objects that you currently have in the database. You can see your middle tier host, its OS, and what services are running on that tier. Further, you can see the information about your database tier, including its host name, SID, version, language

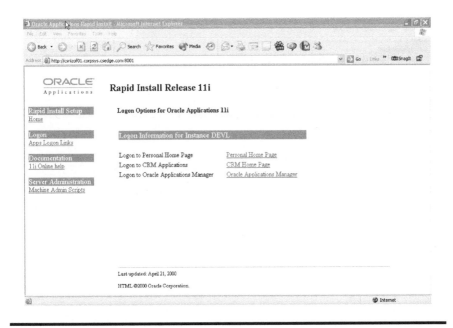

**Figure 13.1   Administration Navigation Choice**

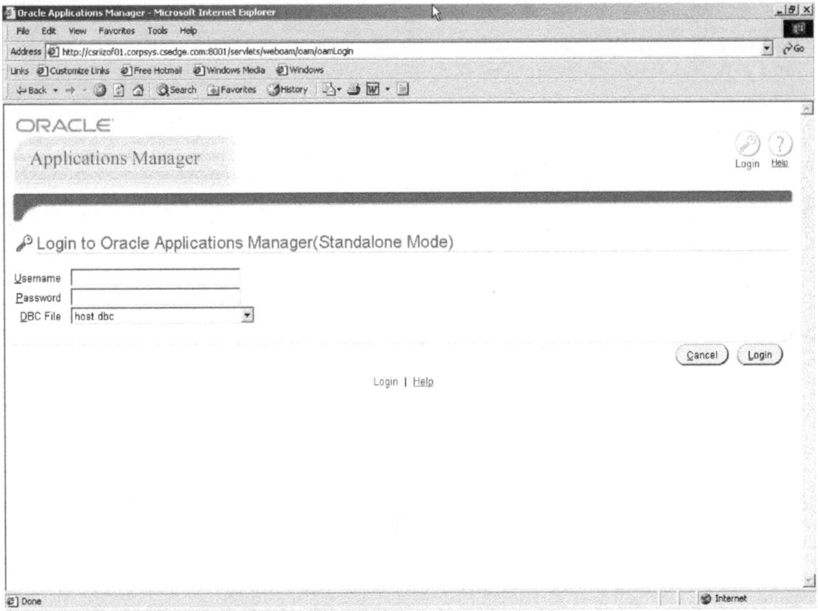

**Figure 13.2   Applications Manager Logon Screen**

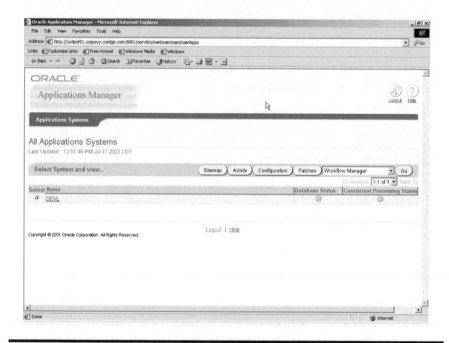

**Figure 13.3   Oracle Applications Manager Home Page**

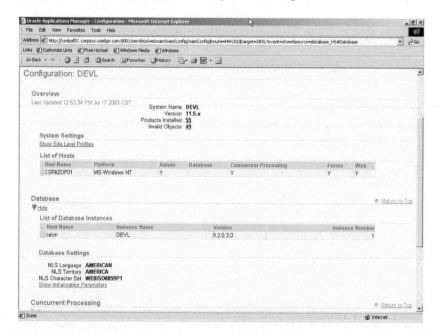

**Figure 13.4   Configuration Screen Top**

and character set, and (at a click of the link) all initialization parameters. These interfaces look a lot like the 9iAS browser-based OEM interface. Figure 13.5 (the other half of the Configuration screen) shows you the access to the configuration settings for the Concurrent Managers, Forms Server, and the Web Server settings. While these, at this time, will not give you full access to all settings and allow you to change some of what is there, it does provide a quicker look into the configuration than might be available in other fashions.

### Activity

Figure 13.6 shows a sample of the Activity Monitor page. It presents, graphically, the current state of the database and all active sessions of the database. Not only can you see that it is up, but what sessions are active, and what the resource usage is for those sessions. By selecting the bar in the graph or the color associated with that bar from the legend, you can drill out for further information on that particular aspect of the database. The same is true for the Concurrent Requests graph. In this case, there are pending requests, but none currently running on the system, no inactive managers, no requests completed in the last hour, and none that are waiting on locks. You will notice that many of the monitored aspects correspond to the tests in the OEM version of OAM, but the one that is accessible through the Oracle E-Business Suite is licensed with the product and not acquired through an add-on license. As such, it is less robust than the OEM model, but it is efficient at what information it provides to you.

### Patches

The OAM interface provides at-a-glance information on patches that have been applied to the system. You first have to provide search criteria (see Figure 13.7) and based on the criteria, OAM returns a list of all patches that were applied that meet those specifications (see Figure 13.8). There is a more advanced search capability and the ability to search by what files were overlaid by the patch, if that is the information you are looking for, which is often the case when there are customized versions of forms and reports on a system.

You can make this search as broad or as narrow as you choose. If you know what file you are looking for, that can be your criteria in the Search Files search. If you want all patches applied to the system or all patches applied this year, you can provide date ranges for that as well. You can even narrow the search to all patches for a particular language and compare those results with another language so that you can see where you might have holes.

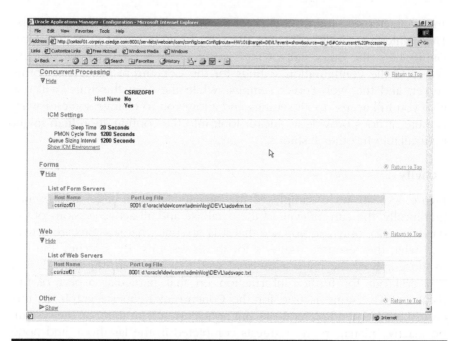

**Figure 13.5   Configuration Screen Bottom**

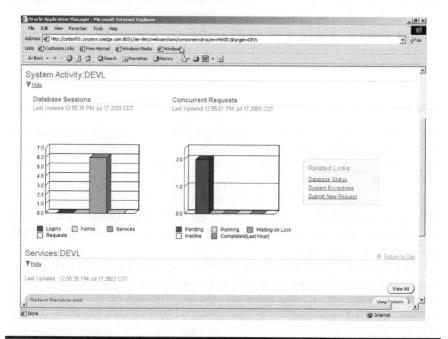

**Figure 13.6   System Activity**

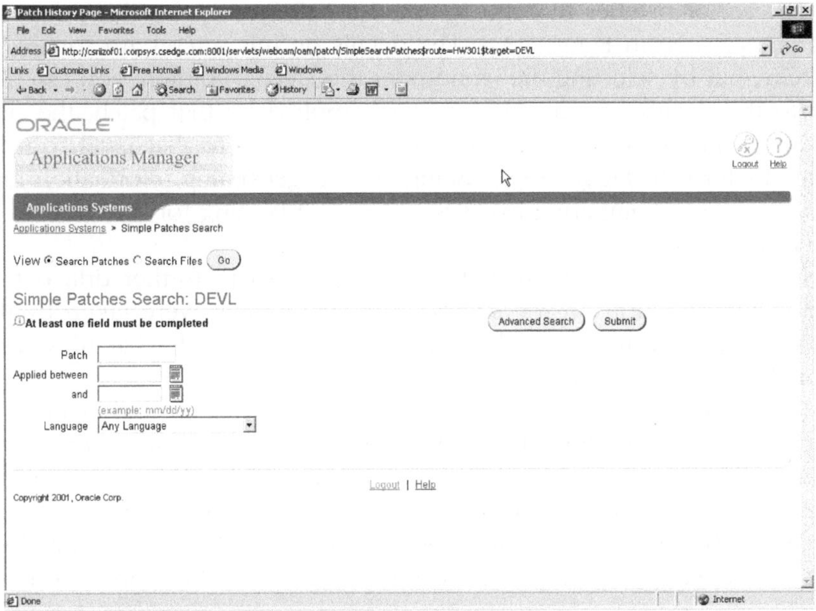

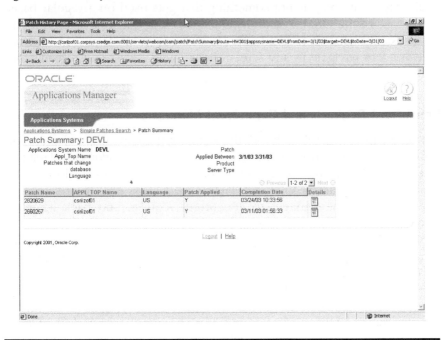

**Figure 13.7   Sample Search Screen for the Patches Search**

**Figure 13.8   Results Returned by the Search in Figure 13.7**

The set of patches that are returned for the search on this particular system are seen in Figure 13.8. The details on this screen are somewhat sketchy, but by selecting the icon under the Details column, you can drill out to the details of what drivers were applied by that patch, the start date and time of the patch, and the directory where that patch can be located later (see Figure 13.9). Being able to get timing information may prove useful in comparing two systems or in planning for the next set of patches.

From the Details screen in Figure 13.9, you can further drill out to find out information on the summary of actions that were taken by the patch driver selected, what bugs this patch fixed, and what files were copied by the copy driver.

Having the ability to report on this information quickly and in a format that prints nicely and formats well for presentation will allow you to show, in just a few minutes, what actions have been performed on your system. You may find that this information is also in a format that is easily sent to Oracle Support for assistance on trouble cases. This is the interface that I have, so far, spent the most time using in real life applications.

## Site Map

Ordinarily, a site map is not something that gets used on a regular basis. In the case of the OAM, it is an invaluable tool in quick navigation if you know exactly what you want to do. As you can see in Figure 13.10, from here you can navigate to any screen directly and access that screen's tool set.

## Concurrent Requests and Concurrent Managers

Not only can you graphically see the status of the concurrent requests on your system, you can examine the settings of the Concurrent Managers and the details on the concurrent requests as well. You can do detailed searches for concurrent jobs (see Figure 13.11) and drill from screen to screen, Concurrent Manager to concurrent request, and back again to determine what exactly is taking place in many cases.

One of the most useful tools in the whole Concurrent Manager/concurrent request part of this system is the ability to easily find and pull up the out files created by the job and the log files (replete with error message in a printable or savable format) associated with a particular concurrent request. Be careful who has access through sysadmin rights to this information; some out files may be sensitive. It saves a great deal of time being able to navigate to that functionality here, rather than having to go to the log and out directories and hunt for the files to provide in support

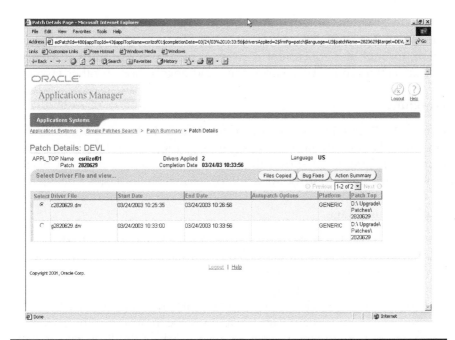

**Figure 13.9   Details of the Patch from the Results Screen**

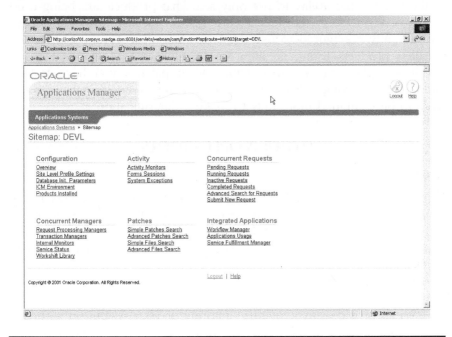

**Figure 13.10   Site Map**

of an iTAR. Where, in applications, you cannot select portions, save the file as another name, or even print a log file to support error documentation, through the concurrent requests screen, you can quickly navigate to that section and save yourself time and aggravation in other tasks.

## Workflow

In the 11.5.7 and 11.5.8 versions of the Oracle E-Business Suite, configuration and administration of workflow is accomplished through the OAM interface. Figure 13.12 shows the new interface screen that will be the central launching point for all workflow management tasks.

## Applications Usage

The Applications Usage Screen (see Figure 13.13) allows you to determine what products are on your system and in what status they currently exist or determine how many users you have configured on the system that are using each product group.

Has anyone ever asked what products are installed as shared or fully licensed on your system? Have you ever been faced with having to determine just how many people are using each of the licensed products and not been able to easily provide those answers. Another neat feature of the OAM is the ability to not only see what products are being used in any way on the system (see Figure 13.14), but also how many users are currently configured to use those products (see Figure 13.15). The installed products listing is often very useful when looking at patch installation planning and determining what patches you have to pay attention to applying, what can be ignored completely, and what patches need to be examined more fully to make a determination.

# OTHER PEOPLE'S TOOLS

## Quest

Quest Software, Inc. brings its own set of products that were specifically designed for the monitoring and tuning of Oracle E-Business Suite applications. I/Watch™ for Oracle E-Business Suite allows you to examine in-depth historical trends in apps processes that will help you optimize performance of queries. It provides facilities for continuous monitoring of Concurrent Managers and Concurrent Processes and analyzes poorly performing SQL statements by tracing the offending statements to their source.

I/Watch provides unattended monitoring of your system on a continuous basis while not adversely impacting the system itself. You can configure the system to alert a number of individuals if a problem should arise or an error in processing should occur. Its monitoring extends to

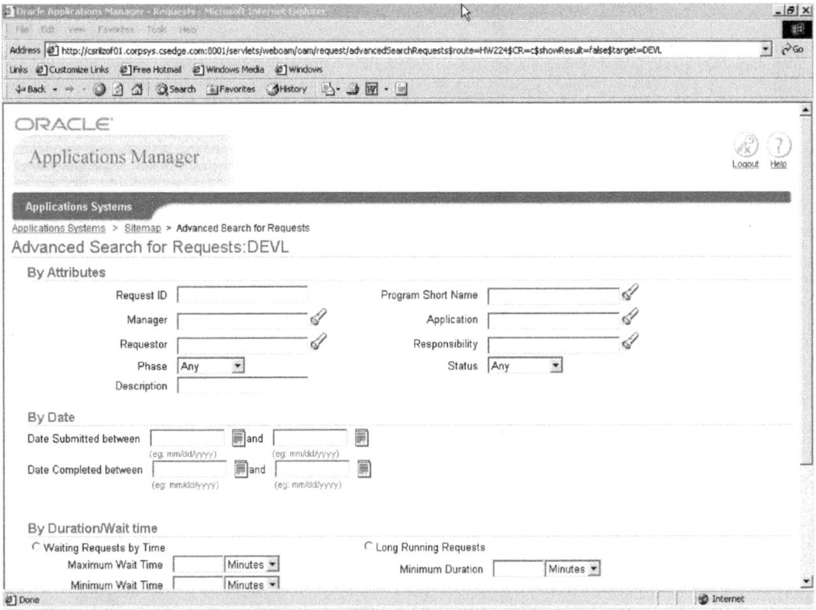

Figure 13.11    Concurrent Manager Advanced Search

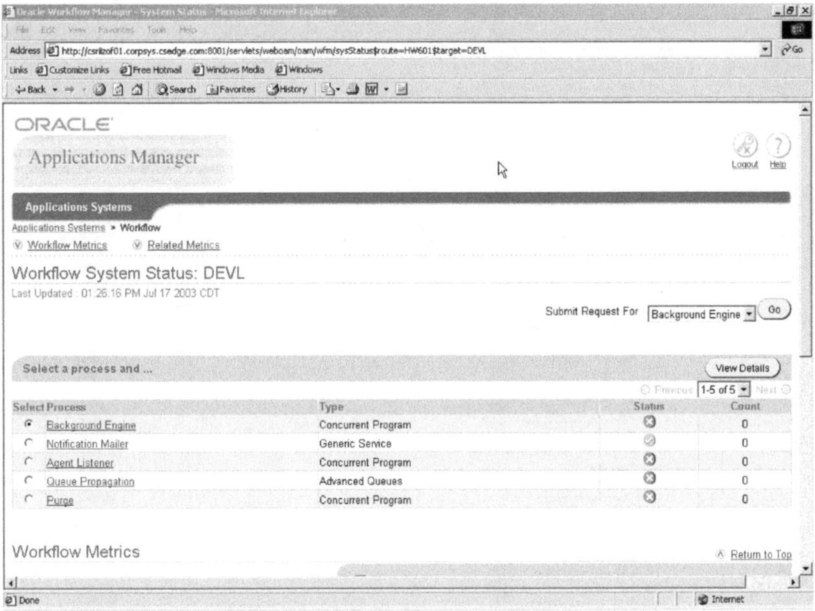

Figure 13.12    Workflow Main Page

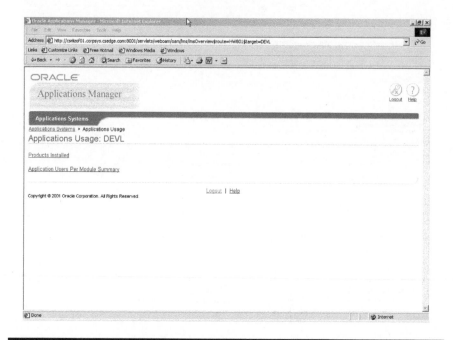

**Figure 13.13  Applications Usage Choice**

| Short Name | Application Name | Version | Status |
|---|---|---|---|
| ABM | Activity Based Management | 11.5.0 | Inactive |
| AD | Applications DBA | 11.5.0 | Shared |
| AHL | Oracle Advanced Service Online | 11.5.0 | Inactive |
| AHM | Oracle Hosting Manager | 11.5.0 | Inactive |
| AK | Oracle Common Modules-AK | 11.5.0 | Installed |
| ALR | Oracle Alert | 11.5.0 | Installed |
| AMF | Oracle Fulfillment Services | 11.5.0 | Inactive |
| AMS | Oracle Marketing | 11.5.0 | Inactive |
| AMV | Oracle MarketView | 11.5.0 | Inactive |
| AP | Oracle Payables | 11.5.0 | Installed |
| AR | Oracle Receivables | 11.5.0 | Installed |
| AS | Oracle Sales | 11.5.0 | Shared |
| ASF | Oracle Field Sales | 11.5.0 | Inactive |
| ASG | Oracle CRM Gateway for Mobile Services | 11.5.0 | Inactive |
| ASL | Oracle Mobile Field Sales Laptop | 11.5.0 | Inactive |
| ASO | Oracle Order Capture | 11.5.0 | Inactive |
| ASP | Oracle Field Sales/PalmTM Devices | 11.5.0 | Inactive |
| AST | TeleSales | 11.5.0 | Inactive |
| AU | Application Utilities | 11.5.0 | Shared |
| AX | Global Accounting Engine | 11.5.0 | Installed |
| AZ | Application Implementation | 11.5.0 | Installed |
| BEN | Oracle Advanced Benefits | 11.5.0 | Inactive |
| BIC | Customer Intelligence | 11.5.0 | Shared |
| BIL | Sales Intelligence | 11.5.0 | Shared |
| BIM | Marketing Intelligence | 11.5.0 | Shared |

**Figure 13.14  Installed Products**

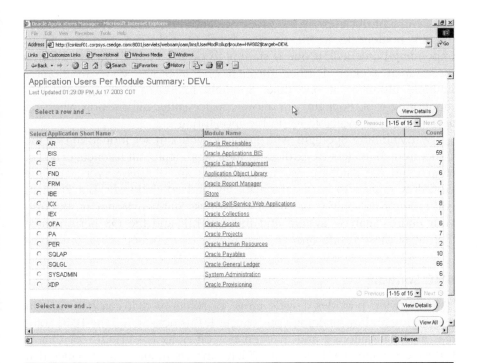

**Figure 13.15   Applications Users per Module**

tablespace growth, user load, and other functions within the suite that are likely targets for problems. With the assistance of I/Watch, you can easily monitor not only Concurrent Manager processes, but the application server itself, the ConText Server, all involved listeners, and objects with a high likelihood of having space related issues.

Trend analysis on key processes in the system (e.g., Concurrent Managers, workflow, and SQL statement performance) allows you to determine the best places to apply tuning efforts and allows you to easily determine if your efforts are having a detrimental or beneficial effect.

Quest furthers its offerings in the monitoring and tuning arena with the Spotlight® on Oracle E-Business Suite product. The graphic Spotlight tool displays real-time data on the actual server processes and dataflow within the system. This can allow you to quickly identify bottlenecks and attempt to correct the contentions. If you see a problem in real time and have the ability to drill down and eliminate much of the guesswork from the process, you will be able to provide longer mean time between failure and shorter mean time to recovery, not from a database recovery standpoint, but from an end user perceived problem area standpoint.

Spotlight is not simply an extension of another product into the Apps monitoring area, it was designed specifically for the Apps administrator to provide an overview of the processes and flows within the system and identify bottlenecks in the process faster (it will even alert you to an impending bottleneck if one is starting to occur) so that you can address those areas sooner. Further, through one interface, you can monitor multiple instances at one time. Spotlight interfaces with Quest's 24/7 monitoring tool, Foglight®, to allow you to gather information when no administrator is available to do the monitoring.

By combining Spotlight with Foglight, you can set monitoring of the Concurrent Managers (regardless of their work shift), all listeners (fndfs, forms, and the database listeners), Reports and Forms Servers, and the workflow engine to occur automatically and continuously. But Foglight will monitor not only your Oracle E-Business Suite environment, but also your entire database system and the network and the OS performance that all of these reside on.

## BMC Software

BMC Software provides a wide range of solutions that can help you in monitoring and maintaining your Oracle E-Business Suite. The BMC solution to the monitoring and maintenance dilemma is PATROL® for Oracle E-Business Suite. PATROL is a widely known monitoring product that provides mechanisms to alert the administrator when error or user defined near error situations occur. It can save you time and effort by locating problems and identifying their root cause before they have a chance to impact your system. To accomplish this, it monitors the Forms and Web servers, the internal system, and all related underlying components. This automated monitoring in turn helps you to ensure availability and reliability of all of your application modules, the database, and underlying resources and infrastructure. PATROL is available for Versions 13.7, 11.0, and 11i of Oracle E-Business Suite (allowing you to monitor current systems clear through an upgrade) and is available for the database and OSs that support both the apps tier and the database tier. It will monitor and manage the most common Oracle E-Business Suite product modules and measure the end to end response time and performance as it occurs on the system and will report proactively on potential trouble spots.

Through one interface, you can centralize the management of all applications components, including the database instance, OSs, and middle tier services. You can proactively monitor all critical failure points in the environment (be they the database, any of the Concurrent Processes, or the Forms and Reports Servers) and identify and resolve resource conflicts with a minimum of manual intervention or system intrusion. And, using the PATROL interface, you can better plan for maintenance (reorganizing the database or rebuilding indexes), which allows you to maximize availability and minimize downtime.

The PATROL interface for monitoring and maintaining the Concurrent Managers will allow you to address wait times by identifying peak usage times and will alert the applicable people if that wait time exceeds acceptable limits. You can track overutilization and underutilization of Concurrent Managers and determine if all Concurrent Managers that are supposed to be active during a given work shift are indeed available and active on the system. PATROL allows you to startup and shutdown the Internal Manager, activate or deactivate any other Concurrent Manager that has been identified to the system, determine why any particular request errored out, and attempt to address those error conditions. The trend analysis that is available to you, as administrator, on the requests running on the system and the performance of those requests, long running and immediate, will allow you to better plan and load balance for the peak times without adversely affecting the rest of the system.

## Precise

Precise Software Solutions also provides a product, Precise/Interpoint, that allows Applications administrators the ability to monitor and tune Oracle Applications by helping you to identify and track problematic SQL statements to their root origins, be they forms, reports, or ad-hoc queries created by end users. Further, Precise/Interpoint can help you to perform impact analysis on database objects that are changing and imact analysis on database version upgrades.

Precise/Interpoint is, primarily, a performance management soution that allows you to tune apps through the sql that is occurring on it. Through this interface, it allows you to break down resource intensive transactions returning to you the username program involved (be it transactional or batch), the application name under which that program was running, and the sql statement involved.

Precise allows you, instead of tuning the Oracle E-Business Suite code to which you have no supported access, to tune the underlying objects in the database by providing you with all relevant indexes for any given SQL statement and, if none exist, will suggest a new one that would have a beneficial effect on the given statement. It goes further by letting you simulate the creation, deletion, or modification of an index to determine the impact that any side effects might have on your system.

# 14

## ODDS AND ENDS

This chapter is dedicated to all of the things that I have stumbled on that are interesting, that have come in handy for me to remember when I am enmeshed in my Apps DBA duties, and that I have found out the hard way.

### ALERTS

Oracle Alerts can be one of an Apps administrator's best friends. Alerts will keep you regularly informed of critical information concerning activity in your database in a format that you choose and assist you with automating system maintenance and in scheduling and performing online tasks. Through Oracle Alerts, you can monitor and control exceptions and react quickly when an exception presents itself. Not only can you create Alerts that monitor critical database activity, you can utilize the same facilities to monitor critical data driven activity that can impact your business processes.

Alerts can take two formats: an Event Alert or a Periodic Alert.

An Event Alert notifies specified administrators about activity information in the database as that activity occurs. The information that is required by the Alert system is a database event that you want to monitor for, a SQL statement that will retrieve the information that is a result of that event, and an action that you want the Alert system to perform as a result of that event. An action can include anything from sending an e-mail message to a list of users, sending a digital text message to a pager, running a Concurrent Program or an OS script, or running another specified SQL statement. If your database throws an ORA-00600 error, your Event Alert can send you an e-mail that contains the string following the alert message to assist in creating iTARs. But an Event Alert can take other forms other than just monitoring the physical running state of the database. It will alert the specified person of any event in the database: an insert, update, or delete on a particularly sensitive table, for example. It can be used for business logic as well as technical monitoring. It does not have to be a simple error condition; it can be a unique combination that would only occur if something out of the ordinary had occurred or if there were some unusual condition happening in the company. Further, it can alert you to the fact that there are currently no error conditions in the database.

A Periodic Alert periodically checks the database per your specified schedule. The same information is required when setting up a periodic alert as is required when setting up an Event Alert, but instead of an event, you provide the period on which you want the information retrieval query run. With a Periodic Alert, you can have current performance measurements at a glance. A Periodic Alert can provide you with trouble spots that you can zero in on to provide performance enhancements. There are several predefined Alerts that you can make use of or you can define your own and you can define them on even your custom modules so that you can be able to see what is occurring there, as well. Your business can define Periodic Alerts that will run and alert a manager as to the number of outstanding invoices or purchase orders that require attention. Periodic Alerts also tell the manager how many were processed since the last time the Alert ran in a given time period or ever.

Not only can you receive Alerts, you can query the Alert history and receive a total picture of what has been occurring on your system and make determinations based on the total overall picture.

You may find that, if used well, Alerts can be one of your biggest assets in monitoring and maintaining your database and your overall system.

## INVALID OBJECTS

Invalid objects, in Oracle Applications, are inevitable. Patching, cloning, upgrading, and sometimes just running applications cause invalid objects. Getting rid of most of them is fairly simple. $ORACLE_HOME/ rdbms/admin/utlrp.sql will eliminate the majority of them. Those that are able to be validated can be gotten rid of by the following set of scripts. Create the scripts in Table 14.1, Table 14.2, and Table 14.3 where they can be easily run on any instance.

Then from the SQL prompt, as in Table 14.4, you can call scripts 1.sql through 5.sql as follows, repeatedly until the output of 5.sql no longer produces a smaller number.

**Table 14.1   1.sql SQL Script for Validating Invalid Objects**

```
set head off
set pagesize 0
set linesize 132
set feedback off
set termout off
set echo off
spool 2.sql
select 'ALTER '||object_type||' '||object_name||'
compile;' STRING
from user_objects
where status='INVALID'
and object_type in ('VIEW', 'PACKAGE', 'TRIGGER',
'PROCEDURE', 'FUNCTION')
order by object_type desc
/
spool off
set feedback on
set termout on
set echo on
```

**Table 14.2   3.sql SQL Script for Validating Invalid Objects**

```
set head off
set pagesize 0
set linesize 132
set feedback off
set termout off
set echo off
spool 4.sql
select 'ALTER PACKAGE '||object_name||' compile
body;' STRING
from user_objects
where status='INVALID'
and object_type='PACKAGE BODY'
/
spool off
set feedback on
set termout on
set echo on
```

**Table 14.3 5.sql SQL Script for Validating Invalid Objects**

```
select count(*) from all_objects where status =
'INVALID'
```

**Table 14.4 Calling Validation Scripts**

```
SQL>@1
SQL>@2
SQL>@3
SQL>@4
SQL>@5
```

## GATHERING STATISTICS

Remember, you are dealing with the CBO. If you have migrated from an earlier version of Apps, this transition may be a big one to make. Oracle strongly suggests that, since you are using Oracle E-Business Suite, you use the fnd_stats package to gather your statistics on your system. You can invoke this package indirectly through Concurrent Programs like Gather Schema Statistics or Gather Table Statistics. Gather Schema Statistics takes one parameter: the schema name on which you want to gather the statistics. All is a valid parameter, but depending on the size of your data and the number of products in which you have larger amounts of data stored, using this parameter may cause the process to run for several hours. You need to make sure that, when you are running something of this magnitude, you set it to run when there is a minimum of users accessing the system. Gather Table Statistics takes the schema name of the owner of the table as well as the table name on which you want to gather the statistics. Optionally, if you have a partitioned table that you want to gather statistics on in this manner, you will want to pass in the PARTITION parameter as the granularity. This will cause the package to not only calculate the global statistics on the entire table, but the statistics on each partition as well.

Alternatively, you can script the running of these packaged procedures from the SQL prompt to remove the extra load from the Concurrent Managers.

To gather statistics on the entire GL schema:

```
Exec fnd_stats.gather_schema_statistics ('GL');
```

To gather schema statistics on the entire system (except the SYS and SYSTEM tables):

```
Exec fnd_stats.gather_schema_statistics ('ALL');
```

To gather table statistics on the FND_PROFILE_OPTION_VALUES table:

```
Exec fnd_stats.gather_table_stats ('APPLSYS',
FND_PROFILE_OPTION_VALUES');
```

To gather table statistics on a partitioned table:

```
Exec fnd_stats.gather_table_stats (owner=> '<table
owner>', tablename => '<partitioned table>',
granularity=> 'PARTITION');
```

It is important to remember that if you have never run any statistics gathering processes on a given object (i.e., table, index, schema), the CBO makes certain assumptions. Primarily, CBO assumes that if you have not gathered statistics that you want to use the default statistics. You probably do not.

There is a freely available script that will assist you in automating statistics gathering if you have a Metalink account and you wish to make use of it. The coe_stats.sql script is included in and well documented by Note 156968.1 from Metalink. This script is for use with Oracle E-Business Suite as it makes extensive use of the FND_STATS package procedures. It dynamically, based on table size, changes the estimation percent that it uses (a higher percent for smaller tables, a smaller percent for larger ones), which can allow you to limit the overall runtime of the statistics gathering without causing you to sacrifice accuracy. When the need to limit the size of the statistics gathering window is an issue (e.g., on a 24/7 implementation where users from all over the globe are accessing the system at any given time), using coe_stats.sql will limit the overall impact to the system and to users.

If you want to get a good overall idea of where your system stands in reference to statistics and how the CBO views them, you can download from Metalink another script (bde_last_analyzed.sql from Note 163208.1) that will summarize by schema name and date when and from where at least one or all schemas had their statistics gathered. It will further warn you of statistics that have been gathered on objects owned by SYS, of stale statistics, or on statistics gathered on partitioned tables where the global statistics and the partition level statistics are no longer in sync with each other. It provides a summary page at the beginning of the report that it produces that gives you a quick, concise overview of your system as well as a more detailed listing following.

## PERFORMANCE ISSUES

The first thing to do when you are faced with troubleshooting performance issues is to clearly document the issue. Document, if you can, when the poor performance started (or at least when the end user first really noticed it); what the symptoms are; if it occurs in one product, one form, or program; or is suddenly a systemwide problem. Is it just in one system (e.g., Production, the Vision instance, Test) or is it in all instances? If it is not happening in all instances, what is different between the ones where it is and the ones where it is not? Does it only happen at certain times of day (8:30 A.M. when most of the users are suddenly logging on) or at certain times of the month (financials closing)? Can it be attributed to peak load times? How many users, that you are aware of, are affected by this performance hit? Are all locations equally affected or can those users that are affected be separated into one location? Has anything recently changed at that location? Can it be reproduced consistently? Have the users found creative ways around the problem, and if so, what are they? What on the system has changed recently (e.g., new software, change in the network, OS upgrade, apps patches, upgrade)?

Further, this document can be viewed as a living document of your ongoing tuning efforts in reference to the particular issue that you are dealing with because it contains information relevant to the particular problem set.

Determining the version of a module or modules in question can be accomplished with the following command:

```
strings <form name or report name or program name>
|grep '$Header'  |more
```

To obtain a listing of modules contained within a Pro*C program you can run the following command and examine the resulting text file (modules.txt) to find the list:

```
Strings <Pro*C module> |grep '$Header' > modules.txt
```

If you are not on the latest patch set and you have to raise this issue with Oracle Support, they will undoubtedly ask you what version you are on and if you are not on the most current version, why you are not. Be aware that, if you are not on the latest patch set, you will likely be requested to apply the latest patch set, as the latest usually addresses any known performance issues.

The electronic documents in Table 14.5 and Table 14.6 are not only a record of what you are doing so you can let anyone know what progress you are making, it is also a document that allows you to maintain a record of what issues you have seen and what your processes and resolutions were on those issues as well as allowing you have a running record that you can provide to Oracle Support if you should have to raise an iTAR. Document as many hard facts as you can obtain and capture as many user perceptions of the issues as you can.

Tuning can typically be broken into categories that describe the location of the problem and by extension, the type of tuning that you have to do on account of those problems. These apparently broad categories usually translate into much narrower focus of ultimate tuning.

### Table 14.5 Performance Problem Resolution Document

*Performance Analysis/Problem Resolution Document*

DateAnalyst(s) involved:

Who reported the issue?

Is anyone else reporting same or similar issue? If so, who?

Are all users reporting the issue in a single location or department or spread across areas?

When was it first reported?

What application group and modules are affected (e.g., AR, all Financials, Form paxtrax.fmx, or list all transactions)?

Environment(s) in which it is appearing (i.e., Production, Development, Test, Vision):

What time of day, if attributable to a particular time, are you seeing this occur?

Does it occur only when load is high?

Does it occur only when load is low?

Is the issue reproducible?

Steps required to reproduce.

Is there currently a workaround for it?

When was the last time that you noticed this working correctly?

Notes:

Upgrades since last worked correctly (e.g., OS, Network, patches, database, third party, other):

How long did transaction used to take?

How long does transaction take now?

How long is transaction supposed to take?

Customizations to component in question:

Module name (short and long name):

Module version:

Form name:

Form version:

Patch set level:

Pro*C program modules (if applicable):

Org ID involved (if multi-org):

Debugging enabled?

Trace file created?

Trace filename:

TKPROF name generated from trace file:

Log file created?

Log filename:

Errors observed:

Notes:

**Table 14.6   Applications Tuning Document**

*Applications Tuning Document*

1.  Detailed description of the performance issue:
2,  TAR Number:
3.  Application Product Name:
4.  Application Product ID number:
5.  Environments on which problem is occurring (i.e., Test, Development, Vision, Production, All):
6.  If poor performance on multiple environments, is it consistent regardless of system load or is it occurring more often in some situations?
7.  How many users are affected?
8.  If more than one, are users at more than one site equally affected?
9.  Can it be reproduced?
10. If yes, explain conditions and steps taken to reproduce:
11. Available workaround:
12. When did this complete correctly without performance problems?
13. Any software (e.g., RDBMS, OS, Apps, Third Party) that has been installed or upgraded since problem started:
14. Any software (e.g., RDBMS, OS, Apps, Third Party) that has been installed or upgraded since last worked correctly:
15. Patches (e.g., OS, RDBMS, Apps, other software patches on same system) applied recently:
16. Patches required to fix the issue:
17. Currently running certified configuration?
18. Most recent patches or minipacks applied?
19. Frequency of statistics gathering:
20. Method of statistics gathering:
21. Tool used to gather statistics:
22. Estimate percentage used:
23. Last time statistics gathered:
24. Are all initialization parameters set at Applications required levels? (To check, run `bde_chk_cbo.sql`, which can be obtained through Metalink Note 174605.1)
25. Initialization parameter changed due to resulting report:
26. How long does it take for the offending process to complete?
27. How long did it used to take (performance expected)?
28. Any customizations that may be affecting this process:Module short name:
29. Module descriptive name:
30. Module version:

*-- continued*

**Table 14.6 (continued)   Applications Tuning Document**

31. Latest module version available:
32. Patch set level for module:
33. Latest patch set for module:
34. Operating unit used (only applicable if you are multi-org):
35. Parameter names and passed values for Concurrent Programs:
36. Form and Field navigation involved:
37. Transaction involved:
38. Applications trace file created?
39. Has TKPROF been done on resulting trace?
40. SQL statement performing poorly (per TKPROF)?
41. Event 100046 trace done?
42. Wait events for poorly performing transaction?
43. Metalink Search done for transaction?
44. Resulting note numbers (attach printouts of relevant notes and results of trying suggestions):
45. Any custom indexes on tables involved in SQL found in trace?
46. If iTAR created, list files uploaded?
47. Suggested fix steps with results:
48. Back end tuning specifics:
    a. Architecture information:
    b. Hardware profile of database server:
    c. Hardware profile of middle tier:
    d. Server workload profile:
    e. Do other transactions on same server report performance problems?
    f. Current system load:
    g. Projected system load:
    h. Concurrent Processing policies:
    i. Known resource contention (e.g., SAN, Memory, IO, CPU)? Event 10046 trace may alert you to existing contention issues.
    j. Apps modules installed and minipack level of each and latest available for each?
    k. OSs involved, their version numbers, and patch levels:
    l. Existing hardware recommendations:
49. Tech Stack Tuning Specifics:
    a. Form version:
    b. Report version:
    c. JInitiator version:
    d. Browser used and version:

Transaction tuning focuses on a transaction or a group of transactions. A transaction can be a specific as a list of values that used to show up almost instantly and now the three users that use this screen have to wait 30 or 45 seconds for it to come back. A broader problem might be that a department in finance and accounting is seeing the posting of journals now taking 10 minutes and it used to only take 2. It can be as broad as AR has been incredibly slow since the application of the latest minipack. Document this category as closely as you can. It may turn out that what appears to be an overall slowdown in all of AR is actually only one or two processes that have actually slowed down noticeably; it may eventually turn out to be one change that fixes them both or you may have to change several things (each addressing one issue) to ultimately rid the system of all of the symptoms. With transaction tuning, the ultimate solution typically focuses on tuning the underlying SQL, addressing indexes, or gathering statistics.

Database and Network Tuning is usually the target when there is an overall slowdown in the performance of the entire system. This is where you will typically focus if multiple user groups across multiple departments are reporting the performance issues. A typical red flag in this case is if you are getting similar reports of slowdowns happening at peak load times. A common complaint might be: What is wrong with the system? Every day at 11:00 A.M. (or at 3:30 P.M. on Friday afternoon), it suddenly takes 2 minutes to do what took 20 seconds to do at 10:00 A.M. At 11:00 A.M., users are trying to finish up a bunch of things so they can have them done when they go to lunch or Friday at 3:30 P.M. so they can get finished up for the weekend. It might be a networking issue, it might be that a set of sysadmins did an OS patch and did not realize there might be ramifications, or it may be attributable to a database upgrade. Typically, these are the areas where you look for these kinds of issues.

Issues with the middle tier are the final broad area to break the problem down into. Has navigation between Forms or opening any form in a product group suddenly started taking an inordinately long time? Have all of the users in a particular location suddenly started noticing the problem? Are all complaints coming from a segment of the network with a common IP address scheme? Might it be an Apache/JServ load issue? Is everyone in one department seeing generalized slowdowns? Have you ruled out issues with the database and its surrounding environment and not been able to determine any particularly poorly running sql statements? You may find that, once you have ruled out other issues, your final avenue of attack is at the technology stack (or middle tier) level.

One safe place, usually, to start is to gather statistics. If you are new to 11i and the Oracle 8i database, but (especially if) you have been around Apps for a long time, remember that you are now dealing with the CBO and it depends almost exclusively on the availability of good statistics. Run the Concurrent Programs that gather and analyze statistics. Your best time to run these kinds of jobs is when there is no one on the system or when the number of active users is low. You can do this while you are searching Metalink for any documents that might show similar issues and resolutions. Put into your documentation how often you are gathering statistics, particularly on the poorly running processes or products. Add to the frequency the approach taken (e.g., analyze table, schema, all schema) as well as the tool used (e.g., `analyze`, `dbms_stats`, `fnd_stats`, `dbms_utility`, or which concurrent job you have running to accomplish this feat) and the estimate size that you are using to estimate sample size.

## Forms Trace

If you are having form specific issues, you can have the user run a form level trace. You may want to not phrase the request quite that way, however, as many of the end users will feel intimidated by the request: "You want me to do what? I could never do something like that."

It is a simple thing to do and many users have been able to accomplish a significant amount of tuning diagnostics without even knowing they have done it. To turn tracing on, have the user navigate to [Help -> Diagnostics -> Trace -> Trace with binds and waits] on the Applications menu. You will often find that you will require quite a large trace file and you may need to have the user set the trace file size to unlimited. To accomplish this, they would simply navigate to the help menu again and go to [Help -> Diagnostics -> Trace -> Unlimited Trace File Size]. Once these have been done, the user can perform the offending transaction as they would regularly and then go back through the steps they just performed to shut off forms tracing (or else have them log out); otherwise, you will capture everything the user does subsequently and the trace file will be less useful and far bigger than necessary.

Initialization parameters helpful in tracing include the following:

```
max_dump_file_size = Unlimited
timed_statistics = true
```

Alternatively, you can set these parameters by using the `alter system` command in later releases of the database.

The resulting trace file should be located in your `User_Dump_Dest` location from your `init.ora` file.

If you have performed the trace with binds and waits, you can use another Oracle designed tool to help in the analysis of the resulting trace file. TRCANLZR.sql will analyze the trace file for you and present it in a more understandable format. You can obtain this tool through Note 224270.1 and run it at the command line as follows:

```
Sqlplus apps/apps
Start trcanlzr.sql UDUMP <trace_file_name>
```

## 10046 Trace

Cary Milsap of HOTSOS (http://www.hotsos.com) has done significant research on the use of the 10046-trace level 8 for finding bottlenecks in a given SQL session. By turning trace on for a session, you can determine what that session's top wait events are both statistically (by the number of times that that event occurred) and by the amount of or total time that the session spent in that wait event and apply your efforts to correcting those that will provide the most improvement to the transactions that were involved during that time.

### Tracing Your Own Session

You can turn Event 10046 trace on for your own session to determine what that session is doing and find all of the places it is waiting and what significant points are causing your problems. If you can perform the actions that the end user is performing or if you can convince the user to work with you through tracing the problem, you can capture all of the parts of that session by either having that user log in and setting trace at their session level or you can log in as them and do it.

Because it is often difficult to determine which Apps session belongs to which user, tracing that session as an outside person looking in is often difficult. Apparently Oracle is also a fan of the 10046 trace, because it allows you to turn trace on at your session's level from the session level.

From the main application window, select Help/Diagnostics/Trace/Trace with Waits (or Trace with Waits and Binds) from the main menu bar. This will set Event 10046 trace level 8 (or 12) on for the session that performs these actions, effectively turning trace on at the session level for the session calling it.

### Tracing Someone Else's Session

You can trace someone else's session, but due to the way that Apps logs into the database with the APPS ID, doing so can become extremely difficult, especially for a busy system. The means by which you can accomplish this can be gotten from the HOTSOS Web site.

### *Using a Special ID to Run 10046 Trace*

In Apps, you can create a special user ID that an end user will log in with that has the profile of being used specifically to detect wait events. The 11i Oracle E-Business Suite provides an option that will allow a user to execute customized code at the beginning of every session that that user initiates. This option allows for the linking to a particular form, package, Concurrent Program or any other piece of code that requires the code to access the database. You can make use of this feature to create a user whose only purpose is to generate trace files for tuning long running processes to run whatever process is giving you problems under a session set to gather 100046 trace.

The first thing that you need to do is to make sure that the profile option Initialization SQL Statement — Custom is available on the system and is accessible to both users and to programs. To accomplish this, you will need to log in as a user to whom the responsibility of Application Developer has been granted. As this user, choose the Profile option on the Applications menu and query profile FND_INIT_SQL. Make sure that the User Access section has both Visible and Updateable checked, that the Program Access has both Visible and Updateable checked, and that under System Administrator Access, both Visible and Updateable are checked for the User row (not for the Site, Application, or Responsibility rows, however). Once you verify that the profile option FND_INIT_SQL has the required values, you can switch to the sysadmin user and create a new user. Make the name for this user something that will obviously point to its purpose. Suggestions would be to call it Trace or Tuning or Waits, something that will obviously designate it as special. For the remainder of this example, I will use the user "Tuning." Assign to this user the transactions that you wish to trace using Event 10046. I suggest you assign this user all responsibilities and guard the password to it, changing it before and after every use so the ID is not misused. Alternatively, you can assign it different responsibilities every time it is needed to run a transaction. Once the user is created, you can navigate to System Profile Values Form (Profiles -> System) and query up the profile option Initialization SQL Statement — Custom for the user you just created (Tuning) and within the Editor panel place the following code string:

```
Begin FND_CTL.fnd_sess_ctl ('', '', 'TRUE', 'TRUE',
'LOG', 'Alter session set events ''10046 trace name
context forever, level 12'''); end;
```

It is important to remember that all quotes in this command are single quotes and anywhere that more than one occurs, it is multiples of one and never a double quote. This tells the system to create a trace file for everything that is done by this user from the time the user logs on until the time it logs off and create it with all wait events and bind variables that are relevant to this session. For tuning slow running SQL, both waits and bind variables are important. Minimally, to determine what waits a statement is encountering, you need to set the number following the LEVEL portion of the statement to 8.

Now that you have this user, it can be used any time you need to create a trace file. Never use this ID to do anything for which you do not deliberately want to have a trace file created as these traces can get quite large and could quite quickly fill up the dump directory. Typically, this trace file will be created in the UDUMP destination from your initialization parameters. Never, while logged in as this user, turn tracing on at the menu level, as this will nullify the command that you put into its profile and turn all tracing off.

## SECURITY

One significant thing to notice is that Oracle E-Business Suite installs with a complete set of predefined passwords. This is not necessarily a bad thing; it does install 150 plus schemas and trying to creatively come up with that many passwords during an installation would be difficult. It is not completely a good thing, however. That means that anyone who has ever been connected with an installation of the software and anyone who has had access to documentation or an article knows what these passwords are. It also means that if you have an interface to the Internet, you are potentially leaving yourself open to someone being able to simply log into your system with one of those passwords and have access to much or all of your information.

### Changing Passwords

One of the most important things to know about security is that it is critical that you change the apps password, the applsys password, and the passwords for all schemas that are responsible for licensed or shared products in your implementation. There are two methods for changing passwords — the Manual Method and the Batch Method. The Manual Method requires that you follow all instructions to the letter and in the exact order specified. You are highly discouraged from following the Manual Method if you have more than just a few licensed products, as the act of changing the passwords can get long and tedious.

First (and probably by far the most important step) back up the FND_ORACLE_USERID table and the FND_USER table. This needs to be done regardless of what method you use (Manual or Batch) as a precaution to enable you to back out anything that might go awry. As the apps user:

```
create table FND_ORACLE_USERID_BAK as select * from
FND_ORACLE_USERID
create table FND_ USER_BAK as select * from FND_
USER
```

This will allow you to get back your previous settings if you totally mess up your system and no one can log on. Yes, it is that important. Otherwise you would have to restore from the previous good backup. Once the table is backed up, you are safe to follow the following procedure exactly as stated.

1. Make sure that all users are logged out of the application.
2. Shutdown the Concurrent Managers and make sure that any running concurrent jobs are finished.
3. Log into the applications' front end as a user with sysadmin responsibility.
4. Navigate to Register Oracle IDs form by following Security/Oracle/Register.
5. Query up into the form all available Oracle IDs in your version.
6. Log into SQL*Plus as SYSTEM or as SYSDBA (preferred).

```
$ sqlplus '/as sysdba'
```

7. In your applications session, enter your new password for the APPLSYS user in the following manner:
   a. View/Query by example/Run
   b. Change password of applsys/press down arrow.
   c. Verify password of applsys/press down arrow.
   d. File/save. Do not under any circumstances requery or exit the form at this time.
8. In the SQL*Plus session, run the following command:

```
SQL> alter user applsys identified by <same new
password as you entered into the screen>;
```

9. Back in the open applications session, enter the new password for APPS (the same one that was for applsys):
   a. View/Query by example/Run
   b. Change password of apps/press down arrow.
   c. Verify password of apps/press down arrow.
   d. File/save. Do not under any circumstances requery or exit the form at this time.
10. In the SQL*Plus session, run the following command:

```
SQL> alter user applsys identified by <same new
password as you entered into the screen>;
```

11. Exit entirely out of the application.
12. Completely close all of your browser sessions and empty the cache.

13. Log completely out of SQL*Plus.
14. Open a new browser session and log into the application as a user with sysadmin responsibility again.
15. Restart your Concurrent Managers after making sure that you changed the batch Concurrent Manager startup script password (remember, this script uses the APPS password).

You have now changed the two most critical passwords. You have up to 180 others that you will now have to change individually in exactly the same manner to make sure that your system and data are protected not only from anyone trying to gain unlawful access to your data, but from well meaning users or developers who want to see how things are done or who want quick access to just one little thing. It is important to note that this can take several hours if you have many modules implemented.

Fortunately, there is a simpler method. Oracle provides a utility called FNDCPASS that allows you to change passwords in batch mode. Patch 1685689 provides you with this utility (check for new versions that include FNDCPASS through the patch download screens).

After you have installed the patch, you can run the following command to change the passwords:

■ Format:
   ■ FNDCPASS apps/<apps password> 0 Y system/
     <system password> SYSTEM APPLSYS APPS1

■ Examples:

   ■ FNDCPASS apps/apps 0 Y system/manager SYSTEM
     APPLSYS APPS1
   ■ FNDCPASS apps/apps 0 Y system/manager ORACLE
     BIS BIS1
   ■ FNDCPASS apps/apps 0 Y system/manager USER
     CUSTOM_USER USER1

The first example would be used to change the applsys password. By specifying SYSTEM parameter, you are telling FNDCPASS to expect the next argument in the string to be the applsys name and the password you want to assign to the applsys user. The steps that Oracle RDBMS and Financials together make at this point are:

1. Validate the applsys username is correct.
2. Reencrypt all of the passwords in the FND_USER table based on the new applsys password (it is used as a seed value from what I understand).
3. Reencrypt all passwords (again based on the value of the applsys password) in the FND_ORACLE_USERID table.
4. Updates the applsys password in the FND_ORACLE_USERID table and sets all IDs with the read only flag that refers to the fact that the associated user IDs have to have the same password as applsys. It sets those passwords the same as the applsys password at this point.
5. Runs an alter user <username> identified by <new password> command for all affected users at the database level.

Example 2 (Oracle with BIS) passes Oracle as a parameter, telling FNDCPASS that it is an Oracle user ID and password (not an apps one) so all it needs to do is update and reencrypt the password in the FND_ORACLE_USERID table and run the alter user identified by script at the database level.

*Note:* APPLSYS's password and APPS's password always have to be identical.

## Other Security Issues

But this is not the only place where you are vulnerable. Your entire system resides on a set of servers. It sits on a network and is communicated to by means of a series of workstations (either PCs or thin clients) and is likely developed against by programmers and developers. Much of the information in the system is personal information, much more is information that only certain people within the company should really have access to read, let alone alter. There are security holes that people rarely consider and several others that sometimes are simply allowed to exist. Any of these holes could potentially mean disaster for your implementation. Many of these holes are simple to fix.

On the Development server, any of the developers and programmers who work with the system should have rights to alter the data via the apps interface. They should have the ability to compile their forms and reports and PL/SQL code and have their own play area in which they can freely work. They should probably not have the same privileges in Production. It is not so much that anything would happen to the Production server due to maliciousness, but a badly formed SQL statement could have devastating effects.

Oracle E-Business Suite is a complex and complicated set of objects with interconnections and interdependencies; that means that something that might not be devastating in another database could potentially mean a complete restore of the system in Apps (a malformed `drop` command could drop a custom interface table instead of dropping a column on the same table).

Maintain a secure central environment where you can maintain copies of all custom objects. If you have interface tables that allow information from other systems to be brought into the Applications environment, keep the `create table` script somewhere central and, if relevant, version those scripts. If there has to be a change made to the table structure, alter the `create table` script to reflect that. Have you created any new indexes in your tuning attempts? Keep copies of those scripts, as well. You do not usually know ahead of time all of the changes that a patch or a minipack will bring with it. You may have to recreate your index or you may have to change it because columns that used to be available (columns that you built indexes on) are no longer found on the table. Control versions and maintain a code repository for at least the Production versions of any customized forms, reports, and PL/SQL program units. This way you can determine what changed, when it changed, how it changed, and have a way to unchange it if for some reason a change causes unreliable output from a previously useful reporting program.

There are directories that you cannot completely control access to. Log file directories and out file directories have to be writable to anyone running a concurrent request. You may not want someone to have the ability to map a drive across the network to that directory, because if they have write access, they also have read access and, therefore, can see the output of any report that has been run. There is certain information that is maintained by HR that other people may not be supposed to have complete access to. The interface controls what those people can and cannot see online, but you (or your sysadmin or your network administrator) have to control the access to the text files that are created on a network accessible machine.

There are directories you may want to have complete control over. The places where the Forms and Reports source code is stored probably needs to be readable by developer and programmers, but it might not need to be writable by them in Production. It will become necessary to compare two versions of a form or report to determine what changed or if anything changed between the Production version and a customized version before anyone starts making other changes. It may not be a good idea to allow them to edit the Production version directly, however.

Does your company have a policy for leaving a workstation unlocked when a user walks away from it (e.g., to use the bathroom, to go to lunch, or to a meeting)? Is there a mandate that screensavers have to be password protected in case someone forgets to lock their workstation when they walk away? That way the window of opportunity for someone to come and access their computer is at least limited. Do all employees follow this mandate? Do you always follow this mandate? You can use Oracle's built-in features of Profile options to automatically make a user log back into the application if that user's session goes unused for a company specified period of time. This will cause the user to have to log back in, but will not cause any work that that user might have had happening in the session to be lost. Once there is a successful relogin, the user gets taken back to exactly where they were. Closing the application or choosing to not log back in will cause any changes made and not committed to be lost. If it does not, you should implement one at the profile option site level.

Do your users have to change their passwords? Again, does your company have a policy that all passwords have to expire at some point in time or after an elapsed amount of time? A common situation is one where a company will implement a password expiration policy company-wide where a password is only good on any system for a maximum of 60 or 90 days. If the user does not change their password within that time, the system makes them change at the end of the specified time. This can be controlled at the profile option site level as well.

## DOCUMENTATION

I am not a fan of creating documentation simply for the sake of documenting. However, with an animal this big and this complex that requires this much attention, it is always a good idea to take good notes when you are dealing with a patching session or troubleshooting issues or just with getting answers to questions that you need to have answered.

Once you have taken the notes, transcribe them into an electronic format and put them in a central location (one that routinely gets backed up) so that you can easily find them later and remember what you did in a certain situation (when you are faced with a frighteningly similar situation later) and so that someone else who might run into a similar situation will be able to look at your document and have some idea where to start looking if they happen to be the one called for a problem that they have never seen. If nothing else, it will likely be a place for them to start instead of calling you or paging you several times simply because they do not know where to start or what might have already been tried.

No matter if you are dealing with Oracle Support, answers to questions from colleagues off of a listserv, or, if you're lucky, from someone in-house helping you with the installation, whatever they tell you, take notes, and keep them. Something someone said might be one of the most useful pieces of information later, when everyone is gone and all you can remember is that you heard something sometime, but cannot remember who or even why you asked. If you are one of the key people on the implementation team and you know what you are doing, you are ahead of the game. If you do not know what you are doing or only have a vague idea of what really is going on, you will probably be very tired by the time your go live date arrives and so much will have happened that you will not be able to completely remember what happened early on. If there was a patch that broke badly in one environment and you fixed it, you should find a way to remember what broke, what you did to fix it, and where you looked to find the answer. It seems a lot like documentation, but there is a good chance that this documentation is for you and you will be much better off if you have it. And if it is not for you, but someone else that you work with, passing on well documented fixes will mean less frantic phone calls later when maintenance of the system is under the watchful eye of someone else.

This advice is not just for the technical people. Functional people on the team are probably more likely to take notes. Make sure that you do. Again, if you have a company in to help you through the implementation and with training of key people, you have this help at hand. They are captive and they will likely show you tricks for taking shortcuts, different ways of doing the same thing, or give you quick little hints that you will find useful after they are gone. The tips are great unless you cannot remember them when you are on your own and have to figure out how to do the very same thing. Do not let anyone say, "I'll fix it, wait a second." If they do the fix, you will not catch everything because it will happen too fast. Make them let you do the work with them prompting you. You will remember it much better that way.

In your notes, keep track of your contacts. Get names, addresses, and e-mail addresses of the people that you have found most helpful. Pick their brain later if you have questions that you think they can answer. Do not be a pain in the neck; they will tire of endless questions that you could find easily in a manual, but they will be glad to answer questions if you think ahead about what you are asking. Many times you will find someone who knows a lot about one particular part of the system. You may find someone who is an expert at printers or at Concurrent Managers. Make note of that. Later you may have a question on that very subject and while you are searching manuals and Web sites for answers to your question, take five minutes and send the person an e-mail. They may shed light not only on your question, but on surrounding questions as well.

Notes will help you answer questions going forward, too. If you know that you installed the D driver for the 11.5.8 upgrade patch and it took

13 hours to run on your upgrade of the Vis instance, you can be fairly sure that it will not take 5 hours on Prod, even if you have a faster machine or put more workers to work on it. When you plan for your next upgrade or major, regularly scheduled patching session, you will have a better idea that, if a 100 MB patch took 2 hours before, and a 75 MB patch took an 1½ hours before, then that 95 MB patch that you are looking at installing next time will likely take somewhere either around or between those two times. It is easier to justify a 3-day outage for patching or upgrade if you have the historical statistics to back you up. Notes will give you those statistics.

Along the same lines, keep logs of what patches you installed; when you installed; which instance they have been applied in; how long it took for each driver; any prepatch, midpatch, or postpatch steps that you had to do; the times that each of the additional steps took; and any problems (with resolutions) you had. Keep this information together in tables in the database or in an Excel spreadsheet that you maintain every time you patch, clone, or upgrade. This way you can quickly look back at what you did where and when and learn from what broke in another patch. If you have seen an error before, you might save yourself the time and aggravation of an iTAR. It will also help you with planning going forward.

Make the documentation fit you and fit your situation. Every situation is different. Every company is different. Every implementation is different. This is one of the wonderfully terrible things about Oracle Financials as it is in this iteration of its life; it is so flexible that there is rarely one absolutely definitive answer. I can give you some ideas that I have seen tried and some that might work in your situation. They are at least a place to start.

## Create and Maintain a Patching Log

Yes, the newer maintenance releases of 11i come with some really neat new tables and interfaces that allow you to see what you have installed in your environment. It will let you see what minipack level you are on, what bugs were taken care of by patches that you have installed, and will even allow you easy access to how many times you started each driver in a particular patch. It will not tell you what you did to resolve the issues, who you talked to (especially if you have worked with a particularly good analyst), it will not track iTAR information that might have been created for an issue that came up, and it will not currently maintain information on exactly how long it took for each driver to run, and the differences in runtime between your different environments. Any of this information you may find interesting or helpful or critical at some point. If you maintain this information in a central location, it will be easier for you or others to go back and see what went on when.

Relevant iTAR information may be particularly important to keep if you want to track that kind of information, because Metalink only keeps a certain amount of iTARs listed online and then only for a certain period of time. After that, you will at least have to know the iTAR number and then you may not be able to retrieve the desired information.

## Use Self-Documenting Log Filenames

There are many default log names that you will encounter in your illustrious career. When you run ADADMIN, there is a default log name; when you run adctrl, there is a default log name; and when you run ADPATCH, there is a default log name. They are short, fairly concise, and have a measure of usefulness. They are not very descriptive and they cannot easily be used for self-documentation. Personally, I thank my lucky stars for the ability to use long filenames. I am not a big fan of typing. I was a COBOL programmer and got a lot of practice with typing. I would much rather use three keystrokes over five if I can. But meaningful, self-documenting filenames are the best thing I have found yet to quickly tell me exactly what has happened. This is especially true if you are not the only one running utilities.

When I run ADPATCH, I make the log name as descriptive as possible. Usually the format of the name is something like <sid>_<driver>_<date and time started>_<initials of analyst installing the patch>.log. If it is a restart, you can tell what order you did them in and how many problems you had with each driver. You can infer (from the combination of the filename and the time stamp) how long that driver took to run. If you make the name more descriptive, you can tell why you restarted it or what you fixed in the meantime.

I usually follow similar logic when running ADADMIN. If I am running it to fix a problem, I put the problem in the filename (vis_form_abcd-fmx_recompile_0428031224_ajw, I fixed form abcd on the 28th of April at 12:24 P.M.). If it is a step in the installation of a patch, I put the patch name and where it falls in the patch in the filename (vis_post_d2934565_recompile-flex-fields_0428031224_ajw). Granted, when you have been running patches for 15 or 18 hours straight, the extra typing gets to be a pain, but when you have been running patches for 15 or 18 hours straight, you want to remember later why you did what you did and when you did it.

There are times and places where you cannot change the log names. If a patch's C driver relinks files, the relink and rebase logs are default names. If you are running the D driver, you will have a worker log for every worker that you have running in the driver. When each driver of the patch is done running, rename these logs to something meaningful.

This will help you in several ways. You will know what files get associated together later and you will have files that are not several hundred megabytes in size to wade through.

If you take the defaults, every time the utility that creates that file runs, it appends to the file. This is true for ADADMIN, ADPATCH, adrelink, and all of the other utilities. A single log is not bad if you really want to keep them all together, but it is not the greatest if you need to hunt for an error in a worker log and the log takes 10 minutes to load into your word processor.

### Use the Tools That You Are Comfortable With

You can maintain your electronic version in a file system on whatever platform you choose in text file format so it is easily readable from any text editor. Or you can store it in a Windows-based file server in Word, Excel or Access format, text format, or in HTML/RTF format so it is browser friendly and you can link it and index it through the intranet. I have even seen much of the information on patching and problems with resolutions stored in the database. You can create tables in a users tablespace that store your information relevant to that environment. When that environment gets cloned, the information in those tables goes with it. You can create a documentation instance, independent of the central Applications databases in which you can store information on tuning measures you have tried with their results in each environment and idiosyncrasies that have popped up that you want to maintain ongoing that cloning one environment to another may overlay. Even if you only maintain the information in varchar2 columns, 4000 characters is a considerable amount to be able to store for notes. If you need more than 4000 characters, Clobs should be big enough or even work with bfiles to store the information. If you have Forms, you can even make a quick interface into these kinds of tables to make entering the information easier.

## BACKUP OFTEN AND VERIFY

If you are lucky, you will be able to take your time putting in fixes and patches during your go live, during all of your upgrades, and during all patch application outages along your career. Realistically, you will not. Everyone is going to be in a hurry for the system. In a hurry for you to get done so they can take their time testing. In a hurry to make sure that everything is done and they can go on with life. That everything is back to stable and will not be going down again for quite a while. When you are applying a patch, performing an upgrade, or cloning from one system to another, you are down and down is a bad thing. Being down takes time. Time is money.

But do not get backed into a lose-lose position. Make sure you have a good backup of where your system is (even if it is somewhat broken and fairly unstable) before you start trying to install patches of any significant size. Even small patches are next to impossible to back out, but what if you have a big patch that runs for a while and it fails. Yes, you look on Metalink and you log an iTAR and you try to fix it. What happens when they do not know how to fix it? Do you have time for them to guess and hunt and guess some more and then tell you that they will need time to research it and they will get back to you? At some point, you will probably be in a position where you are at your wits end and frustrated with the lack of support. If you restore from that backup that was taken right before this 150 MB patch, what are you going to be out? A day or ten messing around with Metalink, the time it took to get you to where the patch broke, and the restore time. I have seen just such a scenario: Applying a patch right after restoring the system to where it was right before it broke and the patch ran clean. I'm not saying to restore every time a patch breaks, but if all else has failed, what do you have to lose? If you do not have such a backup, restoring is out of the question. Besides, it is never a bad thing to have a known point to return to.

There is a good feeling that goes along with knowing that you have a good backup to go back to if something should happen to break. Make sure you can get both the applications software and the database to the same point though. Otherwise you could be in worse shape after a restore than you were before you tried. Depending on your backup methodology and software solution, getting a backup to verify, while it will probably take nearly twice as long, will be well worth the extra time if you have to restore, just for the peace of mind that says they got everything, and it was successful.

## DO NOT GET COMPLACENT

You have gone live. You are now a success, right? At least you are until something breaks or it is time to upgrade to stay supported so you should just let something alone that is working, right? Hey if it is not broken, there is no need to fix it. Wrong.

Set up a schedule for applying patches starting with go live and stick to that schedule. Major patch releases generally come out with some regularity; minipacks (the ones that roll up several changes into one patch that targets a product group, e.g., HR, GL, AP, AR) are released when needed and many can be counted on to come out at least on a quarterly basis. That usually means that if you make the decision to start a patch cycle on a quarterly basis, you will have several patches to send through the paces every quarter. This also means that you will make upgrading less time consuming and less painful when the time comes; especially for just upgrading to the next Maintenance Pack Patch (say from 11.5.6 to 11.5.8), because much of the work that the megapatch would otherwise have to do will already have been done.

Okay, I know what many people in this situation may be thinking. You just lived through it and your wounds are just starting to heal. It is not really broken, so we should not have to do anything to it if it is not broken. If you start tinkering with things, something might break. Yes, something might. It might also be that you will have a problem somewhere with a piece of the system and try to get support and they will ask you what version of a minipack you are on, what version of a form you are on, or what version of the system you are on. You may have something broken in Production the week before year-end closing, you are in the middle of a severity 1 iTAR that is waiting on you to get to the current minipack level, and you are trying to shove through patches in Production without testing in the other environments to allow the company to close the books on time. You are patching in fire fighting mode, patches that you could have had already in and taken the time to implement and fully test to ensure that what you are doing is working and not breaking anything else.

The complexity of the system means that you have to try to stay as current as you can.

## ORACLE SUPPORT

Oracle Support and their most recognized tool, Metalink, will become one of your most used tools as well as the bane of your existence. Metalink is the Web site through which you will download patches, investigate bugs, and log service requests (iTARs). It is a lot more, however. There is a vast information pool within Metalink.

You can search the Knowledge Base for your problem or for something that you want to find out more information on. A simple search using "Concurrent Managers on Windows" can return well over 100 notes and forum discussions on that subject and changing "Windows" to "NT" raises the number of documents returned to over 140. Some of the documents returned do not appear to have anything to do with Concurrent Managers or Concurrent Processing, but there are many that appear to be very valuable documents. You will have to sort out the ones that apply to your situation and are relevant to the actual search sometimes, but by changing the search string you can alter what you are returned. If you are having a particular problem, for example, an ORA-00600 occurs periodically and you want to start researching it on your own, start with a broad search and narrow it down progressively as you research. ORA-00600 returns 200 entries. Most appear to be relevant, however many are for older versions of the database or are OS platform specific. After looking through what is returned with the first search, narrow down your search for the next iteration. I would suggest looking through what you get back with your broad search, even though the amount of information may appear to be overwhelming, there is often very good information that you can gather that may not appear in your subsequent searches. The ORA-00600 search that I did returned some interesting information that explained not only that an ORA-00600 is a kernel error, but directed me to other places to retrieve information by pointing me at Oracle Internal Errors Technical Library in the Top Tech Docs section and the Data Server subsection and to other notes on the subject. By narrowing the search, for example, adding the first argument to the ORA-00600 error (in the case I ran, I added [12700] as the argument and searched on the string "ORA-600 [12700]"). This search returned 59 documents and among the documents returned was information on how to further diagnose the problem, forum discussions on what might be done to alleviate the occurrences, and references to further information on block corruption and how to fix the situation. If you navigate to the Advanced Search page (by pressing the Advanced button next to the search box), you can look at Oracle Support's own suggestions on how to search Metalink efficiently. Included in the suggestions are General Tips (see Figure 14.1) and the rules used by the search engine that will help you to make your search more efficient.

## Navigation Links

Down the left side of the Metalink page are a series of buttons. My Headlines will allow you to look at the latest headlines that are relevant to your particular situation. What appears in My Headlines is customizable through the User Profile button (as well as many other preferences that you can set within those screens). You can see News and Notes; get information from the Bug Database; monitor Technical Forums, the Knowledge Base, and Product Life Cycle information; and monitor iTARs for your site and relevant patches that have recently been released. Attempting to see too much in My Headlines will cause you to get further links to further information, as it will only display a limited number of lines in any one section. If what you are trying to monitor exceeds those lines you will only be given the option to link to another page with that information on it.

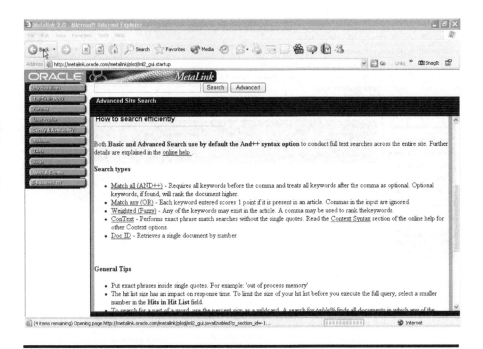

**Figure 14.1    Metalink's Search Suggestions**

## Top Tech Documents

Top Tech Documents will take you to a full list of all of the technical document categories that are available on Metalink, but will not link you to all of the information on everything. From there you will have to search to find some of the information. Included in the list (see Figure 14.2) are documents on Oracle Support's recommended patching strategy, diagnostic tools, upgrade and maintenance information, detailed information on all of the pieces and products in the Oracle E-Business Suite, information on 9iAS, information relevant to current releases of the database on internal errors, upgrades, performance, and backup, and recovery (just to name a few). You can look at information on Data Warehousing, Oracle Enterprise Manager, Internet Products, Networking and Development tools, and a vast array of other Oracle related information.

## Forums

The Forums button will take you to the page from where you can navigate to any of dozens of forums (see Figure 14.3). Many of these are geared mainly toward the functional people in an organization, but many will help you to resolve issues, ask questions, gather more information, and

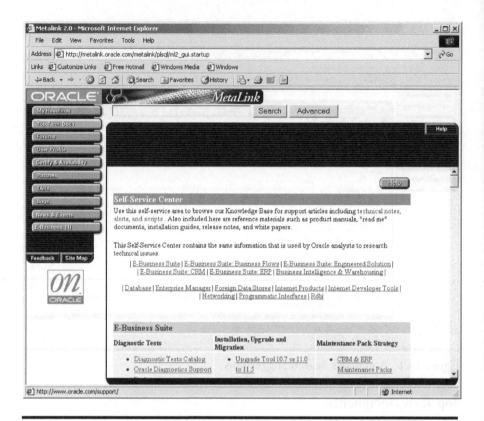

**Figure 14.2   Top Tech Documents**

provide a sounding board from which you can find out answers to questions that may not seem important enough for launching an iTAR, but for which you want answers. In many cases, posting a question to a forum results in the suggestion that you log an iTAR. Oracle Support personnel monitor most of these forums fairly regularly and they know when a request in a forum will require further assistance that can be gathered better in the other venue.

There is a forum dedicated to every product suite, to the Oracle HTTP Server, to Discoverer, to precompiles, to the RDBMS, to SQL*Plus, and everything in between.

## User Profile

The User Profile button will take you to a screen where you can change what your support identifiers are, you can change your password and your personal information, show your license information, list and manage users (if you are set up as an administrator), and take part in occasional

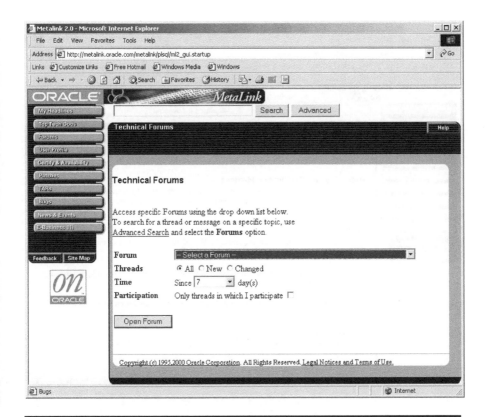

**Figure 14.3    Forums**

user surveys. This is not an area you may be likely to access routinely, but it is a useful tool to check on occasionally so you can make sure you are still seeing those things that you want to monitor and that your information is up to date.

## Certify and Product Availability

This is somewhere that you will want to check periodically to see what versions and OS combinations are still certified together. The most common time to check through the Certify and Availability button is when you are looking at an upgrade to see what version of Applications is certified with your middle tier OS and with your database and what database is certified with your application layer and with your OS, if you are looking at upgrading the database as well. By periodically checking here, you can see when 9iAS becomes certified with 11i on Windows 2000. Figure 14.4 provides an example of the main certifications and availability screen.

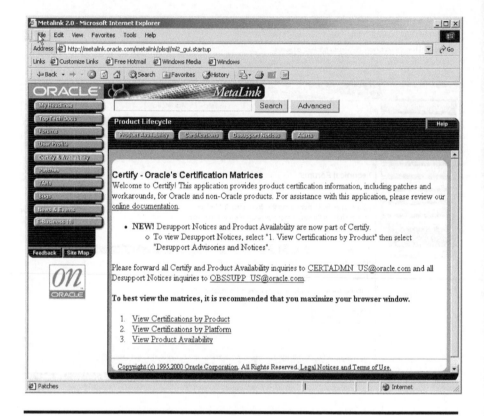

**Figure 14.4 Certify and Product Availablity**

Certifications can be viewed by OS and then by product or vice versa.

Availability shows when the most recent release of Applications that is certified on a platform became available.

You can view product or platform notes to see what server editions are certified at the OS level, see what features can be used with the specified OS–Applications combinations, and link to relevant information that might be applicable in your situation. It is always advisable to view any related documents that link from the certification pages to make sure that there are no caveats involved.

Desupport notices are now part of the Certify and Availability pages.

## Patches

The patches button takes you to the patches search area. From this area, you can search for patches for any of your licensed or shared products, view and print the README files (and any linked documents that the README refers to), and download patches for any portion of your

Applications Suite and your database. Make sure when you are down-loading to choose the correct OS for your patches. This is outlined in greater detail in Chapter 10.

## TARs

The TARs area is where you may find yourself spending the vast majority of your time. TARs are the way that you request assistance with problems that you are having with your system.

When you are creating a new iTAR, the first information you have to provide is your contact information and Support Identifier information. If you have more than one CSI (Customer Support Identifier) number, make sure you use the correct one for the system and product that you are creating the TAR for. Also, make sure that you enter the full version numbers in the OS Version, Product Version, and Database Version fields, so that your request will get routed nearer to the correct analyst. You can choose what form of communication you would prefer between you and the analyst, telephone, e-mail, electronic support services (I think this one is supposed to just be iTAR communication), or fax. Choose the one that you would really prefer. It may not be the way the analyst chooses to communicate, but you have made your preferences known. Figure 14.5 shows an example of the first screen that you will be presented with. This is where you fill in your contact information. If you want to save this set of information for easy retrieval later, you can enter, at the bottom, what profile name you want to give it and it will be saved. You can use that profile later by selecting it from the drop-down box at the top of the page and clicking the go button; that will fill in all of your saved values.

Based on the CSI number that you entered in the first screen, you will be presented with a second screen that contains all of the related products that are available through that CSI number. This is the biggest reason that it is important to choose the right one, if you have more than one. You will not be able to select Applications issues if you use a RDMBS only CSI number. From this screen, choose the area that most closely reflects your issue area. Again, it is important to choose the one that most closely represents your question, as this is the means by which the request gets routed to the analyst. Fill in this page with a descriptive title for your TAR, but make sure that it is under 80 characters and in English. I am not sure if the screen seen by people in other countries is the same, but I will have to infer that it is country specific based on your CSI number. Once you have an English description in the subject statement field, it asks you if you are going to enter the TAR in English. Choose either Yes or No (see Figure 14.6).

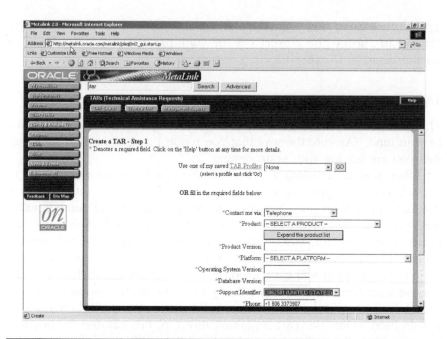

**Figure 14.5    iTAR Contact Information**

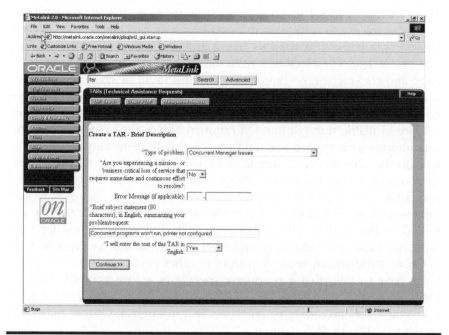

**Figure 14.6    iTAR Minimal Detail Screen**

Navigating to the next page, you are given a rather lengthy list of subjects that the iTAR system feels closely resembles what you have input thus far. In my example, I told the system that I was on Windows 2000 with a 9.2.0.3 database and my Applications layer was Version 11.5.8. Figure 14.7 shows the top suggested documents that the Knowledge Base believes I should look at. The apparently most relevant one in the list (at least it appears as number 1) is for RDBMS Version 7.1.1 and is the release notes for VMS. I chose Patch Applying Issue and none of the documents that I was supposed to try were in any way relevant to patching, although some were actually on both Applications and on a Windows platform. Be careful if you should decide to follow one of these links. If you just follow the link by clicking on it and opening it in the same window, you will have to start entering your iTAR information all over again. Always open these links in a separate window, if you want to attempt to see if they are relevant. The same applies for anything that links out of any subsequent screens as well. It is frustrating to get to a point where you have spent time and thought into getting the descriptions as close to what you are seeing as possible and then have the system throw you back to start all over again.

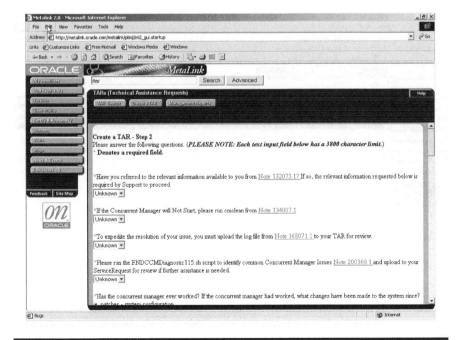

Figure 14.7    Knowledge Base Search Results

The last screen you will need to be concerned with is the one into which you put as much detail on your specific problem as you can (see Figure 14.8), given the questions asked to lead you through the entry. The questions asked on this screen are relevant entirely to the answers you have provided thus far, although not necessarily relevant to your detailed information. Put details in wherever they fit closest. Answer all of the questions that require answers and give as much detail on the problem at hand as you can, while keeping in mind that each question has a 4K size limit (there is not an overall TAR size limit for this screen, however, so the bytes that are not used up by the "yes, no, unknown, does not apply" questions do not carry over to subsequent questions). This does not mean that you will not be asked the same information at least twice more as soon as the TAR is assigned to an analyst, but at least you have all relevant information in the TAR to begin with. Questions that have italic prompts are optional information (I have used these on occasion when a previous question was not fully explained in the 4K allotted as an overflow field referencing the question I was finishing). Prudent use of this is advised and it will annoy some analysts. The final three questions on the TAR creation detail page are Yes/No type questions

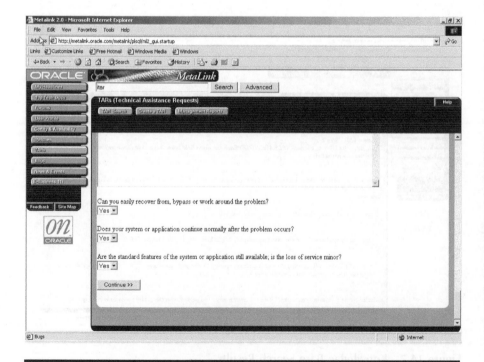

**Figure 14.8   iTAR Detailed Descriptions**

that default to Yes. Your answer to these questions influences the severity assigned to the iTAR, so be honest. The questions are:

- Can you easily recover from, bypass, or work around the problem?
- Does your system or application continue normally after the problem occurs?
- Are the standard features of the system or application still available; is the loss of service minor?

If what you are having troubles with is a standard feature, then the likely answer will be No. If the user's workstation freezes up when the problem occurs and has to be rebooted, but the application still appears to function okay, it is probably safe to say that the application probably does not continue normally.

Once you have finished all screens, your TAR will get assigned a unique number. That will be your means to track your TAR. You will have the opportunity to request that all updates to the TAR be e-mailed to you. If you check that option, you will probably get about half of the updates and the frequencies of e-mail updates usually drops off the longer that the TAR is open, so do not rely on that to alert you when the analyst has made an update. Go out and check on your TAR periodically. If you do not, you are apt to find that the analyst has closed your TAR because you did not hold up your end of the TAR relationship by updating the TAR, even though you did not know that they had updated it in the interim.

Now your TAR gets assigned to an analyst. This assignment is based largely on the first two screens of information that you entered. The assigned analyst may or may not know about your particular situation. If the analyst does not feel qualified to handle the question, the TAR will be transferred to someone else. The TAR system often decides whom to assign it to apparently arbitrarily, as you will often have an analyst who is baffled by the assignment. There is also no apparent correlation between how long it takes an analyst to get back to you with the severity of the iTAR. A severity 1 iTAR is saved for Production systems that are not currently operational or a system that is ready to go live and will receive 24/7 attention from analysts all over the globe. A severity 1 should be answered as soon as possible, as it is usually connected to a downed Production system. Often a severity 2 or 3 or even a 4 will get the attention of the analyst assigned before a severity 1 will. I have opened a severity 1 and a severity 3 at the same time and the severity 3 was answered and a resolution suggested before the analyst addressed the severity 1. If you do not get fairly prompt response on a severity 1, get on the phone to Oracle Support and try to get the analyst on the phone or try to get a duty manager to get someone to start addressing it with you. While the analyst's queues are supposed to be sorted with severity first, I'm not sure that the computer system that handles the assignments and the resulting queues always makes the best judgment.

It is often the luck of the draw with what analyst you are assigned as well. Sometimes an analyst will take a cursory look at the 80 characters of description information that you have entered, make a snap judgment on what documentation you might not have read, and will direct you to read it (or will read it to you on the phone). If you have already exhausted the documentation, do not be afraid to tell them that. The analyst may suggest that you just do not understand what you read and close the iTAR, do not be afraid to push the issue and either reopen the TAR, or call Oracle Support and ask to speak to a duty manager. The same goes if you have a severity 2 iTAR that has not been updated or status changed for several days. Granted, your analyst has several other issues to deal with, but you are paying for support and should have your issues dealt with in a timely manner.

People have often used Oracle Support as a doctor analogy. As an analogy, I guess it is as good as any, however, I'm not sure that I completely agree. Like a doctor, Oracle Support will discuss your symptoms and based on those symptoms will either suggest further tests or a remedy to try. The Support Analyst, like a physician, will likely ask the same questions again over a period of time (they will often ask the question without having read the chart, making the analogy appear like the nurse weighed you, then the doctor weighed you as soon as he came into the exam room, then he walked out for five minutes then walked in and took your weight again, like he was expecting it to balloon up in the intervening time or for you to waste away while you were waiting). It is often useful to take the requests with a grain of salt and answer the questions again, even though the answers may appear earlier in the TAR. If they repeat this too often, it starts to feel like stalling tactics and you might politely suggest that they reread the iTAR for that information (that is probably where you will end up copying it from anyway).

If you need to escalate a TAR (if you believe that you need your situation to receive additional assistance), you can escalate the TAR to a higher severity level. The inference in escalation is that something has not been addressed and you are requesting more attention be given to the issue. This is often the case when you have been working on a severity 2 issue that was not an impending problem when it was first raised, but due to the approach of immovable deadlines, it is now becoming more of a pressing issue. Unfortunately, when a customer makes the decision to escalate, it usually means that there has been an ongoing issue with the iTAR and that either the client wants a second opinion on the solution that may have been suggested or such an extended time has passed that there is a pressing criticality in the system that requires immediate attention. Requesting escalation means that you will be talking to a duty manager and providing him or her with a valid business reason why the iTAR cannot continue to stay in the current status. The duty manager will document within the iTAR the reason for the escalation and a proposed solution for your situation. Escalation needs to be used prudently, as overuse will diminish your credibility in the eyes of Oracle Support and when there comes a time when you really need the extra assistance, it will have the same effect as the boy who cried wolf one too many times. It is important that you not be reticent to use this avenue if you truly believe an issue needs further attention. You are paying for this service, it is up to you to manage the service, and bring issues to the proper people so that your concerns and problems are addressed in a timely manner.

The analysts really do end up being an extension of your own team and you will rely on them to provide the advice and support that you will come to need in your experience with your system. They have, at their dispense, many tools that are not readily available to you and an even deeper set of knowledge bases to draw from. You will find Support Analysts who are very good at what they do and who will help you with your problems and make you feel like you are their only concern. These relationships are important to cultivate. They also have the ability to do remote diagnostics, if you are willing to walk through what you do and allow the analyst to watch. Actually seeing what you are seeing often helps the analyst to make decisions based not on what you interpret, but on what you are, in fact, seeing. This is a great way to diagnose problems. However, it does not always work in all situations. There are often firewalls in the way or extremely slow networks hampering the diagnosis. It is a great help if you can get the chat portions and the interactive session working so that you and your analyst can really become a team and work through the issue together.

One other suggestion I can make is to know your support information, keep the support phone number and your CSI numbers handy. I keep mine electronically on every server that we have involved in any manner with Oracle as well as on the central file server and in my PDA. I keep it in hard copy in my wallet and in an address book on my desk. That way, if something goes horribly wrong with communication and you need to get a TAR going, you can do it via telephone. And if you are at a computer where you do not have the information stored or your PDA's battery goes dead or whatever, you can always get to support.

One final thing you can get do through the iTAR system is to request an enhancement.

Do you think that you have an idea or a useful customization that might be useful to other people or that you would really like to see integrated into a future release of the product? There is a vehicle that will allow you to make this request known to Oracle. Making it known does not guarantee that it will get integrated, but at least it will get it on the docket for discussion in the next semiannual enhancement request review. I have known of one enhancement request that was made and was actually found to be broad enough of a request that would help enough of the user base that the enhancement made it into a future release.

Before the request even makes it to the review board, an engineer will examine the request to see if the request is actually a known defect in the product that is currently being addressed. If that engineer finds this to be the case, the requester is informed of the findings and the workaround (if any) provided.

The process for logging an enhancement request is exactly the same as for logging a request for a support iTAR. One major difference is on the Create TAR Brief Description screen; make sure that you choose Enhancement Request from the drop-down menu. On the subsequent screens, it is important that you describe as completely as you can why the current functionality does not meet your needs and the enhancement that you would like to have included in a future release. If possible, put into words how the current product could be changed to allow your enhancement to be included and any and all justifications that you can come up with for what parts of the business this enhancement would allow your company to more efficiently achieve. The more important that you can make this request to the actual business requirements of your company, the better the chances are that the enhancements will be included.

Once your iTAR has been created, just like any other iTAR, it will be assigned to a Support Engineer Analyst who will check over the information that you have entered, determine if it is a known defect or an enhancement already planned for a future release, and may ask you to provide further information or justification before forwarding the request on to Oracle Development. You will be assigned a number through which you can follow the progress of your request and receive updates on its status. To track the progress of your enhancement request, enter the number into the Bugs search screen into the Bug Number field and click the Search button. On the upper right hand corner of the resulting page, you have the option to click the box next to Monitor Bug link. Selecting this option will allow you to monitor the status of the request by placing a status link on your Metalink start page.

## Bugs

The Bugs button allows you to search for or monitor the status of existing bugs. This feature often returns spotty results as many bugs, including bugs that are associated to your iTARs are considered classified and you are not able to view any information on them. I'm not sure if this classification is considered to be a feature or not, but it is annoying when you cannot look at the details of the bug or find out what the numbers mean that they assign to it.

Figure 14.9 shows the screen where you can search for bugs by bug number, if you know it, or by keywords, product, product version, platform, status or version the bug was fixed in (e.g., to see all bugs fixed in 11.5.8), and you can sort the results by several criteria, so they are presented how you want them.

## News and Events

Through the News and Events link (see Figure 14.10), you can find information on Announcements and Events, Additional Resource links,

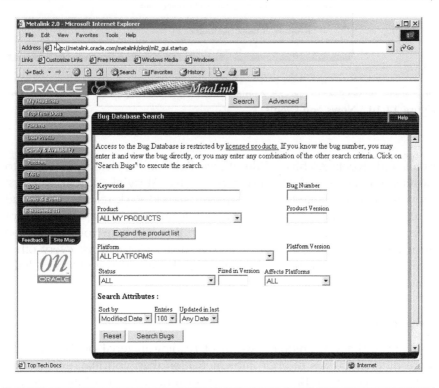

**Figure 14.9  Bugs Search Screen**

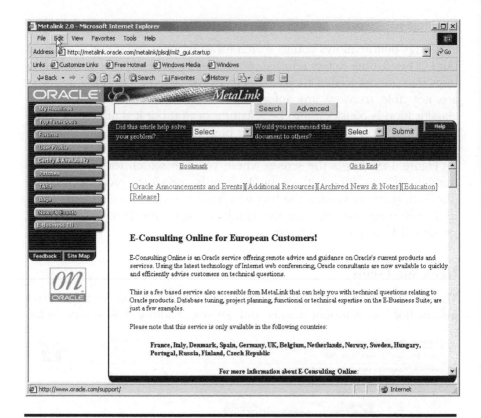

**Figure 14.10   News and Events**

News and Events Archives, Educational links, and Releases. Changes to existing processes and enhancements to the Metalink system will first show up as notes linked from this page. Support Pack releases are found here, as are upgrade and enhancement information. There are dozens of links from this page to useful information that will help you in your job no matter what your job is. It is a page that I visit at least every other week just to see what new information has been added and to find links to notes that have just been added.

## E-Business 11i

You can find several months' worth of reading material on Metalink on more different pieces of your implementation than you may ever realize that you have. The E-Business 11i button on the left side of the page will take you to a page where you can view FAQs on some of the latest releases, check on release availability along with the patch number that will allow you to use those releases, and links to further information and documentation. Four of the most useful follow.

### Alerts

Use the links on this page to find all 11i product Alerts that have been added or updated in the last 90 days. The links from this page include patching strategies for different product groups broken out by product group, advisories and restrictions for installation and configurations, and many relevant notes on the technology stack and on the individual products and product families. Alerts from this page are often breaking information on products that have just come to light on any licensable product. Compatibility issues that may not have made it into any other place and that may not be noticed if you just search on a given product will be linked out of this page. It is a useful page to add to your searches when you search for a problem.

### Documentation

The Documentation link takes you to a quick (although not all inclusive) listing of links to available documentation broken down by product group.

### Top Tech Docs

From the Top Tech Docs page, you can locate the latest diagnostics tests that are available for not only the Applications layer, but for your databases and all of your other systems as well. There is information on upgrading and installing, patching, technical notes, scripts, and access links to other tools that will prove invaluable. There are documents available here for databases, data warehouses, database utilities, development suite, and platform specific information. Links to selected information on virtually any product that Oracle brings to market are accessible from this page.

### Electronic Technical Reference Manuals (eTRM)

The eTRM interface (see Figure 14.11) is a PL*SQL-based utility that reads the design information from a configured Oracle E-Business Suite database and displays the information that it generates in html format that is presented through this page. This interface makes nearly all of the money spent on support worth it, as you can easily find out interrelationships between tables and referential integrity and all attributes of a table at the table level. You can discover the design information that is relevant to your particular version of the application. The relevant tables, packages, and interdependencies are presented in an easily readable and searchable interface. You can search on database object (FND_PROFILE_OPTION_VALUES table) or another search criteria (e.g., Concurrent Processing) and be presented with all relevant objects that meet your search criteria. You can simply select your version of the application and navigate link to link to learn the basic layout of the database and the Application layer. Not only can you indirectly query the information in the Oracle maintained system, you can download information in static format, like the layout of the database, diagrams, and information relevant to the application broken out by product group. There are over 10,000 tables, so it would be difficult to even view a total layout in one sitting. You can view Entity Relationship diagrams showing how tables in one schema relate to not only other tables in that schema, but to tables in other users schemas. It spells out the relationship between the tables (e.g., part of, composed of, contains, is in relationships). These diagrams can be an invaluable resource if you are trying to develop a set of custom reports in Discoverer or in PL*SQL or just trying to get an idea of how your system relates to itself.

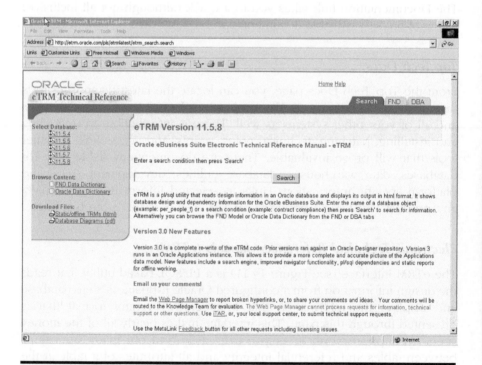

**Figure 14.11   eTRMs**

They have recently rewritten the eTRM system, improving the code and allowing the code to run against a fully functional Apps instance, instead of against an Oracle Designer repository. While the picture that you end up with may appear more complex and complicated, it is a more truly representative picture of what actually resides in the system.

## Self-Service Tool Kits

Oracle's Self-Service Tool Kits is a collection of information that is centrally concerned about product functionality. With these tools, you can quickly locate the information that will help you learn more about your products and assist in resolving the issues that you might find arising in your configuration.

Located via the Technical Libraries button on the Metalink pages, select the product you are looking for assistance with and navigate your way to the tools that will assist you. The Self-Service Tool Kits are continually being updated by the Oracle Support and development teams and include noninvasive tests that will help you determine what steps may be needed when trying to self-troubleshoot the errors that you may be experiencing.

# LEARN FROM YOUR MISTAKES

Okay, now that you have realized that you are responsible for some portion of the Oracle E-Business Suite management, you have landed the job, been assigned to the task, or lived through go live, you can take one last piece of advice to heart going forward: learn from your experiences and learn from your mistakes.

Six months or a year from now (it is hard to tell exactly when), you may be in the position of bringing on more modules to the system, implementing more pieces or some auxiliary add-ons. If you have taken away anything from your experience in getting you to this point in your career, remember your experiences when looking at the next project, looking at ongoing maintenance, or just looking at making it through your job.

Do not try to be in a hurry to get something implemented. Do not pick a company just because it was able to meet the price you quoted and is willing to take on your project. Do not think that if you have had a less than rewarding experience with one contracting company that you had the only one and that you could never be that unlucky again.

Take the time to compare many proposals. It will be worth your time.

Take the time to check references and check the references' references. Make sure that the referenced companies exist and they are not just someone's brothers-in-law trying to help them land the job. There are a lot of people out of jobs and competition is high. Make sure that you cover all of your bases and do not take anything for granted. A company can put up a Web site in a couple days. Make sure that they can provide what it is you really need.

# INDEX

T - #0063 - 101024 - C0 - 234/156/27 [29] - CB - 9780849318610 - Gloss Lamination